READING WORLD LITERATURE

READING WORLD LITERATURE
Theory, History, Practice

Edited and with an
Introduction by
Sarah Lawall

University of Texas Press   Austin

Requests for permission to reproduce material from this work
should be sent to Permissions, University of Texas Press,
Box 7819, Austin, TX 78713-7819.

☉ The paper used in this publication meets the minimum
requirements of American National Standard for Information
Sciences—Permanence of Paper for Printed Library Materials,
ANSI Z39.48-1984.

Library of Congress Cataloging-in-Publication Data

Reading world literature : theory, history, practice / edited and
    with an introduction by Sarah Lawall. — 1st ed.
        p.   cm.
    Includes bibliographical references and index.
    ISBN 0-292-74679-2
    1. Literature—History and criticism.   I. Lawall, Sarah N.
PN51.R35   1994
809—dc20   94-4041

For G. W. L.

Contents

Preface

Reading the world has never been simple, whether in literature, art, or the precarious interactions of diplomacy. It is doubly complicated in today's geopolitical world, where distances have shrunk while independent political and linguistic units have multiplied. With 6,170 different languages currently spoken in 220 countries (Grimes vii), the number of cultural identities pressing for recognition is a reminder of the complex interrelationships to be found in any expression. No reading of any text will ever be complete—but how could it be? As twentieth-century theories of perception from Richards to Derrida have consistently shown, the more it is scrutinized, the more the intriguing otherness that reading tries to pin down evades definition. Indeed, the scrutinizers turn out to be embedded in their readings. Still, there is something challenging in this profusion of information; the data is irrepressibly *there*, impossible to ignore both as an opportunity to scout the unknown and as an invitation to locate ourselves within the context of other global identities. Whether in reading political enigmas or literary works, the increasing availability of new knowledge makes it difficult to accept partial answers, or conventional modes of understanding built on limited information. Yet increased information also spurs a demand for more facts to supplement always-incomplete evidence, and creates a potentially infinite regress that demonstrates how difficult it is to be a responsible (much less, perfect) reader. The more data we collect, the harder it is to coordinate a reading of the world.

This curious situation is exemplified in a specific intellectual-historical phenomenon: the concept and subsequent institutional practice of world literature. The theoretical, political, and educational enterprise known as "world literature" already associates concepts of world with the act of reading. *Reading World Literature* is a joint attempt to examine the idea and academic practice of world literature as a historical and theoretical project. The collection speculates on what world literature ought to be and what it is today, and on the place of the academic course in current controversies over cultural literacy and community values. Throughout, world literature's attempt to "read the world" is conceived as a negotiation between familiar and unfamiliar, or between the reading subject and a world—generally seen as "other"—with which it must come to terms.

As an academic course, world literature has its own special horizons in American educational history. Long a vehicle for citizens to become acquainted with "the best which has been thought and said in the world," tacitly reaffirming a central perspective and mainstream community values, the worldview of the world literature course has been challenged by those who note the exclusions and imbalance of its traditional canon. Their argument, logically enough, addresses itself to the literal misrepresentation of "world" in reading lists that minimize cross-cultural difference and the complicated fabric of social experience. Often the suggested remedy is to include more foreign, marginalized, or non-canonical works so that an enriched canon will more accurately represent global experience. With an increased repertoire and store of knowledge, the course's worldview is less likely to be limited to a single cultural pattern. Others object that adding new books—whatever the catalytic value of unfamiliar works and perspectives—is only tinkering with lists while ignoring the fundamental problem. What do we do with our newfound knowledge? How do we interpret what we read, especially if we are reading a translation? How can we encounter difference of any kind without reworking it into familiar patterns of understanding? World literature courses in the United States have been incorporating a wider span of texts for some time (and teachers have been agonizing over what parts of the world to represent and how to prepare themselves to introduce unfamiliar cultures). Now is a good time to examine the issues involved in reading (and teaching) world literature: its educational mission and the implications of its academic practice.

"World literature" is a portmanteau expression with two different academic allegiances. Located at the crossroads of history and literature, it is both "world" and "literature," history and aesthetics, cultural document and a value-charged model of high humanism. Taught in both world civilization courses and introductions to literature, it is used not only to illustrate issues of personal and social identity and the contrast of cultures but also to exemplify ahistorical concepts like Great Books, aesthetic perfection, and essential human nature. World literature has come into prominence at several points in American academic history: at the beginning of the century, just after the Second World War, and quite recently in unstated competition with international studies, cross-cultural studies, global history, and cultural criticism. The course has been given a special educational position on the assumption that there are particular benefits to be derived from its fusion of two disciplines: as imaginative literature, it conveys structures of experience, and as global history, it offers knowledge beyond local frontiers. In sum, it offers a vicarious experience of the cultural "other." World literature courses (unlike the separate study of "literature") are intended to introduce future citizens to cultural experiences "outside" our own society, usually against the background of an "inside" community experience defined as the Western tradition. Conventionally, these courses present non-Western cultures as the "other" which we must know in order to function effectively in a larger context and to distinguish our own special identity.

"Western" is a convenient label for a complex of values that have been transmitted through the Judaeo-Greco-Roman tradition in a particular geographic and historical location, and under particular power relationships. Historians have known for some time that scrutinizing any specific example of "Western" culture reveals a great many intertwined forces—far more than in the conventional paradigm. The even more local discipline of American studies has developed remarkably complex ethnic, interdisciplinary, and intercultural perspectives in order to describe our national identity. The currency of the term *Western*, however, and the need for a base of some kind ensure that it will continue to be used as a convenient point of departure both for those who uphold the concept and for those who attack it. As both concept and historical phenomenon, the idealized image of the Western core—seen as an impulse to open inquiry and debate, and to publicly accessible knowledge; as the valuing of individual experience and therefore of different personal and cultural beliefs; as openness to change, as an ideal of participatory government, of scientific method as a procedure and also as a means of democratizing understanding—even if all these are idealized, represents a series of enormously important anchor issues. A contemporary "Western" world literature course might appropriately explore the concept and the reality of "Western" experience in its inter- and intracultural frame. It would be assisted in this task by local demographics; the reading audience today is much less homogeneous than it once was. By the year 2000, there will be almost forty million people in the United States for whom English is not the primary language.[1] This figure suggests that there are worlds-within-worlds already grouped in the classroom, able—if authorized—to recognize the diversity of Western experience.

Identifying aspects of "non-Western" experience is similarly challenging, and not merely because West and non-West are intertwined. The separate categorical identities that once gave substance to international studies have lost their firm outline: whether nation, culture, language, art, or race, these categories merge into one another, duplicate or defy definition, fragment into numerous wayward subsets, and generally transgress administrative boundaries. Shifting political frontiers create and merge "national" states around the world; cultures disappear under the pressures of economic or social change. Languages travel and adapt to different contexts, so that former "national-language" traditions imbued with a presumed national essence have been metamorphosed into a variety of Anglophone, Francophone, Germanophone, Lusophone, African, Chinese, or Indian literatures that display, frequently, several linguistic or ethnic identities inside the same work.[2] One cannot even identify one language or culture in these texts as the "dominant" one, and others as foils or contributing elements, without ignoring the new identity of the mix (the significance of creole, gender-oriented, and class-specific languages) and without overlooking the aesthetic and social implications when, for example, one language in a work is used to comment on another, or is given tacit approval over its less "civilized" twin. Abstracting a "world literature" image of this world requires a self-reflexive reading strategy even to begin work, if Wole Soyinka is correct that the African image in European eyes is "a universal-humanoid abstraction defined and conducted by individuals whose theories and prescriptions are derived from the apprehension of *their* world and *their* history, *their* social neuroses and *their* values systems" (x). As George Lakoff reminds us in his examination of reality-structures in language and culture: "The fact is that people around the world categorize things in ways that both boggle the Western mind and stump Western linguists and anthropologists" (92).

Reading the world is, most importantly, a question of *reading*. Texts offer information, but not without an inevitable act of interpretation inasmuch as texts *have to be read*. In practice, a great deal of particularized knowledge about peoples and cultures can be overwhelming. One response is to prune and exclude, to go back to a local "basics" that diminishes interpretation for the sake of proficiency. Yet the discouraging side of this same overabundance—the fact that categories break down and continue to dissolve under the onslaught of increasingly specific information—suggests changes in reading strategy and not simply choices of exclusion and inclusion, familiarity and difference. Models for understanding are more accessible as a set of overlapping dimensions than as an unending progression of facts. Whether canon or anti-canon, literary texts organize a worldview and ask us to believe in its inner and outer boundaries; they are bones of contention not because they have more or less information but because they persuade us of a certain perspective on life. (How much we recognize that hidden appeal is up to us.) The vicarious experience that world literature is expected to provide is constituted as a dynamic composite, not as a fixed vision attached to one or another monolithic culture. The "facts" of this experience are already organized when they come to us, already framed by textual structures that represent fluid and multiple worlds—palimpsests of gender, race, and class, as well as of geopolitical, religious, and economic vision. In addition, the literary and cultural tradition that transmits the text embodies its own worldview; the reader's personal position intervenes with still another. Complex but coordinated, a reader's awareness of the different ways that a work's "world" is constituted provides the closest grasp on texts whose multidimensionality will always defy complete apprehension.

The essays collected here share a common focus: world literature as an invitation to "read the world," and as an academic practice that falls short—when it does—only by failing to read as fully as possible. These are not merely scholarly inquiries based in different areas of expertise (although they are also that); they take positions on a range of ethical and cultural issues involved in literary world-representation. Several essays openly adopt an editorial or collective "we" in order to explore the implications of different frames of cultural identity. Predictably, not all the writers agree on relative priorities, and one can foresee potentially spirited arguments among them. Yet they do agree on reading as an active process of understanding, and they concurrently reject the imposition of any single perspective or methodology when articulating the *world* in literature.

Our correlation of academic and theoretical perspectives on world literature is not accidental, and it should not be surprising. The world literature course is not only a staple of the academic canon with its own place in cultural politics, but it is also a continuously available laboratory sample of strategies, successes, and failures when readers approach cross-cultural or intercultural texts. All of the essayists are experienced teachers of literature, and each of these pieces could also be presented as the topic of a seminar discussion on the cross-cultural or intercultural teaching of literature.

Although the emphasis throughout is conceptual, almost every essay examines a specific text or texts as part of its argument. The authors present not a new menu of recommended selections but rather a range of analyses whose theoretical insights can and should be tested elsewhere. Genres and perspectives change: poetry, drama, fiction, picture books, translation studies, and the analogous literacies of literature and music come into play. The geographic range includes China, Japan, ancient Greece and Rome, the United States, Latin America, Africa, the Caribbean, and Europe, with examples from ancient and modern times; but other areas of the globe and periods of human history are still to be explored. Of the major strategies of cultural criticism, ethnic, regional, race, and gender politics are discussed, but there seems to be less direct mention of class.

Essays after the introduction are grouped to illustrate different aspects of "reading the world," from an early discussion of the concept of world literature to concluding analyses of the reading process itself related to different worldviews. The introduction takes up world literature as a phenomenon and also as a continually provocative challenge to academic practice. Here, I examine the term's origin in Goethe with its orientation toward the future, its relationship to ideas of the canon, its subsequent existence as a specifically American component of the liberal arts education, its relationship to theories of worldview, and its place in recurrent educational debates over a core curriculum and cultural survival. My proposal is that we use concepts of "worldview" together with theories of reading in order to renew the academic practice of reading world literature today.

Establishing "Initial Perspectives," Thomas Greene and Charles Segal explore basic issues of cross-cultural literary education: seeking out and teaching what is unfamiliar, recognizing the contingency of canonical values. Thomas Greene explores the ambivalent position of the world literature teacher mediating between two (or more) cultures. He adopts a consciously Western perspective in examining Chinese, Serbian, and African poetry in order to analyze the concept of otherness as part of the pedagogical situation—and opportunity—of the "Western" teacher of "world" literature. Charles Segal examines the cultural and critical values underlying ancient Greek and Roman readers' expectations of literary works. Their assumptions, he shows, are markedly different from twentieth-century expectations of the same classical canon. His discussion of the cultural ties of classical theory and practice indicates the historically conditioned nature of our own ways of reading, although he finds in both periods a similar tension between notions of aesthetic form and moral value.

In "Canonical Variations," five essayists embed the works under consideration inside different contextual structures and patterns of relationship. The first study takes as its point of departure one of the most canonical authors in the Western tradition: the fifth century B.C. Greek dramatist Euripides. Rejecting the homogeneous audience and presumed universality of "classic" works, Nancy Sorkin Rabinowitz focuses on the ideological shaping of gender roles in Euripides' *Hippolytus* and *Alcestis* and explores the reiterated image of woman as a medium of exchange. Not only does Rabinowitz's essay constitute a feminist rereading of the Euripidean plays, but she also discusses ways that teachers grounded in the traditional canon can simultaneously preserve and reevaluate their texts. In the following essay, Joan Dayan analyzes the powerful adaptation of Shakespeare's *Tempest* by Caribbean writer Aimé Césaire. Stressing common themes of mastery and servitude, of legitimacy and the artifices of language, Dayan describes a "fertile collision" and play of mutuality between the two plays and shows how each writer grasped in his own way the complicated irony of colonial experience. Césaire's redefinition of the relationship between Caliban and Prospero constitutes a major poetic document in modern explorations of cultural identity.

Celtic literature has not received the same kind of visibility, argues Maria Tymoczko, and the reasons have to do with the very processes of canon formation. Tymoczko uses a polysystems approach to describe the way that dominant assumptions about the nature of literature have kept Old Irish texts (even in translation) out of the traditional European canon, despite their survival in the form of buried reference. Introducing classes to issues of historical reception, she proposes, is one means of addressing the broader issue of cultural values—of self and other, familiarity and foreignness—that enters so importantly into notions of world literature. Latin America is the reference point for Doris Sommer, who examines modern concepts of allegory to explain how Latin American romantic novels have established links between erotics and politics in a narrative of cultural assimilation. Subtle messages about cultural image and ideological purpose, she suggests, are structured even into apparently apolitical works such as the "innocent" romance. Finally, Janet Walker takes up the question of genre study across cultures: a particularly pertinent topic inasmuch as many world literature courses are organized by concepts of genre (e.g., epic, drama) that derive from Western scholarship. Walker uses the test case of Japanese autobiography (a genre whose existence has sometimes been denied) to see how genre expectations influence our understanding of texts read across cultures.

"Languages of Community" shifts focus from larger analytic structures to the actual language of literary texts. Eugene Eoyang's essay takes up questions of translation, a central issue for world literature classes insofar as almost all works are taught in translation. In addition to outlining his own typology of translations, Eoyang reminds us that any translation is also a *reading* of the original text, and that the choice of words and aesthetic pattern reflects a translator's own cultural attitudes and expectations. He illustrates his argument (and the proposed typology) with translations from the Chinese *Shi Ching* analyzed as choices of cultural perspective. Readers and teachers alike, he concludes, must recognize that the preexisting worlds within us determine the translations that we find acceptable for ourselves and for the classroom. In the following essay, Chantal Zabus takes as her subject the diverse linguistic worlds that exist in an "original" tongue and the way that textual language is situated inside—and an active participant in—cultural politics. Zabus sketches the "glottopolitics" of the West African novel, where layers of indigenous and European speech in the same work create a new literary medium that communicates a complex cultural identity.

The last section, "Literacies," builds upon the previous essays' collective inquiry into what it means to read "for the world." Literacy—both technical and cultural—is still defined as the *ability to read*, and reading is envisaged as a process of understanding. Reading music, reading symbolic expression in pictures and words, or examining the very process of learning to read all disclose different facets of a literacy that is nothing more or less than understanding how language is used to create meaning. Appropriately, we think, for a study of world literature, this view of literacy implies a move to correlate familiar and unfamiliar, or to read for the *new* in relation to the *old*. It develops the capacity to construct new worldviews by comparing other systems of reality, to imagine and bring about change by examining reciprocal reflections and the possibility of mutual transformation. Such reading does not happen with impunity. It is an investment of the self in the other, and each element of newly acquired knowledge produces a change in the familiar appearance of things. L. S. Vygotsky, speaking about language use and learning through imaginary situations, already notes that "the customary structure of things is modified under the impact of the new meaning it has acquired" (110).

Sometimes analogies help disclose common patterns of understanding. Peter Rabinowitz and Jay Reise draw attention to shared principles of literacy by choosing a starting point outside literature: the listening habits and canonical assumptions of "reading" music. Literacy, they argue, is a *mode of comprehension* that is crucially shaped by the historical context of the reading (or listening) process. They stress the reader's *attribution of value* at every point and demonstrate with both literary and musical examples how selected codes are always invoked in the act of interpretation. Attributions of value begin at an early stage, argues William Moebius, and the subtle tension of word and image in children's picture books shapes adult readers in ways that we are only beginning to recognize. Moebius examines the ambiguous symbolization of experience in this hidden but influential canon and points out different implied (and often competing) world-structures. Finally, Margaret Spencer draws upon her experience as writer, researcher, and teacher of multilingual students to examine the way that the study of language development illuminates both actual and potential reading processes. Spanning the range from her own traditional British education to the recognition, in multicultural classrooms, of the broadly referential symbolic game of discovery that *is* reading, her essay pulls together the threads of literature, literacy, and the making of meaning that are woven into the enterprise of *Reading World Literature*.

Notes

I would like to thank the National Endowment for the Humanities for its generous support of the Institute for the Theory and Teaching of World Literature held at the University of Massachusetts at Amherst during the summer of 1987. Several of the essays in this volume are based on presentations at the institute.

1. Rebecca Oxford-Carpenter puts the figure at 39.5 million (1).

2. See, for example, Christopher L. Miller, Robert J. DiPietro and Edward Ifkovic, and Reinhold Grimm. Braj B. Kachru illustrates "the expansion of the cultural identities of the language" by listing, in addition to the traditional English-speaking countries, "institutionalized non-native varieties of English spoken in regions that have passed through extended periods of colonization" (Bangladesh, Ghana, India, Kenya, Malaysia, Nigeria, Pakistan, the Philippines, Singapore, Sri Lanka, Tanzania, and Zambia), and

locations where English is used in a foreign-language context (including China, Egypt, Indonesia, Israel, Japan, Korea, Nepal, Saudi Arabia, Taiwan, the USSR, and Zimbabwe) (1).

Works Cited

DiPietro, Robert J., and Edward Ifkovic, eds. *Ethnic Perspectives in American Literature.* New York: MLA, 1983.

Grimes, Barbara F., ed. *Ethnologue: Languages of the World.* Dallas: Summer Institute of Linguistics, Inc., 1988.

Grimm, Reinhold. "Identity and Difference: On Comparative Studies within a Single Language." *Profession 86* (1986): 28–29.

Kachru, Braj B. "World Englishes." *ERIC/CLL News Bulletin* 12.1 (1988).

Lakoff, George. *Women, Fire, and Dangerous Things: What Categories Reveal about the Mind.* Chicago: University of Chicago Press, 1987.

Miller, Christopher L. "Theories of Africans: The Question of Literary Anthropology." In *"Race," Writing, and Difference,* edited by Henry Louis Gates, Jr., pp. 281–300. Chicago: University of Chicago Press, 1986.

Oxford-Carpenter, Rebecca, et al. *Demographic Projections of Non-English-Language-Background and Limited-English-Proficient Persons in the United States to the Year 2000 by State, Age, and Language Group.* Rosslyn, Va.: InterAmerica Research Associates, Inc., 1984.

Soyinka, Wole. *Myth, Literature, and the African World.* Cambridge, England: Cambridge University Press, 1976.

Vygotsky, L. S. *Mind in Society: The Development of Higher Psychological Processes.* Cambridge, Mass.: Harvard University Press, 1978.

Reading World Literature

Introduction:
Reading World Literature

Sarah Lawall

I

"World literature" holds out many promises. For the individual reader, it promises vicarious experience and personal growth as well as the excitement of an aesthetic voyage among masterpieces. For society and its educational institutions, world literature offers a pleasurable way to prepare broadly informed, self-confident, and adaptable citizens who are meanwhile educated in the cultural values of the home community. Consequently, the disappointment is all the more severe when the "world" of world literature turns out to be much smaller than the globe, and when anticipated personal growth is not immediately visible—worse, when it challenges the very cultural identity that was to be reinforced through wide learning and comparative judgment. Promising the world is a risky business.

What *is* the "world" of world literature; how, for whom, and to whom is this world represented; and what does the process of representation involve for those implicated in it? Is the focus on works of literature "as such," or on texts in context, or on ourselves as readers processing questions of cultural and personal identity? In what way is "world literature" different from "literature"? Quantitatively, defining the "world" as representative global coverage (chiefly in translation)? Qualitatively, referring to an implied "world-class" standard and universal values?

Such questions complicate the traditional curricular definition, according to which world literature is a list of works from around the globe that represent, in some indefinable manner, the essential experience of human beings in different cultures.[1] This generalized concept lends itself in practice to absolute interpretations. Covering the whole world, it claims totality of vision; offering a manifold yet universally valid canon, it presents an implicit measuring stick (in ancient Greek, *kanon*) for the human condition. The more diverse the models of human experience provided for readers, the more they reinforce a central claim of universal ("world-class") validity. World literature's current place in the curriculum is based on these two idealized images. The geographic scope of international literature educates citizens to function (or "compete") globally, while the canon itself constitutes an idealized reference point, an authoritative sample of human experience and a guide for those learning to know themselves and the world. World literature as a list of works, therefore, promises a centralized base of understanding which is installed through a series of global examples: a canon whose artificial nature emerges only when it is shown to be based in practice on a far more limited national or cultural view.

World literature is often defined by opposition. It is defined in contrast with national literature or "Western literature"—although the literature of the Western heritage has occasionally been called world literature (usually to mark a step beyond European nationalism). Its global horizons also suggest a qualitative contrast with narrow or parochial thinking, and they imply an inherent ability to instill breadth of vision and judgment in the reader. At this point, notions of "world-class" are involved: Calvin S. Brown comments that world literature is "that small part of literature which has proved itself to be intensely alive and viable outside its own country and age" (10). For *The Dictionary of Cultural Literacy*, world literature is "an especially rich and interesting domain of knowledge. Its names are stars in the firmament of thought. . . . An important feature of the writings included in this section is their almost timeless character" (Hirsch et al. 81).[2] Such universal world literature is firmly ensconced in an ambiguous niche of American academia as a commonly required course in "Great Books." In periods of educational crisis, government officials and foundation presidents list basic works of world literature as anchor points of civilization—anchors that are immediately attacked as personal moorings by those who disagree. Institutional practice is scarcely less personal. World literature courses cannot help but reveal individual attachments inasmuch as the enormous size of the potential syllabus imposes, more than for any other traditional course, significant aesthetic, moral, and cultural choices on teachers who must decide for their own classes questions of inclusion, exclusion, context, and point of view.

World literature defined as a list of books does not provide the best measure of the world literature concept or of its potential. Goethe's coinage of the term in 1827, for example, had little to do with universals or lists of masterpieces; instead, the German author imagined an ongoing exchange of perspectives between readers in different countries. Insofar as the academic practice of world literature is bound by lists or canons, it undercuts the intention of achieving worldly knowledge and personal growth.

Reading world literature is a process of reading *for* the world: of recognizing the worlds involved in the text, or in the reading of texts. Not that such worlds can be grasped as homogeneous or unchanging, any more than the literary text; they merge, overlap, metamorphose, and offer multiple layers of inclusion and absence.[3] Moreover, as Edward Said has shown, the textual "world" is not just a scene to be observed but an aggressive participant in the reader's process of understanding. World literature texts are not neutral agents; they do more than invite parochial readers to broaden their minds, for their rhetorical and situational meaning-structures underwrite a particular manner of paying attention. An embedded worldview suggests itself as a mode of experience, either a subliminally "right" way of thinking or the representative model of another culture.[4] For readers outside a particular tradition, samples from the tradition are taken as the expression of an authentic cultural "Other."[5] At home, such book lists form part of the self-image a community elects for its own guidance. If Plato, Dante, Shakespeare, and Goethe (or Jane Austen, Sinclair Lewis, and Harriet Beecher Stowe) are presented as Western exemplars of world literature, their status as a certified introduction to the thinking of the West not only informs the response of other traditions but reinforces their own centrality as a viable model at home. Arguments consequently arise over the "right" model, over canonical inclusions and exclusions. Focusing on a list and its choices, however, entails a serious disadvantage in that it shifts attention away from world-apprehension as a specific aspect of literature, and it ignores basic problems of reading—especially reading cross-culturally.

The canon or booklist is the most visible, concrete, and immediately reformable portion of literary studies. For that reason the list itself—as opposed to the implications of *having* a list, or having it presented in a particular manner—often takes priority in discussions. Until recently, when scholars were deciding the salutary or oppressive effects of studying "masterpieces," most debates over the literary canon fell into a binary opposition: preservation or progress, narrowness or diversity, inherited wisdom or radical rethinking, idealism or social relevance. A tradition of anticanonical criticism beginning with *The Politics of Literature* (1972) demonstrated the largely Anglo-American, white, male, and middle-class identity of the masterpiece-oriented canons in mid-century American academia. Such criticism of "the literary canon" narrowed its object to a single model, however. Its canon was not *the* canon (were we to posit such a thing), but instead a specific version of Western literary tradition that preserved strong links to the theological and social aims of pre–Revolutionary American education. The model texts of this early education were selected from Latin and Greek antiquity not as literary masterpieces or even as literature, but as moral teaching devices for future citizens (male) many of whom would go into the ministry (Levin; Rudolph). While this extremely focused tradition has clearly had its impact on the social mission of American education, it represents only part of the history of canonicity[6] and a small segment of world literature.

As a practical matter, it is difficult to know which world literature canon to pursue since such lists vary from country to country. This divergence is hardly unexpected, given the number of literate cultures as well as Erich Auerbach's reminder that any literary-historical perspective has its own point of departure. Only a "historical perspectivist sense," according to Auerbach, would permit the notion of world literature; modern scholarship, he thought, might achieve such a large synthetic perspective (8).[7] What Auerbach calls "historical perspectivist sense," however, defeats the global claims of any canon. Jan Brandt Corstius has shown how different histories of world literature address their own publics, each awarding more space to its indigenous minor authors and emphasizing foreign literatures according to their importance for local tradition. The nineteenth-century Transylvanian comparatist Hugo Meltzl de Lomnitz used the concept of cultural maturity to list the modern "civilized languages" in which one could expect world literature to be written: German, English, Spanish, Dutch, Hungarian, Icelandic, Italian, Portuguese, Swedish, and French. Surveying international lists of Great Books, Etiemble noted in 1966 that a Japanese canon included works from Western Europe but not from India or the Arab world and that an Egyptian list of two thousand masterpieces constituting the "common patrimony of humanity" ignored Latin literature as well as any mention of India, China, or Japan. Calvin Brown has described a world literature list proposed to English teachers that included thirty-five works, most of which were written in the last century, with twenty-six written in English (11–12); similarly, respondents to a questionnaire from Pléiade editor Raymond Queneau recommended sixty French titles and thirty-nine foreign works apportioned among eight European literatures with one selection from Arabic and Hebrew literatures. None of this implies that there is no such thing as a canon, or even that canons are not useful, but rather that the notion of a universally valid book list is particularly hard to uphold for "world" literature.

There is an undeniable similarity among the previous book lists in one respect: all are attempts to determine a literary "common patrimony of humanity." Underlying the diversity of example is a shared belief in the exemplary value of the work (its common humanity) and its role as transmitter of community values (the patrimony). Yet this agreement only displaces the problem onto concepts of "common humanity" and corollary principles for selecting exemplary books.

Not all canons are meant as general metaphysical or cosmopolitan guidance. Some display a particular category of knowledge, others may be arranged by form, others are selected in view of a special audience or usage. The cuneiform collection of Ashurbanipal (669–630 B.C.) has been considered an early example of canon (in the sense of a collection of texts representing community memory), and it apparently included both archival and general texts. The Greek and Roman texts that form the basis of the conventional "world literature" canon contain lists by librarians following principles that are not fully known: some, it appears, are based on meter, others on subject matter (Zetzel 122–123).[8] Even more: the list-making itself follows an era of enormous scholarly and creative activity that demonstrated a far wider definition of the heritage to be preserved than could be reduced to any specific set of names. According to Eusebius, the aim of the Ptolemaic library at Alexandria was to collect "the writings of all men as far as they were worth serious attention . . . " (Pfeiffer 99). The approximately half million volumes of this international library—surely the first recorded collection of "world literature"—contained in addition to Greek literature, translations into Greek of texts from other Mediterranean as well as Middle Eastern and Indian languages. When the library was destroyed by fire in 47 B.C., only a few works survived to represent the past and to shape Western literary tradition. The model handed down was much narrower than its source and it reflected only part of the original organizing principles: for example, the library's influential canon of Greek poetry was classified strictly by meter, which implies a perspective and measure of value that is not shared by modern collections.

The person who did the most to transmit the Greek and Latin "Great Book" lists underlying the traditional Western canon is Quintilian (c. A.D. 35–c. 95), whose *Institutio oratoria* was rediscovered in the fifteenth century and speedily disseminated throughout Europe as a model of classical learning. Quintilian's list of Greek writers was based on the traditional lists of the ancient grammarians, but his discussion of Latin authors and his comparative analyses were openly selective. He chose from a wide range of recognized authors those whose linguistic purity made them good examples for aspiring politicians learning how to use the right word at the right time. Foreseeing complaints that his book left out important names, he noted that everyone knew who they were: "No one is so far removed from their [the poets'] acquaintance that he could not get a list from the library and transfer it to his own books."[9] Quintilian's strictly pedagogical aim was not to create "whole men" or appreciators of aesthetic effects or even world citizens, but rather to enable a student enrolled in his school of public speaking to win votes in the Forum. Nonetheless, Quintilian's list of well-known writers underlies much of the Western "Great Books" tradition.

Juan Luis Vives (1492–1540), a polyglot contemporary of Erasmus known as the "second Quintilian," is closer to the modern interest in world literature as a body of works of the imagination. Like Quintilian, Vives was interested in language use, in educational processes, and in the selection of appropriate texts. Living fifteen centuries later, however, in a militantly Christian environment that was suspicious of profane authors, Vives was already separated from the classical antiquity which he cherished and would transmit to his contemporary audience. In *De Tradendis Disciplinis* (On Education, 1531), he argued that a common heritage of humanistic wisdom was to be found in profane literature, "e.g. of the heathens, Agarenes [Arabs], Jews," whose writings "contain the knowledge of antiquity and of all human memory . . . that encyclopaedia which leads to the life of greatest usefulness, in which what has been observed and thought has been diligently consigned to posterity" (48).

Vives's argument depends on a Renaissance image of Man. He views society as a common enterprise in which the individual grows only through relation to a larger human community, and through an education whose "branches of learning are called humanistic, since they make us human" (293). Acquaintance with wise books raises the merely average mind above its natural talents, while a brilliant but isolated mind is held back by its ignorance. "Unlearned men, however intellectual they may be by nature, cannot be pervaded by so great a vigour of mind as those who are of average intellectual power, when furnished with learning, for they have many others to help them" (49). The imaginative world of the ancients is transmitted through authors like Homer, whose ability to crystallize and communicate common human experiences renders them accessible to later generations. Homer's "sense of common human feeling is so strong," says Vives, and "everything that he says is so much in accord with the actuality of life" that, "after all these centuries, with their altered customs and habits and changes in the whole way of living, his words, precepts, conversations, speeches, etc. are still suitable to our age and for every other" (145). Not all educators agreed. Many rejected the ancient poets as dishonest and perverse (especially the Latin elegiacs); in the next century, the Czechoslovakian scholar Comenius dropped Greek and Latin poetry and gave his students "realistic" writers with a more practical vocabulary (Watson "Introduction" clv). Vives is talking about a different kind of realism, however. He does not stress the usable vocabulary of everyday things, but an experiential realism that is conveyed by a transparent language of scenario and situation. This view of literary expression has nothing to do with world literature as a collection of aesthetic masterpieces (the "ideal order" of Eliot's "Tradition and the Individual Talent"). It is a linguistic and moral criticism that responds to "words, precepts, conversations, speeches, etc." as if the world in question were actually on stage. Vives's argument for world literature stresses its nature as *speech* rather than as *writing*, and its importance as community memory. He singles out the contribution of individual authors, across time and different civilizations, to the development of a reader's moral and cultural identity.

Similar questions about the educational role of literature permeate American debates in the nineteenth and twentieth centuries, although the argument follows different lines and responds to changed curricular imperatives.[10] Charles Eliot, who had made a reputation for himself as a student of European educational systems before becoming president of Harvard in 1869, noted in his inaugural address the current "endless controversies whether language, philosophy, mathematics, or science supply the best mental training, whether general education should be chiefly literary or chiefly scientific" (quoted in Levin 355). Eliot's response was to eliminate all required courses at Harvard. This champion of the elective curriculum nonetheless sponsored in 1910 his own broad canon, the fifty-volume *Harvard Classics*, as a commercially available compendium of humanistic thought (Rosenberg; Levin). In the thirties, St. John's University at Annapolis based a whole degree program on the coordinated knowledge of a Hundred Great Books, a collection that college publicity described as "the great books of literature, history, mathematics, science, philosophy, and religion" through which "the student earns his intellectual heritage from Homer to the present, and learns to be a free and responsible person" (quoted in Rosenberg 24). The impetus to recognize different categories of modern scientific thinking, and the desire (after Kant) to authenticate different disciplines according to their ability to isolate and define their subject matter, both enlarged and restricted the role of world literature. On the one hand, world literature as the "Great Books" encompassed all the humanistic disciplines: the wisdom of a whole civilization could be found in the right collection of books. On the other hand, the apportionment of diverse categories of thought *within* the Great Books list separated literature from other modes of knowledge whose perspectives it could no longer claim to convey.

The liberalization of the Greek and Latin core to allow for different categories of learning ended by pushing literature into a niche where it not only competed with other disciplines but also required complementary courses in history to fulfill its earlier humanistic role. Civilization courses, emphasizing historical themes, were devised to share in the representation of Western culture. Mary Louise Pratt notes that Columbia's launching of a course in Western Civilization in 1919 was antedated by a "War Issues" course that would introduce newly conscripted soldiers into the European heritage for which they were about to fight (Pratt 8; Graff 135). Ralph Rosenberg's earliest example of a specifically literary course is Philo Buck's "Masterpieces of Western Literature" and "World Literature in Translation" at the University of Wisconsin in the late twenties.[11] The separation of literature and science, or literature and history, as distinct but correlated inquiries was institutionalized on a broader scale as part of Harvard's *General Education in a Free Society* in 1945, a report which, as Harry Levin notes, also popularized the terms "common core" and "core curriculum." The Harvard report, which helped shape the higher education curriculum for two decades, recognized a triad of Humanities, Social Sciences, and Natural Sciences, and established a pair of basic required courses: "Great Texts of Literature" (Humanities) and "Western Thought and Institutions" (Social Sciences) (Levin 358; Graff 133–135, 162–173).

Once their status as separate basic requirements was established, college and university courses dependent on a definably "literary" canon grew proportionally. The proliferation of world literature courses was not without problems, as Calvin Brown complained in his 1953 "Debased Standards in World Literature Courses." Unless those acquainted with other languages and literature took an interest, he declared, the "world" of these courses would soon be limited to the parochial habits of beginning (and monolingual) English faculty. Haskell Block's 1959 Conference on the Teaching of World Literature, held at the University of Wisconsin, was an invitational gathering of current world literature teachers who attempted to formulate principles and practice for an educational enterprise that had gotten out of hand.[12] The proceedings of the conference constitute a valuable overview of the kinds of courses and theoretical issues prominent after more than a decade of rapid growth. Essays such as "The Evaluation and Use of Translations," "Correlating the Teaching of Literature in Translation," "Teaching the Classics in Translation," "The Teaching of European Literature from St. Augustine to Dante," "Non-Western Literature in the World Literature Program," "The Role of Philosophical Texts in a Humanities Program," and "Intensive and Extensive Approaches in the Teaching of World Literature" focus, as one might expect, on questions of coverage, translation, chronological depth, the academic preparation of the world literature teacher, the transmission of cultural values, and the challenge of representing the "world" in a series of literary texts.[13] In general, the world represented is the Western world and the texts are those of T. S. Eliot's "ideal order."

Reaction in the 1960s against the Eliotic canon, and against New Critical emphasis on intrinsic analysis, had special relevance for academic world literature. Revisionary critics attacked the reduction of "world" to the Western hemisphere and to a mainstream that demographic trends belied. They urged a place in the canon for literatures previously marginalized by gender, ethnicity, or class, and they criticized the idea of a universal aesthetic standard based on Western models. Many world literature courses were simply abandoned in favor of interdisciplinary and general-humanities offerings when it appeared that they were not able to deliver their promised "world" experience.

The problem of global coverage linked to Eurocentric bias was not new. Literary anthologies in the first half of the century strove for coverage and ended up with what René Wellek called "snippets from famous authors and great books ranging from the *Rig-Veda* to Oscar Wilde [that] encourage an indiscriminate smattering, a vague, sentimental cosmopolitanism" (*Theory* 41). In some cases, cultural bias seemed largely unconscious; in others, it was announced as a point of departure openly selected in order to organize otherwise intractable material.

The most common approach was to present non-Western literatures as a background for the Western heritage. The next step was even more significant: to present the earlier literatures in terms derived from Western tradition that either distorted or eliminated their significance for their own culture. Ford Madox Ford, in *The March of Literature from Confucius to Modern Times* (1938), found the beginnings of European and American modernity in ancient Egyptian, Hebrew, and Chinese texts. After a rapid, colorful, and detailed overview of international antiquity, the earlier non-European traditions dropped out of sight: reasonably enough, since they were presented as preparation for Western models. Parallels and references to Western tradition permeate the early section, and in spite of the wealth of foreign allusions, the didactic tendency runs consistently Westward; for example, the two Chinese sages Confucius and Lao-tzu (taken together) are said to prefigure the complete image of Christ (70). The book is divided into two parts: "From the Earliest Days to the Elizabethans" and "From the Elizabethans to Modern Times." Ford's literary history clearly demonstrates the unequal discursive relationship that Edward Said has shown operating between cultures and especially between Western and Oriental societies (48), and it does so quite unself-consciously.

A different and more self-conscious approach emerged in Richard Moulton's *World Literature and Its Place in General Culture* (1911). The author, a British scholar who taught for twenty-seven years at the University of Chicago and headed the Department of General Literature, was quite aware of problems of perspective and proposed a solution he based in "cultural studies" and "intrinsic analysis." Moulton planned to follow his book on world literature with another "more formal introduction to literary theory and interpretation," and he argued against the tendency of book lists to assume that "everything knowable is of the nature of information, sure to be found in the right compendium." He recognized that the literary spectrum would look different to readers around the world, and that the foreground and background of diverse literary landscapes would not be the same. Not many readers today would accept Moulton's way of organizing world literature, the unity of his "Literary Pedigree of the English-speaking Peoples," the marginalization of geographic and other categories in "Collateral Studies in World Literature" (Chapter 6), or his arrangement of (Western) world literature in five "literary Bibles," but the book as a whole made no bones about its pedagogical imperative and was quite open about presenting "World Literature from the English Point of View" (v, 1).[14] Its example survives in courses in the Western literary tradition where one of the current tasks is to discover how unified or diverse the "Western" heritage is, and in journals with an openly linguistic basis like *World Literature Written in English*.

By the middle of the century, when world literature courses flourished throughout the United States, discussions of world literature had taken on the pattern of a cyclical debate over the same kind of questions. Against the background assumption of similarity or "one world," the topics raised were typically the place of Great Books in the humanities curriculum, the range of global representation, the need for and accuracy of translations, linguistic qualifications to teach foreign literature, the inclusion of philosophic texts, and what one scholar called "the enlargement of the reader's perspective by . . . the cumulative method" (Alberson 47). The frequent lively discussions of an ideal book list enlisted university presidents, editors, writers, teachers, and respondents to newspaper polls—in part because it *was* obvious that each list merely juggled an impossibly small sample of global literature. Indeed, the problem of the static nature of the book list was frequently raised and provided an opening to many debates, including Haskell Block's address to the Conference on the Teaching of World Literature, in which he agreed with Lionel Trilling that "World Literature is so large a subject that it cannot be studied systematically" (Block 3). Whether as a Great Book list codifying the values of cultural tradition (e.g., the "perspective of the English speaking people") or as the formulation of universal human experience communicated in transparent language,[15] the concept of world literature at this point was trapped in a general paradigm that merely shifted components. The cumulative (or accumulative) method could not address the particularization of experience involved in sensing the "world"—the same irreducible particularity, for example, that Vives adduced to explain Homer's continued appeal.

Lacking, visibly, was any question of the nature of language or of representation in these texts, any suspicion of the listed work's monolithic image, and any inquisitiveness about the cultural values that selected it for listing or suggested how it should be read. Nor was there any real question but that these works *could* be read—in the proper translation. Good professors would have read the text in the original language and be able to point out mistranslations and double meanings, and they would also provide any necessary cultural background. Such optimism was probably premature, even for the best-trained and most sympathetic scholar. Jurij Lotman has described a more complicated picture of the interacting boundaries of "self" and "other" in reading across cultures. The Slavic theorist emphasizes the likelihood of substituting some version of local experience for the foreign text. When a local culture is intensely curious about an "outer sphere," he suggests, it "assimilates what is similar to it, that is to say, what from its position is *recognized as a fact of culture*" (my emphasis). What cannot be recognized as a fact of culture is simply not recognized at all—drops out of sight—so that the perceiving culture is put in the position of assimilating "texts which it does not have the means to decipher." Lotman's argument suggests that world literature texts must be seen as both alien and familiar: they are certifiably foreign and thus fill the role of an oppositional other, but their foreignness has also been domesticated through being channeled into local recognition-patterns (60).

Access to the cultural polyphony or the "worlding" of these books is consequently blocked, unless there is some way of disorienting this substitution of self for other, and unless an (essentially list-subverting) maneuver of literary analysis can be found. Such a maneuver would operate for canonical as well as non-canonical texts, since the problems of interpretation would be the same. Indeed, Dominick LaCapra asserts that

> texts included in canons have critical potentials often occulted in canonical readings of them and that it would be foolish to neutralize these potentials through a quasi-ritualistic condemnation of canons. My approach questions the canonical uses to which certain texts have been put, and one of the incentives of its "noncanonical" readings is precisely to destabilize and contest such uses.

> (209)

II

In seeking to open up the notion of reading world literature, it may be useful to consider the way the term *world literature* came into being, and to ask how its earlier use implied a different and less canon-bound model of literary exchange. This is not to propose an "original" definition as the true one, for that would merely replace one formula (the canon of "Great Books" given global scope) with another one prescribing its own mode of automatic thinking. Juxtaposing the earlier concept, however, has the advantage of setting off one mode of understanding against another, and of testing the *concept* of world literature against the various assumptions and historical perspectives hidden in this portmanteau term.

The term *world literature* was coined by Goethe in 1827, following foreign responses to his own work,[16] and it formed part of a vision of future exchanges among writers and readers that would accompany a new global literature of mutual recognition. While the internationalism of this world literature depends visibly on a number of stereotypes—on Herder's national soul or essence, and on individual writers and languages as microcosms of national identity—there are also aspects that distinguish it from either nationalism writ large or the tradition of world masterpieces with which it was later associated.[17] Goethe's world literature proposed the idea of a literature to come, a literature that was always being written and was simultaneously a manner of *reading* for self and other. It was a leap into the future rather than a recuperation of the past, and it was to be created through the play of refracted identities: personal and linguistic identities that were inescapably colored by their cultural matrix which then became part of the exchange. Creating such an exchange on the level of letters would help bring about a new stage of global awareness and a broader utopia of society and literature that was still only dimly imagined: a coming world of "world literature" whose texts would have the largeness of perspective—as well as the authenticity of deep local roots—possessed until now only by the greatest of masterworks.

As the sage of Weimar who had presented the archetypal saga of human dreams and ambitions in *Faust*, and whose works spanned classicism and romanticism, literature and science, Goethe was already viewed throughout Europe as a prophet, frequently consulted for his views on the future of humanity. Conversing in his home with writers from many countries, and reporting international literary opinion in his journal *Über Kunst und Altertum*, he worked steadily to bring about the international understanding that would usher in an era of world literature.[18] However, he wrote rather little about the topic itself (Fritz Strich, in his 1946 book devoted to the topic, is able to cite only twenty brief passages from all of Goethe's works, diaries, letters, and conversations),[19] and never developed the concept in a single essay as he once anticipated. Goethe's various partial definitions, given in letters, journal entries, lectures, and reported conversations, sketched a tantalizing image whose ambiguous outlines and heroic scope soon achieved a life—and separate career—of their own. In Europe, the image inspired countless writers to try their hand at "world literature," publishers to issue translations of foreign literature past and present, and critics and historians to register and analyze the phenomenon.

Goethe was seventy-eight when he first used the term while describing, in his journal *Über Kunst und Altertum*, the French response to an adaptation of his drama *Tasso*. Pleased by a sympathetic review in the Paris *Globe*, he wrote in January 1827 that the understanding he had met heralded a new era of universal communication, and that a reciprocal knowledge of each others' literature would bring about greater harmony and communication among nations. At this point, world literature is conceived in political terms, a response to the misery brought by the wars following the French Revolution. The social impetus is clear in the writer's introduction, three years later, to Thomas Carlyle's *Life of Schiller* (1830). Goethe explains:

> There has for some time been talk of a Universal World Litera-
> ture, and indeed not without reason: for all the nations that had
> been flung together by frightful wars and had then settled down
> again became aware of having imbibed much that was foreign,
> and conscious of spiritual needs hitherto unknown. Hence arose
> a sense of their relationship as neighbours, and, instead of
> shutting themselves up as heretofore, the desire gradually
> awoke within them to become associated in a more or less free
> commerce.
>
> (quoted in Strich 351 n.18 [trans. by C. E. Norton])

In 1827, Goethe already attributed specific political importance to literature as an agent of human progress, describing it as a civilizing agent that heralded "the progress of the human race, and . . . wider prospects in world relationships between men . . . my conviction [is] that a universal world literature is in the process of formation in which we Germans are called to play an honourable part. The nations all look to us, they praise, blame, adopt and reject, imitate and distort, understand or misunderstand us, open or close their hearts towards us" (quoted in Strich 348 n.2). The nations that are humanized as individuals and neighbors—that are given the capacity to *read*—thereupon recognize each others' existence and take stock of what they see. Reading each others' literature, even in translation, they become further aware of different national characters (and of their own) as so many separate personalities. Here is transactional analysis on a grand scale, with individualized national cultures comprehending one another and consequently *themselves* better through the reciprocal experience of being mirrored ("read") by foreign eyes.

This interpersonal refraction is not only neighborly but familial, creating mutual recognition among different generations. "The happiest transmigration," said Goethe, "is that in which we see ourselves reappearing in another." A continuous and cyclical exchange was initiated when younger readers across Europe discovered Goethe's early work and identified in it their own emotions and aspirations. Goethe wrote contentedly that they "see themselves in our mirror . . . they draw us into their company and delude us with the mirage of returning youth."[20] What was first a point of recognition has become a renewal of the source, mirages within mirrors that link identities and make it unclear (or unimportant) who is the source of the glance.

Levels of identity intermingle again when the nation-as-neighbor is reversed to become the neighbor-as-national-image. If world literature comes into being as the "living, striving men of letters" come to know each other across national boundaries (quoted in Strich 350 n.12), these individuals are also perceived as representative samples of a national or cultural soul. Visibly there is a connection between Goethe's desire for harmonious relations among nations and individuals and the idea—drawn from Herder—that each national community has its own core identity. The core identity is expressed most purely in folk poetry, which both men collected for that reason, but for Goethe—paradoxically, it seems to me—the essence was both inherent in poetic language and simultaneously available for translation. In fact, the third stage of translation for Goethe was precisely this attempt: the highest achievement consisted not in adapting a work to its "target" audience (translating Baudelaire into English, for example, so that he seems a modern American poet), but in successfully transmitting the original "foreign" essence itself.[21] If the translator were sufficiently steeped in the original, this by now almost disembodied essence of national consciousness would be visible without conflict in a perfectly attuned alien tongue. The exchange or blend of identities which Goethe described in the mirroring of his own work would reappear on a larger scale in translation as a blend of linguistic and cultural identities. It is easy to see why Goethe would be so interested in retaining foreignness in translation: world literature will only come about, and do its work of harmonizing the concert of nations, after a preliminary process of displaying otherness takes place. To this end, a medium is needed that faces in two directions at once. Language and identity (like coinage) are both domestic and foreign, unique to a particular society but at the same time exportable and a medium of exchange. "For the characteristics of a nation are like its language or its coinage, they facilitate intercourse and even make it possible."

The personalized identification of national qualities occurs throughout Goethe's comments on foreign literature and criticism, including broad stereotypes used either to make a swift rhetorical point or to categorize different styles of being. In his testimonial for Carlyle's candidacy to the chair of moral philosophy at St. Andrews, for example, Goethe made the relevant argument for his disciple by asserting that "German literature has effected much for humanity . . . a moral-psychological tendency pervades it, introducing not ascetic timidity, but a free culture in accordance with nature, and in cheerful obedience to law. . . ."[22] Essays on the reception of English and French drama in foreign capitals describe the different responses as if they were modes of reading (albeit a theatrical text), and attribute these differences to national character. In an article comparing three essays on his own *Helen*, Goethe observes that "the Scot [Carlyle] tries to penetrate the work, the Frenchman [Ampère] to understand it, the Russian [Shevirev] to assimilate it." Moreover, these three approaches have "exemplified every one of the possible categories of interest that may be taken in any product of art or nature."[23] It is not necessary to belabor the issue—such broad images of national identity were widely accepted, and these are not as destructive as, for example, Philarète Chasles's personification of Chinese society as a Mandarin among porcelain cups who is "after all an incurable barbarian underneath the veneer of civilization" (quoted in Schulz and Rhein 229 n.2). However, since they form part of Goethe's expressed "world" view, it is worth noting that these stereotypes not only contrast with the fluid relationships described earlier but also set up procedural expectations that undermine the previous argument.

Apportioning points of view among national stereotypes—the typical Scot, Frenchman, or Russian—on the one hand merely extends a tradition of philosophical dialogues between people representing particular ideas (the dialogues of Plato or, nearer in time, Friedrich Schlegel). On the other, it also conjures up the structure of an everyday conversation among basically similar beings—*European* beings, as it happens, for although Goethe took an interest in non-European literature his main focus continued to be on European relations. This picture of siblings contributing their complementary perspectives not only lodges the completed scene inside European culture ("every one of the possible categories of interest"), but also domesticates the mode of approach. It would not be fair to imply that Goethe limited his world vision to the equivalent of "European, in other words, World Literature," the title of a proposed *Kunst und Altertum* essay that would have compared the international literary relationships of German, French, English, Scottish, and Italian literature, for he clearly intended to describe a particular stage of internationalism and not its scope. Nonetheless, the Europeanizing impulse remains dominant in both image and paradigm.

Reading translations of the thirteenth-century Persian poet Hafiz, Goethe sees another Anacreon, with erotic themes similar to his own—or he recognizes in Hafiz a similar recoil from political strife.

He disapproves of Indian religion—either the Vedas or Buddhism—because the author of *Hermann und Dorothea* will reject any claim that the world is a delusion; in Indian literature he likes only *Sakuntala*, whose suffering wife, forgetful husband, and other domestic themes he admires (Strich 136–140). Reading works of Chinese literature (in English translation), and especially *Chinese Courtship in Verse* by Peter Perring Thoms (1824), he notes happily that the latter volume's romantic tale and selection of poems by "a hundred beautiful women" show that the Chinese "despite limitations" "still live, love, and write poetry" (*Sämtliche Werke* 101) and he comments elsewhere that the Chinese "think, act, and feel almost as we do" only that with them everything is "clearer, cleaner, more moral . . . reasonable, respectable" (*bürgerlich*) (*Gespräche* 203).[24] We could add other examples, all of which would show that this original concept of world literature as cross-cultural understanding dramatizes others as alternate selves who can then be admired or criticized on familiar grounds. The problem is clearly one of reading, and has been addressed by recent criticism that focuses on the way cultural structures determine reading expectations and hence the perceived horizons of a text.

Is there any room at this point for a less prepackaged view of cultural identity, one that might even adumbrate the dialectic structures of current reader response criticism? Goethe first described world literature as cross-cultural reception inside an evolving *world history*, a concept he (and others) found already developed by Johann Gottfried Herder. He met Herder in winter 1770, and later described the impact of their extended discussions in his autobiography (8–23). Herder's modern reputation is only now beginning to recover from the taint of his popularity in Nazi Germany, which distorted for its own use his fascination with intuitive forces, national tradition, and ethnic character—the *Volksgeist* or national spirit. Such simplified themes scarcely recognize the philosopher's political skepticism, impatience with a Eurocentric perspective and with pseudo-scientific theories of racism,[25] belief in the shaping power of society and circumstance, and intense respect for diversity. Variously understood, Herder's broad concept of a universal world history and universal literary history, his belief in a grand totality of cosmic design, his study of ethnic units and national character, and his description of folk poetry from around the world as a universal language of humanity (*Humanität*), had a strong influence on Goethe and German Romanticism (Koepke 58, 72, 119; Wellek *History* 183–187, 197). The world of this worldview existed as a total organism governed by principles of balance and compensation, which meant that each part could ultimately be explained by a logic of analogy.

The notion of world history as an organic whole, a gradual evolution out of smaller social units into a grand design, is visibly static and lacks the dynamic dialectics of (for example) Marxian history or post-structuralist performative systems. Nonetheless, there are elements in Herder's essays that suggest a greater diversity and tension of contradictory forces than fit inside a narrowly teleological view of history. The national character in which Herder believes is not inborn or instinctive, but the result of complicated social interactions carried on over time. In *Ideas for a Philosophy of History*, he qualifies the assertion that "the history of mankind is necessarily a whole," by noting that the whole is defined as "a chain formed from the first link to the last by the moulding process of socialization and tradition" and that the essential process of this socialization is a "continuous interaction of individuals" (*J. G. Herder* 312–313). Herder's stress on empathy (*Einfühlung*) and experience, his insistence on the plurality of national and ethnic characters, and his belief in the metaphorical quality or intentionality of perceptions, keep his world history from being the mere workings of a perfectly balanced neoclassical machine. Wulf Koepke suggests that the writer's ethnic and evolutionary studies contain anticolonial implications and undercut the Eurocentric focus of nineteenth-century literary history: Herder "emerges as a champion of small nations and of the cultures of other continents. Adhering to his own principle of *nemesis*, he foresees a powerful reaction of the other continents against violent European colonization" (Koepke 72).

The method of synthesis and analogy upon which Herder's universal history is constructed also requires a great deal of material evidence, and thus allows the impact of empirical events to play a role in the writing of history. One of Herder's best-known proposals (which foreshadows the way modern anthropologists record dying languages to preserve knowledge of indigenous cultures) was a project of particularized research: the collection of folk poetry from societies all over the world as a means of recognizing, preserving, and regenerating national cultures. In a less poetic vein, he also wrote about the world-historical effects of technological inventions such as printing, Arabic numerals, the vacuum pump, clocks, and the compass, and he commented on the way such inventions both served and served to alienate the life of the populace at large (Nisbet 288–290).

In trying to assess the rigidity or openness of this influential concept of world history, it is important to recognize a complementary (or contradictory) side to the large synthesizing frameworks, the use of analogy for scientific reasoning, and the generalized images of ethnic and national character by which it is usually known. This other side is represented by the emphasis on concrete particulars and on practical research—on the individuality accorded each piece of evidence and each viewer, even if that individuality will later be interpreted as part of a transcendental design. In "Über Bild, Dichtung, und Fabel," Herder comments on the irreducible particularity of subjective impressions. Every piece of evidence comes to us already shaped by our drive to assign meaning; all life is colored by subjectivity as we project our own vision in a kind of experiential *poetics*. "We don't really see," says Herder, "but we create images for ourselves" (*Sämtliche Werke* 15, 526).[26] Such a recognition of intentionality and the stress on differentiated observation as the basis for research is clearly related to the premises of modern phenomenology (and Herder was once Kant's student even if the latter was not happy at the memory). Herder's universal history and universal literature—these large, reciprocal, and self-balancing frameworks—are supported by global research of extreme particularity, and they incorporate a potentially subversive intentional or "poetic" perception.

Even if Goethe did not exploit the range of Herder's thinking in his own brief discussions of world literature, the world-historical model on which he drew already allowed for openness and exchange. Goethe's receptionist paradigm for world literature, according to which "the living, striving men of letters should learn to know each other,"[27] is (when not frozen into cultural stereotypes) similarly open: a model of continuous reciprocal reading, of mutual reflections and reflectivity, arguably of transference and countertransference. It is a process of mutual recognition around textual exchange, employed toward a cultural (not aesthetic) goal of global awareness, working toward a broader utopia of society and literature that is still only dimly imagined.

This concept of world literature is not associated with the idea of masterworks, except when masterworks are defined as representing the particular essence of their culture and time (as in Eliot's "Tradition and the Individual Talent"). The idea of a universal, changeless, archetypally human expression did exist for Goethe, but only as what he called (after Herder) "world poetry," an essentially human core of creativity found potentially in any society but most clearly revealed in folk poetry and songs.[28] World poetry is a timeless or eternal concept, a single genre defined by its supposed essential humanity. The temporal dynamism and future-orientation of Goethe's concept of world literature begins with the notion of people reading each other's works across cultural boundaries. It is based on a vision of the book not as a canonical object, part of a tradition, but of the text *as read*—as part of cultural practice. This is not to deny that literary works exist inside a tradition, or that they stem from a particular convergence of historical circumstances, or even that they have aesthetic qualities; however, the most relevant practice for this "world literature" is to use texts as a basis for negotiating cultural relationships: to explore a middle ground where the identity of literary works, as of nations, and of individuals, is still to be discovered.

The concept of "world literature" was immediately popular; in fact, excessively popular. Goethe complained in 1828 that the response was "threatening to drown me like the sorcerer's apprentice," and ten years later a German writer traveling in England dreaded being accosted on the subject. Theodor Mundt wrote in his "Letters from London" that he was "heartily sick of all the vague talk about it. The world literature idea pursues me everywhere like the Marlborough-tune; every traveling student carries it about in his knapsack nowadays and airs it at every inn; things will get to such a pitch that wandering journeymen will begin to beg in its name and plead for charity, no longer now for the love of God but for the sake of world literature" (quoted in Strich 350, 281). The notion of a coming world literature gave pleasing shape to hopes for international understanding and world community after the recent Napoleonic wars; moreover, as a grand design, it correlated with the global ambitions of contemporary philosophical and scientific theories. It tapped into the Romantic attraction for universal and ideal concepts, into Romanticism's thirst for exotic or otherworldly experience, and into a prevalent mythology of the artistic genius attuned to archetypal humanity. It even worked its way into the *Communist Manifesto* as part of a bright future of global communication and harmony. "National one-sidedness and narrow-mindedness become more and more impossible, and from the numerous national and local literatures there arises a world literature" (Marx and Engels 84).[29]

III

The reputation of world literature is somewhat different in the United States. Frozen by academic history into the image of a great book list that offers simultaneously the wisdom of the ages and the accumulated experience of societies around the globe, it has not been able to fill either role. And yet, taken as more than a historical curiosity—a nineteenth-century utopian notion that chanced to name an academic canon—the *idea* of world literature has surprising relevance and pulls together many issues that are regularly taken up as issues of educational or national policy. Whether or not "world literature" is the reference point, issues of "world" ("what kind of world?" "whose world?"), of "literature" ("whose texts? in what contexts?"), and of "reading" ("who reads?" "reads what?" "what does it mean to read?") articulate a wide-ranging problematics of cultural identity and values. As "worlded" perception and the "writing" of experience, world literature cannot be divorced from current debates over shifts in values, national identity, the Western heritage, and the decadence or promise of modern society.

Not since Aristophanes' *Clouds* in 423 B.C. has the connection of educational philosophy to society's survival been argued with such heat. Already in the first half of the twentieth century, Paul Valéry's "La Crise de l'esprit," Rabindranath Tagore's *Crisis in Civilization*, and Arnold Toynbee's *Civilization on Trial* had expressed their anxiety over the survival of civilization and the impact of "Western values."[30] Discussion intensified in the United States after the end of World War II, with the expansion of higher education and a rethinking of the nation's international position. The sixties' move to create a curriculum that would reflect the diversity of community experience only increased anxiety for those who feared a loss of community memory and common purpose. Titles of national reports and individual critiques of education proclaimed a clear and present danger to American cultural identity. In 1983, the National Commission on Excellence in Education warned that we were *A Nation at Risk*. The National Endowment for the Humanities planned *To Reclaim a Legacy* in 1984 and in 1990 saw current educational practices ("gone wrong") as *Tyrannical Machines*. In 1985 the editors of *Challenges to the Humanities* asked "Is there no common heritage that belongs to us all?" (Finn et al. 8). The 1987 NEH Report on the humanities in the nation's public school system told us that we had to fear the loss of *American Memory*. In the same year, Allan Bloom described how higher education had "Failed Democracy and Impoverished the Souls of Today's Students," and E. D. Hirsch, Jr. explained how to impart *Cultural Literacy* to every American. The American variety of literary reception theory had already emerged with Stanley E. Fish's proposal that the "authority of community" would define textual meaning, a desire that the *Dictionary of Cultural Literacy* seemed designed to fulfill. In the nineties, appeals to community values have become even more frequent, focused, and sharply divided. Popularized conservative attacks like Dinesh D'Souza's *Illiberal Education: The Politics of Race and Sex on Campus* (1991) and Martin Anderson's *Impostors in the Temple* (1992), or the more detailed revisionary discussions in Robert and Jon Solomon's *Up the University: Re-Creating Higher Education in America* (1993), co-exist with nuts-and-bolts attempts to make the curriculum represent diverse community voices: e.g., Betty E. M. Ch'maj's *Multicultural America: A Resource Book for Teachers of Humanities and American Studies* (1993), or Thomas Hilgers et al., *Academic Literacies in Multicultural Higher Education* (1992). Political action groups organize to help shape educational policy for, as the National Association of Scholars pointed out in a membership letter aimed at classical scholars (September 23, 1992): "As a classicist you know what's at stake in the battle over the curriculum: cultural continuity and consciousness of our civilization's roots."

In world literature as in debates over educational practice, the intertwined categories are those of *community* (global or national) and *model* (canon or tradition). Each term sets in motion a range of implications and inner divisions. The community that unites a group of individuals with the bonds of tradition and common experience is also a diverse and changing entity whose collective definition depends on the involvement of its separate members. A model composed of shared texts or examples depends in practice on interpretations that vary over time and according to available information. In the criticism of world literature, this alternate stress on cultural or canonical qualities crystallizes as alternate approaches to textuality: on the one hand, the attitude of historicism (seen as the desire to historicize, particularize, differentiate, and contextualize discourse), and on the other, a desire to frame reading in terms of transhistorical values (synchronic, "aesthetic," structure-oriented discourse). In teaching, the same issues tend to concretize around priorities of "coverage" or "example." It is hard to decide whether lines are more fiercely drawn in literary-theoretical debates or in national polemics over the degeneracy of American education. What is clear is that the multilayered identity of the world literature concept—its links to texts, to literacy and language, to community values tested in the interface (at home and abroad) of different cultures, and to concepts of "worlding" as a philosophical and imaginative construct—activates versions of all these issues, each with its ideological commitment to a particular solution.

The Great Books canon of the mid-century was a canonical model trusted to provide social continuity and communication, albeit inside a particular brand of humanism. Its shared reference point was available not only for community self-definition but also for individuals to situate themselves in relation to that community. When belief in that canon's representative quality was lost, however, either a new set of texts was needed, or new manners of reading, or both. The plaintive question raised by *Challenges to the Humanities* (Finn et al.) shows how far uncertainty had progressed since Goethe's assumption that we merely read another nation's literature to glimpse its cultural essence and subsequently obtain an "other'ed" image of ourselves.

In their search for a humanities curriculum to express a cultural heritage "common to us all," editors Chester E. Finn Jr., Diane Ravitch, and P. Holley Roberts acknowledge the diversity of cultural experience but emphasize the primary importance of the Western heritage for humanistic education. Essays in the volume characteristically resolve the dilemma by postponing consideration of diversity to the modern era where it really matters, by relegating the discussion of diversity to the secondary role of context, or even by moving it outside the schools. Stephan Thernstrom, in fact, suggests that such topics are best raised elsewhere. "Ethnic awareness is not necessarily benign and colorful. It can be enormously destructive if cultivated to the point at which a sense of the ties that bind a nation together is lost" (77).[31]

Challenges' general attempt to postpone or absorb the discussion of diversity is not intended to simplify issues. The editors stress the need for a richer and more inclusive reading of texts, one that would avoid the interpretive rigidity of newly fashionable creeds. Their own effort to avoid this rigidity carries its own hidden categories, however, including categories of reading. The introduction imagines "a course in American literature or one in American history that represents the true richness and diversity of our heritage without becoming merely a numbers game based on gender, race, and ethnicity" (Finn et al. 8–9). In the editors' search for true richness, they are uneasy before pre-set categories such as the conventional "gender, race, and ethnicity" ("class" is omitted). The example they give illustrates how hard it is to move from an abstractly stated (and therefore probably traditionally conceived) "richness and diversity" to the actual task of identifying this diversity. Questioning the need to teach about women's roles and concepts at the time of the Constitution, they emphasize the text itself, and the need to "learn about the Constitution, even though it was written by men, since women's claims for equality are based on its letter and spirit" (Finn et al. 9). It is a quibble, perhaps, to note the slip in academic categories between examining social history and construing a text's letter and spirit, or to perceive a continuing image of dependency when women's "claims for equality" exist as *claims* and are based on the earlier document. More important is the antithesis and its exclusions; the suggestion that to learn about domesticity for women at the era of the Constitution is not to learn something about the semantic expectations of the document itself, and about a current in intellectual history that continues to be "read" along with the Constitution and complicates acceptance of its "letter and spirit."

The question of the heritage "common to us all" remains to be addressed. How is this Western or American heritage to be identified and taught as a unit, and how can it be distinguished from what it is not? The scope of the issues emerges even more inside the concept of *world* literature: how do we map out Western culture in relation to the rest (what "rest?") of the world? how useful (or possible) is it to separate a "Western" heritage from its simultaneous global connections? Since the impossibility of absolute distinctions is widely acknowledged, many find the attempt to distinguish neither useful nor possible.[32] Others argue for the usefulness of some concept of Western heritage as a flawed but necessary starting point. Whether the framework is "Western" or "global," two modes of inquiry are usually proposed, each of which has implications for the other and both of which pertain to notions of cultural identity and world literature.

The first emphasizes pluralism (the book list's "coverage") in its search for an authoritative community, and the second stresses repeatable examples: models of experience or analogous acts of reading. The "authority of community" that Fish described, which is already close to E. D. Hirsch's authority of history in *Validity in Interpretation*, is proposed by Hirsch as a way to resolve the conflicting claims of cultural diversity and common purpose through a base vocabulary of currently shared "maturely literate" references that would serve as a canon of common *knowledge* for American education. *Cultural Literacy: What Every American Needs to Know* (Hirsch), announces the establishment of a database of terms that come from consensus and may be enlarged at any time: in principle, a quantitative solution that obviates the need for subjective interpretation and lays claim to a collective—if fragmented—authority.

Hirsch's thesaurus of issues and references that "every American should know" is to be a verbal treasure house that stores the community's cultural knowledge. In its collective wisdom, it disperses the ability to read into a series of prepackaged mind bites, just as it defers the interpretation of individual terms to an ultimately inaccessible historical model (authoritative but remote, like the model of authorial intention in Hirsch's *Validity in Interpretation*). The analogous procedure for world literature would be the attempt to provide knowledge by coverage, representing the broadest possible geographic and demographic diversity. In each case, there is a sophisticated effort to avoid subjective narrowness by accumulating samples from the community: samples that subsequently become a starting point for reading comprehension as well as for communication inside and across cultures. This move to incorporate diverse reference points, however, actually diverts attention from structures of decision-making or *reading*. It defers responsibility for the inevitable act of interpretation, which becomes, by default, the implied or potential reading of the maker of lists.[33] The complementary approach assumes that texts function as exemplary or repeatable world views, as reproducible structures of perception and analysis that can be experienced by generations of different readers. This concept of reproducibility—shared by traditionalists and reformers alike—depends implicitly on the belief in a universal humanity that permits human beings to have analogous experiences. Exemplary reading is valuable because it allows readers to inhabit other subjective patterns, and thus to develop richer personal and social identities.[34] Texts and readers may be positioned inside different cultural systems but they also exist in an analogous existential framework. There is even an oblique similarity between the paradigms of *example* and *list*, since exemplary readings point to a larger pattern of shared experience and so do representative lists. In practice, however, the approach to the text as repeatable *model* is more closely tied not to lists and coverage but to concepts of great literature as an instrument of personal enlightenment, of self-definition, and of the transmission of cultural values.

Such a view aims to be active and exploratory rather than static or prescriptive, and it regards literary works as small-scale, specifically focused, dynamic models of reality. Close reading of such elements as the arrangement of details, patterns of imagery, an implied logic of events, available choices and their consequences, voice and presumed audience suggest recognizable and therefore advisory patterns of "real" consciousness. In "The Teaching of Values," Joel Kupperman uses formal criteria like "sense of detail and of character structure" and the perception of a text's "internal logic" to support his discussion of the way literature provides a model for vicarious experience and informed decision-making (139). Literature exemplifies reality, he suggests, if it is viewed as "problematic, rooted in responses to a cultural context or a set of problems, and if it can be seen as representing a contingent choice among alternatives" (129). Analyzing literary structure as part of cultural dynamics thus compensates for the limitations of a *Dictionary* approach. In contrast (or at least in principle), the *Dictionary*'s pluralist enterprise keeps a model-oriented argument from being too satisfied with its own boundaries. The fact that Kupperman's examples are Dostoevsky and Brecht does not mean that his argument is confined to white European males writing in the nineteenth and twentieth centuries, but neither does his essay show any need to confront a broader set of challenges to its humanity.

The problem expressed by most writers is how to recognize and express diversity, and not whether or not it exists. Advanced technologies of information storage and retrieval have multiplied the raw material available for processing into cultural arguments. Even those who, like Allan Bloom, see diversity as a distraction from the exemplary core cannot leave it out of their calculations.[35] One result is the growth of new academic programs in cultural studies, and another even more striking sign is the fact that new editions of standard reference material—handbooks, and encyclopedias of literature—boast of their broader scope and pluralist vision. Anthologies of "world literature," even when subtitled the "Western heritage," situate themselves in relation to the enormous body of omitted texts. They know that their audience has only to consult a map (or even a flawed "world history") to be aware of problems of representation. International collections of any kind commonly include a discussion of principles of selection along with an open or implied apology for their inevitable limitations. Such modesty has become all the more visible in the last decades as critics have noted that the representable "world" expands beyond geographical dimensions to include racial, religious, economic, and gender-specific mapping.

International coverage is less problematic for editors of dictionaries and encyclopedias, who can define their enterprise in geographic and linguistic terms. The 1981 edition of the Ungar *Encyclopedia of World Literature in the Twentieth Century* adds material on African and Asian literature as well as on "minor" European literature.[36] The revised edition of *Cassell's Encyclopedia of World Literature* prides itself on having reflected

> the changed attitudes of the last twenty years . . . added importance has been given to non-European writing . . . [including] the larger treatment of the literatures of Africa and Asia. Under Africa (Subsaharan) will be found new articles covering the major

indigenous literatures, Ethiopian, Hausa, Yoruba, Southern Bantu, and Swahili (with a separate section on Oral Literature) and the literatures of both Anglophone and Francophone Africans to accompany the articles on Afrikaans and South African writing in English.

(1 vii)[37]

While the encyclopedia's accumulation of geographic and ethnic sources makes it an indispensable resource as well as catalyst for discussion, its nature as a quantitative summary limits its usefulness as a guide to reading.

The sixties' attempt to reform the traditional humanities curriculum objected first to *what* was taught: to a mainstream canon that did not reflect the differences of gender, class, and ethnicity in the audience for which it was a requirement (recalling Rimbaud's wry mention of the way a French colonial education required Africans to read about their "blue-eyed ancestors, the Gauls"). Bruce Franklin's polemic address, "The Teaching of Literature in the Highest Academies of the Empire" (read in 1969 at the Modern Language Association Convention), attacked the theoretical, political, and pedagogic narrowness of traditional literary studies by satirizing his experience as an undergraduate English major at Amherst College.

Many of the courses in Great Books of Western Literature were dropped or adapted to fit inside interdisciplinary humanities courses, indicating perhaps that one didn't expect much contemporary relevance from literary studies but that examples of literary high culture could profitably be read inside a broader civilizational context. Such contexts were readily available in new area studies programs that emulated the interdisciplinary scope and structure of American Studies in the previous decade (Smith; Sklar). Some embodied specific cross-cultural projects, such as Tufts University's "African and New World Studies" program which currently coordinates courses in anthropology, art history, dance, economics, English, history, modern languages (Swahili), music, political science, Portuguese, and Spanish and offers literature courses taught in French and Portuguese as well as in English. Combinatory programs possessed a diplomatic advantage over individual reforms in that they could be seen as an enrichment of tradition and not necessarily its wholesale rejection. Antagonism was predictable, however, when the change took place inside a single "core" category, and such antagonism erupted between champions of the traditional Western curriculum and of a more broadly representative "world" context when Stanford revised its traditional Western civilization course. Adopted in 1935, dropped at the end of the sixties, reinstituted in 1978 and required in 1980, the 1988 revision of the latest "Western Culture" sequence into a pluralist "Cultures, Ideas, and Values" program had the distinction of being attacked as decadent by the secretary of education.[38]

Recent models of curricular reform emphasize the way patterns of thought permeate structures of presentation in academic courses, and emphasize the fact that these structures are tacitly proposing approved manners of understanding the material. The first item on a list cannot help but be a reference point for later works, and often this priority becomes the key to a hierarchy of attention and value. The order itself implies its own plot, characters, and even quasi chapters in a proposed story of civilization: in her discussion of the Stanford program, Mary Louise Pratt described the way the conventional paradigm of historical studies (the division into ancient, medieval-renaissance, and "modern" eras) reaffirmed a specifically Eurocentric "canonical narrative of origins." *The Politics of Literature* (Kampf and Lauter 1972) collected essays attacking the narrowly conservative cultural assumptions embedded in conventional English teaching, and Frances Fitzgerald's *America Revised: History Schoolbooks in the Twentieth Century* described the recurrent paradigms governing American history texts read in the public schools. Equally as value-laden as chronology is the practice of treating some works as central and others as peripheral, where the "core" works possess greater importance than "related" texts presented as challenge, analogy, or setting for what is really important. These are not abstract or passing concerns: the same issues were raised in 1987 by participants in an NEH-funded Institute in the Theory and Teaching of World Literature when they noted the different implications of starting a course in world literature with Homer, *Gilgamesh*, or a non-literary work; of equating or subordinating non-canonical material; and of grouping texts in centrally thematic patterns or in conflictual groups seen as opportunities for mutual subversion.[39] Similar issues recur in Paul Lauter's excellent *Canons and Contexts*, and in his description of a "canonical criticism" (opposed to "formalist or speculative criticism") that is "focused on how we construct our syllabi and anthologies, on the roots of our systems of valuation, and on how we decide what is important for us to teach and for our students to learn, or at least to read" (134).

Commenting in 1983 that "a decade ago, it would have been virtually impossible to undertake the pedagogical tasks" of the sixty-seven syllabi collected in *Reconstructing American Litera-*

ture (xxii), editor Lauter hoped that their example would "change the teaching of American literature and, therefore, the definition of what we call American culture" (xi). The syllabi and their accompanying pedagogical notes proposed to increase readers' understanding of a text by taking them closer to the world of its production and initial reception, and by shifting their attention "from interpretation of the text itself to re-creation of the cultural, social, and performance contexts that shape it" (xxi). Essays collected by Robert J. DiPietro and Edward Ifkovic in *Ethnic Perspectives in American Literature* show a similar concern. Other studies made direct connections between the positioning of the reader and strategies for multiplying modes of understanding in the classroom: books with titles like *Gendered Subjects: The Dynamics of Feminist Teaching; The Resisting Reader; The Black Presence in English Literature; Gender and Reading: Essays on Readers, Texts, and Contexts; Textual Power;* and *Theory in the Classroom.* In each case, a narrow or distorted perception of the text's "world" is to be corrected through a better understanding of the dynamics of reading.[40]

The dynamics of reading are closely related to the dynamics of *literacy*, whether as technical competence in reading and writing or as a broader "cultural literacy." Nor are the two necessarily distinct; many composition courses (and textbooks) now diversify their models by including ethnic texts and works by women, and a survey of American literacy from 1880 to the present notes the continuing existence of various literary subcultures and reading communities (Kaestle 279). Recent theoretical and historical studies of literacy show that its definitions and measurements have been remarkably arbitrary, and vary according to period and social context. Carl Kaestle's *Literacy in the United States* documents the difficulty of affirming the rise or decline of literacy in America given unreliable statistics, dissimilar target groups, unsophisticated methods, and changing criteria for judgment.[41] Yet essays in the book also testify to a common assumption that literacy is measured by the degree to which one can recognize language and linguistic concepts in order to function adequately in society: hence the tests for "functional" and "survival" literacy (92, 95) that combine rudimentary reading and writing with some knowledge of cultural context.

This "survival" literacy is a favorite of governmental officials who see it as a reliable, unambiguous, "back-to-basics" category of instruction.[42] Yet even technical competence runs into the question of how and for what this competence exists. Today's *functional* literacy involves more than a narrowly defined set of basics. Myron Tuman shows that in the 1860s "reading was taught as decoding and writing as encoding," with an emphasis on memorization (37), but modern survival literacy is more complex. The study of literacy—like the study of literature—has broadened its base, moving away from memorization and towards processes of understanding. Kaestle argues that American print culture is much more diversified than presupposed by the "basics" of earlier literacy tests.

> Standardized reading material leans toward maintaining the status quo and assimilating people to a mainstream culture. Conversely, cultural diversity in print is aligned with choice, challenge, and individual self-growth. But America's history is, in reality, a tangle of subcultures and myriad patterns of cultural self-definition. . . . each individual's cultural identity is acquired by reconciling or choosing among these cultures. . . . Literacy can expand the thoughtfulness of such choices. . . .
>
> (Kaestle 276)

Literacy in the United States focuses on literacy as technical competence, as the literacy *skills* taught in composition classes whether readings are standardized or diverse. Both Kaestle and Stephen North, in different ways, demonstrate the way that ideas of technical competence have broadened to include various models of communication. North's examination of the "emerging field" of Composition depicts a variegated inquiry into different ways of articulating the world and its relationships. Writing is seen as a process of "naming the world," language as a "speculative instrument," and reading as the "confrontation of more or less coherent and systematic opposed world views" or, by extension, "the mind studying its own operations."[43] The need for world-apprehension is everywhere assumed as an inevitable aspect of language use. North's discussion of the "ethnographers of composition" who mediate between different speech communities describes them, in fact, as "alternate reality brokers" juxtaposing "one imaginative university with another . . . to make both more intelligible" when each is interpreted in terms of its own rules for meaning-making (119, 279, 285).

What North sees more narrowly as an aspect of composition theory, the mediation between different worlds of speech, Myron Tuman considers typical of literacy itself. For the latter critic, modern theories of literacy define a problematic and even philosophical enterprise that is far removed from nineteenth-century dependence on canonical memory and the repetition of community norms. Tuman's theorizing of *literacy* (which he opposes to the "boundaries of illiteracy") examines primarily the processes of understanding connected with the written word. He is not concerned with the broader sense of "cultural literacy" that includes oral cultures, and in fact his analysis tries to make distinctions between cultures that depend on the written word (and thus have a larger and more heterogeneous community memory) and those that do not.[44] We may or may not accept Tuman's view of the limitations of oral culture. Yet the repetition of written forms does not constitute literacy in his eyes. For him, literacy depends on the written word but not on memorization (one can memorize a ritual, but that does not make one literate). Literacy deals in symbolic or open-ended meaning, and it encourages a hermeneutic process of discovery and change. Tuman stresses the therapeutic effects of literacy as a defamiliarizing and recuperative process in which readers go back and forth between new and old frames of reality. He anticipates that *literate* readers have the power to substitute an unfamiliar mental universe for their own.

Tuman's emphasis on adapting to different structures of meaning recalls Lauter's image of American literature, or North's account of communication between alternate mental universes. To the latter more combinatory approaches, however, Tuman adds the importance of *subjective* learning through an engagement that forces the reader out of habitual patterns to engage new modes of being. Reading always involves some unfamiliarity, he says, because texts are already separated from the initial circumstances that gave them meaning; understanding a written work, consequently, entails a leap of the imagination or "essentially the same skills as the effort to understand forms of cultural experience different from our own" (15, 47). Both North and Tuman describe views of literacy that include a form of world-apprehension, and both veer sharply away from a canonical, proficiency-oriented "back-to-basics" definition that depends on memorization. Literacy as they describe it has much in common with concepts of reading as a multidimensional activity that constantly adjusts its perspective on reality. Its goal, says Tuman, is to "break free from the mold of ordinary conversation in order to be able to learn what one would never hear and to assert what one would never say" (99).

When theories of literature and literacy began to attribute educational, ethical, and intellectual value to integrating unfamiliarity rather than to reinforcing community norms, many who hoped for a peaceful renewal of educational tradition were profoundly shaken. Government officials noted belatedly and often with outrage that curricular reform (perhaps funded by national and local grants), had changed not only institutional structures but also modes of understanding. Official and unofficial reports proposed retroactive remedies, such as the 1989 NEH Report outlining a fifty-hour core curriculum (which minimized literary study), and a conservative foundation's "common sense" guidebook to higher education that promised "tough-minded and straightforward appraisals" of a college's core curriculum and its "ethical and social climate."[45]

IV

No matter how "tough-minded" we may be, it is not really possible for curricular reformers to pretend that twentieth-century literary, linguistic, and historiographical theory has not existed or does not count. From the Prague School's early descriptions of structures of norms and value to contemporary semiotic, psychoanalytic, and philosophical investigations into modes of knowledge, the articulation (or deconstruction) of linguistic worlds is part of contemporary patterns of understanding. Nor is this recognition of different communicative economies a decadently modern claim: for anthropologist Dell Hymes, it continues "an intellectual tradition, adumbrated in antiquity, and articulated in the course of the Enlightenment, which holds that [man]kind cannot be understood apart from the evolution and maintenance of its ethnographic diversity" (41).[46] Sociolinguist George Lakoff argues that different cultures and languages are different conceptual systems, "diverse ways of comprehending experience [whose diversity is] necessary to our survival as a species" (337). It is not surprising, then, that so much work on the "meaning of meaning" asks how different communities construct or "authorize" meaning, and how readers or speakers situate themselves inside available horizons of signification. Wolfgang Iser's account of the phenomenology of reading moves from the description of a closely interactive process of textual structures and individual reader to the larger interaction of implied (cultural) horizons of expectation; Hans Robert Jauss sets reception aesthetics inside literary and social history.[47] The interpretation of texts has moreover already begun, according to Edward Said, "by virtue of the exactness of their situation in the world," so that any reading must recognize a text's cultural embedding in order to decipher the way it displaces and overrides competing texts with other world views.[48] Adrienne Rich uses a "politics of location" and of physical identity to describe the cultural positioning embodied in texts (literary or not): "When I was carried out of the hospital into the world, I was viewed and treated as female, but also viewed and treated as white . . . located by color and sex" (and also, presumably, by having been born in a hospital). To escape the reduced reality of habitual reading, she suggests, we must always ask "when, where and under what conditions has the statement been true?" (10–11).

One of the great contributions of deconstructionist theory to cultural criticism has been to display the "supplement" embedded in a text's rhetorical structures, and thus to uncover hidden value-paradigms operating through omission and implied natural processes. The related tactic of describing a text's internal conflicts also presents a world whose categorical contradictions, once laid bare, induce readers to select their own positions in relation to conflicting values. In the best criticism, even assumptions of difference are cross-examined; Barbara Johnson's *A World of Difference* analyzes the complicated inner play of literary texts (e.g., by Zora Neale Hurston) where the nature of cultural difference initially seems unquestionably clear—perhaps taken for granted.[49]

The closer the reading, the more it pursues networks of signification which—even though they momentarily fix meaning—are never fixed themselves. Such, at least, is the picture given by George Lakoff when he describes the constantly adjusting systems of thought and perception in human experience. Exemplary models exist as a tentative framework for understanding but are quickly unsettled by the interference of local detail (local "domains of experience"). Lakoff's intricate discussion of the cognitive categories and radial structure of thought, *Women, Fire, and Dangerous Things: What Categories Reveal about the Mind*, is a remarkable attempt to "read" the shifting texts of different cultures as dynamic or self-adjusting systems that hold in balance a universal conceptualizing capacity on the one hand, and disordering local factors (such as climate and indigenous tradition) on the other. Lakoff includes within his own conceptual model the check and balance of externally derived variation: the globe, for him, is a space of cultural difference that enables us to envisage alternate realities, and such plural comprehension is in itself a cultural imperative. "Diverse ways of comprehending experience are necessary to our survival as a species. . . . Like Whorf, I think we have a lot to learn from other ways of conceptualizing experience that have evolved around the world" (337).[50] For the researcher considering modes of understanding, an abstract model of "worlding" with rigorously pursued networks of *internal* difference is not enough; it must be accompanied by a continual test of that model in the light of different conceptual patterns around the globe. Lakoff's willingness to re-interpret a central paradigm on the basis of its actual concrete variations echoes the alternation between canon and community, or universal and plural reference points, that recurs constantly when readers take seriously the notion of reading the "world" in world literature.

These dual reference points indicate a play of self and other that engages the reader simultaneously as individual (related to an inner "world" of reading) and as member of a cultural community (part of a perceived social world with its global variations). I am not attempting to map out separate identities here: distinctions of inner and outer, or of individual and society, are meant only as heuristic conditions, conventional terms employed as a basis for exploration and inquiry. They are additionally useful in that they acknowledge the expectation that "world" literature will situate the reader somehow "in the world," or that it will clarify a sense of personal identity through awareness of one's "situation in the world."

Perhaps unavoidably, this reading for the self verbalizes the world in spatial terms, mapping it with inclusions and exclusions that etch boundaries between areas of experience. The self who is to be illuminated will draw on the entire globe organized as an instructive Other: the world is everything "out there" separate from the perceiving self and available to enrich it with glimpses of different ways of being. Arguments for global studies and "world" literature conventionally depend on the existence of such a geographic or cultural Other existing now or in the remote past. The wisdom to be gained from these encounters is a securely distanced and totalized body of experience whose alien qualities can be catalogued in greater or lesser abundance and whose study entails no real invasion of the perceiver's self-identity. Such a separatist quest not only implies that the world is *out there* waiting to be found, but also that any individual self is incomplete without the guidance of the larger entity. Evoking access to a promised "other" world, this view encourages readers to substitute a larger controlling paradigm for their partial—and therefore inferior—individual judgment. Yet incompleteness is not by definition inferiority, nor does it guarantee an inferior reading stance. It may, instead, be the corollary of that multiplicity which is also a staple of "world" and "world literature" images.

According to Hans-Georg Gadamer, the concept of worldview itself implies variety and difference, incorporating "multiplicity and the possible change of worldviews" (442). If "worldview" generically encompasses myriad separate worldviews, none is a total or complete vision. Instead, each worldview, like any view, is limited by incomplete awareness, its "truth" as truly finite as the historical condition in which it is situated. This finite condition also entails a partial blindness in self-images, which is just as well to remember when "reading" the world or construing its relation to the self. *"To be historically means that knowledge of oneself can never be complete"* (302).[51] Maurice Merleau-Ponty had already noted that the world that we perceive is only indicated and not grasped; put otherwise, "the perception of the world cannot be assumed to be true but is defined for us as access to the truth" (xi).[52] The subjective impasse of the worldview is dramatized by poet Yves Bonnefoy as the "lure of the threshold," in which the threshold promises entry into a realm beyond, while it remains the only domain we can truly inhabit, a space of unending access.

This space of perpetual access and limited awareness is also the relational space of reading, where each reader's incomplete perspective constitutes one part of a web of relations that simultaneously separate and connect.[53] Psychoanalytic studies have done the most to spell out the negotiated understandings of self and world, whether as part of ego-analysis or in a Lacanian tradition that decenters selfhood and denies fixed identity. Reading in the latter perspective emphasizes the way that meaning is necessarily suspended or perpetually negotiated by an awareness that is always oriented towards what it is not and cannot fully grasp. A more palpable image of the space of access is D. W. Winnicott's experimental space of play, where the child's incipient "I" constitutes its personal identity by testing out separation from and attachment to the world. This self/ other scenario involves more than the famous teddy bear as a transactional object, and it extends easily to any situation that allows for separation and attachment. The world of cultural values, Winnicott asserts in *Playing and Reality*, enters into developmental play inasmuch as these values provide and restrict the space of action, enabling or limiting the free play that assures imagination, creativity, and growth.[54] Much the same social function was attributed to play by sociolinguist L. S. Vygotsky when, as part of his discussion of language use in analyzing and mastering reality, he noted how children create imaginary situations in order to try out rules for dealing with real-life tensions (35–37, 94–95).

"World" and "self" are inextricable parts of a dynamic network of correspondences, notes the French philosopher Jean-François Lyotard. Although one would not ordinarily link Lyotard's postmodernist views with the more centered work of Winnicott and Vygotsky, each writer stresses the importance of perceiving relationships as a key to understanding. Lyotard's *Postmodern Condition* strikingly reformulates a literary image—the religious personalism familiar to English readers as John Donne's "No man is an island"—

inside the rhetoric of intertextuality. "A *self* does not amount to much, but no self is an island; each exists in a fabric of relations that is now more complex and mobile than ever before. Young or old, man or woman, rich or poor, a person is always located at 'nodal points' of specific communication circuits, however tiny these may be" (Lyotard 15). What is noticeable throughout these discussions of multiplicity and shifting identifications is that the gathering-term *world* continues to play a part in definitions of identity—that is, it remains an anchor or reference point—but it is used *only* as an intuited reference point and not as some unitary *thing* grasped in itself. In whatever form the relation of personal self and exteriority is assumed to take place, the world that was initially offered as a touchstone of difference disappears in a web of connections once it is "read" or put to the test. Similarly, the self previously understood as a separate entity to be "discovered" or drawn out now disappears inside the definition of its dynamic relationships with the world.

The same pattern of exchange operates on a broader level when the "self" is a larger or plural entity: for example, a nation or community seeking the security of cultural self-definition as part of its search for survival. The urgency of educational policy proposals to reassert the Western tradition is based on the same survivalist opposition of self and other, and on the need to rediscover a community self by pruning away whatever is alien to it. Minus the poetry, it is a modernized version of Herder's quest to regenerate fallen cultures by rediscovering their national essence. The cry "Is there no heritage common to us all?" implies nothing else than this search for the cultural bonding that might be achieved through an agreed-upon vision of the Western heritage.

Clearly what has been called the Western tradition does in fact exist as a particular set of cultural habits, an inherited framework operating to link segments of the community and to keep alive a group of (however debated) perspectives. The geographic and social continuity of this tradition is visible: it is "the continuity between Greek and Roman literatures, the Western medieval world, and the main modern literatures; and, without minimizing the importance of Oriental influences, especially that of the Bible, one must recognize a close unity which includes all Europe, Russia, the United States, and the South American literatures" (Wellek *Theory* 41). Subtending this cultural unity are persisting shared values, generally described as the belief in open inquiry and debate, in publicly accessible knowledge, participatory government, and openness to change, in the valuing of individual experience, and in scientific method as a procedure and also as a means of democratizing understanding. This ideal version remains a useful convention even for those who deny static images of historical influence. Indeed, a contemporary historian who affirms that "history does not exist" and "facts have no absolute dimensions" also finds that the study of cultural diversity is a typically Western concern. "From Montaigne to *Tristes tropiques* or to *L'Histoire de la folie* of Foucault, the variety of values from nation to nation and from century to century is one of the great themes of Western sensibility" (Veyne 6).[55]

Examples of the "Western heritage" complicate themselves under close scrutiny, however, following out global networks of historical, economic, and cultural affiliation that crisscross maps of inclusion and exclusion. Even the Arnoldian view of Western culture is more complicated than would be suggested by his image as the upholder (after Swift) of a canonical "sweetness and light." The famous passage in *Culture and Anarchy* recommends a continued activity— the "pursuit of our total perfection"—and not a unique model of perfection. Matthew Arnold wishes to disseminate knowledge of "the best which has been thought and said in the world," but he does not propose a book list. Instead, he reasons that culture is renewed by the influence of "fresh and free thought upon our stock notions and habits, which we now follow staunchly but mechanically, vainly imagining that there is a virtue in following them staunchly which makes up for the mischief of following them mechanically" (xi).[56] In other words, it is not the repetition of customary values that enables the renewal of community or cultural identity, but rather the reforming impact of unfamiliar ideas.

Both supporters and challengers of the Western heritage alike find it difficult to avoid referring to a monolithic image. Fredric Jameson's "Third-World Literature and International Capitalism" uses such a reified perception of the West in order to attack Western literary canons and build a "cognitive aesthetics of the third world" based on national allegories. He founds his attack on a set of geopolitical assumptions that Aijaz Ahmad, in a dismayed response, calls oversimplified and paradoxically colored by the same first-world thinking that Jameson wishes to escape. To the American critic's categorization of readers as Western or non-Western, Ahmad counters that this distinction alienates Ahmad's own identity and reduces it to that of Jameson's "civilizational Other." Rereading the essay's binary Western/non-Western, first world/third world opposition in order to assert (partly through his own intercultural experience) the claims of the excluded middle, the Pakistani critic urges a more precise understanding of texts that would involve the "utter historicity of multiple, interpenetrating relations." What is striking, at least in terms of conventional academic practice, is the pragmatic equation of both literary and historical readings. Ahmad rejects Jameson's division of the globe into three worlds both as cultural critique and as a basis for literary criticism,[57] and he reaffirms the need for *any* definition of "world" identity to be part of a web of relations.

The shifting boundaries of world-apprehension appear in a different light when they leave the speculative forum of scholarly debate and move into daily educational practice. The harsher focus does not result only from the artificial closure of calendar constraints and the limited availability of texts. (Such closure, however, clarifies the workings of an underlying value system as nothing else could do.) Demographic changes and a wide range of institutional settings have discredited the picture of a standard reading context in the schools or an accepted interpretation that would be equally meaningful to all students. Reading guided by a single worldview lacks credibility when audiences are more diverse,[58] students less generally knowledgeable,[59] and the quest for common learning itself occurs in a fragmented "postmodernist" society where fifty different purposes for general education have been promulgated since 1918.[60] Although society still expects education to provide cultural continuity and social bonding, educators have become increasingly aware of the complicated circumstances that influence the way these goals can—or cannot—be pursued.

It is not surprising, therefore, that so much rethinking of ideas about reading, community standards, and inherited tradition has gone on in educational institutions, among people who confront these issues as part of their daily responsibility and must weigh the impact of their work on students as individuals and as future citizens of the community. The reform movements of the sixties have visibly changed curricular patterns and influenced publishers' lists towards the inclusion of more diverse material and points of view. Even if the move towards a world-oriented curriculum is incomplete (and the current "back to basics" movements implicitly rejects much of that larger perspective), its more comprehensive vision has put an end to sharp divisions between humanities and the human sciences. Current patterns of understanding are reflected in the emergence of interdisciplinary programs (more recently, "centers"), as well as in literature courses that draw on material culture, cognitive science, and new modes of historical inquiry. These are not eccentric experiments. National and regional organizations award curriculum planning grants to implement our changed understanding of how people learn; professional associations hold lengthy seminars on literacy (both technical and cultural), on reading (related to gender and class), and on new audiences and different patterns of learning; national journals break down these general issues into a plethora of more specialized articles.

Teachers of world literature are engaged in many aspects of this reappraisal, for they are tacitly charged not only with transmitting a particular cultural heritage through major texts but also with introducing readers to global history.[61] The potential contradictions of this task soon emerge in practice and serve as a point of departure for rethinking methods in the light of common aims. A group of college and university teachers examining the theory and practice of world literature express the difficulty as follows: "A sense of this diverse world is something our students have a right to expect from us . . . Any narrower view will only hinder their understanding of their own and others' cultures, and render them less able to act in a world whose diversity they do not expect" ("Report on World Literature" 1). Moreover, they note,

> Courses that stress Western literature under a 'world literature' title implicitly present the West as the center of the world, with other cultures in a dependent position. Clearly such a centering presupposes its own hierarchy of values, and in itself requires appropriate classroom discussion. . . . Western culture is not a monolith. The history, culture, and economics of the West are interdependent with the rest of the world, and nowhere is this relationship more obvious than in the diversity of ethnic backgrounds and ethnic literatures within the United States itself.
>
> (2)

The courage and dedication of this statement emerge more clearly when the authors remind us that their own preparation falls short of this goal.[62]

> Most faculty members are likely to be trained in the traditional Western canon described by T. S. Eliot; they rise in their careers through specializing in aspects of that canon; and they are understandably uncomfortable in speaking not only from a vantage point of lesser authority but also with less cultural knowledge.
>
> ("Report" 2).

Uncomfortable or not, these are the teachers who are reworking their world literature courses towards a more cross-cultural model, whether by learning about material and modes of perception in other societies or by employing the diversity of their own classroom to introduce a measure of "worlding" in teaching literature.

That there is no single cross-cultural model for teaching is clear; moreover, individual reworkings always reflect the way in which the course is situated inside academic patterns and different institutional needs. Usually one of a series of introductory requirements, the world literature course does not exist in a vacuum and is at least partially defined by its relationship to other types of requirement. English? History? Civilization? Humanities? Taught inside an English department where they form a minor part of a program dedicated to British and American literature and to composition, world literature courses are often a mildly international equivalent of the conventional introduction to literature, taught in invisible translation. If the institution requires a separate grounding in the "Western heritage" (assuming that world literature is not defined *as* that heritage), then world literature draws its texts from the "rest" of the world: the non-West, used as foil and complement to a presumedly indigenous tradition. Needless to say, such a division risks prolonging a monolithic image of both "West" and "rest." If Great Books are the model, the selection usually includes a larger proportion of philosophical or religious works. Some humanities programs take the world literature course as an opportunity for teamwork among different departments—art, history, music, philosophy, literature—so that selected (major) texts become the focus of an introduction to the relationships of the arts. Conversely, area or gender studies programs that aim to introduce images of diverse cultural experience through literature may include texts from around the world that are neither "great books" nor aesthetic documents. When the world literature course is linked with "world civilization" or situated inside a program of global studies, the historical syllabus with its emphasis on chronology often dictates the format and thematic pattern of literary study.

Physical settings also play their role in influencing the perceived horizons of the world literature course. Urban, suburban, or pastoral, public or private, commuter or residential, religious or secular, large or small, cloaked in tradition and ivy-covered stone or joined to the landscape by full-length plate glass, the material circumstances of different academic institutions already suggest their own horizons of expectation and contexts for reading. The effects of social privilege or deprivation have often been demonstrated; what is worth noting here is the way that architectural space suggests its own correlated views—of a solid, harmonious, stable set of values built on ancient foundations; of modular wisdom given temporary housing and accessible to current needs; of speed, motion, and shifts between sharply demarcated units; of overlapping boundaries and shared areas of concern.[63] These latent frameworks of value extend an invisible invitation to participate in their perspectival order, whether of physical space or the arrangement of a mental world. The opposite situation occurs when the physical context is so striking a factor that it becomes a perspective to be confronted in reading or even used as a point of departure. Such was the opportunity taken by a teacher[64] on a military base in Adana, Turkey, when she devised a world literature course that would not only integrate Turkish history and literature into the general reading list but, through further analogies and perspectives, indirectly provided an interpretive framework for an audience of servicemen who were almost totally unprepared by their previous schooling to encounter a different set of norms. Here both texts and associated reading expectations mediated between an unfamiliar cultural setting and an uprooted, newly "foreign" reader whose first reaction was usually to retreat into the reassuring enclave of his home away from home.

In some instances, the mission of individual institutions and the nature of the contemporary audience dictates a more pluralist sense of identity. World literature courses in a college like Spelman, historically dedicated to the education of black women, are enriched by the institution's need to define its intellectual and cultural position inside the larger community (which community?) and in relation to traditional educational models. Denominational institutions, like any institution addressing a particular audience, are already positioned in a certain way and can use that location as a point of departure for courses that promise an introduction to the "world." No syllabus is impervious to student scrutiny, which in some cases may see something quite different from the professor's canonical intentions. An ethnically diverse class is more likely to look for different traditions intertwined in the "Western" heritage, and be able to read the oppositional "non-Western" texts with a less bifocal vision.[65] Similarly, the reliability of translated material is perceived differently by students who speak several languages and by those who know only one. The provocative "otherness" to be incorporated into world literature, as well as the anchoring outlines of a "Western heritage," is as difficult to locate as the "stock notions and habits" that according to Matthew Arnold must always be challenged by "fresh and free thought."

The teaching paradigm is thus a shifting or dialogic one in which initial versions of self and other are constantly complicated as part

of the process of discovery.[66] The most frustrating aspect of this conclusion is that it disallows any fixed answer to questions that invariably recur whenever a world literature syllabus is created. Each
time, a range of possibilities arises that cannot be ignored but can
never be finally adjudicated. I have already mentioned the importance of relative position on the syllabus—the anchoring status of
the first text, or of the "core" works to which all else is ancillary.
Other issues include the relative proportions of modern and pre-
modern works, the number of works written in English or read in
translation, the competitive relationship between coverage and exemplarity (with "coverage" also encompassing representation by
chronology, gender, class, and ethnicity), the advantages and disad-
vantages of chronological order, the use of oral as well as written
texts, the central or marginal positions of "literature," "history,"
and "non-literary" texts, and the value of familiarity as a point of
departure compared to the therapeutic shock of difference. With
each syllabus, similar choices are decided with greater or lesser conscious intent. As a result, world literature in academic practice re-
solves into an example of W. B. Gallie's "essentially contested concepts," indicating that the only response to these questions may be
to recognize that answers are *enacted* rather than *ascertained*.

In fact, such individual enactment takes place each time students
of "world literature" are asked to experience the text as vicarious
knowledge of other cultures, or encouraged to relate their worlds to
an alternate picture of human experience. The assumption is that
literature projects worlds of the imagination that are temporarily
adopted and matched with our own. When a scene or manner of
acting is unfamiliar, readers draw on their own experience to project
a hybrid reality that "makes sense" so as to be able to continue reading. A process of correlation is engaged that builds a newly coherent
whole and enlarges the reader's intellectual scope and sense of identity; it emulates Goethe's notion of a literary conversation of cultural identities over their common curiosity about sameness and
difference, and it shares the generous optimism of Kant's description
of the humanities as *Teilnehmung*, "taking part" in and "impart-
ing" humanity in a fundamentally social act.[67] Yet the act of reading
does not always produce a harmonious whole, and sometimes the
very need to adjust discrepant horizons also emphasizes difference
and sharpens the exclusion of the other world. A potentially vicarious experience may be forced to assume the outlines of a cherished
familiar reality, or the fusion of different cultural horizons may be
rejected because a particular disparity cannot be assimilated without endangering familiar concepts of self. Reading world literature

in its full web of relations must all the more be understood as *reading*, as construing overlapping worlds whose inescapable interaction problematizes individuals, texts, and community horizons.

A complicated set of assumptions enters into reading "for" the world: a manifold knot of language, history, aesthetics, and truth. Gadamer calls aesthetics a "history of worldviews" which he immediately equates with a "history of truth" manifest in the work of art. He dates the concept of *Weltanschauung* to Hegel's *Phenomenology of Mind*, but adds that its "special stamp" in aesthetics comes not from an expanded model of moral order—a fixed or exemplary image—but from the representation of multiplicity and change. Language in all its variety corresponds to the idea of worldview because language formulates the perception of reality, because it mediates the relationship of human beings to themselves and to the world, and because it surpasses individual formulations to become a larger world of expression: a sociolinguistic universe contextualizing and embedding individual speakers. In Gadamer's paraphrase of Humboldt, *"a language-view is a worldview"* (442) and language and perception are equally active in their structuring of the truth. The insistence on a structure of truth that incorporates multiplicity and change distinguishes this hermeneutical position— even as it emphasizes the incompleteness of individual reading experiences—from postmodern strategies that derive their sense of world from within the network and eschew any larger coordination or context.

Criticism of the literary world view seems to alternate between the world as geographic or cultural "globe" (with corresponding implications of wholeness and representation), and the less finished experience of "being-in-the-world." It moves between quantifiable, unitary, and plausibly representative structures (a semiotic or positivist vein) and a manipulation of perceptions, qualities, and value whose dense and open-ended interplay attests to its "truth." This alternation does not simply oppose images of wholeness and incompletion, for semiotic analyses frequently play with the dynamics of fragmentation, and phenomenological analyses project the image of a (at least potentially) complete being. Moreover, the boundary line between cultural and personal identity always retreats upon approach. What is noticeable is that the implied guarantors of worldliness are different in either case. On the one hand, the "global" perspective lays claim to authenticity through the multiplicity and accuracy of its categories of representation, whether geographic or cultural. The world is a mappable geographic object with observable cultures and conventions: the more you represent their diversity, subtle relationships, and confrontations, including the way that textual production suggests its own pre-reading, the closer you come to reality. Adrienne Rich suggested as much in her "Politics of Location," and "worldliness" is the term adopted by Edward Said in *The World, the Text, and the Critic.* It is deceptive, suggests the latter, to find worlds *inside* texts or even inside the reader's mind, for the "real" world cannot be contained in that way. Said does not accept a categorical difference between written texts and speech, in which the text would have infinite and infinitely free networks of intertextuality whereas speech would always be embedded in a real-life communicative situation. To Paul Ricoeur's proposal (in "What Is a Text?" 138) that "a text is somehow 'in the air,' outside of the world or without a world" and that "by means of this obliteration of all relation to the world, every text is free to enter into relation with all the other texts which come to take the place of the circumstantial reality shown by living speech," Said retorts that "worldliness does not come and go," and "texts have ways of existing that even in their most rarefied form are always enmeshed in circumstance, time, place, and society—in short, they are in the world, and hence worldly" (34–35). Clearly both Ricoeur and Said in this instance are using "world" not in the sense of a world of individual consciousness, however grounded it may be, but in a more distanced application as the referential "real world" of historical materiality. If a critical promise of attaining the "world" is to have any force, it must find a way of making links to this more comprehensive situation. For Ricoeur, the task of literary interpretation is to "actualize" a hitherto suspended reference. For Said, however, the world of reference pre-exists and determines reading.

Guaranteeing the other, less easily documented perspective is a philosophical integrity whose coordination with formal strategies of literary analysis (otherwise known as practical criticism) is sometimes difficult to articulate. It may depend on intuited existential categories which are then combined to form a world of prereflexive consciousness (as in the second Geneva School),[68] or on psychoanalytic negotiations of self and other (personal, cultural, and absolute Other) that compose a world of symbolic order. Criticism intent on recuperating a world of consciousness projects its world-frames in various directions: into the embeddings of the implied author, or the imbricated worlds operating between text and reader, or into the world-potentials disclosed by successive readers and their diverse contexts. It may hypothesize an oracular appreciation of intuited Being in the house of language, or articulate the relationship of being and language in concepts of density and activity that could conceivably be called the postmodern equivalent of New Criticism's "efficient cluster of meanings" but instead stakes out the world under a specially open and dynamic paradigm. Gianni Vattimo proposes just such a concept to explain how aesthetic experience constitutes a model of the worlded "experience of truth." The aesthetic model consists of "intensely concentrated nuclei of meaning," nuclei that "constitute the only possible point of departure for any discourse that does not just duplicate what already exists, but rather claims to be able to criticize it." In a later section of *The End of Modernity*, the Italian philosopher suggests (after Heidegger) a further distinction: the world, he says, "is the system of meanings which are read as they unfold in the work," but the "earth is that element of the work which comes forth as ever concealing itself anew, like a sort of nucleus that is never used up by interpretations and never exhausted by meanings" (Vattimo 13, 71). The inexhaustibility of "earth," read as an always open and continually recreated play of relationships, gives life to static patterns and to literature when it promises the world.

There is no guarantee that world literature can keep the promises that have been made in its name, and it certainly cannot do so without attention paid to the "worlded" act of reading. Yet the variety and complexity of theories devised to account for the presence (or absence) of "world" in the text have had little impact on the most visible example of the study of world literature: its solidly established presence in the academic curriculum. This traditional presence, reinforced by current fears for community survival if that tradition is endangered, tends by its weight alone to delay changes in methods or material. Its success has much to do with the fact that many of the works included in the mainstream canon are dense and active enough to find their own subversive route to the reader's imagination, and they are thus able to survive unimaginative pedagogy and limiting interpretations. Efforts to rethink the study of world literature will continue, nonetheless, as long as there is a discrepancy between the lively expectations generated by the term "world" and the pinched reality elicited by conventional approaches.

For world literature to evoke the multiple, changing *worldview* that Gadamer calls the experience of "truth," worldly multiplicity and difference must become a part of the reading process. That process is also a recognition of *incompleteness*: an incompleteness that impels the search, if not for completion, at least for connection with a world constituted by similarly incomplete points of view. With a different vocabulary and imagery, this model of interaction and change is reminiscent of the interconnected society and world view that Goethe hoped to bring about through the community discourse of world literature. In principle, this latter world is not fixed by the canons or texts of the past but is constituted as a future-oriented process of transformation and change, brought about in a continuous rereading of one identity through the eyes of another. Mention of Goethe is not indispensable at this point, but it continues to be relevant inasmuch as his name and reputation are associated with the term he popularized, and because there is such a paradigmatic discrepancy between his concept of world literature and the static or canon-bound view that has defined it as a staple of the American curriculum.

The inquiry could start anywhere: a question of literary theory, analysis of a poem, any example of reading *in situ*. Here, we have focused on two areas: the juxtaposition of the already-problematic terms *world* and *literature*, and an academic practice that has the apparently paradoxical aim of making readers feel at home in the world while consolidating their sense of local community. In each case, it seems clear that solutions to existing dilemmas are not found in the closure of static models, and that a more dynamic approach that also considers the audience part of the evolving world-view will be part of any hoped-for "experience of truth." The difficulty in practice is to avoid cutting short or disabling the entire enterprise—to set in motion a process of inquiry and cross-reference that does not bog down in the accumulation of exotic data or an invisible recycling of familiar beliefs.

Rethinking the world literature curriculum too easily falls into an impasse between the unlimited possibilities of a representative book list (coverage) and the paradigmatic value of selected texts (exemplarity). It may be less important, however, to settle on certain texts than to think carefully about how they will be presented—or reciprocally *negotiated*—and in what context of values. This is not to ignore issues of "major" and "minor" texts, or the way texts are selected or deselected in the first place. Choosing texts follows a variety of imperatives, some of which have been mentioned earlier, and any collection can and probably should be examined for what it excludes or pushes to the margin. The important thing is to provoke that examination and to encourage the more comprehensive inquiry. Combinations of texts from various cultures usually elicit a sense of difference faster than one book, or than five books describing the traumas of adolescent males in modern American society. There is no foolproof selection, however, for anything can be interpreted in a reassuring rather than disorienting perspective. Exotic texts may be read in familiar terms, and even the common practice of selecting translations for their "accessibility" further domesticates the original text's patterns of understanding. Insufficient knowledge, unrecognized customs of speech, or the desire to rely completely on one's own cultural expectations, noting only where they are upset by strange elements that are not further explored: all invisibly foreclose the interrogation of internal and external difference. Whether cross-cultural or intracultural, a successful catalyst initiates an "othering" process that obliges readers to match their own frameworks against different systems of reality, in the course of which they acquire the worldliness that is aware of itself as a finite perspective positioned inside a complicated and dynamic worldview.

It is ironic that so much faith should be invested in major canonical texts without corresponding energy being put into insuring that they are read. Even if a community has a vested interest in having its members share knowledge of a series of common texts (for example, "masterpieces"), issuing a book list does not suffice. I. A. Richards's *Practical Criticism* demonstrated how easy it is *not* to read canonical texts and to let a set of assumptions concerning "Shakespeare," "Donne," or "D. H. Lawrence" substitute for close reading in a fill-in-the-blank school of interpretation. Non-canonical works, film and interdisciplinary texts, and documentary material have been used effectively to start the process of world-apprehension. Non-canonical questions may initiate a more far-reaching inquiry than others whose predictable nature allies them with conventional approaches to the texts they study. Themes of love, heroism, fate, or coming to maturity, used typically to unify the world-literature syllabus, are double-edged; their universal scope encourages an initial comparison of differences around the world, but it is easy to prioritize the familiar model and measure "other ways" against it. If these notions are not particularly new, they nonetheless redirect attention to the fact that a text has limited meaning unless it enlists the reader's continued and multifarious curiosity.

Canonical texts are at an initial disadvantage insofar as their reputation precedes and often defines them. This reputation in itself is one reason to include them in a list of readings; they provide an opportunity to display and to analyze a specific image that society wishes to preserve of itself.[69] If they are "masterpieces," the presumption is that they generate a particularly full experience of value in their readers. This presumption once again is subject to investigation. It may be examined in a historical perspective for its conjunction of ingrained cultural attitudes and for the ideological activity carried out in its name. It may also be analyzed for its conceptual claim to be a catalyst of multiple insights operating through a specially efficacious use of language. The latter argument depends, visibly, on a concept of artistic language as a web of potential references that are more easily accessible to the reader than is true for other works, whose power to engage exploratory thought is limited to the repetition of familiar patterns.

Ascribing to language the power to set in motion different world views implies a particular kind of literacy, one that combines the cultural literacy of broad reference and the primary literacy of reading and writing. It engages a problematics of knowing and *naming* in which experience of the world is made a subject of consciousness after being approached as the unfamiliarity of cultural difference. Goethe's picture of a reciprocal reading that progressively illuminates identity finds an echo in contemporary theories that examine how meaning is negotiated among different domains of experience. In both instances, more is at stake than a cyclic exchange: the encounter and mutual transformation of different points of view opens up new directions and makes possible the creation of new identity. This possibility of directed change may well be what is meant by the adaptability and self-confidence traditionally promised in the name of world literature. The literacy of world literature is consequently the ability to read for a *new* world in relation to the *old*: to construct new worldviews by comparing other systems of reality, to imagine and bring about change by examining reciprocal reflections and their intervening space of exchange. The boundaries of this intervening space have not yet been fixed; it is a potential world that problematizes issues and adds an initiatory dimension to the perception of otherness. The world of world literature is not a canonical model because it is and always has been a process of global discovery.

Notes

1. Various distinctions are made between the related categories of world, general, and universal literature. Albert Guerard subdivides literature as follows: "*Universal Literature* . . . embraces all literatures, of all ages, in all languages, without insisting on their unity or their relations. *World Literature* is limited to those works which are enjoyed in common, ideally by all mankind, practically by our own group of culture, the European or Western" (*Preface to World Literature* 16). A. Owen Aldridge defines world literature as "the great works or classics of all times selected from all of the various national literatures" and universal literature as "the sum total of all texts

and works throughout the world, or the combination of all national literatures" or alternately "all works that contain elements cosmopolitan enough to appeal to the average person in any literate culture" (*The Reemergence of World Literature: A Study of Asia and the West* 55–56). René Wellek finds the distinctions theoretically unimportant: world literature is the "study of literature in its totality, with 'world-literature,' with 'general' or 'universal' literature. . . . The term 'world literature,' a translation of Goethe's *Weltliteratur*, is perhaps needlessly grandiose, implying that literature should be studied on all five continents, from New Zealand to Iceland" (*Theory of Literature* 40–41). The basic study of Goethe's idea of world literature and its impact on European society is Fritz Strich's *Goethe and World Literature*. Strich makes the following distinction: "When in ordinary speech we talk of world literature we mean . . . the choice literature which has gained for itself a significance transcending nationality and time. . . . Goethe meant by it something quite different from our colloquial use of it. World literature is, then, according to Goethe, the literature which serves as a link between national literatures and thus between the nations themselves, for the exchange of ideal values" (4–5).

2. The celestial image recalls both the phrasing and the essentialist thought of Irving Babbitt in his "Ancients and Moderns": "In like manner some of the ancients and a few of the greatest of the moderns may be regarded as the fixed stars of literature. We may safely take our bearings with reference to them and be guided by them in deciding what is essence and what is accident in human nature" (194–195). Religious and philosophical writings are specifically classified under "world literature" in the *Dictionary*, and the entire section is distinguished from "Literature in English."

3. See Aijaz Ahmad, "Literature among the Signs of Our Times" and "Literary Theory and 'Third World Literature': Some Contexts."

4. Or, as Christine Brooke-Rose has pointed out in her "Palimpsest History," it suggests itself as a "magic realist" tissue of history and fantasy that provides still another interpretation of the world.

5. An introduction to Yukio Mishima's *The Temple of the Golden Pavilion* comments that the novel "could only have been written by a Japanese and a member of a race whose cultural heritage is essentially Buddhist. This is one of its great values to the Western reader. . . . Through the pages of a novel like Yukio Mishima's, one is able to perceive some of the elements that have gone into the creation of this rare, paradoxical, and long-enduring civilization" (Nancy Ross 18). The jacket description of Mishima's *The Sailor Who Fell from Grace with the Sea* perceives a different civilization in "a Novel of the Homicidal Hysteria that Lies Latent in the Japanese Character."

6. See the excellent collection *Canons*, ed. Robert von Hallberg (University of Chicago Press, 1984).

7. Auerbach's aim in this essay (which was first published in a festschrift for Fritz Strich in 1952) is only obliquely related to Goethe's more future-oriented concept; the twentieth-century critic "accepts as an inevi-

table fact that world-culture is being standardized" (7) and would preserve the recognition of cultural pluralism through a "scholarly and synthesizing philology of *Weltliteratur*" (9).

8. In his edition of Quintilian's treatise on the education of an orator, W. Peterson notes, after Usener, that the traditional list of historians was arranged by pairs, possibly with the inclusion of a final fifth pair to make up the conventional total of ten names (xxxvii).

9. "Nec sane quisquam est tam procul a cognitione eorum [plurimorum poetarum, 56] remotus, ut non indicem certe ex bibliotheca sumptum transferre in libros suos possit" (X, I 57).

10. For a useful discussion of European and American ideas about the cultural value of literary education, from the Enlightenment to the present, see Gossman. For a more sociological approach, see Joan Shelley Rubin's description of the development and commercialization of "Great Books" programs in twentieth-century America (*The Making of Middle-Brow Culture*, 1992).

11. Rosenberg also quotes a description (taken from a 1953–1954 Wisconsin catalogue) of a subsequent "graduate course in 'Great Books of World Literature,' in which the ideas and philosophies of ten masterpieces are studied each semester" (27): an excellent illustration of the way that reading practices at the graduate student level often derive from and feed back into undergraduate teaching methods—including, in this case, teaching methods for world literature.

12. "In virtually all of our major universities, there is a lively interest in the special needs and problems which have arisen in response to the rapid development of basic courses and programs embracing an increasing part of world literature" (Block 1).

13. See Block, *The Teaching of World Literature*: Frederic Will, "The Evaluation and Use of Translations" (23–30), Walter R. Agard, "Teaching the Classics in Translation" (31–34), John C. McGalliard, "The Teaching of European Literature from St. Augustine to Dante" (35–44), Hazel S. Alberson, "Non-Western Literature in the World Literature Program" (45–52), H. V. S. Ogden, "On Defining the Humanities" (53–64), M. Isenberg, "The Role of Philosophical Texts in a Humanities Program" (65–72), Weldon M. Williams, "Intensive and Extensive Approaches in the Teaching of World Literature" (73–82), and Ralph Freedman, "Correlating the Teaching of Literature in Translation" (109–119).

14. The "literary Bibles" are more than single texts: Moulton identifies "1. The Holy Bible. 2. Classical Epic and Tragedy. 3. Shakespeare. 4. Dante and Milton: The Epics of Medieval Catholicism and Renaissance Protestantism. 5. Versions of the Story of Faust." He also discusses "Comparative Reading" (Chapter 7) and concludes with "The Place of World Literature in Education." Selections from the Introduction and Conclusion are reprinted with an introduction in the Winter 1993 *Yearbook of Comparative and General Literature*.

The third chapter of Moulton's promised introduction to literary theory,

"Literary Evolution as Reflected in the History of World Literature," is organized on broadly generic lines (*The Modern Study of Literature* 117–218).

15. Terry Eagleton's description of the ideological impulse behind studying "English" could easily apply to the study of world literature. "English was . . . *the* supremely civilizing pursuit, the spiritual essence of the social formation. English was an arena in which the most fundamental questions of human existence—what it meant to be a person, to engage in significant relationship with others, to live from the vital centre of the most essential values—were thrown into vivid relief" (31).

16. Hans-J. Weitz reports an earlier use of the term in Wieland (206–208).

17. "The term *world literature* is Goethe's invention. It suggests a historical scheme of the evolution of national literatures in which they will fuse and ultimately melt into a great synthesis. Today the term is used in a sense which was not in Goethe's mind. It means all literature from Iceland to New Zealand, or the classics which have become a common heritage of all nations" (Wellek *History* 221).

18. "The matter is rather this—that the living, striving men of letters should learn to know each other, and through their own inclination and similarity of tastes, find the motive for corporate action" (Goethe in an address to the Congress of Natural Scientists in Berlin, 1828; quoted in Strich 350).

19. He notes also a reported conversation with Willibald Alexis in August 1829 (351).

20. Note to *Scientific Writings*, vol. 6, p. 221 (quoted in Strich 20).

21. "The first is that, abandoning the artistic form, one can convey in simple prose the bare sense and content of a foreign work. . . . The second is that at which one assimilates the sense of the foreign work and tries to reproduce it in one's own manner. . . . At the third stage however, the highest and the last, the translator's national characteristics are surrendered and [the translator] tries to make a translation identical with the original in form and content" (quoted in Strich 7).

22. Letter of March 14, 1828 (quoted in C. E. Norton 77).

23. "Helen in Edinburgh, Paris and Moscow" (1828; quoted in Strich 76–77).

24. January 31, 1827 conversation with Eckermann. My translations.

25. Herder, in the *Ideas for a Philosophy of History*. "If we take the idea of European culture for our standard, we shall, indeed, only find it applicable to Europe" (Book IX). " . . . I should like to express the hope that distinctions that have been made—from a perfectly laudable zeal for scientific exactitude—between different members of the human species will not be carried beyond bounds. Some, for instance, have thought fit to employ the term *races* for four or five divisions, according to regions of origin or complexion. I see no reason for employing this term. Race refers to a difference of origin, which in this case either does not exist or which comprises in each of these regions or complexions the most diverse 'races'" (Book 7) (Herder, *J. G. Herder* 313, 284).

26. "Unser ganzes Leben ist also gewissermassen eine Poetik; wir sehen nicht, sondern wir erschaffen uns Bilder." (Herder, *Sämtliche Werke*, 15, 526).

27. From a lecture to the Congress of Natural Scientists in Berlin, 1828 (quoted in Strich 350, n. 12).

28. "If, however, we wish to preserve Goethe's idea of world literature in its true sense, we must realise that it is not identical with literature of universal and changeless human content. . . . Great works of this kind were, however, reckoned by Goethe as belonging not to world literature but to world poetry, and the two should never be confused" (Strich 14).

29. "Die nationale Einseitigkeit und Beschränktheit wird mehr und mehr unmöglich, und aus den vielen nationalen und lokalen Literaturen bildet sich eine Weltliteratur" (Marx and Engels 84).

30. Paul Valéry, "La Crise de l'esprit" (*NRF*) 71 (1919), 321–337; Rabindranath Tagore, *Crisis in Civilization* (Calcutta:Visva-Bharati, 1941); Arnold Toynbee, *Civilization on Trial* (New York: Oxford University Press, 1948).

31. The corollary of Thernstrom's argument is that the United States has successfully fused its diverse population to create, unlike less fortunate nations, essentially "one people" as a valuable "deeper reality" that overrides discussion of cultural differences in the schools. He stresses "the overwhelmingly strong blending and melting influences that have absorbed dozens and dozens of distinct groups and made them into one people, processes of integration and absorption that have operated more feebly or not at all in most other countries" (Finn et al. 77).

32. See *On Cultural Literacy: Canon, Class, Curriculum*, Robert Boyers, ed.

33. What are the interpretive prospects for Rabelais, Rimbaud, or Maya Angelou in the light of a *Dictionary of Cultural Literacy* that includes "mainstream" in both editions but recognizes the margin only as "marginal cost" and "marginal tax rate"? Moving away from the edge, the revised *Dictionary* introduces the more unifying term "multiculturalism" and subsequently reassures us that there is a "growing consensus over multiculturalism" (vii). Moreover, "over ninety percent of what one needs to know has remained stable in all subjects except the obvious ones of recent history, science and technology" (viii).

34. Paul Lauter's revisionary Introduction in *Reconstructing American Literature* rests on a similar assumption of communicable "paradigms of human experience embodied in a work. Literary study can become central once more to the academic enterprise precisely because it provides students imagined opportunities to learn of experience and cultures not their own and to encounter differing values" (xvi).

35. Bloom's attack on the "recent education of openness" (27), his worry about the place of non-Western courses in the curriculum (36), and his assertion that cultural relativism is destroying the West and that all civilizations are *not* equal (37, 374), clearly dissociate him from "world literature" as well as from Comparative Literature (399). Classical scholars like Martha

Nussbaum have likewise taken him to task for an eccentric and uninformed interpretation of the Greek philosophical heritage.

36. Leonard S. Klein, ed. *Encyclopedia of World Literature in the Twentieth Century*, rev. ed., 4 vols. (New York: Frederick Ungar, 1981).

37. The original work published in London in 1953 was titled simply *Cassell's Encyclopedia of Literature*; the 1954 New York publication and all subsequent publications changed the title to "World Literature."

38. Secretary of Education William Bennett's attack on the new program at Stanford was reported in the editorial section of the *New York Times* on April 19, 1988. Mary Louise Pratt reviews the Stanford debate and its implications in "Humanities for the Future."

39. See "Report on World Literature." In *A World of Difference*, Barbara Johnson wishes to see in history and biography "not answers, causes, explanations, or origins, but new questions and new ways in which the literary and nonliterary texts alike can be made to read and rework each other" (15).

40. It would be interesting to pursue Richard Lanham's suggestion that the electronic text, with its capacity for interactive reading and rewriting, marks a qualitative change in an act of reading which is no longer focused on a codex seen as "crystal goblet." One could argue, however, that Lanham's model, despite its picture of different reading habits and expectations, is only an electronic extension of the earlier interactive paradigm.

41. "Much of the data is unreliable, unrepresentative, or noncomparable over time" (Stedman and Kaestle 77). "The army Alpha tests [psychological testing during World War I] were field tested on graduate students and officer-training-school candidates, and items that did not favor them were discarded. Later, the psychologists 'proved' their test's validity by showing that scores were highly correlated with education and income" (102).

42. Alfred Kitzhaber mentions a congressman's fears that Project English money might be used "to teach novels and poems," and the commissioner of education's reassurance that "the money would be used to teach only reading" (quoted in North 12–13).

43. As he points out, there is a difference in perspective between Janice Lauer, for whom composition is a creative process, "the process of naming the world," and Ann Berthoff, for whom language is "a speculative instrument, our means of creating and discovering those forms which are the bearers of meaning" (North 110).

44. "Writing transforms the world. No longer is verbal knowledge embodied in social relations; now, for the first time in human history, knowledge can be codified and stored in autonomous academic disciplines, independent of the beliefs of the population at large. The study of the past thus becomes formalized as history. . . ." (Tuman 71).

45. Chester E. Finn, Jr., president of the Madison Center founded in 1988 by William J. Bennett and Allan Bloom, as cited in the *Chronicle of Higher Education* (January 31, 1990) A33.

46. Hymes continues: "A satisfactory understanding of the nature and unity of [humans] must encompass and organize, not abstract from the di-

versity. In this tradition, a theory, whatever its logic and insight, is inadequate if divorced from, if unilluminating as to, the ways of life of [human]kind as a whole."

47. Kaestle even includes a capsule description of reader-response approaches (chiefly American) in *Literacy in the United States* (43–48).

48. "All texts essentially dislodge other texts . . . take the place of something else" (Said 39, 44).

49. Teasing apart the interplay of visible and repressed cultural values from Molière to Zora Neale Hurston, and drawing on history and biography in relation to the literary texts themselves, Johnson's deconstructionist critique responds in exemplary fashion to Kupperman's call for readings of great detail and sensitivity that would display literature's modeling activity as problematic, related to real life and cultural values.

50. See his examination of the concept *mother* as a cluster model whose meaning changes according to radially structured and localized subcategories (74–85). Lakoff discusses the conceptualizing capacity itself (280ff.) and recurrent "human" patterns of consciousness. His discussion of self-adjusting systems (minus the generic patterns of consciousness) recalls the dynamic networks described by Jean-François Lyotard as a "postmodern condition," where the mobility of relationships ("language games") forms part of "the self-adjustments the system undertakes in order to improve its performance" (Lyotard 15).

51. Compare Vygotsky's "*To study something historically means to study it in the process of change*" (64–65).

52. "Chercher l'essence de la perception, c'est déclarer que la perception est non pas présumée vraie, mais définie pour nous comme accès à la vérité."

53. "We are not outside of reality. We are part of it, *in* it. . . . What is possible is knowledge of another kind: knowledge from a particular point of view, knowledge which includes the awareness that it is from a particular point of view, and knowledge which grants that other points of view can be legitimate" (Lakoff 261).

54. See Murray Schwartz in *Memory and Desire* (1–12).

55. Veyne draws an analogy between the perspectivist truth of history and that of literary criticism. "Every 'fact' is surrounded with an implicit margin of the non-eventworthy, and it is that margin that leaves room to arrange it otherwise than has been done traditionally. Finally, since the 'fact' is what one makes of it if one has the necessary flexibility, the discipline with which history can be compared is literary criticism. For we well know that what textbooks say about Racine is the least part of what could be said about that writer; a hundred critics writing a hundred books on Racine would write them all more differently, more truthfully, and more subtly than each other. Only the ungifted critics would be satisfied with the school Vulgate, with the 'facts' " (46).

56. Arnold's celebrated "best which" has two endings in *Culture and Anarchy*: the preface's "best which has been thought and said in the world"

and the assertion in the first essay, "Sweetness and Light," that culture "seeks to do away with classes; to make the best that has been thought and known in the world current everywhere." A third version occurs in a separate essay, "The Function of Criticism at the Present Time," as "the best that is known and thought in the world." When Alexander Nehamas attacks Gertrude Himmelfarb for misquotation and for the reactionary ideological blunder of "her replacement of Arnold's present-tense 'is' by the perfect-tense 'has been,'" he follows the often-anthologized third essay (Nehamas 157–158).

57. Ahmad, "Jameson's Rhetoric of Otherness and the 'National Allegory.'" Jameson's reworking of his essay the following year retains the binary oppositions challenged by Ahmad. Ahmad's book reprints the original response and, remarking on the history of the by-now celebrated exchange, expresses irritation that his specific criticism of Jameson (that his Marxist theory was not rigorous enough, and that he defined nationalism as the dialectical opposite of imperialism) was pressed into service as part of broader attacks: "the sort of thing which we hear nowadays from the fashionable poststructuralists in their unbridled diatribes against nationalism as such" (10–11).

58. Taking fluency in the English language as their base, a recent demographic study projected that the number of people of "non-English-language background" would be almost 40 million by the year 2000 (Oxford-Carpenter et al. 1). Using color as the criterion and referring only to the University of California at Berkeley, Richard Lanham noted that the 1989 undergraduate class was more than fifty percent non-white (29).

59. A staple complaint of all eras, but knowledge of the world is clearly not increasing. A *New York Times* article reported in 1988 that young adults (18–24) averaged 6.9 out of a possible 16 points on a geography test, and that over a third could not determine the westernmost city on a map. *New York Times* Thursday, 28 July, 1988: A16.

60. Ernest L. Boyer and Arthur Levine, *A Quest for Common Learning*. Appendix A (53–58) lists excerpts from different reports: e.g., "to integrate a swarm of newly arrived 'immigrants' into the mainstream of their new country," "to reduce 'individualism,'" "to develop the 'whole man,'" "to end the free 'elective' system and overspecialization," "to provide a global or 'worldwide' perspective," "to bring back the national 'solidarity' of the war years," and "to educate people to a 'common' heritage rather than their individual differences."

On the last page, however, the authors synthesize what is clearly seen as a continuity of concerns. The reports have promoted generally "the preservation of democracy, the sharing of citizen responsibility, the commitment to ethical and moral behavior, the enhancement of global perspectives, and the integration of diverse groups into the larger society. They also sought to eliminate a common set of perceived ills—overspecialization, free electives, vocationalism, unethical conduct, selfishness, and anti-democratic behavior" (58).

61. Almost all statements by applicants to the Institute on the Theory and Teaching of World Literature emphasized this dual function of the world literature course. See my discussion in "The Alternate Worlds of World Literature."

62. Paul Lauter echoes these concerns when advocating a "comparative approach to the literatures of the United States." "We need to learn about, study, be sensitive to a far broader range of audiences, conventions, functions, histories, and subjects than has in general been the case in literary analysis. In pursuing such tasks, I think we must acknowledge the limitations of our own training" (*Canons and Contexts* 86).

63. "The aesthetics of the community colleges are similarly dualistic—a drab physical reality communicating a depressing ideological message. The architecture of worker-campuses signals to four million non-elite students how unimportant they are" (Shor, 49).

64. Johnnie Lee Aldrich, of the NEH Institute, who taught until recently in the University of Maryland extension program at Adana, Turkey.

65. The University of Leiden (Netherlands) openly recognizes the implications of studying the "non-West" with Western cultural and linguistic perspectives. Included in the catalogue description of their non-western studies programs is the caveat: "One should really bear in mind the fact that, at Leiden University, a non-Western language and culture is primarily approached from a Western point of view, and that it is studied with the aid of American, English, or even German grammars and study books." *Leiden University . . . Guide* (38).

66. See the definition of worldview cited earlier from Gadamer (442), and also Dominick LaCapra's discussion of dialogism in his *History, Politics, and the Novel* (205–208).

67. They are "' . . . called the humanities (*Humaniora*): presumably because *humanity* signifies on the one hand the universal *feeling of taking-part* (*Teilnehmungsgefühl*), and on the other, the power of being able to *impart oneself* (*mitteilen*) in the most inward and universal manner: which properties in combination comprise the *sociability* of human beings, by which they distinguish themselves from the limited character of animality.' (*Critique*, Section 60, p. 201. Translation modified)" (Samuel Weber, *Institution and Interpretation* 143).

68. The works of Marcel Raymond, Albert Béguin, Georges Poulet, Jean-Pierre Richard, Jean Rousset, and Jean Starobinski. The main figure in the Geneva School, Georges Poulet, is known for his intricate reconstructions of a literary *cogito* (implied authorial self) based on the coordination of time and space perceptions in the text. Many of Poulet's books have been published in translation in the United States, and he influenced the early work of J. Hillis Miller from *Charles Dickens: The World of His Novels* (1958) through *Thomas Hardy: Distance and Desire* (1970). See Lawall, *Critics of Consciousness* (1–217).

69. "At least in limited respects, reading 'classic' texts with a sensitivity to the way they negotiate relations among symptomatic (or ideologically

reinforcing), critical, and transformative effects may itself be one way to reopen the canon and to counteract the hegemonic functions it may serve" (LaCapra 5).

Works Cited

Ahmad, Aijaz. "Jameson's Rhetoric of Otherness and the 'National Allegory.'" *Social Text: Theory/Culture/Ideology* no. 17 (1987): 3–25. Reprinted in *In Theory: Classes, Nations, Literatures*. London: Verso 1992. 95–122.

———. "Literary Theory and 'Third World Literature': Some Contexts." In *In Theory: Classes, Nations, Literatures*. London: Verso, 1992. 43–71.

———. "Literature among the Signs of Our Times." In *In Theory: Classes, Nations, Literatures*. London: Verso, 1992. 1–42.

Alberson, Hazel S. "Non-Western Literature in the World Literature Program." See Block 45–52.

Aldridge, A. Owen. *The Reemergence of World Literature: A Study of Asia and the West*. Newark: University of Delaware Press, 1986.

Anderson, Martin. *Impostors in the Temple*. New York: Simon & Schuster, 1992.

Arnold, Matthew. *Culture and Anarchy*. New York: Macmillan, 1924.

Auerbach, Erich. "Philology and *Weltliteratur*." Translated by Maire and Edward Said. *The Centennial Review* 13 (1969): 1–17.

Babbitt, Irving. "Ancients and Moderns." In *Literature and the American College: Essays in Defense of the Humanities*, by Babbitt, pp. 184–214. Boston: Houghton Mifflin Co., 1908.

Bennett, William. *To Reclaim a Legacy: A Report on the Humanities in Higher Education*. Washington, D.C.: National Endowment for the Humanities, 1984.

Block, Haskell M., ed. *The Teaching of World Literature (Proceedings of the Conference on the Teaching of World Literature at the University of Wisconsin, April 24–25, 1959)*. University of North Carolina Studies in Comparative Literature 28. Chapel Hill: University of North Carolina Press, 1960.

Block, Haskell M. "The Objectives of the Conference." See Block 1–7.

Bloom, Allan. *The Closing of the American Mind: How Higher Education Has Failed Democracy and Impoverished the Souls of Today's Students*. New York: Simon and Schuster, 1987.

Bonnefoy, Yves. *Dans le leurre du seuil*. Paris: Mercure de France, 1975.

Boyer, Ernest L., and Arthur Levine. *A Quest for Common Learning: The Aims of General Education*. Washington, D.C.: The Carnegie Foundation for the Advancement of Teaching, n.d.

Boyers, Robert, ed. *On Cultural Literacy: Canon, Class, Curriculum. Salmagundi* 72, 1986.

Brooke-Rose, Christine. "Palimpsest History." In *Interpretation and Over-*

interpretation. Edited by Umberto Eco, et al., pp. 125–138. Cambridge, England: Cambridge University Press, 1992.

Brown, Calvin S. "Debased Standards in World Literature Courses." *Yearbook of Comparative and General Literature* 2 (1953): 10–14.

Cassell's Encyclopedia of World Literature, rev. ed. London: Cassell, 1973.

Chasles, Philarète. "Foreign Literatures Compared." 1835. In *Comparative Literature, The Early Years: An Anthology of Essays.* See Schulz and Rhein 13–37.

Cheney, Lynne. *50 Hours: A Core Curriculum for College Students.* Washington, D.C.: National Endowment for the Humanities, 1989.

———. *American Memory: A Report on the Humanities in the Nation's Public Schools.* Washington, D.C.: National Endowment for the Humanities, 1987.

———. *Tyrannical Machines: A Report on Educational Practices Gone Wrong and Our Best Hopes for Setting Them Right.* Washington, D.C.: National Endowment for the Humanities, 1990.

Ch'maj, Betty E. M., editor. *Multicultural America: A Resource Book for Teachers of Humanities and American Studies: Syllabi, Essays, Projects, Bibliography.* Lanham: University Press of America, 1993.

Corstius, Jan Brandt. "Writing Histories of World Literature." *Yearbook of Comparative and General Literature* 12 (1963): 5–14.

Culley, Margo, and Catherine Portuges. *Gendered Subjects: The Dynamics of Feminist Teaching.* Boston: Routledge and Kegan Paul, 1985.

DiPietro, Robert J., and Edward Ifkovic, eds. *Ethnic Perspectives in American Literature.* New York: MLA, 1983.

Douglas, George H. *Education without Impact: How Our Universities Fail the Young.* New York, N.Y.: Carol Pub. Group, 1992.

D'Souza, Dinesh. *Illiberal Education: The Politics of Race and Sex on Campus.* New York: Free Press, 1991.

Eagleton, Terry. *Literary Theory, an Introduction.* Minneapolis: University of Minnesota Press, 1983.

Etiemble. "Faut-il réviser la notion de weltliteratur?" *Proceedings of the International Comparative Literature Association* (1966): 5–16.

Fetterley, Judith. *The Resisting Reader: a Feminist Approach to American Fiction.* Bloomington: Indiana University Press, 1978.

Finn, Chester E. Jr., Diane Ravitch, and P. Holley Roberts, eds. *Challenges to the Humanities.* New York: Holmes and Meier, 1985.

Finn, Chester E. Jr., Diane Ravitch, and P. Holley Roberts, eds. "Introduction." In *Challenges to the Humanities.* See Finn et al. 3–18. New York: Holmes and Meier, 1985.

Fish, Stanley E. *Is There a Text in This Class? The Authority of Interpretive Communities.* Cambridge, Mass.: Harvard University Press, 1980.

Fitzgerald, Frances. *America Revised: History Schoolbooks in the Twentieth Century.* Boston: Little, Brown, 1979.

Flynn, Elizabeth A., and Patrocinio P. Schweickart, eds. *Gender and Read-*

ing: Essays on Readers, Texts, and Contexts. Baltimore: Johns Hopkins, 1986.

Ford, Ford Madox. *The March of Literature from Confucius to Modern Times.* New York: Dial Press, 1938.

Franklin, Bruce. "The Teaching of Literature in the Highest Academies of the Empire." *College English* 31,6 (1970): 548–557; reprinted with additions in *The Politics of Literature.* See Kampf and Lauter.

Gadamer, Hans-Georg. *Truth and Method.* Translated by Joel Weinsheimer and Donald Marshall. New York: Crossroad Publishing Corporation, 1989.

Gallie, W. B. *Philosophy and the Historical Understanding.* New York: Schocken, 1964.

Goethe, Johann Wolfgang von. *The Autobiography of Johann Wolfgang von Goethe.* Translated by John Oxenford. New York: Horizon Press, 1969.

———. *Gespräche mit Goethe in den letzten Jahren seines Lebens, von Johann Peter Eckermann.* Edited by Fritz Bergemann. Wiesbaden: Insel-Verlag, 1955.

———. *Sämtliche Werke, Jubiläums-Ausgabe in 40 Bänden,* vol. 38, *Schriften zur Literatur.* Stuttgart, Berlin: J. G. Cotta, 1912.

Gossman, Lionel. "Literature and Education." In *Between History and Literature,* pp. 30–54. By Gossman, Cambridge, Mass.: Harvard University Press, 1990.

Graff, Gerald. *Professing Literature, An Institutional History.* Chicago: University of Chicago Press, 1987.

Guerard, Albert. *Preface to World Literature.* New York: Henry Holt, 1940.

Hallberg, Robert von, ed. *Canons.* Chicago: University of Chicago Press, 1984.

Harvard Committee. *General Education in a Free Society.* Cambridge, Mass.: Harvard University Press, 1945.

Herder, Johann Gottfried. *J. G. Herder on Social and Political Culture.* Translated by F. M. Barnard. Cambridge, England: Cambridge University Press, 1969.

———. *Sämtliche Werke.* 1888. Edited by Bernhard Suphan. Hildesheim: Olms, 1967.

Hilgers, Thomas, Marie Wunsch, Virgie Chattergy, eds. *Academic Literacies in Multicultural Higher Education: Selected Essays.* Honolulu: Center for Studies of Multicultural Higher Education, University of Hawaii at Manoa, 1992.

Hirsch, E. D., Jr. *Cultural Literacy: What Every American Needs to Know, with an Appendix, What Literate Americans Know [by] E. D. Hirsch, Jr., Joseph Kett, James Trefil.* Boston: Houghton Mifflin, 1987.

———. *Validity in Interpretation.* New Haven: Yale University Press, 1968.

Hirsch, E. D., Jr., Joseph F. Kett, and James Trefil. *The Dictionary of Cultural Literacy.* Boston: Houghton Mifflin, 1988; 2d ed., 1993.

Hymes, Dell. "Models of the Interaction of Language and Social Life." In *Directions in Sociolinguistics: The Ethnography of Communication*, edited by J. J. Gumperz and D. Hymes, pp. 35–71. New York: Holt, Rinehart & Winston, 1972.

Iser, Wolfgang. *Prospecting: From Reader Response to Literary Anthropology*. Baltimore: Johns Hopkins University Press, 1989.

———. *The Act of Reading: A Theory of Aesthetic Response*. Baltimore: Johns Hopkins University Press, 1978.

———. *The Implied Reader: Patterns of Communication in Prose Fiction from Bunyan to Beckett*. Baltimore: Johns Hopkins University Press, 1974.

Jameson, Fredric. "Third-World Literature in the Era of Multinational Capitalism." *Social Text* no. 15 (1986): 61–88. Revised "World Literature in an Age of Multinational Capitalism." In *The Current in Criticism*, edited by Clayton Koelb and Virgil Lokke, pp. 139–158. West Lafayette, Indiana: Purdue University Press, 1987.

Jauss, Hans Robert. *Toward an Aesthetic of Reception*. Minneapolis: University of Minnesota Press, 1982.

Johnson, Barbara. *A World of Difference*. Baltimore: Johns Hopkins University Press, 1987.

Kaestle, Carl F. "Standardization and Diversity in American Print Culture, 1880 to the Present." In *Literacy in the United States*, edited by Kaestle et al., pp. 272–293. New Haven: Yale University Press, 1991.

Kampf, Louis, and Paul Lauter, eds. *The Politics of Literature: Dissenting Essays on the Teaching of English*. New York: Random House, 1972.

Klein, Leonard S., ed. *Encyclopedia of World Literature in the Twentieth Century*, revised ed., 4 vols. New York: Frederick Ungar, 1981.

Koepke, Wulf. *Johann Gottfried Herder*. Boston: Twayne-G. K. Hall, 1987.

Kupperman, Joel. "The Teaching of Values." In *Challenges to the Humanities*. See Finn et al. 128–144.

LaCapra, Dominick. *History, Politics, and the Novel*. Ithaca: Cornell University Press, 1987.

Lakoff, George. *Women, Fire, and Dangerous Things: What Categories Reveal About the Mind*. Chicago: University of Chicago Press, 1987.

Lanham, Richard. "The Extraordinary Convergence: Democracy, Technology, Theory, and the University Curriculum." In *The Politics of Liberal Education*, edited by Darryl J. Gless and Barbara Herrnstein Smith. Special issue of *South Atlantic Quarterly* 89.1 (1990): 27–50. Duke University Press, 1992.

Lauter, Paul. *Canons and Contexts*. New York and London: Oxford University Press, 1991.

———. "Introduction." In *Reconstructing American Literature: Courses, Syllabi, Issues*, by Lauter, pp. xi–xxv. Old Westbury: Feminist Press, 1983.

Lawall, Sarah. *Critics of Consciousness: The Existential Structures of Literature*. Cambridge: Harvard University Press, 1968.

———. "Richard Moulton: Literature and Cultural Studies in 1911." *Yearbook of Comparative and General Literature* 39 (1990–1991): 7–15.

———. "The Alternate Worlds of World Literature." *ADE Bulletin* 90 (1988): 53–58.

Leiden University: An Introductory Guide. Leiden, Netherlands: Leiden University, 1989.

Levin, Harry. "Core, Canon, Curriculum." *College English* 43.4 (1981): 352–362.

Lotman, Jurij M., B. A. Uspenskij, V. V. Ivanov, V. N. Toporov, and A. M. Pjatigorskij. "Theses on the Semiotic Study of Cultures (as Applied to Slavic Texts)." In *The Tell-tale Sign: A Survey of Semiotics*, edited by Thomas A. Sebeok, pp. 57–83. Lisse, Netherlands: the Peter de Ridder Press, 1975.

Lyotard, Jean-François. *The Postmodern Condition: A Report on Knowledge*. Translated by Geoff Bennington and Brian Massumi. Minneapolis: University of Minnesota Press, 1984.

Marx, Karl, and Friedrich Engels. *Manifesto of the Communist Party. On Revolution*. Edited by Saul Padover. New York: McGraw Hill, 1971.

Meltzl de Lomnitz, Hugo. "Present Tasks of Comparative Literature." Parts 1 and 2. 1877. In *Comparative Literature, The Early Years: An Anthology of Essays*. See Schulz and Rhein 53–62.

Merleau-Ponty, Maurice. *Phénoménologie de la perception*. Paris: Gallimard, 1945.

Miller, J. Hillis. *Charles Dickens: The World of His Novels*. Cambridge, Mass.: Harvard University Press, 1958.

———. *Thomas Hardy: Distance and Desire*. Cambridge, Mass.: Harvard University Press, 1970.

Mishima, Yukio. *The Sailor Who Fell from Grace with the Sea*. Translated by John Nathan. 1965. New York: Berkley, 1971.

Moulton, Richard. *The Modern Study of Literature: An Introduction to Literary Theory and Interpretation*. Chicago: University of Chicago Press, 1915.

———. *World Literature and Its Place in General Culture*. Norwood, Mass.: Macmillan, 1911.

National Commission on Excellence in Education. *A Nation at Risk: The Imperative for Educational Reform: A Report to the Nation and the Secretary of Education, United States Department of Education*. Washington, D.C.: The Commission on Excellence in Education, 1983.

Nehamas, Alexander. "Serious Watching." In *The Politics of Liberal Education*, edited by Darryl J. Gless and Barbara Herrnstein Smith. Special issue of *South Atlantic Quarterly* 89.1 (1990): 157–180. Durham, N.C.: Duke University Press, 1992.

Nelson, Cary. *Theory in the Classroom*. Urbana: University of Illinois Press, 1986.

Nisbet, H. B. *Herder and the Philosophy and History of Science*. Cambridge, England: Modern Humanities Research Association, 1970.

North, Stephen N. *The Making of Knowledge in Composition: Portrait of an Emerging Field*. Upper Montclair, New Jersey: Boynton/Cook Publishers, 1987.

Norton, Charles Eliot, ed. *Correspondence Between Goethe and Carlyle*. 1887. New York: Cooper Square Publishers, 1970.

Nussbaum, Martha. "Undemocratic Vistas." *NY Review of Books* 34 (Nov. 5, 1987): 20–26.

Oxford-Carpenter, Rebecca, et al. *Demographic Projections of Non-English-Language-Background and Limited-English-Proficient Persons in the United States to the Year 2000 by State, Age, and Language Group*. Rosslyn, Virginia: InterAmerica Research Associates, Inc., 1984.

Parker, Kenneth. "The Revelation of Caliban: 'The Black Presence' in the Classroom." In *The Black Presence in English Literature*, edited by David Dabydeen, pp. 186–206. Manchester, England: Manchester University Press, 1985.

Peterson, W. "Introduction." In *M. Fabi Quintiliani, Institutionis Oratoriae Liber Decimus*, by Quintilian, pp. i–lxxx. 1891. Hildesheim: Georg Olms, 1967.

Pfeiffer, Rudolf. *History of Classical Scholarship from the Beginnings to the End of the Hellenistic Age*. Oxford: Oxford University Press, 1968.

Pratt, Mary Louise. "Humanities for the Future: Reflections on the Western Culture Debate at Stanford." In *The Politics of Liberal Education*, edited by Darryl J. Gless and Barbara Herrnstein Smith. Special issue of *South Atlantic Quarterly* 89.1 (1990): 7–25. Duke University Press, 1992.

Quintilian, M. F. *M. Fabi Quintiliani, Institutionis Oratoriae Liber Decimus*. Edited by W. Peterson. 1891. Hildesheim: Georg Olms, 1967.

"Report on World Literature." *ACLA Newsletter* XIX, 2 (1988): 1–3. Summary statement of the NEH Institute in the Theory and Teaching of World Literature (directed by Sarah Lawall), Summer 1987, at the University of Massachusetts at Amherst.

Rich, Adrienne. "Notes Toward a Politics of Location." In *Women, Feminist Identity and Society in the 1980's: Selected Papers*, edited by Myriam Diaz-Diocaretz and Iris M. Zavala, pp. 7–22. Amsterdam/Philadelphia: John Benjamins, 1985.

Ricoeur, Paul. "What Is a Text? Explanation and Interpretation." In *Mythic-Symbolic Language and Philosophical Anthropology: A Constructive Interpretation of the Thought of Paul Ricoeur*, by David Rasmussen, pp. 135–150. The Hague: Nighoff, 1971.

Rosenberg, Ralph P. "The 'Great Books' in General Education." *Yearbook of Comparative and General Literature* 3 (1954): 20–35.

Ross, Nancy. "Introduction." In *The Temple of the Golden Pavilion*, by Yukio Mishima. Translated by Ivan Morris, pp. 5–18. 1959. New York: Berkley, 1971.

Rubin, Joan Shelley. *The Making of Middle-Brow Culture*. Chapel Hill: University of North Carolina Press, 1992.

Rudolph, Frederick. "The English College on the American Frontier." In his

Curriculum: A History of the American Undergraduate Course of Study since 1636, pp. 25–53. San Francisco: Jossey-Bass Publishers, 1977.

Said, Edward. *The World, the Text, and the Critic*. Cambridge, Mass.: Harvard University Press, 1983.

Scholes, Robert. *Textual Power: Literary Theory and the Teaching of English*. New Haven: Yale University Press, 1985.

Schulz, H. J., and P. H. Rhein. *Comparative Literature, the Early Years, An Anthology of Essays*. Chapel Hill: University of North Carolina, Studies in Comparative Literature 55 (1973).

Schwartz, Murray. "Introduction." In *Memory and Desire: Aging—Literature—Psychoanalysis*, edited by Kathleen Woodward and Murray M. Schwartz, pp. 1–12. Bloomington: Indiana University Press, 1986.

Shor, Ira. *Critical Teaching and Everyday Life*. Boston, Mass.: South End Press, 1980.

Sklar, Robert. "American Studies and the Realities of America." *American Quarterly* 22 (1970): 597–605.

Smith, Henry Nash. "Can 'American Studies' Develop a Method?" *American Quarterly* 9 (1957): 197–208.

Solomon, Robert C., and Jon Solomon. *Up the University: Recreating Higher Education in America*. Reading, Mass.: Addison-Wesley Publishing Company, 1993.

Stedman, Lawrence C., and Carl F. Kaestle. "Literacy and Reading Performance in the United States from 1880 to the Present." In *Literacy in the United States*, edited by Carl F. Kaestle, et al., pp. 75–128. New Haven: Yale University Press, 1991.

Strich, Fritz. *Goethe and World Literature*. Translated by C. A. M. Sym. Westport, Conn.: Greenwood Press, 1971. Orig. *Goethe und die Weltliteratur*. Bern: Francke Verlag, 1946.

Thernstrom, Stephan. "The Humanities and Our Cultural Heritage." In *Challenges to the Humanities*. See Finn et al. 66–79.

Thoms, Peter Perring. *Chinese Courtship in Verse*. London: Parbury, Allen, and Kingsbury, 1824.

Tuman, Myron. *A Preface to Literacy: An Inquiry into Pedagogy, Practice, and Progress*. Tuscaloosa: University of Alabama Press, 1987.

Vattimo, Gianni. *The End of Modernity: Nihilism and Hermeneutics in Postmodern Culture*. Translated by Jon R. Snyder. Baltimore: Johns Hopkins University Press, 1988.

Veyne, Paul. *Writing History: Essays on Epistemology*. Translated by Mina Moore-Rinvolucri. Middletown, Conn.: Wesleyan University Press, 1984.

Vives, Juan Luis. *Vives: On Education. A Translation of De Tradendis Disciplinis of Juan Luis Vives*. Translated with an Introduction by Foster Watson. 1913. Totowa, N.J.: Rowman and Littlefield, 1971.

Vygotsky, L. S. *Mind in Society: the Development of Higher Psychological Processes*. Cambridge, Mass.: Harvard University Press, 1978.

Watson, Foster. "Introduction." In *Vives: On Education. A Translation of*

De Tradendis Disciplinis of Juan Luis Vives, by Vives, pp. xvii–clvii. 1913. Totowa, New Jersey: Rowman and Littlefield, 1971.

Weber, Samuel. *Institution and Interpretation*. Minneapolis: University of Minnesota Press, 1987.

Weitz, Hans-J. "'Weltliteratur' zuerst bei Wieland." *Arcadia* 22 (1987): 206–208.

Wellek, René. *A History of Modern Criticism: 1750–1950. Vol. 1: The Later Eighteenth Century*. London: Jonathan Cape, 1955.

Wellek, René, and Austin Warren. *Theory of Literature*. New York: Harcourt, Brace and Co., 1949.

Winnicott, D. W. *Playing and Reality*. New York: Basic Books, 1971.

Zetzel, James E. G. "Re-creating the Canon: Augustan Poetry and the Alexandrian Past." In *Canons*, edited by Robert von Hallberg, pp. 107–129. Chicago: University of Chicago Press, 1984.

Part 1.

INITIAL PERSPECTIVES

**TEACHING THE UNFAMILIAR;
LOCATING CANONICAL VALUES**

Introduction

Sarah Lawall

Academic world literature has long been based in a very local vantage point: the Western tradition. Most teachers of world literature have been trained in the traditional Western canon and its models: that is, in Great Books, Greek and Roman classics, English and American literature, and translated European texts. The models they think of, the comparisons to which they return, and the genre definitions they use, come out of that tradition, which in itself is often seen as a monolith: *"the* classics," *"the* Western tradition," *"the* canon." Yet the curiosity of these readers to explore a world beyond—this desire to make contact with various other cultures and their instructive differences—raised practical questions of interpretation even before anyone challenged the twinned image of "West" and "non-West." Clearly language barriers intervened when works were read in translation; in addition, teachers needed some knowledge of history, religion, traditional art forms, and general culture to explain references in a foreign text. As later scholarship brought out the complexity of any cultural identity and the chequered history of literary canons, the need for information multiplied. Many readers, newly aware of the differences composing Western society, found that a monolithic *we/they* opposition did not provide a satisfactory base for understanding.

What, then, was the traditionally prepared teacher of world literature to do? How might such teachers convey the cultural complexity of different texts, or negotiate relationships between familiar and unfamiliar literary worlds? How might they use their knowledge of traditional culture not as an obstruction but as an opening wedge, the reference point for an attempted cross-cultural reading? Implicit in these questions is the notion that all teachers who move outside their areas of expertise are negotiating the unfamiliar. It is an anxious step. In the first essay in this section, Thomas Greene considers the theoretical and practical situation of those world literature teachers (and they are the majority) who are trained only in the Western canon and yet wish to explore non-Western works in an appreciative and professionally responsible manner. The second essay, by Charles Segal, returns to the ancient literary tradition that is the foundation of "Western" culture, comparing and contrasting the world of its readers with our own.

Professor Greene, a Renaissance scholar and teacher deeply versed in occidental tradition, takes up the question of negotiating otherness from inside a traditional Western perspective. His remarks are aimed at the many readers and teachers of world literature who are hesitant about approaching foreign texts without broad knowledge or relevant cultural experience. Appropriately, his essay is based on an address to a group of representative world literature teachers (almost all of whom were trained in English and were teaching in English departments) participating in a 1987 NEH Institute on the Theory and Teaching of World Literature. Greene consciously adopts the position of a Western-based world literature teacher starting from a sense of "our" cultural identity vis-à-vis the intriguing opacity of another mental universe. Given this awareness of limitation (that is, of monocultural training faced with multicultural texts), how does one begin to negotiate the relationship of self and other? Examining translations of Chinese, Serbian, and African poems or chants, Greene leads his readers through a series of steps in which they register the fact of difference, describe and articulate it in terms of familiar categories, and gradually become more aware of their own identities inside local and global contexts. Rejecting extremist positions that would either absorb everything into familiar categories or insist on absolute and irreconcilable dissimilarity, he opts for a dialectics of contrast and comparison. The common denominator, he suggests, is our shared humanity—and finding out how complex this shared humanity can be.

If the teaching of world literature involves a look outward toward other regions of the globe, it also presupposes a look back in time—to the literary and philosophical classics that still provide, in some ways, a touchstone for modern thought. Yet they are purely touchstones nowadays, and no longer an unambiguous source of values. Indeed, classical antiquity has been a cultural standard for so long, the symbol of an establishment "high" culture, that it can hardly escape re-evaluation in current critiques of Western society. The twentieth-century Battle of the Books has shifted ground from previous quarrels over aesthetic preferences, or the superior value of modernity, to a bitter argument over the ethical and cultural implications of the works founding the Western tradition. A certain mythmaking is involved: on the one hand, a traditionalist view (chiefly associated with Allan Bloom) that sees in Plato and the fifth-century B.C. dramatists a model of heroic, disciplined thought that could redeem modern decadence; on the other hand, a revisionary approach that finds classical texts responsible for a destructive patriarchal society riddled with racist and sexist bias. In one guise or another, ancient Greek and Roman culture continues to fascinate contemporary writers and critics, whether they be Jacques Derrida and Luce Irigaray commenting on Plato, Christa Wolf using the figure of Cassandra to shape a novel, genre theorists redefining Aristotelian models, or cultural historians uncovering the roots of Greek culture in Asian and African society. Variously understood, "the classics" reappear in the most contemporary discussions of canon, literary criticism, cultural identity, and ethical or aesthetic issues.

Classicist Charles Segal offers an analytic survey of ancient literary criticism as an antidote to simplified ideas of the classical tradition. Examining ancient ideas of artistic form, the representation of reality, and the relationship of text and reader, Segal concurrently outlines a self-conscious process of canon-building throughout Greek and Roman antiquity. Ancient critics were quite conscious of making ethical and aesthetic choices when they selected their (different) canons, and they distinguished between different artistic world views. Comparing and contrasting classical attitudes with modern concepts of art and human experience, Segal remarks on a continuing tension between the ideals of aesthetic form and moral value. He makes the point that both periods, in their similarities and difference, are expressing a variety of historically shaped attitudes towards art and experience.

1. Misunderstanding Poetry: Teaching outside the Western Canon

Thomas M. Greene

The challenge of teaching world literature is nothing if not daunting. If one takes the expression "world literature" at its face value, one realizes that teaching it is literally impossible, and that all one can hope is to reduce that impossibility to the merely very difficult. "World literature" traditionally has been taken to mean the literature of Western Europe and North America, with perhaps a few Slavic or Latin American texts thrown in. Once one begins to take Goethe's phrase seriously, in a more literal sense, doubtless, than he himself intended, then one finds oneself confronted with the universal human activity of verbal creation on our planet, and as a teacher, one's heart is likely to sink. But there is also something liberating in that phrase and that conception, and perhaps we have reached a moment in history when they must be faced.

There are clearly many reasons why the time is propitious to expand our notions about what world literature involves. I am speaking for that majority of teachers in the United States whose roots and training are Western. The traditional literary canon is undergoing radical scrutiny, and we're becoming much more aware of all the voices that canon has tended to filter out. Even our notions about what is properly called *American literature* are expanding as we try to reclaim those texts heretofore neglected, whether because of their author's language or dialect or gender or race or access to written inscription. Twenty years ago the name of Zora Neale Hurston (to take only one familiar instance) was little known in or outside the classroom, but today it receives the respect it deserves. A few years ago Benjamin Harshav and Barbara Harshav published a superb anthology of American Yiddish poetry with facing translation, a book that opens up an entire chapter of our cultural history that was closed to many of us. We are gradually becoming aware of Hispanic-American literature written within our borders. And we are beginning to learn from our anthropologist colleagues something about the superb verbal creativity of native Americans which for so long didn't even exist as literature at all, as letters inscribed on paper, but only within the memories and imaginations of tribal elders. If we have to learn so much about the neglected creativity of our own country, how much more is there to learn about the verbal creativity of other regions! Even if we managed to read it all, we couldn't begin to teach it in *four* years, let alone one.

Nonetheless there is something exhilarating about that wealth of texts which is newly available to us; there is something heady in knowing they are there, whether or not it is possible to assimilate that wealth as we would like. The expansion of a canon of masterpieces that once seemed firmly fixed is a healthy development. But there are other reasons why it makes sense at this moment of history to rethink our conceptions of world literature. Sixty years ago the world was dominated politically and militarily by the nations of Western Europe; it seemed inevitable to accord a special privilege to *their* literatures. Today those nations have undergone a political decline; other nations like China and Japan are beginning to challenge or eclipse them in our vision of the world we live in, and that conscious or unconscious political factor privileging Western Europe is no longer so compelling.

Let me digress for a moment to say that anyone who thinks that cultural prestige is divorced from political prestige is naive. The most visible example is the burgeoning of American Studies throughout the world since World War II. When I was young I thought of my own American culture as marginal and provincial from a global perspective; lately I've been surprised when I travel to discover that the study of American culture is a worldwide industry. What is perceived as American political and military hegemony has produced what the Renaissance called a *translatio studii*. So as the political alignments of our world continue to shift, as the so-called third world forces itself upon American consciousness, as front pages evoke places many have to locate in the atlas, as the economic interdependence of all nations becomes ever more obvious, people of this nation have many more reasons to think in terms of their common humanity and their common experience as *literary* animals.

But in reaching out to embrace pedagogically the actual globe and not simply a Eurocentric version of it, it's impossible not to confront the formidable challenges this widening of horizons entails. Those non-Western cultures are alien to Westerners in a profound and disturbing way which, as readers and as teachers, most are not prepared to deal with. Unless one happens to be a specialist in one of those cultures, one is likely to feel lost, bewildered, presumptuous in pretending to interpret them to one's students and, still worse, privately to oneself. Does one have the *right* to invade that alien territory as though one could absorb and transmit its texts in good faith? Even within the limits of their vast heritage, Westerners are constantly obliged to deal with the alien, the remote, the mysterious codes and habits of feeling of distant periods that resist their facile assimilation. That uneasy sense of remoteness is only compounded when they are striving to reach out to an implacable, ostensibly opaque otherness. How do readers and teachers deal with that inherent resistance?

There are several answers to that question, none of them wholly satisfactory, answers that introduce, each of them, issues of psychology, ethics, and literary theory. One response of course is simply to give up, turn one's back on all that textual hocus-pocus, and continue to read and teach what is already familiar. That choice would constitute a mutilation of the experience potentially open to us; it would also condemn the reader to a kind of parochialism increasingly inappropriate to the world he or she inhabits. Another much more tempting if arduous enterprise would be for Westerners to attempt to rid theirselves of all their Western biases and prejudices and mind-sets, in order to approach the alien text as a kind of human *tabula rasa*, stripped of all their ingrained occidental categories and expectations. This enterprise would assume their freedom to assimilate the alien civilization with a kind of free-floating, meta-cultural negative capability. That solution would indeed spare them a good many problems, if they were capable of achieving it. To most it will seem Utopian, if not naive. And yet it seems to me that an influential book of the seventies implicitly demanded that kind of ethnographic purity from its readers. I'm thinking of Edward Said's *Orientalism*, an interesting and important study of occidental perceptions of the Orient over the last two hundred years.

Said's book, radically polemical, exposed the ethnocentric prejudices which have colored all accounts and descriptions and travel journals and scientific monographs on the Near East written by European observers, even those who strove most earnestly for scientific objectivity, even those who lived in the Orient for much of their lives and came to think, as they believed, like Orientals. Said renders Westerners a service by exposing their own unconscious biases to themselves, even the biases of great writers like Nerval and Flaubert. He is in fact merciless as he pounces on the ethnocentric remark that gives the Occidental away, and nobody passes under his lens unscathed. Every Occidental is guilty of ethnocentrism, and "guilty" is indeed the right word, since this bias is for Said very much an ethical matter. There is much bitterness in that book, the understandable bitterness felt by the victim of the ethnic stereotype, and yet I wonder if the author is ultimately not subject to that naiveté I mentioned a moment ago. He wants Westerners evidently to attain that condition of the ethnic *tabula rasa*, that purity from the Occidental categories that have been bred into them and which organize inevitably their perceptions of the world, both positive and negative. He is furious at their failure to transcend ethnocentrism, even the most enlightened and sophisticated brand. But the implicit demand he makes on them is itself misguidedly Utopian. Without the values of our cultures, interpreted scrupulously and self-consciously, we would be hollow, since we are all of us, for better or worse, cultural animals. The person who shed *all* cultural perspectives would be unthinkable, would in fact be a monster. In our encounters with the alien, we can never utterly free ourselves from the responses and the standards we have imbibed from infancy, although we can strive to be self-conscious about those standards; we can strive to avoid the kind of crudity and mistrust and hostility the alien tends to elicit; we can try to be *aware* of the pitfalls Said documents so tellingly. But we cannot ultimately cease to be Occidentals.

Said is not primarily concerned with Western responses to oriental *literature*, but I think that the problems posed by his book are altogether relevant to our problems as readers and teachers of alien texts. We can learn from him what we need to learn and what he wants to teach us. We can learn to scrutinize our responses to traditions we are estranged from. But we can also learn what he did not intend to teach us, namely that we cannot escape the horizons of our own place in history even as we try to widen those horizons and recognize their limiting constraints. Reading texts from remote cultures might be said to *train* our ethnocentrism, enlighten it, discipline it, broaden it, but never altogether dispel it. And so it must be for our students. Once we have recognized that, we have set useful parameters for teaching world literature.

I have been arguing that the ideal of cultural neutrality in reading alien literary texts is unattainable and inhuman, and that we can come better to perceive our biases and thus ourselves by our contact with the alien. But this argument obviously should not be used as an alibi for absorbing the alien into our own world of discourse, as though there were no distance to cross, no interesting and enlightening mystery to cope with. That passivity in facing the alien would be the mirror opposite of the *tabula rasa* fallacy. Neither of those extremes is really feasible, and so we're left to search for a third approach which would oblige us to try to bridge a division that we know in advance is not completely bridgeable. Formulating that third solution will not be easy, any more than working it out in practice. But given the operative parameters, we can try to determine what procedures are available.

In order to do that, a few examples will be necessary. I cite first an ancient Chinese poem, a short lyric by a certain Meng Hao-Jan, who lived in a period corresponding to our eighth century A.D. (To facilitate discussion, all of the examples I shall cite will be lyrics.) Let me say at the outset that I don't read Chinese. My source for this text and its translations is a book entitled *Chinese Poetry: Major Modes and Genres* by Wai-Lim Yip.

As even Occidentals know, the Chinese language uses very little grammar. Poetry in that language essentially provides a series of nouns, verbs, and adjectives without connectives, so that the reader is obliged to make the connections himself or herself. One can judge the kind of difficulty involved from this little example by Meng.

Line 1   移   move (v.)

舟   boat (n.)

泊   moor (v.)

煙   smoke (n./adj.)

渚   shore (n.)

Line 2   日   sun (n.)

暮   dusk (v.)

客   traveler (n.)

愁   grief (n.)

新   new (adj./v.)

Line 3   野   wild/wilderness (adj./n.)

曠   wilderness/far-reaching/empty (n./adj.)

天   sky (n.)

低   low (v./adj.)

樹   tree/s (n.)

Line 4   江   river (n.)

清   clear (adj.)

月   moon (n.)

近   near (v./adj.)

人   man (n.)

(Yip 2)

Those twenty characters arranged vertically constitute the poem for
the Chinese reader. From our Western point of view, accustomed as
we are to connectives—conjunctions and prepositions, as well as
other helpers like article adjectives, pronouns, and verb tenses—this
is scarcely a poem at all. Some of our twentieth-century poets have

experimented with reduced syntax or suppressed syntax, but even
they tend to give us more direction than this poet who wrote twelve
centuries ago and who was by no means experimental or unconven-
tional according to his own poetic traditions.

What should an English translator do with this elusive list of
twenty characters, some of them capable of being read alternatively
as noun or adjective, adjective or verb? And what should an English
language teacher do in presenting this supposed poem to a class of
American students, if he or she chooses to try it? The simplest response would be to turn to one of several existing verse translations.
I cite three of the several available versions. All have been published
over the years from 1919 to 1944.

> Our boat by the mist-covered islet we tied.
>   The sorrows of absence the sunset brings back.
>   Low breasting the foliage the sky loomed black.
> The river is bright with the moon at our side.
>
>   (John Gould Fletcher)

> While my little boat moves on its mooring mist,
> And daylight wanes, old memories begin . . .
> How wide the world was, how close the trees to heaven!
> And how clear in the water the nearness of the moon!
>
>   (Witter Bynner)

> I move my boat and anchor in the mists off an islet;
> With the setting sun the traveler's heart grows melancholy
>   once more.
> On every side is a desolate expanse of water;
> Somewhere the sky comes down to the trees
> And the clear water reflects a neighboring moon.
>
>   (Roger Soame Jenyns) (Yip 7)

What we learn from these alternative translations is the amount of
emotional logic, the amount of coherence, motivation, and rational
connection, that the English-language poet feels he has to bring to
the bare bones of the Chinese original in order to make it acceptable
to the Western reader. The translator feels obliged to do this even if
in effect he is writing a new poem. Some elements in the original
clearly posed more problems than others. Thus the last line seems
to have looked fairly straightforward to these three translators, al-

though they vary in their willingness to make explicit the very last character in the Chinese, the character that means "man." Fletcher assumes more than one person present, presumably a pair of lovers with the moon "at our side." The others assume a solitary speaker, unaccompanied, and the moon is said to be "near," but the actual person alluded to in the original disappears.

More troublesome is the word *grief* in the second line of the Chinese; the grief is unaccounted for, or rather the poem offers several possibilities without forcing any of them upon the reader and essentially leaves the emotion, so to speak, in suspension. That indeterminacy seems intolerable to the English translator. The first version attributes the grief to absence, the second to nostalgia for happier years, the third to the melancholy of the landscape. Each translator assumes that the Western reader will find this psychological indeterminacy or vacuum intolerable, and I think one can learn from this professional judgment. All three translations were probably right about the great majority of their readers, at least the English readership between the two wars. A text that fails to specify a cast of characters, fails to supply connections, motivations, spatial and emotional coherence, is bound to disturb us, bound to seem incomplete. The kind of free-floating vagueness that denies us those elements is radically foreign to our sensibility. We don't even know whether the Chinese poem is inviting the reader to make the connections it deliberately omits, or whether the reader is expected to live with the indeterminacy, to sacrifice the coherence that we Western readers seem to require. Perhaps the very absence of connections for the Chinese is what constitutes the poetic element.

I append a version produced by a student of Professor Yip which would seem to approximate more closely the impressionistic character of the original.

> A boat slows, moors by beach-run in smoke.
> Sun fades: a traveler's sorrow freshens.
> Open wilderness.
> Wide sky.
> A stretch of low trees.
> Limpid river.
> Clear moon close to man.

> (Yip 8)

This version moves closer to the Chinese suppression of connectives. But in order apparently for this to happen, the four-line structure of the original has had to be jettisoned. And even here the English language has forced the translator to make certain arbitrary decisions. The adjective *low* in the Chinese could refer either to sky or trees; the English translator has to choose, and opts for the trees. The word *freshens* in the second line corresponds to the symbol for "new," which is variously applicable and which the other translators had tended to ignore. The image of the moon reflected in the water has been suppressed, although arguably it should be there. And so on. What we can learn from this exercise of comparison is that *no* English version, however brilliant, however sensitive to the smoky semantic mistiness of Meng's poem, is wholly capable of finding equivalents to it. It will be fundamentally incapable not only because of the limitations of the English language but also (what amounts to the same thing) because of the limitations of the Western reader. Reading a poem like this one can alert Westernized teachers and students to a division between our habits of mind, our fundamental linguistic assumptions, our literary epistemology, and those of another civilization.

Our methodology for dealing with alien literature now contains at least a first step. Rather than gliding over the signals of our estrangement from the text, rather than concentrating on what we can assimilate and explain, it may be useful to pause precisely there where our conventional habits of reading desert us. We need to look for the feature that defeats our ingrained habits; we need to be alert to that violation of our expectations and pause over it. In that very puzzlement may lie precisely the potential enlightenment the text can offer us.

Having made that point, let me digress to raise the question how in fact one would teach a poem like Meng's in the classroom, assuming that one wanted to tackle it. Whether or not one had access to the vertical transcription available in Professor Yip's book, the most effective way of presenting such a poem might be to tell one's students what the original probably looked like. One could explain the relative lack of grammar in the Chinese language, and ask students to turn the Westernized version into what each considered to be the essential bare bones of the Eastern version. If one could provide several English versions, the students could then try to work out the common denominators. The value of the exercise would lie in the students' contact with a radically different sensibility and a radically different means of verbal expression.

Sometimes of course we don't have to seek out the alien trait; it overwhelms us from the beginning. I want to quote the beginning of a traditional Serbian poem which is also a folk-charm against jaundice, *jaunisse*, the yellow disease. This particular version of the charm is spoken by the mother of a boy afflicted with the disease, a boy whose name is Milan.

> Yellow cock
> Beat your yellow wings three times
> Over a yellow hen.
> A yellow hen in a yellow year
> In a yellow month
> In a yellow week
> On a yellow day
> Laid a yellow egg
> In yellow hay.
> Let the yellow hay stay
> And the yellow fever leave our Milan.
>
> Yellow bitch
> Whelp your yellow pup
> On a yellow day
> In a yellow week
> In a yellow month
> In a yellow year
> In a yellow wood.
> Let the yellow wood stay
> And the yellow fever leave our Milan.
>
> Yellow cow calve a yellow calf
> On a yellow day
> In a yellow week
> In a yellow month
> In a yellow year
> In a yellow field.
> Let the yellow field stay
> And the yellow fever leave our Milan.
> Hooh!
>
> (Rothenberg 71–72)

Here presumably we have no trouble noticing what is alien to us. The difficulties begin when we go beyond the act of registering difference, when we try to understand that difference—in this case, understand what motivates the blizzard of yellowness in relation to the illness of a little boy. The first thing to notice in a text like this is that it cannot be considered as an autonomous aesthetic object, self-contained and self-justifying. It is not in the traditional sense a poem at all; it is quite clearly a charm, which means that it is intended to get results in a world outside the poem. When the mother refers to her Milan, that signifier does not point toward a signified, the idea of the boy she carries in her head, but to a concrete referent, to the boy himself, that specific boy who needs help urgently. How is the text going to supply that help? It attempts apparently to create intense magnets of yellowness outside of Milan; it creates a network of magnetisms, connections, and mysterious forces that share magically the invisible quality of yellowness which will draw the yellow out of Milan's body and make him whole again. It may be that in the Serbian world of magic certain days, months, years, are matched with certain colors, in which case Milan may have to wait a while for his cure. But it seems more likely that the text is *assigning* yellowness to the units of time, designating them as yellow so that they can operate as the speaker wants them to. The day, the week, and the month are endowed with power because the language itself has power to endow them. All those images of yellowness are operative metaphors, and the Occidental reader has to accustom himself or herself to that unspoken assumption of operational language. The optative subjunctives in this little charm—"Let the yellow wood stay," "Let the yellow field stay, and the yellow fever leave"—those optatives are not simply expressions of a wish or a fantasy, as they might be in our linguistic world; rather, they have force. Spoken in the correct way, accompanied perhaps with the correct actions or gestures, they are expected to be efficacious. Thus Occidental readers have to confront a conception of language which may not have disappeared altogether from their own, but which has, so to speak, gone underground. They confront language whose incantatory repetitions and imagistic density embody literal power. The very repetition of the adjective *yellow* in this text is a technique of multiplying its efficacity; repetition enhances its substance, fortifies its *mana*, its energy, creates that universe of yellowness which will demonstrate its effectiveness.

There are other suggestive elements in this little text: for example, the imagery of procreation which has the cock mating with the hen, the bitch whelping her pup, the cow calving. Are those primal events necessary to trigger the yellow magic? The climactic "Hooh!" appears to have the force of an "Amen" or a "Selah," ensuring that all those things spoken will indeed occur. Whatever we choose to look at, this Serbian text, not quite so remote as the Chinese, will permit us to pass beyond that first step I suggested we should take as alien readers. We will not only be noting those elements that raise problems for our Western eyes; we can formulate explicitly what is different. That, I submit, should be our second step: not only registering estrangement but describing it, putting it into words which will, let us not forget, remain *our* words, *our* terms, reflecting *our* understanding of the cultural division we are hoping to begin to bridge. But even if these terms reveal our categories, our ways of understanding, we have nonetheless made a beginning.

What should be the next step, if in fact there are any more steps? I quote a text from a funeral rite of the pygmies of Gabon, a text which addresses at the end the spirit named "Khvum," the father of the forest especially associated with the afterlife of the dead. This chant is ritually spoken alternately by the eldest son of the deceased and the maternal uncle.

A: The animal runs, it passes, it dies. And it is the great cold.
B: *It is the great cold of the night, it is the dark.*
A: The bird flies, it passes, it dies. And it is the great cold.
B: *It is the great cold of the night, it is the dark.*
A: The fish flees, it passes, it dies. And it is the great cold.
B: *It is the great cold of the night, it is the dark.*
A: Man eats and sleeps. He dies. And it is the great cold.
B: *It is the great cold of the night, it is the dark.*
A: There is light in the sky, the eyes are extinguished, the star shines.
B: *The cold is below, the light is on high.*
A: The man has passed, the shade has vanished, the prisoner is free.
Khvum, Khvum, come in answer to our call![1]

This is a text which was produced by a traditional, tribal society, and we can recognize it as such. There is a sense of kinship between animal, bird, fish, and man which our own society appears to have lost. There is the appeal to a spirit of the forest, a forest peopled by spirits, which is not our forest. There is a primitive symbolism of light and dark, warmth and cold, which correspond to a quality of darkness and of cold most of us are not likely to have encountered. And yet having registered all this, having registered our distance from this text, what is remarkable about it to me is its extraordinary accessibility. We are of course dependent on the translation, which has detoured from the original African language through French to the English of C. M. Bowra. We don't know how much assimilation has occurred in that double rewriting. But something presumably of the original remains, something of the starkness of life and of death, something of that kinship with the natural world which we *are* capable of responding to, something of the mingled concept of death as frozen immobility and release, as terror and hope, something of the hovering of the numinous which the most sophisticated civilizations have not quite been able to dispel. And despite our sense of cultural division, we do respond to all that. The movement from the utter cold and darkness to the release of the soul and the appearance of the star, this movement does have, after all, its analogies in our own elegies, in the movement, say, from "Lycidas is dead" to "Weep no more." And the haunting effect of the ritual repetition in the African text does after all have its counterpart in the solemnity of our own litanies. There is ultimately a human continuity that persists in spite of the cultural chasm, and we must not, in our effort to confront that chasm, deny the existence of the continuity. We are in fact in a better position to measure the continuity, even to wonder at it, *after* we have registered and explored the division.

This recognition of community with a remote society, a recognition over and against our sense of remoteness—this might be considered a third step in our response to the alien. If there were no community of human experience, then presumably we couldn't read the remote text at all. It's important to begin by acknowledging our estrangement, by taking note of what is mysterious and uncomfortable to us; it's important to try to formulate as lucidly as we can what the assumptions and beliefs and mental habits are that make our reading difficult; but then finally it's important to grope for what in the foreign text does speak for a humanity that we can recognize. When we have finished doing that, and even when we have done it over and over again, we will not have lost the mind-set of the particular perspective we began with. We will not have ceased to be Occidentals. We will not have exorcised our own habits and biases. But we can hope at least to hold them more self-consciously; we can begin to see them *as* arbitrary, contingent, culture-specific, and indeed that might be the very last step in one's confrontation with the alien: the question, posed both to one's self and one's students, of what this effort of understanding has clarified. The effort of understanding, if it is going to be fruitful, has to be double: in trying to understand the alien, you come better to understand yourself. Thus in reading that Serbian text, one might begin to look for ways in which our own poetry tries to acquire a numinous power which our rationalistic semantic theory denies it. Theoretically, we believe, most of us, that words are lifeless, passive, purely conventional signifiers. But our poetry may carry with it vestigially a repressed striving for that efficacious power the Serbian mother calls upon so consciously. And in teaching the Chinese poem, we come to understand our Western need for verbal and conceptual coherence, our resistance to the suggestively indeterminate. We can learn precisely from those elements that disturb us or baffle us; those are the elements that mark the borders of our Western consciousness.

In teaching world literature of the twentieth century, there is a special dilemma whch I have not yet touched on—a dilemma of the teacher, certainly, but far more poignantly a dilemma of the writer. I've been speaking of the division between Western reader and non-Western text as though there were no middle ground conceivable, but of course there is a kind of middle ground, the space precisely where the post-colonialist writer of the so-called third world finds himself or herself. The contemporary third-world writer is indelibly marked by European or American civilization, even if he or she is in revolt against it, even if it constitutes a demonic system to be purged from the land and the mind. As we know, there are few remaining places on this planet where the traces of Western society cannot be found, for better or for worse, and these are not only traces on the landscape or the cityscape; they are also traces within the consciousness. Post-colonialist writers have to wrestle with that ambivalent heritage, and in many cases they are obliged to use the language of the colonizer if they want to reach a wide audience. This very compromise imposes further painful decisions: are they to adopt that language as though it were their own, as though they accepted the European heritage obediently, docilely, eagerly? Or should they try to introduce a distortion, signal a linguistic protest, dramatize their compromise by reconstructing the language they are bound to feel has been imposed on them? And what, on the other hand, should be their posture toward their native traditions, shrinking as they so often are before the onslaught of the Western invasion, corrupted as they are, infected, isolated, in the process of becoming quaint folklore? Should post-colonialist writers wage a defensive battle to preserve what remains; should they become archivists? And how exactly can they hope to do that if they have already accepted the language which denies the native past its specificity? This dilemma of the uprooted intellectual is plain enough in the writing of blacks and native Americans in our own country, but it can really be found everywhere beyond the walls of established dominant cultures. It should certainly be a concern of any course in world literature that includes the twentieth century.

One writer who has written passionately and eloquently about this impasse is the Caribbean poet and playwright Derek Walcott.

As an epigraph to his remarkable play, *Dream on Monkey Mountain*, Walcott has the courage to quote Jean-Paul Sartre's scathing anatomy of the post-colonialist outlook. Here is the passage, taken from Sartre's preface to Frantz Fanon's *The Wretched of the Earth*:

> Let us add . . . that other witchery of which I have already spoken: Western culture. If I were them [members of third-world societies], if I were them, you may say, I'd prefer my mumbo-jumbo to their Acropolis. Very good: you've grasped the situation. But not altogether, because you *aren't* them—or not yet. Otherwise you would know that they can't choose; they must have both. Two worlds; that makes two bewitchings; they dance all night and at dawn they crowd into the churches to hear Mass; every day the split widens . . . The status of "native" is a nervous condition introduced and maintained by the settler among colonized people *with their consent*.
>
> (quoted in Walcott 277)

Walcott has the courage to include those damning last three words in his quotation, and in the long, tormented overture to the collection of his plays, he quotes the whole sentence again. His harshness in that overture toward those who would idealize the native past is equaled by the pathos he evokes of the supposedly liberated native. "Our visionary plays about the noble savage [he writes] remain provincial, psychic justifications, strenuous attempts to create identity." The identity clearly remains to be created; it seems to fall for Walcott precisely within that cultural no-man's-land which lies between the Western and the non-Western, that gulf which earlier I was trying to bridge. "Once we have lost our wish to be white," writes Walcott, "we develop a longing to become black, and those two may be different, but are still careers" (20). By the word "careers," I think he means difficult, life-long enterprises. To be black, truly black, in these terms would mean achieving a rootedness in the land which the post-colonialist intellectual feels himself cheated of. "The migratory West Indian feels rootless on his own earth," says Walcott (20–21), and he offers no facile prescription for a deeper rootedness. That struggle for belonging to a land scarred by imperialism will need to be represented in any course that includes the literature of the third world. And even in that phrase *third world*, which is used so formulaically, there may be more than a touch of condescension; there may also be a hint of that deracination the writer has to deal with. This world lies not so much between the capitalist and Soviet blocs as it lies between industrial and tribal. We cannot do much to help such writers, but we can try to help our students understand their situation.

There is one more question posed by the advent of a new, expanded study of world literature, whether or not contemporary, a question whose answer I am by no means sure that I know but which has to be posed anyway. This has to do with the status of our traditional Western classics in a curriculum that is suddenly exploding. What do we do with Virgil and Dante and George Eliot and Proust and Faulkner as we welcome *The Tale of Genji* and the *Shih Ching* and Chinua Achebe to our classrooms? What do we do with the Western past which has, for better or worse, produced the modern present? Ideally there should be world enough and time for all the texts we think it desirable to teach, but of course there never is. One can make an argument for a larger fraction of the curriculum devoted to literature, Western and non-Western, since we are in fact finding ourselves with a far larger body of material to teach than we realized twenty years ago. That argument for a larger share of the undergraduate's attention can and should be made, but it is safe to predict that it will not always succeed, and we need to think about the crunch that results when and if it fails. I ought to make it clear that I speak as one who still believes in the classics of the Western tradition. I still believe in Homer and Shakespeare and Austen and Joyce, and it pains me to think of sacrificing any of them. Yet sacrifice we must if we are to teach our students the universality of human creativity in language. One way to choose, out of the virtually infinite wealth of texts available, would be to look for works that illustrate the radical differences of experience and perception and verbalization in literary production while still revealing the underlying common obsessions of men and women in all cultures—love, heroism, community, the supernatural, evil, time, death. Any one of those obsessive themes of our existence on this earth could serve to bring together an array of texts representative of the boldest and noblest human imaginations.

There is one last aspect of teaching world literature that needs to be stressed, and it has to do with the original status or function of the works such a course is likely to group together. Thirty years ago André Malraux pointed out that most of the so-called artworks gathered in a modern art museum were never intended to be collected there. Our museums homogenize works that were intended for devotional or political or commemorative or familial or even intensely private purposes. So it is likely to be in the case of a course in world literature. If we include in such a course only those texts composed with what we might call a "literary" intent, we would have to exclude almost all the Bible; we would have to exclude Greek drama and sacred drama from around the world; we would have to exclude incantations and spells like the little Serbian charm; we would have to exclude personal correspondence and history and hymns and myths and thus a very great deal of the material most valuable to us and our students. We need to include those works, but we also need to be aware of their very different social functions at the moment of their composition (if indeed the given text was composed at a single historical moment). Part of the challenge of such a course lies in the responsibility *not* to homogenize any more than its structure requires us to. Part of the job lies in evoking the immense variety of occasions, and the particularity of each specific occasion, insofar as we can learn it.

The goal of teaching outside our Western canon might be said to reduce as far as possible the betrayals we know that we will anyway be guilty of. We have to grope our way as best we can, trying to preserve the uniqueness of the occasion and the culture as well as the text we want to share. We will never know enough; we'll make mistakes; we can't cross all those ethnic divides; we can't cease, most of us, to be incurable Occidentals. But we can strive to make that effort of imaginative interpretation which will never entirely succeed, an effort we have to make unless we want to remain provincial in a world that no longer tolerates provinciality. It is indeed daunting to try to gauge the breadth of recorded human experience, bewildering and bizarre and vast and elusive and finally unknowable, but we need to try, for ourselves and our students; we need to try to discern, at the end of this unhappy century, across all those gulfs of ignorance, whatever it is we share with one another.

Note

1. Quoted and translated by Bowra (202–203) after R. P. Trilles, *L'Ame du Pygmée d'Afrique* (424).

Works Cited

Bowra, C. M. *Primitive Song*. Cleveland: The World Publishing Company, 1962.

Fanon, Frantz. *The Wretched of the Earth*. 1963. New York: Grove, 1968.

Harshav, Benjamin, and Barbara Harshav. *American Yiddish Poetry. A Bilingual Anthology*. Berkeley: University of California Press, 1986.

Rothenberg, Jerome, ed. *Technicians of the Sacred*. Berkeley: University of California Press, 1985.

Said, Edward W. *Orientalism*. New York: Pantheon Books, 1978.

Trilles, R. P. *L'Ame du Pygmée d'Afrique*. Paris: n.p., 1945.

Walcott, Derek. *Dream on Monkey Mountain and Other Plays*. New York: Farrar, Straus and Giroux, 1982.

Yip, Wai-Lim, ed. and trans. *Chinese Poetry: Major Modes and Genres*. Berkeley: University of California Press, 1976.

2. Classical Criticism and the Ca or, Why Read the Ancient Critics

Charles Segal

I

For the modern critical endeavor, alienation is central. It may account for the flurry of discussion about aims, methods, and legitimations of criticism of which this volume, I suppose, is part. We fear, perhaps rightly, that literature has lost its central role in our culture. Redefining the canon is an attempt to come to grips with the consequences of losing that centrality. Classicists' professional concern is a closed corpus of well-established texts, and so they may seem to be on the sidelines of these debates. Yet classical studies also offer a valuable perspective. Studying the critical practices of a remote time and place can help us understand the historically conditioned nature of our own ways of reading and therefore our reasons for selecting what we read. Our fascination with the discontinuities, silences, ellipses in literary texts, for example, is in part a heritage from movements like cubism, surrealism, and abstract expressionism and from the general fragmentation of our image of ourselves and our world in writers like Kafka, Musil, Joyce, Eliot, Pound, etc. The writers of classical antiquity, on the whole, sought a greater and more direct continuity between the moral and the aesthetic effect. When Aristotle described tragic reversal in the *Poetics*, for instance, he hoped to establish universally valid ethical as well as aesthetic principles; Dionysius of Halicarnassus or Longinus could dwell on the beauty of a particular sound or a particular image without anxiety that he was engaging in an outmoded, effete aestheticism or being taken in by a pretty surface that was masking some monstrously evil cause.

The ancient critics, however, were also engaged in a continuous process of establishing canons, and they did so with a vengeance. They selected nine lyric poets, ten orators, five tragedians, and three poets of Old Comedy. The term "canon" itself seems to go back to Aristophanes of Byzantium at the end of the third century B.C. and to have meant a list of selected authors.[1] The basis of the selection is literary excellence as these critics saw it, but the aesthetic criteria have ethical resonances. Aristotle, for example, placed the *Iliad* and *Odyssey* above the so-called Cyclic Epics (the continuations of the story of the fall of Troy and its heroes) because the former were more unified and less episodic (*Poetics* 23.1459a30–b7). But for Aristotle this aesthetic unity also clarifies ethical meaning, revealing the tragic shape of human life, a pattern in which suffering and reversal of fortunes bring new awareness or "recognition" (*Poetics* cc. 11, 13). Longinus (whom for convenience we shall call the author of the treatise *On the Sublime*) ranked the occasionally flawed brilliance of Homer, Pindar, and Sophocles above the smooth, sustained skill of Apollonius of Rhodes, Bacchylides, and Ion of Chios (*On the Sublime* 33.4–5). But this admired brilliance, realized in the inimitable, breathtaking metaphor or the overwhelming power of *pathos* (intense emotion), is not just an aesthetic effect. It partakes of the grandeur of the great heroes of the past and is the clearest sign of humanity's participation in the divine.[2]

These critics also voted with their feet, as it were, and so directly shaped the history of literature: the Cyclic Epics and the tragedies of Ion of Chios have disappeared, except for a few sparse fragments quoted by later epitomizers and grammarians. The choral odes of Stesichorus or Bacchylides would scarcely be known today were it not for the chance finds of papyrus rolls over the course of the past century. The dry sands of Egypt are also responsible for a good deal of what we now possess of Sappho, whom the scribes of early Byzantium quietly condemned to oblivion. Whereas all four books of Pindar's odes celebrating male athletic victors survive almost intact in a number of Byzantine manuscripts, there is no manuscript at all of Sappho or of any other archaic lyric poet, with their erotic and sympotic themes.

The ancient critics have formed our own notions of literary excellence. One of their greatest legacies to us is the notion of literary form itself; that is, the concept of literary art as defined by clear norms and formal properties, such as symmetry, proportion, decorum, grandeur, clarity, sublimity.[3] Each of these criteria also implies its opposite (e.g., meanness of style, frigidity, the unsuitable or inappropriate) and thus provides values for discriminating between good and bad writing. Yet, with the possible exception of Aristotle's dense remarks on tragedy, there are no comments on patterns of imagery, on the conscious or unconscious intentions of the author, or underlying narrative structure, or on the interrelation between the microcosm of local verbal effects and the macrocosmic design.[4] Symbolism as an interpretive tool appears only late in the tradition and, as we shall see, in a relatively restricted form. Aristotle singles out the *Oedipus Tyrannus* as the best model for tragedy, but his critical comments on the structure of the play are far less searching than, say, those of Voltaire in his *Lettres sur Oedipe*.[5]

Ancient literary criticism bears the mark of the special status and social function of ancient literature. The critics expect the works they discuss to be useful to their readers. "Useful" means serving as a model of style or expression, considerations that are always important in a culture where the spoken word has power and is not in competition with other media such as film or television. These works also provide models of behavior and criteria of ethical judgment. The critics can assume a continuity of values between the works they discuss and the values of their society because those values are derived, in large part, from the "classical" works themselves.

Modern critics have had no difficulty in extrapolating poetics from authors like Pindar, Euripides, and even Hesiod.[6] But only when the literary works have been formally canonized and set apart as school texts (largely from the Hellenistic period on) does criticism in antiquity develop as an activity independent of literary creation itself. Indeed, it would be hard to find a Greek word for "literary critic" as we understand the term.[7]

Four points are important for understanding the differences between ancient and modern approaches to literature. They are as follows:

1. the cultural continuities within ancient literature;
2. the homogeneity of cultural values for the ancient audience, in contrast to the pluralism to which modern critics are accustomed;
3. the status of the ancient reader as what I shall rather vaguely call "the included reader," as opposed to the modern excluded or alienated reader; and
4. the greater hermeneutic self-consciousness of the modern reader.

1. Cultural Continuity.

Many works of ancient literature are not only what we call literary texts. They are also cultural texts. They are part of a continuous cultural tradition, and they constitute the mark of education for all free (male) citizens. Until the late fifth century, Greek culture was still largely oral, even though writing was in use almost from the beginning of the archaic period. This means that the Homeric texts, to take the most prominent example, were regarded not just as examples of literary art but as a source of wisdom and as a repository of cultural values.[8] In this period literary works were an integral part of the values of the community and were experienced in largely communal contexts, in living performance, even as late as Plato's *Ion*, which shows the rhapsode in action.

The great bulk of surviving ancient criticism comes from the post-classical period, when a canon of famous works was codified for the schools and for commentaries, whether in the learned fashion of the Alexandrian editors or in a more humble fashion for young students. But even in this period, when literature was experienced to a greater extent than earlier through reading and the formalized instruction of the rhetorical schools, authors cited Homeric passages as models of proper or improper behavior. The heroic ideal, for instance, as exemplified in Achilles, Ajax, or Hector, retained a strong hold on the ancient mind long after the demise of the small, independent city-state, where the outstanding warrior and the sacrifice of his life in battle had an immediate social value. This continuation of the heroic ideal as a stylistic ideal is apparent in Longinus's treatise on sublimity.[9]

I need not dwell on the obvious point that prior to the Industrial Revolution, to say nothing of the Nuclear, Computer, or Sexual Revolutions, the rate of change is far slower than anything in our experience. Few of my readers are likely to recall a time when there were not electric lights, automobiles, radios, typewriters, or movies; and relatively few will know of a life without television or antibiotics. The technological changes between Homer and Porphyry are negligible in comparison to the changes between Keats and Helen Vendler. Television has brought enormous changes to reading habits (where it hasn't annihilated them), and even such obvious, everyday conveniences as the electric light, the printed book, or central heating change our way of reading. Lucretius spoke of serene nights that he spent in composing his Epicurean poem, but (I would venture) it is far more common for the modern critic to ponder over his or her author in the solitude of the wee hours, seated comfortably in a well-lighted and well-heated study, than it would have been in the ancient world. We should remember, too, that much of the "reading" in the ancient world was done aloud. Even within relatively recent times the basic physical setting for reading has undergone radical change. Readers in sixteenth- and seventeenth-century Europe, for instance, often read standing at high lecterns, and in the libraries books were chained to the desks (a practice that many contemporary librarians would doubtless regard with envy).

On a less material level, however, there is no doubt that the ancient reader, like the ancient poet, was saturated in his pastness in a way that can never be true for the modern reader. Even in the age of Alexander, and even under the Romans, classical Greek culture showed remarkable tenacity of its traditions and conventions. For St. Augustine, writing in the twilight of the classical tradition, Virgil's *Aeneid* was still a powerful, indeed dangerous, force (*Confessions* 1.13). Whereas classical readers had firm roots in the past, the past for us seems to send up a little tendril that we can just barely grasp, knowing that if we pull too hard it will break. For the logocentric culture of ancient Greece and Rome, as still for its rediscoverers in the Renaissance, the study of literature was the key to the collective wisdom of the society; for us literature is in intense competition with many other disciplines and many other sources of knowledge.

For the ancients the very composition of poetry was under the sign of continuity with that past, that is, under the aegis of the goddess of memory, Mnemosyne. The ancient critics were still the disciples of the poets they studied. For both these critics and their poets, the underlying model was a figure of Presence. For the poets, the Muse emerged into visual clarity in the radiant dance or procession on Helicon or Olympus, and spoke clearly and directly to the poet, as in the proem to Hesiod's *Theogony*. For the ancient critic the canonical writers had something of that quasi-magical closeness: heroized or idealized, they were studied in minute stylistic detail in order to realize in the present the excellence that they were felt to embody. The process was a kind of dialogue with a realm felt to be both timeless and familiar. Greek critics like Dionysius, Demetrius, and Longinus even experimented with recasting sentences of "classical" authors like Demosthenes in different ways (with a resultant demonstration of the excellence of the original version).

For the contemporary critic the underlying model is the figure of absence, be it the deconstructive concern with the gaps between signifier and signified inherent in language or the psychoanalytic concern with the truth that the text refuses to speak, or the marxist or feminist concerns with the hidden, subsurface ideologies, class privileges, or gender prerogatives that the text consciously or unconsciously masks. The ancient critic did not begin with the modern's painful awareness that the work under discussion will be unfamiliar, arcane, or perhaps even repugnant to large segments of the audience.

We have to be careful not to mythicize the ancients here; and there are, to be sure, ancient critics who felt the distance between themselves and the works that they were studying. To lament the loss of energy, grandeur, and power in writing and speaking was a common topos in the first century A.D., and the Elder Seneca, Quintilian, Tacitus, and to some extent Longinus all expatiated on it, citing the lethargy, hedonism, self-indulgence, and slackness of public life under the emperors. Yet even those tones of nostalgia were qualified by the feeling that the great writers of the past were still living, shining models of literary excellence. The very nostalgia of the retrospective glance carries with it the cultural recognition of assured values.

In a culture more continuous than ours, mere survival is an index of value. One can have some confidence that what "pleases all men and through all time" will be good (Longinus *On the Sublime* 7.4). In the modern world survival in an eternity of fame has become as shaky as the belief in progress. A nuclear-age audience is uncertain of how much of "all time" our battered planet may have left.

Although the ancients, from Hesiod on, reiterated that poets tell lies, they nevertheless retained a strong belief in the truth-value of poetry in general. The task is always to sort out the lie from the truth, to distinguish the true poets from the false. This is the task that Plato and in a very different way Plutarch, half a millennium after, set themselves. Or, like the allegorists Pseudo-Heraclitus and Porphyry, the critic can see his work as clearing away the covering of fiction and myth that overlays a valid spiritual meaning concealed beneath. Even a poet like Lucretius (middle of the first century B.C.), expounding a highly rationalistic and materialistic philosophy, could drink from the pure fountains of the Muses and hope to pour forth utterances that had greater sanctity than the pronouncements of the Pythian priestess on her tripod (*De Rerum Natura* 1.926–930, 5.110–112). The underlying assumption of Lucretius, as indeed of the entire classical literary tradition, was that the poet is endowed with the capacity for a wisdom that extends beyond his or her individual circumstances or individual personality, whether that capacity is defined as divine inspiration, poetic madness, special talent, or inborn nature (*physis, ingenium*). But once you unmask literature as ideology, as a form that cannot escape serving the interests of a certain class or gender, or as a set of operational techniques for manipulating signs, its truth-value becomes far more problematic.

2. Homogeneity.

Perhaps the modern critic's heaviest burden is the freedom to choose among a multiplicity of alluring and competing theories, approaches, and techniques. And that is also a choice among competing audiences. You write, and doubtless think, differently if you are aiming to publish in *Critical Inquiry, Rheinisches Museum für Philologie, Philological Quarterly,* or *Diacritics.* This is the kind of choice which the ancient critics, by and large, did not face, except perhaps insofar as they wrote as a member of a philosophical school: Theophrastus writing as a Peripatetic, Plutarch as a Stoic, Porphyry as a Neoplatonist. For the modern critic the very existence of such choices brings the uncomfortable awareness of the relativism or even the arbitrariness of the interpretive act.

The Greek or Roman critics not only wrote within a homogeneous cultural setting, with more or less agreed-on moral and aesthetic standards. They also wrote for an audience that still belonged to the same linguistic culture as the works that they were describing. Latin in the West had not yet fragmented into the vernacular languages, and Greek remained the standard in the East for many centuries. Thus the ancient critic did not have to deal with the problems of cultural difference or of translation versus original (Longinus was the only major ancient critic who even began to confront this question). He was less interested than his modern counterpart in exploring alien modes of self-representation. Herodotus, for all his commentary on the otherness of Egyptian theology or Scythian sex-life, was not much interested in the literature of these peoples.

3. The Included Reader.

Precisely because the ancient critic lived in a world more or less continuous with that of his texts, he was more able to accept their surface meaning in their own terms, and he felt less pressed to search for meanings beneath that surface (I shall speak later of the allegorists).

I say "he" advisedly here, for of course there were very few women critics of ancient literature, or at least very few whose names come down to us.[10] The discussion of literary texts belonged to the largely male arena of public life, for one of the functions of literary study was to improve one's skills in public speaking and public comportment, and this was an area reserved for men alone. Indeed, one of the reasons that feminist criticism of classical Greek literature has been so illuminating is precisely because it exposes to view just those hidden assumptions that the male-oriented author (and often audience) cannot see.[11]

Ancient criticism, as a branch of rhetoric, tended to be normative, communal, and on the whole practical. Yet there was a curious division in ancient views of literature between the femininity of the sources of inspiration (the Muses or their evil imagos, the Sirens) and the wholly masculine enterprise of criticizing or discussing literature. Women are associated with inspiration and with the hidden, private, and mysterious sources of the word, before it has the formed, authoritative power of the spoken or written text, and also with the capacity of language to charm, deceive, or seduce us by its mimetic power—language as magic. As Piero Pucci has shown, the roots of this association of mimesis and the female go back to Hesiod, whose Pandora is a creature of pretty adornment and "likeness."[12] Even Homer intimated the connection between mimetic deceptiveness and female wiles in the figure of Helen in the *Odyssey*, especially in the divergent tales about her behavior at Troy in Book 4.[13] Some three centuries later, Euripides and Gorgias made Helen a focal point for the charm and deceptiveness of art.[14] Yet the restrictions of political life kept women from any public exercise of verbal skill. Women in Greek culture may have discussed love and death, as Diotima does in Plato's *Symposium*, but they did not talk much about literature. Formal Greek literary criticism is far from any conscious awareness of this excluded (female) reader.

4. Hermeneutic self-awareness.

The modern self-awareness of our activity as interpreters begins with the early centuries of the Christian era and the work of assimilating both the pagan and Hebraic sacred writings to Christian thought. The ancient critics wrote from within a unified culture and had no hesitation in labeling those outside as barbarians, even though (as in the case of Herodotus and Plato on the Egyptians) they occasionally recognized their high cultural achievements. The long process of fitting pagan to Christian culture and assimilating another culture by reinterpreting its texts in the light of a new worldview has a profound effect on the modern critical sensibility. It produces, among other things, a charged hermeneutic atmosphere. In this atmosphere there is an awareness that meaning can, and indeed, must exist at two levels. Armed with the proper interpretive tools the reader can move from, say, an Old Testament prophet to the Gospels or from a pagan text like Virgil's Fourth *Eclogue* to its

Christian meaning as a prophecy of the birth of Christ. In a famous passage of the *Purgatorio* Dante depicts Statius's pity for his (and Dante's) pagan master, Virgil, for failing to grasp the deeper, and most important, meaning of his own text.[15] We are all the heirs of this hermeneutic tradition. There are some glimmers of the process in the allegorizing of Homer within the traditions of classical literary study, but this enterprise is far less massive, unified, serious, or self-conscious about the alterity of the traditions being confronted than the Christian hermeneutic is. The classical allegorists, after all, were still working within their own culture, and did not bring to their interpretation of the texts so radically different a set of values.

II

To turn now to the critics themselves. The bulk of ancient literary criticism consists of two kinds of analysis: the discussion of formal features of style and language, such as sound patterns or rhetorical figures, and moral concerns. Not infrequently the two strands come together, as in Aristotle's combination of formal structure and moral categories in his discussion of tragedy in the *Poetics*: the formal structure of reversal and recognition (*peripeteia* and *anagnorisis*) and the essentially ethical definition of the best type of tragic hero as a decent man who, through some *hamartia*, changes from good fortune to bad.

For all the differences between them, Plato and Aristotle ultimately agreed on the ethical role of literature. Its function is to improve life, to make us better. They differed, of course, in their views of what kind of literature makes us better; Plato took a dim view of the emotion-arousing power of tragedy and epic, while Aristotle allowed their cathartic function as beneficial.

Aristotle is here more traditional than Plato, for from the time of Hesiod, poets describe the benefits that poetry confers: it consoles and cheers us in times of trouble, and it reminds us of life's uncertainties and dangers in times of reckless overconfidence. Cicero and Plutarch put this tradition to practical use, citing excerpts from Greek literature to console or exhort (e.g., *Tusculan Disputations* and *Consolation to Apollonius*, respectively). Plato reversed the procedure, citing passages from Homer and Hesiod to illustrate the harmfulness of the traditional poets.

The practice of citing exemplary passages and labeling them as to their ethical value rests on the underlying assumptions about the community of culture and experience that the citations evoke and communicate. In such a climate, the critic's task is to bring the literary work into contact with a common ground of human experience which is felt to be expressed by the literary tradition. Thus the ancient reader turned instinctively to Euripides or Menander for reflections on the fragility of fortune, to Homer or Sophocles for the incentives to nobility and fame, to Anacreon and Alcaeus for the festive mood, and so on. Montaigne's citation-studded essays are the heirs to this tradition. For him, too, the common bond of "humanity," of a recognizable and relatively constant human nature, could span the barriers of the centuries. He found the advice of Lucretius or Horace or Seneca as useful as that of a neighboring landowner.

"Poetry," wrote Plutarch, "is rather like the head of an octopus or squid: it is sweet to the taste, but it causes bad dreams and strange imaginings" (*How the Young Man Should Study Poetry* 1.15 B–C). The antidote is to be ever mindful of the poet's tendency to relate false tales, like the myths about the terrors of the Underworld or the immoral behavior of anthropomorphic gods (16B). Regarding Achilles' maltreatment of Hector's body, for instance, Plutarch remarked, "Homer does well to use his closing line of comment [i.e., *Iliad* 23.23f., 'Achilles devised unseemly deeds against Hector'], as if casting his own vote against the things being done and said" (19D). In like manner, he rejected the allegorical explanation of Demodocus's risqué song about Aphrodite's adultery with Ares and viewed the episode as characterizing the soft, luxurious Phaeacians, in contrast to the enduring hero of stony Ithaca, who calls for a song about the capture of Troy (19E–20A).

Plutarch's moralism is an open-minded one. He believed in evil, and he believed that literature reveals evil alongside the good in humans and shows us how to choose. Thus we owe to him alone the preservation of the shocking lines of *Iliad* 9.458–461, in which Phoenix tells how he wanted to kill his father in an oedipal quarrel over the father's concubine to whom the son had made love. The Hellenistic editor, Aristarchus, had deleted the lines, Plutarch remarked, "in fear" (*phobetheis*), but they correctly suit the occasion (*kairos*), Plutarch argued, as Phoenix is "teaching" (*didaskein*) Achilles what anger is and what harm it can do (*How the Young Man Should Study Poetry* 26F).

About a century earlier, another Greek polymath, the geographer Strabo, had defended Homer's learning against Eratosthenes' charge that it was all old-wives' tales. In a vein that almost anticipated Vico, Strabo suggested that the poets are akin to the ancient lawgivers: both are teachers of their people. The poets use humans' natural curiosity and love of stories and novelty as an incentive toward education (1.8). From such passages we can appreciate how radical is Plato's expulsion of the poets from the city and how partial was its influence in the later history of Greek views of literature.

Behind this discrepancy of attitudes lie different notions of *mimesis*, imitation. By *mimesis* both Plutarch and Strabo meant the depiction of life and manners in an ethically adequate way. Literary mimesis does not necessarily reflect the petty details of everyday events back to us with photographic realism, but, Plutarch said, it shows us, in persuasive and plausible form, the mixed, complex quality of life, the constant interpenetration of good and bad, and the constant need for ethical judgment and discrimination (*How the Young Man Should Study Poetry* 25C). When the ancient scholiasts on Homer remarked on the graphic, pictorial, or mimetic scenes in the *Iliad*, like the meeting between Hector and Andromache or the baby Astyanax's fright at his father's helmet, they had in mind not only lifelikeness but also exemplarity: these scenes are distillations of something representative of suffering humanity.[16] For Horace, too, the poet's imitation of life lies in knowing the proper social behavior, obligations, characters, roles, and stations (*Ars Poetica* 317f.). Because these writers insisted on the primary reality of this world, especially the social world, to "imitate" its mixed moral qualities is not (as in Plato) to wander in the error of the transient, shifting senses.

Apart from Plato's definition, with its hostility to the mimetic power of literature, "imitation" refers to the process by which aesthetic form makes visible an otherwise invisible or intangible quality of character, personality, or ethical disposition. "Imitation of a serious action," in Aristotle's definition of tragedy, also contains the idea of rendering by formal means some otherwise invisible set of relations between acts and final effects. When Xenophon's Socrates asks some celebrated painters and sculptors how they "imitate" the soul of a man, "imitation" approximates the notion of aesthetic representation (*Memorabilia* 3.10). The visual artist, like the poet, makes visible *êthos*, the moral character that a man manifests in his private actions, his comportment in society, and his behavior toward the gods.

The concern of both poetry and visual arts, however, is not primarily the unique, idiosyncratic particularities of individual psychology but rather the paradigmatic and typical features of a situation, behavior, status, or time of life, especially as these bear on basic human situations of mortality, suffering, the precariousness of happiness, the importance of family ties and obligations, and the like. Hence characters in epic and tragedy often extrapolate from their immediate circumstances to large, recurrent phenomena of nature. In a celebrated passage of the *Iliad* the Lycian warrior Glaucus compares the generations of men to the falling and sprouting of leaves; the Sophoclean Ajax and Deianeira each compare the innocence of youth to a sheltered grove or meadow (Homer, *Iliad* 6. 145–149; Sophocles, *Ajax* 558–559 and *Trachiniae* 144–150). In this ability to reveal and portray human circumstances in universal, exemplary forms, poetry is, as Aristotle says, more "philosophical" than history, which deals in particulars (*Poetics* 9.1451b3 ff.).[17]

The tendency for the Greek critics after Aristotle to regard the primary task of mimesis as the rendering of manners, character, or ethical comportment (all included in the Greek term *ethos*) may have something to do with their failure to develop an adequate theory of fiction and their tendency to confuse representation with imitation. There are, of course, other reasons for the limited concern with fiction: myths rather than individually invented narratives were the main substance of narrative, and (as Aristotle noted) individual fictional subjects for tragedy were very rare. Comedy used narratives invented *ad hoc*, but it also lacked the prestige of tragedy or epic. The Greek literary vocabulary also tends to identify "fiction" with "lie" (*pseudos*) or "fabrication" (*plattein* and derivatives).

The Greek poets and philosophers frequently call attention to the problem of whether language is an adequate mode of communicating the invisible forces of emotion or thought; and they explore the ways in which language deceives or immerses us in a realm of surface appearances.[18] The critics, on the other hand, paid relatively little attention to these issues. Because of their normative and ethical concerns, derived in great part from the classical works themselves, the ancient critics, by and large, did not treat literature as an autonomous category of what we may call the aesthetic. Thus they are interested in language less as a system of signs and structural patterns than as a practical way of describing and influencing behavior. One possible reason for this lack of epistemological concern was the division between rhetoric and philosophy that developed from the early fourth century, with Plato's attacks on the Sophists and their successors, the school of Isocrates. Thus Dionysius of Halicarnassus begins his treatise *On Literary Composition* precisely with this division. What Dionysius called *theoria* (i.e., philosophy) was too difficult for his young addressee, who should rather have busied himself with the *praxis* that the stylistic study of language, *onomata* ("words"), provides (Chapter 3). Language not only describes character: it manifests character. For nearly all the ancient critics, form always stood in the closest relation to content, both as beautiful, harmonious, or appropriate expression of material and as the ethical outlook that pervaded the material and determined its level of elevation, range of application, breadth of view, and so on.

One of the underlying principles of ancient criticism, from Aristophanes on to Cicero and Longinus, is that a noble spirit will produce a noble style, and that a pusillanimous heart can create only a puny style. Excellence of style is never a matter of form alone. "As is a man's speech, such is his life" is a famous dictum of the younger Seneca (*talis oratio qualis vita*); and Longinus was thinking along similar lines when he wrote that "sublimity [of style] is the echo of grandeur of spirit" (*hypsos megalophrosynês apêchêma, On the Sublime* 9.2). But half a millennium earlier Aristophanes could already get good comic mileage from the mimetic relation between style and spirit, outer form and inner essence. In *Frogs* the subtle Euripides weaves ethereal strands of "wordlets" and "thoughtlets," whereas the grand, martial Aeschylus tosses about his big words, the size of mountains like Parnassus and Lycabettus, that correspond to his big ideas (*Frogs* 1056ff.). In the first scene of the *Thesmophoriazusae*, the effeminate tragedian Agathon appears on stage in appropriate dress to make the point, with comic concreteness, that the tragedian puts on womanish garb when he wants to portray womanish subjects. Longinus not only ranks thought and passion above technical proficiency in the tropes of rhetoric but also cites as his examples rhetorical figures whose *content*, as much as their form, embodies the stylistic quality of sublimity that he is defining. His first extended example of lofty style, for instance, is Homer's account of the Aloades boldly piling Pelion on Ossa to unseat the gods from their high mountain eyrie of Olympus.

At the beginnings of formal literary criticism in Aristophanes' *Frogs*, the battle of the prologues between Aeschylus and Euripides is settled not by the metrical or lexical dexterity of the contestants but by the physical weight of what the verses say. Aeschylus's line on death easily defeats Euripides' verse on persuasion because death is the heaviest experience we have and it easily sinks the scales. Behind the humor lies the deep-seated notion that the content is more decisive for the judgment of literary quality than the form. The scales on the stage act out the metaphor and decide the issue in terms of the tangible "weight" not of style (*onkos* is the rhetorical term) but of the matter. For Longinus "sublimity" not only cut across generic or stylistic categories but even transcended the signifying process of language itself, as in his example of the "sublime" silence of Ajax in the *Odyssey*, Book 11.

From Homer to the Christian apologists the power of an effective speaker to change the course of events was always a factor to be reckoned with in the assembly, in court, or on the battlefield. The ancient emphasis was therefore on pragmatics; it is audience-centered rather than author-centered. Longinus is a partial exception, as he regarded the sublime largely in relation to the grandeur of thought and feeling of the author; but he, too, was concerned with the ways in which that intensity is communicated from the author to the audience.

It is characteristic of this affective orientation that the chief virtue of style, on which almost all the ancient critics agreed, is clarity of expression, *sapheneia*; that is, the ability to communicate clearly and directly with your audience. The high value that the ancients set on force and clarity of communication is the heritage of centuries of a largely oral culture. In such a culture, as scholars like Eric Havelock and Jack Goody have pointed out, the literary work served to validate the norms and to reaffirm social solidarity rather than express personal idiosyncrasies.[19] The oral poet, seeing his audience in a face-to-face situation of performance and competition, was at least as much concerned with their reactions as with his own feelings.[20] *Pathos* was seen as the emotion conveyed *to* the audience rather than as the emotion depicted *within* the character or even between one character and another.[21]

In his treatise *On the Education of Children* Plutarch included the style of speaking as an essential part of education. The child (implicitly, the male child) should avoid the extremes of the flamboyant, theatrical style and the low, mean style. Turgidity in speaking was unsuited to public life (*apoliteutos*), while the too low or "thin" style made a feeble impression (Chapter 9, 7A). Plutarch went on to develop a three-way analogy between the health of language, body, and soul. Such a passage illustrates how much the ancients viewed speaking not only as an educational instrument but also as an essential mode of action in the public realm, a form of self-advertisement and self-presentation in the political arena. A little later in the treatise Plutarch advised the father to pay special attention to the training of his son's memory. He thereby incidentally revealed the continuing influence of the oral mentality. Memory, he suggested, is a benefit both for general culture and for practical success in worldly affairs (Chapter 13, 9F). The practical view of literary study, closely tied to the importance of oratory, has no precise equivalent in the modern world. Our rift between literature and the mass media has (*inter alia*) created literary criticism as an autonomous discipline and also separated the teaching of literary art from the teaching of style or "prose composition."

These considerations help us understand why some questions so important to modern criticism were relatively uninteresting to the ancient critics, even though the issues may be implicit in the ancient literary works themselves. Thus while the practicing poets repeatedly explored the sources and the nature of artistic creativity—one need only think of the descriptions of the Muses in Hesiod, the meeting with the Muses in the biography of Archilochus, or the recurrence of the mythical figure of Orpheus as a symbol of the power of poetry—the ancient critics paid little, if any, attention to this subject. Their concern was more with the external form of the work than with the quality of the personality that had shaped it. When Aristophanes, for instance, used the term "creative poet," *gonimos poêtês*, to describe his longed-for Euripides in the *Frogs* (96), the notion of individual genius was not uppermost. The speaker is Dionysus, god of the theater, and what he has in mind is a "generative" benefit for the community, something akin to fertility, social renewal, and cosmic regeneration. His "generative poet" should be able to "utter a noble saying" (*gennaion*, 97), a language that can put the audience of Athenian citizens back in touch with the traditional values of the civic greatness, power, confidence, and self-respect implied in the value word *gennaion*.

When the early writers did describe this source of poetic energy, they projected it outward, onto the divine, rather than inward, onto the self. It is a sacral power rather than a trait of personal psychology. Democritus was one of the earliest authors to make an explicit pronouncement on the subject: "Very fine indeed are whatever the poet composes with the inspiration of the *holy* afflatus."[22] Yet in the older tradition the personalizing of creative energy as a gift of the Muses is friendly and familiar rather than alien and irrational. Harold Bloom's interpretation of sublimity as something akin to the Freudian "uncanny," however suggestive for the Romantic poets, is not the ancient view, which allows a greater continuity between the "creative experience" and the rational processes of ordinary life.[23] The sublimity of Longinus, for example, is emphatically composed of teachable skill as well as vehement emotion, and it opens outward into the communities of both men and gods, culminating in the famous section on the "theater of the universe" in which man is a noble spectator (Chapter 35). In the only explicit reference to "inspiration" in the Homeric epics, the bard Phemius pairs this divine, non-rational gift with the personal and human effort of one who is "self-taught" (*autodidaktos*, *Odyssey* 22.347f.).[24]

Concern with something approaching our notions of creativity, however, does occur at a late stage of the rhetorical tradition, when the communal and cultural functions of literature are weakened and there is a parallel collapse or weakening of belief in the mythical or sacred origins of poetry. The first full-blown, explicit statement of something resembling our notions of the artist's creative imagination seems to occur in Philostratus's *Life of Apollonius of Tyana* in the early third century A.D. (6.19). The speaker adduces *phantasia*, the inner vision of imagination, as the source of Phidias's and Praxiteles' statues of the gods. This inner vision, he suggests, and not "imitation" from life (*mimesis*), is what produced these works. This emphasis on the superiority of imagination to imitation is new;[25] and it constitutes, in effect, a reversal of Plato's attack on the verbal and visual arts as an "imitation" of a lower, derivative, or earthly reality, in contrast to the vision of truth contained in the suprasensual realm of the Forms or Ideas.[26] In this late phase of the rhetorical tradition, and again in close association with the visual arts, there also emerges a more fully articulated interest in the artist's shaping power over the material substance of his work. The late sophistic rhetorician Callistratus (perhaps late third century A.D.) lavished his flowery rhetoric on the metamorphic process by which form is infused into matter through art, and the warmth of life miraculously fills the lifeless substance: "Indeed words cannot describe"—he said of a statue of Narcissus—"how the marble softened into suppleness and provided a body at variance with its own essence; for though its own nature is very hard, it yielded a sensation of softness, being dissolved into a sort of porous matter" (*Descriptions* 5.5 [393f.]). Similarly, in a bronze statue of Eros "it was possible to see the bronze coming to obey the passion and easily receiving the imitated appearance [*mimesis*] of laughter" (3.2). The power of mimetic plasticity to dissolve the boundaries between solid and liquid, inanimate and animate, and to make matter flow with supple vitality defeats the representational power of language itself. Elsewhere Callistratus notes with triumph how we are "smitten with speechlessness" (*aphasiâi plêgentes*) at the sight of bronze that "blushes" and "hard though it is by nature, flows softly as it yields to art and to whatever art wills."[27]

Conversely, Callistratus is interested in cases where the material resists and even defeats the artist's mimetic drive for full plastic expression. Thus, apropos of the statue of an Indian Dionysus in black stone, he observes that "the color of the stone gave no indication of the drunken state [of the god], for [the artist] had no device [*mêchanêma*] to redden the cheeks, as the blackness covered up the drunk-

enness, and he revealed the emotional state [*pathos*] by the gesture"
(*schêma*, 4.3). The underlying principle of this process is not so
much the classical notion of the controlling power of form and
thought as it is the magic of metamorphosis inherent in matter. In
this last passage, Callistratus calls attention to a quality in the material over which the artist has no control. Indeed this metamorphic
potentiality of material substance seemed to fascinate Callistratus
as much as the shaping vision of the artist's mind. In his *Descriptions* the artist is often absent, and it is the marble or the bronze by
itself that is undergoing the change, putting off hardness for vital
fluidity.

This shift of emphasis goes hand in hand with changes in artistic
taste. As in Baroque literature and art, there is a new appreciation of
illusionistic effects, which a Baroque sculptor like Bernini expresses
by rendering cloth in marble or vaporizing stone into a shimmering
haze of golden light. In this rhetorical approach to the shifting play
of appearance that emanates from the surface, the artwork is viewed
as process rather than finished structure. There are some affinities
with contemporary deconstructionist attitudes. It is the fluidity of
origins that the interpreter seeks to recover, the indeterminate, contingent features by which a work comes into being; and these are
determined by the material (or, one could say, the process of signification) rather than a separable meaning or signified that stands
apart from the process itself. Yet the dominant interest of ancient
criticism, heavily influenced by Aristotle and by the highly formalized "classical" artworks of the fifth and fourth centuries B.C. that
formed his judgment, was the work as a finished product, with a
clearly definable structure and a clearly definable and limited set of
meanings.

Even allowing for this later rhetorical interest in the creative
transformation of matter, there remains another fundamental difference between ancient and modern views of creativity. This is
probably due to the differences between the pagan and the Judaeo-
Christian culture. In the latter, the creative activity of the artist has
an importance analogous to the creativity of God, bringing new life
into being and breathing vital force into what was hitherto inert.
Though Ovid's myth of Pygmalion seems to approximate this view
of artistic reation, the pagan emphasis is on giving shape and form,
rather than bringing new matter into being. Indeed, "making" per se
had a pejorative connotation in the classical world, as the activity of
manufacture, which was often the task of slaves.

Even more modern-looking than such texts are the allegorical
interpretations of the traditional poets.[29] This approach has a mod-

ern look, thanks to the interpreter's dissatisfaction with surface meaning and his search beneath the literal. Yet ancient allegorical interpretation is a direct outgrowth of the moral tradition of ancient criticism and thus has a rather different function from the allegorical or symbolical study of literature in modern times. It also derives much of its impetus from the strong cultural continuity and uniformity which I discussed earlier. The most frequently allegorized text is the *Iliad*, precisely because it is the cultural text par excellence and the test case for the worthiness of the old literary culture. If this text cannot be "saved," that is, defended against charges of rudeness or immorality, there is no hope for the rest of the literary heritage. Homer is to emerge as the vehicle of an "ancient wisdom" that anticipates contemporary knowledge or science, not a crude survival from a morally and intellectually primitive epoch. Mutatis mutandis, Christian and Jewish interpreters of the Old Testament struggle with the same problems.

To the modern critic the allegorical interpretations are interesting more for their methods than for their results. The most extensive work of this nature is Heraclitus's (or Pseudo-Heraclitus') *Homeric Problems*, perhaps of the first century A.D. His method was to explain in naturalistic, rational terms irrational or apparently arbitrary events caused by divinities. This he did by interpreting the divine phenomenon in question as a natural force, thereby rendering the text acceptable to an audience that no longer believes in direct divine intervention in human affairs. The plague in the *Iliad* is a natural event, not the result of an anthropomorphic god's wrath; Apollo is merely "the same as the sun" (6.5–6.6, 8.5–8.6). By close reading of a number of passages, Heraclitus proves that summer, the natural season for plague, is in fact the season of the *Iliad* (11.1). He notes, for example, the dustiness of the earth and the sweatiness of various heroes (Chapter 10). The terrible clang of Apollo's arrows is the effect of the natural movement of the heavenly spheres (Chapter 12). Homer, therefore, "allegorically calls the rays of the sun 'missiles'" (13.1). Apollo is "like to night" because the foggy air in the sky is pestilential (13.2). The nine days of the god's attack refer to the nine-day crisis common in many illnesses (14.6). Achilles can end the plague because of this medical skill, learned from the wise Centaur, Chiron, mentioned in *Iliad* 11. The fact that Hera "put this thought in his mind" (*Iliad* 1.55) is explained by the allegorization of this goddess as air, identified also with intelligence and with the clearer air that replaces the pestilential murkiness of the plague (15.7). The sacrifices and paeans offered to Apollo when the plague ends confirm this interpretation (16.1).

Heraclitus's approach seems artificial today because he was determined to make Homer logical and because he freely called on material extraneous to the text, as when he identified Apollo with the sun. Yet the method creates some of the underlying principles and practices of modern literary criticism, at least in its predeconstructive phase. The underlying assumption of the method is the coherence of the text: there is unity of thought as well as unity of narrative form, and it is possible to draw upon this coherence to link a particular episode with another located at considerable remove. The critic circles carefully around the text, interweaves more and more of its details into his interpretation, and calls upon other parts of the text (or sometimes upon material from outside) whenever he needs to support factual details like the setting of the *Iliad* in summer or Achilles' medical skill in Book 11. Such an approach draws on earlier views of the structural and logical coherence of the work of art, especially in Plato and Aristotle.

The most famous and perhaps most successful use of the allegorical method is Porphyry's treatise *On the Cave of the Nymphs*, referring to *Odyssey* 13.[28] Porphyry did not merely select items at random over the whole corpus but instead paid close attention to the surface detail. He noted, for instance, that the orientation of the cave is north-south, whereas east-west is the normal orientation for worship. The divinities, he pointed out, are not just any Nymphs, but Naiads. His starting point is the obscurity, incoherence, or contradictoriness of the details at the surface level (Chapters 3, 4). And he paid great attention to these details. The inadequacy of the text to explain itself in literal terms is the justification for another order of explanation. His basic critical principle is that nothing in the work is accidental.

At the outset, Porphyry set forth and countered possible alternative explanations for the contradictions, inconsistencies, or difficulties that he had observed. Either the poet has merely invented these details at random, without any further intention than to entertain his audience (Chapter 4), or else he is giving a historical account of an existing geographical reality, a bit of local topography. Porphyry opted for a third possibility. He suggested that these details conceal an underlying spiritual meaning which has to do with the cave as a place of rebirth and renewal, where the soul is liberated from the realm of the senses, matter, and earthly becoming. The content of the interpretation comes, of course, from outside the text, but the necessity for the interpretation is grounded in the notion of the coherence of the text, the rationally based relationship of all the parts.

A second, equally important principle is that the poet is in touch with "nature" and is the vehicle of an "ancient wisdom," of which he need not necessarily be fully conscious himself. Homer expressed this wisdom, Porphyry suggested, through the "mystic symbols" that appear in his details about various ritual elements, that is, elements concerned with man's contact and communication with divinity. "The ancient wisdom of Homer," he wrote, "tells its truths under the covering of mythical fictions" (Chapter 36). With this notion that the poet has access to a special wisdom about the soul through a language of symbols and figures contained in the myths that he tells, Porphyry was a forerunner of archetypalist criticism. For him the language of the soul's secrets was a language of symbols and images rather than of abstract concepts, forces, or natural processes.

At the same time Porphyry was heir to a long tradition, going back to Hesiod, Democritus, and Plato: the poet is in touch with a divine power, be it Muse, inspiration, or madness. But for Porphyry, unlike Homer and Hesiod, this power gives the poet not just the technical skill to sing his songs but also the spiritual depth that makes those songs meaningful, "wise," to generations centuries after his own time. One may recall Strabo's remark about the ancient wisdom of the poet as a proto-lawgiver, or Horace's lines in the *Ars Poetica* about the poets' ancient *sapientia*, embodied in Orpheus' charming of wild beasts by his song, turning men from their savage and violent life in the forests to civilized behavior (391–399).

This notion of an all-pervasive wisdom that the poet shares with the philosopher through the symbols of the soul's journeys from the earth toward the divine enabled Porphyry to resolve Plato's "ancient quarrel between poetry and philosophy" (*Republic* 10). Instead of being expelled because they could speak only immoral foolishness and could give no logical account of what they may be saying, the poets were in fact valued for a wisdom that transcends rational knowledge or explicit formulation. Already for Longinus the corpus of great writers constituted a reservoir of spiritual energy or greatness of soul in times which themselves permit no other access to such qualities (Chapter 44). For Porphyry the wisdom of the ancients, hidden from our own minds, could be revealed by the interpretive depth of the philosopher-critic.

Conclusion

Every complete literary creation is both a work and a text. Because it is a construction of words, it will reveal the constructed patterns that can be followed back, deconstructively, to their fluid moments of origins, in all their contingent, indeterminate possibilities. Because literary works also shape language into more or less coherent images of reality—depictions of objects, places, events, and emotions—they comment on human experience, and they pattern these mimetic representations into structures that convey and embody interpretations of life. Readers can be helped by the different perspectives that other times and other cultures offer for understanding this process.

Specifically, recognizing the evolution of interpretive procedures from the early phases of our own culture reveals how many of the assumptions made about the nature of literary representation and reception are conditioned by the technological developments of the last century and their social consequences. Looking over the centuries since classical antiquity, we can see how men and women in different cultures and different historical moments have made very different definitions of the ways in which literary works can be read.

Throughout the entire corpus of ancient criticism, as I have shown, the interpretive activity has social purposes and has to answer to society. Longinus, Plutarch, "Heraclitus," and Porphyry all wrote, with different emphases, in the philosophical-moralistic mode of ancient criticism. But in one way or another, each of these writers also raised the question of the tension between the practice of criticism as a technique for the formal analysis of language *and* the practice of criticism as a locus for ethical or spiritual values. Contemporary critics struggling with the problem of what we should be reading and how we should be reading it are grappling with this pull between aesthetic form and moral value—that is, between the study of literature as a discipline with its own laws, history, and principles *and* the study of literature as a commentary on how to live. Revising the canon of literary works is an attempt, at some level, to assert that literary study is not marginal to current social and political debate on the equality of races and genders and on the relations between the West and the third world.

These conflicts are present, embryonically, in Aristophanes' contest between Aeschylus and Euripides in the *Frogs*, which is a conflict between skillful technique that produces aesthetic pleasure and socially useful moral and/or political advice. They are still more prominent in Longinus' malaise about the relation between the heroic spirit of the grand style and the craftiness of artful technique. And of course, as with almost everything of the Greeks, they remain very much with us still.

Notes

1. See P. E. Easterling in *The Cambridge History of Classical Literature,* vol. 1, *Greek Literature* (35), with the further literature there cited. Translations of classical texts are my own.

2. See Charles Segal, "Writer as Hero: The Heroic Ethos in Longinus, *On the Sublime"* (especially 210).

3. See, for example, W. J. Verdenius, "The Principles of Greek Literary Criticism" (16ff.). It is important to keep in mind that there is a span of some seven centuries between Aristophanes' *Frogs,* the earliest sustained piece of literary criticism, and (for example) Porphyry's treatise *On the Cave of the Nymphs.* Needless to say, I am aware of the blurring of particulars in the attempt to arrive at an overall picture. I can only hope that the resultant overview justifies the risks of generalization.

4. On this point see G. M. A. Grube, "How Did the Greeks Look at Literature?" (13ff.).

5. For example, Paul Fry remarks in *The Reach of Criticism,* "There is no evidence in the *Poetics* of the subtlety of modern formalism or of the attention to detail traditionally lavished on sacred texts and eventually on Shakespeare by German and English Romantic readers" (38).

6. See, for instance, the collection of comments on poetry in the anthology of Giuliana Lanata, *Poetica Preplatonica.*

7. On the term *kritikos,* for example, see Robert Lamberton, *Homer the Theologian* (13); also James Porter, "Aristarchus and Crates on the Exegesis of Homer" (85).

8. See E. A. Havelock, *Preface to Plato* (Chapters 3 and 4); also Bruno Gentili, *Poetry and Its Public in Ancient Greece and Rome* (3–23).

9. See Segal, "Writer as Hero."

10. Athenaeus, *Deipnosophistae* (11.490E) mentions one Moero of Byzantium who wrote a work entitled *Mnemosyne* (*Memory*), interpreting verses of Homer.

11. Two recent books represent several: Eva Keuls, *The Reign of the Phallus* and Page duBois, *Sowing the Body.* For an abundant recent bibliography see Synnove Des Bouvrie, *Women in Greek Tragedy.*

12. P. Pucci, *Hesiod and the Language of Poetry* (85ff.). Compare also Hera's combination of devious persuasion, sexual seduction, and the meretricious adornment of her body in her deception of Zeus in Homer, *Iliad* 14.197–221.

13. See Ann Bergren, "Helen's 'Good Drug,': *Odyssey* 4 1–305" (201–214).

14. See Segal, "The Two Worlds of Euripides' *Helen,"* (263–266).

15. Statius in *Purgatorio* 22.67ff. See also Leonard Barkan, *The Gods Made Flesh: Metamorphosis and the Pursuit of Paganism* (98).

16. See Jasper Griffin, *Homer on Life and Death* (6f.).

17. For an approach to mimesis along these lines see L. Rosenstein (562).

18. One need only think of Euripides' *Hippolytus* or Sophocles' *Oedipus Tyrannus* or of Gorgias' *Helen* or Plato's early Socratic dialogues.

19. See Havelock; Jack Goody, *The Domestication of the Savage Mind.* See also Marcel Detienne, *L'Invention de la Mythologie* (translated as *The Creation of Mythology*), especially Chapter 2.

20. See, for instance, Joseph Russo and Bennett Simon, "Homeric Psychology and the Oral Epic Tradition."

21. Christopher Gill, "The *Ethos/Pathos* Distinction in Rhetorical and Literary Criticism" (especially 152–155), and "The Character Personality Distinction" in Christopher Pelling, ed., *Characterization and Individuality in Greek Literature.* Many of the essays in this collection are also relevant here, particularly P. E. Easterling, "Constructing Character in Greek Tragedy," and Simon Goldhill, "Character and Action, Representation and Reading: Greek Tragedy and Its Critics."

22. Fragment 68 B18 in H. Diels and W. Kranz, eds., *Die Fragmente der Vorsokratiker.* For the earlier identification of what we would call creativity and divine inspiration see Homer, *Odyssey* 22.345–348, with Segal, "Poetry, Performance, and Society in Early Greek Literature" (136ff.) and "Bard and Audience in Homer."

23. Harold Bloom, "Freud and the Sublime: A Catastrophe Theory of Poetry," in *Agon* (91–1180, apropos of Sigmund Freud, "The 'Uncanny,'" (1919), in *The Standard Edition of the Complete Psychological Works of Sigmund Freud* (219–256). Closer to Bloom, however, are the well-known statements on the "divine madness" of the poet in Plato, *Ion* 533E–534E and *Phaedrus* 245A. But for Plato the irrationality of poetry is a reason for dismissing it as a valid source of knowledge of reality.

24. For recent discussion and bibliography see Verdenius (38f.) and note 22.

25. The notion, however, may be somewhat foreshadowed in Longinus' treatise *On the Sublime*: see D. A. Russell, *Criticism in Antiquity* (109f.), on what he calls the "poetical" *phantasia*.

26. See. J.-P. Vernant, "Naissance d'images" in *Religions, histoires, raisons* (136f.).

27. *Descriptions* 6.3; see also 8.2, 11.1, 13.3. With Callistratus's phrase compare the rhetorical *ekplexis*, the effect of "smiting one out of his senses" by means of the power of language.

28. For the nature and development of allegorical exegesis, with extensive bibliographies, see Felix Buffière, *Les Mythes d'Homère et la pensée grecque*, and Lamberton, *Homer*, passim; also Porter, passim.

29. For further discussion and bibliography see Lamberton, *Homer*, 119–133; also his *Porphyry, On the Cave of the Nymphs: Translation and Introductory Essay*; and his essay, "The Neoplatonists and the Spiritualization of Homer" (especially 123ff.).

Works Cited

Aristotle. *The Poetics.* In *Aristotle's Poetics: A Translation and Commentary for Students of Literature*, translated by Leon Golden and O. B. Hardison Jr. Tallahassee: University Press of Florida, 1981.

Barkan, Leonard. *The Gods Made Flesh: Metamorphosis and the Pursuit of Paganism*. New Haven: Yale University Press, 1986.

Bergren, Ann. "Helen's 'Good Drug': *Odyssey* IV 1–305." In *Contemporary Literary Hermeneutics and Interpretation of Classical Texts*, edited by S. Kresic, pp. 201–214. Ottawa: Ottawa University Press, 1981.

Bloom, Harold. *Agon*. New York: Oxford University Press, 1982.

Buffière, Felix. *Les Mythes d'Homère et la pensée grecque*. Paris: Belles Lettres, 1956.

Callistratus. "Descriptions." In *Philostratus, the Elder, the Younger; Imagines; Callistratus; Descriptiones*, translated by Arthur Fairbanks, pp. 375–423. Loeb Classical Library. London: Heinemann, 1930.

The Cambridge History of Classical Literature. Vol. 1, *Greek Literature*. Edited by B. M. W. Knox and P. E. Easterling. Cambridge: Cambridge University Press, 1985.

Des Bouvrie, Synnove. *Women in Greek Tragedy. Symbolae Osloenses Supplement*, vol. 27. Oslo: Universitetsforlaget, 1990.

Detienne, Marcel. *The Creation of Mythology*. Translated by M. Cook. Chicago: University of Chicago Press, 1986.

———. *The Cuisine of Sacrifice among the Greeks*. Translated by P. Wissig. Chicago: University of Chicago Press, 1989.

Diels, H., and W. Kranz, eds. *Die Fragmente der Vorsokratiker*, 5th ed. Berlin: Weidmann, 1952.

Dionysius of Halicarnassus. *On Literary Composition (De Compositione Verborum)*. In *Dionysius of Halicarnassus, The Critical Essays*, edited and translated by Stephen Usher, vol. 2, pp. 14–243. Loeb Classical Library. Cambridge, Mass.: Harvard University Press, 1985.

duBois, Page. *Sowing the Body*. Chicago: University of Chicago Press, 1988.

Easterling, P. E. "Constructing Character in Greek Tragedy." In *Characterization and Individuality in Greek Literature*, edited by Christopher Pelling, pp. 83–99. Oxford: Oxford University Press, 1990.

Freud, Sigmund. "The 'Uncanny.'" 1919. In *The Standard Edition of the Complete Psychological Works of Sigmund Freud*, edited and translated by James Strachey, et al., 17: 219–256. London: Hogarth Press, 1954.

Fry, Paul. *The Reach of Criticism*. New Haven: Yale University Press, 1983.

Gentili, Bruno. *Poesia e pubblico nella Grecia antica*. Rome and Bari: Laterza, 1984. *Poetry and Its Public in Ancient Greece and Rome*. Translated by A. T. Cole. Baltimore: Johns Hopkins University Press, 1988.

Gill, Christopher. "The Character Personality Distinction." In *Characterization and Individuality in Greek Literature*, edited by Christopher Pelling, pp. 1–31. Oxford: Oxford University Press, 1990.

———. "The *Ethos/Pathos* Distinction in Rhetorical and Literary Criticism." *Classical Quarterly* 34 (1984): 149–166.

Goldhill, Simon. "Character and Action, Representation and Reading: Greek Tragedy and its Critics." In *Characterization and Individuality in Greek Literature*, edited by Christopher Pelling, pp. 100–127. Oxford: Oxford University Press, 1990.

Goody, Jack. *The Domestication of the Savage Mind*. Cambridge, England: Cambridge University Press, 1977.

Griffin, Jasper. *Homer on Life and Death*. Oxford: Oxford University Press, 1980.

Grube, G. M. A. "How Did the Greeks Look at Literature?" In *Lectures in Memory of Louise Taft Semple, 1966–1970*, edited by C. G. Boulter, pp. 87–129. Norman, Oklahoma: University of Cincinnati Classical Lectures, Second Series, 1973.

Havelock, E. A. *Preface to Plato*. Cambridge, Mass.: Harvard University Press, 1963.

Keuls, Eva. *The Reign of the Phallus*. New York: Harper and Row, 1985.

Lamberton, Robert. *Homer the Theologian*. Berkeley and Los Angeles: University of California Press, 1986.

———. *Porphyry, On the Cave of the Nymphs: Translation and Introductory Essay*. Barrytown, New York: Station Hill Press, 1983.

———. "The Neoplatonists and the Spiritualization of Homer." In *Homer's Ancient Readers*, edited by Robert Lamberton and John J. Keaney, pp. 115–133. Princeton: Princeton University Press, 1992.

Lanata, Giuliana. *Poetica Preplatonica: Testimonianza et frammenti*. Florence: La Nuova Italia, 1964.

Longinus. *On the Sublime*. In *Longinus, On the Sublime*, translated by D. A. Russell. Oxford: Clarendon Press, 1965.

Porter, James. "Hermeneutic Lines and Circles: Aristarchus and Crates on the Exegesis of Homer." In *Homer's Ancient Readers*, edited by Robert Lamberton and John J. Keaney, pp. 79–114. Princeton: Princeton University Press, 1992.

Plutarch. *How the Young Man Should Study Poetry*. In *Plutarch, Moralia*, edited and translated by F. C. Babbitt, vol. 1, pp. 74–197. Loeb Classical Library. London: Heinemann, 1927; reprinted Cambridge, Mass.: Harvard University Press, 1969.

———. *The Education of Children*. In *Plutarch, Moralia*, edited and translated by F. C. Babbitt, vol. 1, pp. 4–69. Loeb Classical Library. London: Heinemann, 1927; reprinted Cambridge, Mass.: Harvard University Press, 1969.

Pucci, Piero. *Hesiod and the Language of Poetry*. Baltimore: Johns Hopkins University Press, 1977.

Rosenstein, Leon. "On Aristotle and Thought in Drama." *Critical Inquiry* 3 (1977): 543–565.

Russell, D. A. *Criticism in Antiquity*. Berkeley: University of California Press, 1981.

Russo, Joseph, and Bennett Simon. "Homeric Psychology and the Oral Epic Tradition." 1968. In *Essays on the Iliad*, edited by James Wright, pp. 41–57. Bloomington: Indiana University Press, 1978.

Segal, Charles. "Bard and Audience in Homer." In *Homer's Ancient Readers*, edited by Robert Lamberton and John J. Keaney, pp. 3–29. Princeton: Princeton University Press, 1992.

—————. "Poetry, Performance, and Society in Early Greek Literature." *Lexis* 2 (1988): 123–144.

—————. "The Two Worlds of Euripides' *Helen*." 1970. In *Interpreting Greek Tragedy*, by Charles Segal, pp. 222–267. Ithaca, New York: Cornell University Press, 1986.

—————. "Writer as Hero: The Heroic Ethos in Longinus, *On the Sublime*." In *Stemmata: Hommages à J. Labarbe*, edited by Jean Servais, Tony Hackens, and Brigitte Servais-Soyez, pp. 207–219. Brussels and Liège: L'Antiquité classique, 1987.

Verdenius, W. J. "The Principles of Greek Literary Criticism." *Mnemosyne*, Series 4, vol. 36 (1983): 14–59.

Vernant, J.-P. *Religions, histoires, raisons*. Paris: F. Maspero, 1979.

Part 2.

CANONICAL VARIATIONS

**WORKING WITH TEXTS AND
THEIR COUNTERTEXTS**

Introduction

Sarah Lawall

This section offers a group of literary texts seen as part of a network of literary and cultural relationships. These texts are not explained away by historical reference, nor do they dissolve in continually deferred associations. Nonetheless, they appear inside patterns of intertextual reference that call alternately on cultural, literary-historical, ideological, and formal systems. The governing assumption is that one learns more about the "world" of world literature by tracing the different ways it is embedded in the linguistic and social structures that energize meaning. Essayists take up works from a range of sources including ancient Greece, medieval Celtic Europe, Elizabethan England, nineteenth-century Latin America, the modern Caribbean, and Japanese literature.

Nancy Rabinowitz's study of Euripides is part of the current revisionary analysis of classical antiquity that derives from cultural studies and focuses on interrelated structures of gender, power, and race. As a teacher of ancient Greek drama, she is conscious of a dual obligation: to transmit major works whose impact on generations of readers has shaped Western tradition, and to disclose—in those works—the functioning of ideological structures that have also shaped tradition but in less visible ways. Rabinowitz's rereading of the *Hippolytus* and *Alcestis* notes the female protagonists' silences, absence, repression, sacrifice, and death that define women as objects of exchange and encourage a similar definition by the audience. Examining the sense of human community represented in each play, she argues that it is a male-oriented community that achieves its final idealized harmony only by excluding the resistant Other: that is, women. If modern readers absorb the classical tradition in terms of such an idealized male experience, they are obscuring real power and gender distinctions that are already demonstrated in the ancient plays and have not disappeared from contemporary society. Deconstructing the implied world of ancient drama, she suggests, gives students a more accurate picture of their own ideological inheritance and helps them understand the play of forces in modern society.

Joan Dayan takes up intertwined issues of race, power, and the complex perspectives of art in her discussion of Caribbean writer Aimé Césaire and his portrayal of Caliban. For the traditional canon, Caliban is a figure in Shakespeare's play *The Tempest*: a minor character who unsuccessfully opposes the all-powerful and wise magician Prospero. Prospero is the rightful duke of Milan, who has been exiled to a savage and remote island by his usurping brother, Antonio. Here he finds and enslaves the island's only inhabitant, Caliban, a savage creature "not honour'd with a human shape" and son of the dead witch Sycorax. Among Prospero's servants is Ariel, a spirit of air whom the magician had freed from Sycorax's imprisonment and bound to his own service. The malicious and rebellious Caliban plots his master's destruction throughout the play but is forced to submit to Prospero's superior power at the end, while the obedient Ariel is freed. Given this triangle of master, good slave, and bad slave, it is small wonder that Caliban became a symbol of disinherited black identity, or that the "Caliban complex" would be a central theme in twentieth-century analyses of colonialism. Césaire's adaptation of Shakespeare in *A Tempest* (1969) takes its place in these analyses: indeed, it is probably the most influential literary statement and vindication of Caliban's position. Nonetheless, argues Dayan, the play offers much more than a symbolic reversal in which Caliban triumphs and Prospero, the self-interested defender of "civilization," remains besieged in his cave on an island overrun by the jungle. The texture of Césaire's play deconstructs mere role reversals and expresses a complex mutuality of opposed images: civilization and savagery, speech and silence, illusion and reality, knowledge and ignorance, weakness and strength, beauty and ugliness, mastery and servitude. Dayan observes that Shakespeare had already incorporated considerable irony into his portraits of Prospero and Caliban, and their complicated relationship becomes in Césaire an overt part of Caliban's struggle for self-knowledge.

The literature of the ancient Celts—early inhabitants of western and central Europe, covering the British Isles and modern France—is familiar to modern readers chiefly through themes and images. King Arthur, King Lear, the lovers Tristan and Isolde, Merlin the magician, fairylands and otherworlds, fantastic journeys to lands populated by strange and magical beings: all have become part of world literature in a range of works influenced by Celtic sources and written in different European languages. Yet the Celtic texts themselves have been excluded from such transmission, and rarely appear in anthologies or the classroom. Maria Tymoczko argues that this exclusion demonstrates an important truth about canon-formation: that societies accept what they need, recognize, and want from other cultures, and that they transmute or filter out resistant material. Documenting the mixed attraction and repulsion of archaic Celtic texts for various European societies, she suggests that reading across cultural boundaries is always a *process* that involves matching up the reader's worldview with the horizons of an unfamiliar text. Sometimes this process excludes strikingly different ways of seeing the world: Victorian readers, for example, could not process the overt sexuality, violence, and scatology of many Celtic tales. Generalizing from the example of Celtic literature, Tymoczko suggests that students should learn to recognize the processing factors at work in the creation of literary canons so that they themselves may become more informed and accurate readers of any text.

One phenomenon of modern canon processing is the global popularity of a group of Latin American novelists who gained fame in the "Boom" period of the 1960s and 1970s: for example, the widely taught Colombian Gabriel García Márquez (best known for *One Hundred Years of Solitude* [1967]), the Mexican Carlos Fuentes, the Argentine Julio Cortázar, and the Peruvian Marios Vargas Llosa. The "magical realist" style of many Boom works—a mixture of realism and fantastic imagination—conveyed both actual historical events and a dreamlike, interpretive vision that gave a symbolic picture of political and psychological conflicts in Latin American society. Yet the Boom writers were not new in their blending of realist and symbolic structures; as Doris Sommer shows, popular novelists in the nineteenth century used a more subliminal form of symbolism that may have made their works even more effective as political instruments. The historical romances she examines have a dual role as political program pieces, because the erotic and domestic conflicts they describe in traditional realist style are also persuasive allegories for broader social issues. A marriage between two characters recommends the fruitful reconciliation of two aspects of national identity; the subjection or death of another character indicates the disapproval of the related ethnic or economic element in an approved national narrative. These immensely popular novels helped shape the national communities of modern Latin America: as widely read literary works, they were the canon and they also constructed a canon of social relationships. Sommer's discussion takes its place among recent analyses of the cultural implications *and effects* of symbolic structure in literature. She provides another example of the need to read symbolic structures as part of the work's world if readers are to be aware of the "whole story."

Janet Walker approaches world literature from a different perspective, and asks about the possibility of studying genre across cross-cultural boundaries. In doing so, she takes up a common starting point for many world literature courses which organize material under the genres of drama, lyric poetry, or versions of "the novel." Such comparisons are risky, as she points out: they start from a Western paradigm and try to find cognates in other literary traditions. These other traditions may favor quite different forms, however, so that the genre analysis ends by imposing Eurocentric definitions on resistant texts or finding no comparable material at all. Walker's test case of autobiography is especially significant because the genre has been said not to exist outside the Western tradition. If other cultures do not have a similar concept of the individual, as some have argued, it may be sheer cultural imperialism to look for autobiographies as such. How, then, can one proceed, and is it worthwhile to try? Walker suggests that we should not start from current literary definitions of autobiography, which are based on Western models that privilege linear, historical narratives of complete lives. Instead, we should decide what *functions* autobiography fills in those paradigmatic Western works and attempt to discover if works in other cultures possess similar "autobiographical intent." One of the unique genres of Japanese literary tradition, she observes, consists precisely of accounts of personal experience aimed at self-understanding. Yet the form is different: Western autobiographical conventions of realism and completeness are replaced by an aesthetics that permits mixed forms and fragmentary, intensified (sometimes fictionalized) experience. Examining these "autobiographical" works of Japanese literature—a major genre, and one dominated for over a century by women writers—Walker proposes that genre studies employ a broader understanding of the ways different societies use literary form to explore personal experience.

3. Men Working: Community under Construction

Nancy Sorkin Rabinowitz

Academia seems to be seriously fragmented as it faces the next century; contests rage over who will control the curriculum and the classroom. At a time when a major university could be accused of capitulating to "a campaign of pressure politics" in revising its Western culture requirement (*Chronicle of Higher Education,* April 27, 1988, p. A2), the pressure is clearly on; colleges and universities are caught in the conflicting force fields of those demanding a multicultural curriculum and those demanding a traditional one. In such a context teachers of world literature need to think through some of the assumptions behind our treatment of ancient works, and particularly the Greek tragedies, the center of what we have taken to be the flowering of Athens.

The old-style reasons for literary study are summed up in this 1899 passage from the *Ridpath Library of Universal Literature:* "Literature is the highest blossom of the human spirit. . . . Such is the nature of literature that it is susceptible of being translated from language to language, from race to race, from century to century, and, it may be, from world to world" (Ridpath vii). Such thinking has not disappeared, and despite post-structuralist pronouncements to the contrary, the humanist position survives. Thus, for instance, Bernard Knox introduces the 1987 *Norton Anthology of Masterpieces of the Ancient World* with the comment that "the literature of the ancient world . . . is still the background of our institutions, attitudes, and thought" (2). The classics ought to be retained, then, simply by virtue of their place in "the tradition." What do we imply when we call texts "classics"? Twenty years ago, *Classics of Western Thought* informed its readers that it contained only "what is truly *classic,* that is to say, valuable both for its intrinsic merit and for having exerted a paramount influence on its own and later times" (Hirschfeld v). It would seem then that the "classics" gain their status from their "universality," from the eternal human values believed to be found in them.

The very term is a misnomer, however, since, as others have observed, each literature has its own classics and its own classical period (Haley "Classics and Minorities"; Hallett "Feminist Theory"; Rabinowitz "Introduction"). The stress on humane values that transcend their time is in effect a form of nostalgia for a nonexistent past, based on its supposed wholeness and sense of community. Certainly I grew up with the cliché that Greek tragedy depended on the audience's shared beliefs; modern tragedy was problematic because of the lack of such a cohesion. But was Athens cohesive? Only because we ignored the groups excluded—metics, slaves, and women—to make possible that ideological whole. But the Athenian law of 451 B.C. requiring that citizens have two Athenian parents shows that membership in the *polis* or city-state, and the question of who was in and who was out, was a problematic issue that had to be resolved. By design, the Athens of the fifth century B.C., the Athens of tragedy, was first and foremost a men's club, and as Jacqueline de Romilly points out, the democracy was based on an ambitious empire with economic advantages for Athenians (86). Teaching the plays without reference to the cultural struggles behind them creates a fantasy of homogeneous citizenry. This work of construction arises in part out of critics' desires for a community like that of this fantasized Athens, one that would deny North Americans' own historical divisions along race, class, and gender lines. As the work of Judith Hallett attests, early republican French and United States idealizations of antiquity were based on such an identification; contemporary assertions about what all educated people should know, along with current tests for U.S. citizenship requiring knowledge that "natives" don't have, suggest that the current intellectual climate acts as a hothouse for the forcing of an elite, without regard for the power dynamics encoded in words like "classic" and "best."

If the dominant order has such an investment in classics, what about the opposition? Why in a time of limited resources would a progressively minded scholar want to teach these texts with their particular history? Whether designing a course or proposing a book for publication, such scholars do not have infinite time or money and thus must make choices. On what basis do we continue to focus on antiquity? At times, given the phrasing of the curricular debates, I have felt that there was in fact no way for a self-respecting feminist to work in classics, that the contradictions between the discourses was such as to be irresoluble (see also Skinner "Classical," "Expecting"). The conflict between classics and feminist studies is even more pointed given current efforts to construct a meaningful analysis of race, class, and sexuality, as well as gender; that is, to take into account differences among women. A 1992 conference on "Feminism and Classics," however, gave me hope and renewed energy; marginal groups, excluded by the racism, sexism, homophobia, and classism of society, have our own subversive interest in studying these founding cultural texts—precisely because of the force that the texts have exerted in the past.

There are several ways in which to proceed. First, we can understand classics' complicity in sexist and racist constructions of knowledge by analyzing the history of the discipline. By considering what scholars of the past have found in antiquity, we can be more critical of our own motives for the study, recognizing that, as Ruth Padel says about opera, the turn to "the Greeks" is "rather, to their own idea of the Greeks, as their own epoch mirrored itself in that fragmented heterogeneous lot of male texts which we call Greek culture" (201). Second, other scholars could help to resolve the contradiction between the two claims on our loyalty by rescuing classics from its old definition. Teachers of classics face the challenge of deconstructing the universalizing interpretations, removing their texts from a static Eurocentrism and taking seriously the multiplicity of cultures represented in the United States today. A further possibility is to stress the relationship between ancient Greece and ancient Asia Minor and ancient Africa instead of the West (Bernal). Recent work by Shelley Haley ("Black Feminist Thought") and Bella Zweig ("Primal Mind") have shown how current modes of cross-cultural analysis can open up antiquity, in particular by problematizing a continuing tendency in feminism to assume that male domination has been universal. Zweig, using Native American models, and Haley, using black feminist thought as a hermeneutic, reveal some of the possibilities of decentering the hegemonic view.

Even those remaining within the more narrowly defined Greek and Roman tradition can handle the dissonance between feminism and classics by turning their attention away from the much read and studied canonical literary texts and looking instead for women authors and a women's tradition, perhaps in non-literary remains.[1] But are there reasons (beyond brute economics—this is what classicists were trained to do and are paid to do) for continuing to study Homer and fifth-century Greek tragedy, for instance? In the past I was convinced that the dominance of the Greek myths and their ability to reinscribe themselves in our subconscious necessitated feminist deconstruction, but as fewer and fewer students have classical education, I have become concerned that that argument might be largely bogus, and that I might be the one inscribing Greek tragedy in my students' minds. Nonetheless, there is a level on which cultural valorization of the Greeks continues and may be more potent if students do not have any concrete information to support or counteract its effects. So, my first reason for continuing to work on canonical texts is to provide a non-hegemonic point of view on material that forms the deep backdrop to modern culture. Second, feminists have not yet sufficiently analyzed canonicity itself. So much work in feminist criticism and theory has focused either on women writers or on the modern period that the position of privileged authors in antiquity has been relatively untouched. It is not enough to challenge the canon(s) without understanding the force behind the construction, and feminist classicists are uniquely positioned to study the ancient texts from both perspectives. Third, tragedy remains an appealing subject for literary criticism because of the complexity of these high art texts. In current academic circles, obscurity is a valued commodity; while feminists may recognize the ideological implications in the training that leads to such evaluation, the discipline does discipline us, and many continue to find interest and value in such relatively dense works.

Finally, tragedy remains an attractive subject for feminist critique because the female characters and the gender issues are so prominent in them. Given that appeal, I find it nonetheless frustrating to study because the form is relentlessly masculine (actors, writers, and judges, if not audience, were all men). How do instructors handle the contradiction between masculinity and gender prominence? Is it possible to argue that Euripides speaks for women, for example, through Medea (Knox "Medea"; Page *Euripides*), or, as Froma Zeitlin does in "Playing the Other," that tragedy was a feminine form? In post-structuralist discussions, the feminine has been deployed in interesting ways. To the extent that Derrida, in Mary Poovey's phrase, investigates the possibility that the woman constituted as Other destabilizes "the entire metaphysics based on presence and identity" (53), his work may seem to valorize the feminine. As Poovey and others have pointed out, however, this tactic is problematic since even within post-structuralism it implies a biologism "all too compatible with conservative arguments about female nature" (60), and it may do so even more strongly when applied to ancient Athens, which assuredly did not validate the feminine.

Another strand of post-structuralism seems more profitable, namely, work on subjectivity. As a teacher, I try to make the case for the relevance of the tragedies by marking not their revelation of

some humanist universal truth but the ways in which current ideologies of gender, sexuality, and to some extent class and race, were
constructed by and in the plays my students are studying. In the rest
of this essay, then, I will analyze Euripides from this perspective; by
articulating the relationships between gender, power, and sexuality
it is possible to interrupt the easy reinscription of the plays' dynamic on the modern audience. It is my hope that by illuminating
the political agenda behind some Greek tragedy, I can play a role in
enabling readers to sidestep the ideological and gendered effects of
the plays.

Looking at tragedy through the lenses provided by Louis Althusser, Michel Foucault, and Teresa de Lauretis shows more clearly that
the values of tragedy are not timeless verities but rather a form of
ideology. Althusser's definition of ideology as the "imaginary relation of those individuals to the real relations in which they live"
(165) recognizes that ideology is essential to the reproduction of the
relations of production because it brings into being "subjects," who
act and choose on the basis of what they perceive as an identity
(162–175). Foucault, like Althusser, points out the double role of
the subject who is also subjected, but neither is particularly attentive to the differences between subjects of different classes, races, or
genders. De Lauretis, rereading these theorists, refines Althusser
thus: "Gender has the function (which defines it) of constituting
concrete individuals as men and women" (*Technologies* 6). I would
argue that Greek myth, as formulated in tragedy, is, to use de Lauretis's phrase, a "technology of gender," that is, one of the sites where
sexuality and gender are constructed. Every time the audience gets
the point or makes sense of the play, they are also constructing
themselves. It would seem that tragedy, in its own time, created
subject positions for men in the audience, and a differential subject
position for women.

Representation under male dominance—for example, in ancient
Athens—places women in a position analogous to what Claude
Lévi-Strauss, in *Elementary Structures of Kinship*, identified as the
exchange of women, the corollary of the incest taboo. To put it
simply, his related claims are that, one, the incest taboo is universal
(and thus a feature of nature), but it is a Law (and thus a feature of
culture). Two, the exchange of women among men acts to enforce
the incest taboo. Three, by exchanging women with another group,
men establish relationships beyond the family and thus establish a
social order beyond biology (esp. 42–43, 60–61, 67–68). His theory
is problematic, to be sure (for critiques see, e.g., de Lauretis *Alice
Doesn't*; Rubin; Arripe). Lévi-Strauss, like Freud, tends to make

what is historical and contingent sound natural and universal; the descriptive then becomes prescriptive. For instance, the exchange of women that Lévi-Strauss observes is a feature of *patriarchal* culture; it exists because of male power and simultaneously supports male power, but it is not self-evidently true that the exchange had to go that way: why did women not exchange men? Nonetheless, or even as a result, Lévi-Strauss is very useful for understanding the functioning of patriarchy, particularly in ancient Greek literature, since both gift giving and the exchange of women were at work in the culture. Further, his analogy between the circulation of women and the circulation of language (496) encourages the reader to make connections between male power over female sexuality and male power over discourse and female speech. It further suggests that feminists should look carefully at representation to see how patriarchal power manifests itself and reproduces itself.

Recent feminist analysis of signifying practices, and of pornography as one especially vexed example of such practices, may indicate the ways in which texts exert an epistemological power to make the male point of view seem like what IS. As Catharine MacKinnon has said, "The parallel between representation and construction should be sustained: men *create* the world from their own point of view, which then *becomes* the truth to be described. . . . *Power to create the world from one's point of view is power in its male form*" (249). Given the structure so established, women will continue to be inscribed as the object, not a subject, no matter who is doing the writing or viewing. A significant congruency emerges then between structuralism and feminist critiques of representation: the triangle constituted by the exchange of women between men works to prevent women from acting as sexual subjects; representation can constitute such a triangle between author, audience, and character in the production of gender.

In order to see what use this elaborate theoretical framework has, I will turn to Euripides, the tragedian whose reputation has been most changeable, and who alone of the three has a reputation on the "woman question." I will not look to his plays for images of women, grouped by T. B. L. Webster under the rubrics of good and bad, but will try to be more subtle, for there is more to reading or viewing than the passive reception of images; by taking into consideration structures of representation and effect, I will demonstrate the plays' work as technology of gender. Both *Hippolytos* and *Alcestis*, one depicting a "bad" woman, the other a "good" one, are exemplary of strategies for controlling female desire, through a pattern reminiscent of the Lévi-Straussian paradigm of the exchange of women. Female sexuality and female speech are threatening to an order based on the exchange of women, yet female sexuality is also necessary for procreation; therefore, heterosexual desire is posited for women, but eliminated except where controlled by men. A community of men is established by these two plays, and taking them simply as models of timeless abstractions or human problems obscures their role in perpetuating a particular hierarchy. In each play the central female character is displaced so that at the end we are left with a tableau of a male dyad which represents the male homosocial desire at the base of society (Sedgwick). Although the plays work out different techniques for accomplishing this task—Phaedra commits suicide, while Alcestis is fetishized and turned into a veiled object of male desire—both women end up in very similar predicaments.

Let me touch on the salient features of Euripides' *Hippolytos*.[2] The play opens with the goddess Aphrodite announcing her plan for revenge on Hippolytos, which she has already set in motion by making Phaedra fall in love with him. Phaedra gives up her initial choice of silent starvation at the insistence of her Nurse, who then approaches Hippolytos on her behalf. After overhearing his misogynist diatribe, Phaedra vows revenge. She leaves a suicide note accusing him of rape, then hangs herself. Her husband, Theseus, returns, reads the note, and condemns his son Hippolytos. The play ends with Artemis appearing *ex machina* to promise a marriage ritual in Hippolytos' honor, and with an embrace of father and son, Hippolytos dies on stage in his father's arms.

Humanist structuralist readings of the *Hippolytos* stress the binary oppositions resolved by the embrace of father and son, or by the marriage ritual promised to Hippolytos.[3] But although the play centers on marriage, this marriage is significant because it is an arrangement between men, in which the desired relationship is not between husband and wife, but between father and son. The play effects the displacement of Phaedra and the facilitation of male bonds through its depiction of male and female desire, through Euripides' particular formal choices in the ending, and through its desired effect on the audience. The cultural imperative is to secure marriage and rule of Athens. If we look at the play's story, we see that the woman is made the recipient of overwhelming heterosexual desire, ascribed to her by the goddess, myth, and playwright. That desire is then seen as excessive (even monstrous in the case of her mother's passion for the bull): it is a goad (39, 1300) driving Phaedra (see Padel 121–122). At first the plot makes Phaedra an innocent victim who fulfills the expectations of her society. Her body (made strikingly fleshly for tragedy) and its desire are problematic for the culture; Phaedra accepts the value system that blames her for her physicality. She begins by controlling herself and assuming a stance of absolute interiority: silence and starvation. Thus, in her case two openings, two sets of lips, are clearly connected: chastity and silence/starvation are both closings of the lips (Sissa; cf. Irigaray 23–33, 205–218).

Hippolytos's misogynist sentiments, like Phaedra's noble pattern of behavior, link speech and desire, the emergence of the woman from the private into the public space, and make them the problem for men (616–668). Hippolytos wishes that Zeus had arranged some other means for reproducing the race, so that men would be rid of women's rampant sexuality. And in the plot, Phaedra's desire threatens as soon as she begins to speak or act on it—a process that begins with the Nurse's first mention of Hippolytos's name (352) and ends with the inscription of the *deltos*, or tablet. Language and sexuality come together in the tablet on which she writes her story, since the word can stand for both female sexual parts and surface for writing.[4]

This dangerously desiring woman is controlled and objectified in subtle and not-so-subtle ways. First, throughout the play, Phaedra is a vehicle, not the purpose of the action, for playwright and goddess—Aphrodite merely uses her to take revenge on Hippolytos. Second, having nonetheless actively desired Hippolytos—she has the gaze and falls in love when she looks on Hippolytos (27)—Phaedra must depict herself as a victim.[5] Because women cannot act directly, she needs the power of a man, one of the Fathers, to achieve her ends; she motivates Theseus through a story of her rape, in which she is an object, for only thus can she act as the subject of her desire for revenge. Third, and most obviously, she has to be her own murderer in order to kill Hippolytos, for her corpse makes her an unassailable witness. Moreover, although her suicide at least looks like an action, it is an action which ends up gratifying Hippolytos's longing for a world without women.

The pattern of objectification and use has significance beyond the play, for Hippolytos's desire is not completely idiosyncratic but is in fact consistent with later Greek philosophy, which in turn laid the basis for much of Western thought. The Platonic ideal of love, the relationship to the physical in both Plato and Aristotle, finds merely exaggerated expression in Hippolytos's slogans.

As I argue more extensively in *Anxiety Veiled* (Chapter 6), the double form of the ending (Hippolytos outlives Phaedra and dies on stage; Artemis promises him a marriage ritual in his honor) simultaneously promotes male homosocial desire and eliminates the female principle. First, the ending restores father to son, making the male the true parent. The eros associated with Aphrodite in the earlier portions of the play is enacted on stage as the loving embrace of the two men. By this device not only is the woman displaced, and the action of mothering taken up by the father, but even the goddess is appropriated in a script of the two men.

Second, Hippolytos will be remembered by maidens on their wedding day. While there was such a cult, its existence does not totally explain Euripides' use of it, which is both problematic and prominent. And placing ritual and play in the context of ancient initiation practices merely highlights the asymmetries of both (on initiation, see Zeitlin "Power"; Burnett). The sexes are out of phase: men are initiated by sexual relations with men and prepared for a long youth (indeed life) passed in groups of men. Women are initiated, possibly by sexual relations with women, but for individual heterosexual relationships with men that would follow immediately upon coming of age (Calame). Moreover, men gain power from these relationships with older men; women do not gain power from older women. If they gain status from a particular older man, it is contingent on remaining inside his household. The play, like the cults, juxtaposes an enacted union of two men, with a prescribed union of women with men. Hippolytos is being initiated not into heterosexuality but into a relationship with the father, through the murder of the mother (Delcourt 64).

Just as the woman is replaced by the father-son dyad in the play, so woman is displaced from the audience by the structure of its experience. The text makes it difficult for us to give Phaedra the admiration she desires; Artemis links her with Aphrodite and Theseus as part of the force destroying Hippolytos, then bids the son forgive his father. Phaedra is not the worst kind of villain because she does not consciously give in to her desire, but even her memory is tarnished because she falls short of her ideals, even though only at the Nurse's urging and through her stratagem (1305). The play is strong in its guidance: Hippolytos is explicitly praised by chorus and father (1122, 1454, 1459–1461), whereas Phaedra is given only a conditional recognition ("some kind of nobility," 1301). The play thus reasserts the aristocratic values of honor that she fails to uphold, but that he maintains. In this way, an additional male-male dynamic is set up between the audience and the playwright, or between audience and characters, one where the woman is again devalued and eliminated to make those ties possible. It is clear, therefore, that the play participates in shoring up the patriarchal men's club. It is significant that it is not even certain that women were present at the

Dionysian festivals; from what subject position would they have watched the plays if they were there? If modern women spectators/readers wish to establish ourselves as subjects when we read these texts and not experience re-subjection to the gender hierarchy, we must be conscious of the import of this representation of gender, which would constitute females as exclusively heterosexual and loose-lipped, or starved and mute. A reading which simply takes consolation from the kindness of son to father and father to son runs the risk of ignoring the violence to Phaedra; such a reading simultaneously risks creating a future like the past, and doing the modern equivalent of the work of the ritual.

What does the *Hippolytos* have in common with *Alcestis*? Even a brief summary seems to reveal their total dissimilarity: *Alcestis* after all enacts the story of its namesake, who has volunteered to die for her husband, Admetos, when no one else would, but who is instead rescued in the end by Herakles in gratitude for Admetos's hospitality. In this case, the play is named after the woman, and she is the one who seems to be validated by the tradition, whereas he is of questionable (and often questioned) morality. Nonetheless there are important similarities; in particular, taken without reference to gender, this play, too, seems to provide "human" consolation. As is clear from extensive funerary art depicting her (Keuls), Alcestis's return from the Underworld was reassuring; but is her promise to humanity or to men? On the more realistic mortal level, what precisely does she promise? That the wife will sacrifice for her husband? Looking for meaning instead in the lesson that Admetos learns (and which Alcestis knew already), we once again make the woman a means for the development of a man.

The *Alcestis* also functions as part of the female disappearing act, with a concomitant bolstering of male bonds to other men. In the story, patriarchal needs are all too clearly worked out. Repeatedly called the "best of women," Alcestis is emptied of all desire, for life or children, so that she can stand for life for Admetos. Standing for life, extending his life: giving men life is a traditional female role. Alcestis sacrifices herself so that Admetos can live; like her virginal corollary, Iphigenia, she demonstrates the higher value placed on male life. She prefers to leave Admetos to be both father and mother rather than bring up the children herself as a widow or as another man's wife. But why must either partner die young? In the tradition that Euripides does not give, a wedding sacrifice to Artemis was overlooked; snakes in the chamber foretold an early death; thus, Alcestis's sacrifice replaces that sacrifice (Hesiod fragments 59–60 [West ed.]; Apollodorus *Bibliotheca* 3.10.3–4, 1.9.15; Plutarch

Amatores 761e). In other words, she goes from being the most valuable gift at the wedding (à la Lévi-Strauss) to being the wedding sacrifice itself. This slippage highlights an element of the system of exchange, in which the bride is given in order to facilitate ties between men. Admetos won his bride in a contest; thus, Alcestis was first a prize exchanged between Pelias and Admetos, and she functions in this way repeatedly: as Admetos's surrogate, she is fought over by Death and Apollo, and she returns to life as a gift that Herakles gives to Admetos.

Her disappearance through death is only stage one of her displacement from her position; Euripides' rhetoric emphasizes the replaceability of the wife. When Alcestis requests that Admetos not marry after her death, he makes extravagant promises, for instance that he will have a sculptor make a statue of Alcestis to take to bed with him (348–354). The statue is difficult to understand. On one level, it seems to point to funerary art, statues or reliefs that memorialize the deceased and mark the burial place. But on another level, given its prominent location in Admetos's bed, the replica suggests that the wife can be replaced by an object. The statue is not a perfect substitute, but it will provide a "cold pleasure."

Alcestis is further displaced by Herakles himself and through the working out of the hospitality theme that dominates the play from the beginning since Admetos owes his extended life to Apollo's appreciation of his hospitality (10–14). Admetos is characterized as a great host, and he enacts this role on stage when Herakles happens to be passing through the Pheraian land: Admetos will not be any less than a perfect host and insists that Herakles stay with him even though he is in mourning (509–550). However, to focus on *xenia*, or guest-friendship, as an unequivocal good is to accept Admetos's point of view, and there are other positions, namely, that of Alcestis. In the scene following the funeral procession, Admetos further reneges on his promises to his wife by welcoming Herakles despite the obligation to mourn her. This interpretation gains strength since, in order to persuade Herakles to stay, Admetos must deny that it is his wife who is dead (533, 535, cf. 805); the wordplay that makes such a deceit possible pointedly emphasizes Alcestis's ambiguous status in the house. The nameless deceased household member is literally "from elsewhere" (*othneios* or *thuraios*) because of virilocal marriage rules; she is not technically a member of the family or of the house of Admetos even though she is essential to it. The exchange of women puts the men into relation in the first place, but here the displacement of the outsider/exchanged woman makes possible a further relationship between men.

Alcestis moves from being imitated and replaced by a statue to coming back from the dead, but without making much real progress. Admetos does not recognize her when Herakles first brings her on stage, although he thinks that she resembles his wife (1061–1063). Since he accepts her from Herakles before he recognizes who she is, Alcestis is for all intents and purposes once again replaced by an imitation. She is still an object to be passed from man to man—a prize that Herakles has won. The suggestion of funeral rites in the middle of the play gives way to suggestions of a wedding. Herakles makes the traditional gesture of giving away the bride and makes a point of giving her into Admetos's hand. Alcestis has regained her "virginal" status, is veiled and speechless, suitable for one who must wait to be opened by her husband in matrimony. Statue and veil are Euripides' devices for representing Alcestis as a blank, which she must be in order to be exchanged between men.

In the fifth-century tragic contexts, the poets presented three tragedies and one non-tragic satyr drama; since the *Alcestis* was performed fourth (which would typically have been the position of a satyr drama), there is an extensive debate about its form. Ascription of form is of course related to effect, and that depends on perspective, in particular on the audience's perception that Alcestis is better off alive. Critics have located its "comic" quality not only in the "happy ending" but also in the play's manner, identifying many humorous scenes, including the finale.[6] The mistaken identity at the basis of Herakles' teasing of Admetos turns Alcestis into the object for a mildly salacious joke—on the order of "that was no lady, that was my wife." But would Alcestis watching Admetos betray his promise to her find it funny? What is the source of the comedy? The scene bears analysis from at least two points of view, that of Herakles and that of Euripides—but we must ask whether either of them is up to something more than a simple increase of pleasure. If there is such an increase, whose pleasure is increased? Why, after all, does Euripides/Herakles not simply hand Alcestis over with a long description of the battle with Death (a description notably missing, by the way)? Even if Herakles "means" nothing by this game, this is not a totally innocent joke, if analyzed through Freud's taxonomy in *On Jokes and Their Relation to the Unconscious* (90, 142, 143). There may be two butts of the joke, and there is an on-stage audience that "gets the joke." Admetos is clearly made to look foolish in the process, and so must be the primary target of the humor. What about Alcestis and the chorus—do they just get an innocent laugh from this "innocent" joke? But Alcestis is not simply the audience, she is rather a necessary part of the joke work itself: it depends on her presence. It seems more likely, then, that this is an example of Freud's second category, the tendentious joke, one that gratifies an aggressive desire. In this interpretation, Herakles' hostility at having himself been made a fool of satisfies itself by drawing out to equal length his deception of Admetos. This explanation leaves Alcestis out of the account, however, and I must have recourse to another type of tendentious joke, which Freud calls the smutty, in order to place her. In Freud's explanation of these jokes, a verbal pleasure replaces denied sexual pleasure; interestingly enough for my purposes, while the described/denied encounter is heterogendered, the enacted one is between men.

To put it bluntly, then, Euripides is using Herakles' rhetorical ploy to further efface Alcestis; she is hidden behind the words as she is hidden behind the veil. His audience may, even while sympathizing with Alcestis, take pleasure in Herakles' joking unmasking of Admetos; moreover, the tactic of the "joke" still expands Herakles' relationship to Admetos as it excludes Alcestis. Euripides gives Herakles a game to play that is inscribed within a larger picture of male power, represented by Alcestis's position on stage, shuttled about between men and the pretext for a joke, or at best the audience for one. The comic effect, like the tragic effect of *Hippolytos*, depends on and establishes the audience's pleasure at the solidarity of men, on the ground of the invisibility of women.

Using the terms of discussion set up by feminist film theorists, I would argue that Alcestis is first turned into a fetish, the statue; then, like the images in pornography and Hollywood film, her veiled presence focuses the male gaze apparatus, and male subjectivity. She literally brings life, while these images give the feeling of life to an audience. The structure of the play brings together Herakles and Admetos in a form of *xenia* founded on a woman as an item to be exchanged; a similar structure is established with the audience. The "men" (in the sense of those participating in the dominant structure of representation) are reassured that women willingly sacrifice themselves for men, so that the male bonding necessary for the polis and the heterosexual bonding necessary for the family can coexist. But what about an actual woman, either ancient or modern, who has identified with Alcestis? What positions are available to her?

Tragedy has been idealized and taken as a representation of the "human," but as a cultural artifact, it participated in the subordination of women in the forms appropriate to its own time. By eliminating women as subjects, each of these plays establishes a community of men within the play and between the play and the audience. To take them as about self-other, chastity, and sexuality, or life and death, overlooks the strongly marked engendering of each member of these pairs and effectually continues to prevent women as subjects from constituting an appropriate audience for the plays. Women will either have to be "men" and subjects, or women and objects. Modern readers may be able to resist the binaries of active and destructive or masochistic and self-destructive ascribed to the female characters of Euripidean tragedy by focusing instead on the strength that necessitated such strategies of control.

To return to my earlier framing of the question, it is not clear that our students are familiar with the "tradition" that critics so confidently assert is "theirs." Thus, as I said earlier, students may read Euripides for the first (and only?) time in a course on feminist criticism with me! I find myself in the position of preserving the texts of antiquity even as I criticize them. That means that such a class has a great deal of unpacking to do, first presenting what I have here labeled the traditional, humanist, reading, then deconstructing it. Moreover, my students—predominantly female—are likely to assume feminism without examining what it means, and to assume that what they see in a text is "self-evident." Work on the history of interpretations is productive of a necessary tension, and can prevent students from thinking that Euripides in fifth-century Athens meant exactly what they mean, or thought exactly what they think; one task of reading must be to explicate the belief system "intended" by the text even though that will not exhaust the work of interpretation. By attending to the material and political environment that produced the texts, and in particular to what is excluded to make the apparent whole, students can learn about the Western tradition which *is* theirs (if only by virtue of their attendance at an institution of higher education), at the same time that teachers acknowledge the violence that has been done in the name of that tradition. In short, even when reading male canonical authors, scholars need to interrogate the silences as well as the speech/acts.

Notes

Portions of this essay appear in very different form in my long study of Euripides, *Anxiety Veiled: Euripides and the Traffic in Women* (Cornell University Press, 1993), and in "Feminism and the Re-production of Greek Tragedy," *Theatre Studies* (Winter 1989) 1–12.

    1. The works of Jane Snyder and Marilyn Skinner ("Greek Women," "Sapphic Nossis," Sappho *Thēluglōssos*) are most notable for seeking out a female literary tradition; Phyllis Culham has most strongly articulated the position that it is necessary to turn away from these canonical authors (or

totemic icons). Her essay is part of an issue devoted to Ovid, *Helios* 17 (1990), which elaborates some of these issues.

2. References to the plays will be given in parentheses in the text; I have used W. S. Barrett's edition of *Hippolytos* and A. M. Dale's *Alcestis*; all translations are my own.

3. Optimistic readings of the ending may be found in the following, to cite just a few: Knox, "Hippolytus" 31; Winnington-Ingram 191; Segal, "Tragedy" 156; Conacher, *Euripidean Drama* 46; Reckford, "Phaethon" 419; Segal has returned to the *Hippolytos* in a study which "views language and communication as the area where meaning is created or destroyed. It thus moves outward from language to other areas that participate in this struggle for order" ("Signs" 421). His early article is nonetheless still important to me for its cogent statement of a widely held position.

4. Aristophanes, *Lysistrata* 151; Artemidorus, *Oneirocritica* 2.45. For modern discussion, see Zeitlin, "Travesties" 326; "Power" 76–77; duBois 41–42. For a more detailed consideration of speech and sexuality, see Rabinowitz "Female Speech"; Segal "Signs."

5. The looking is prominent, since *idousa* occupies the first word in the line. On *looking* see Zeitlin, "Playing" 90–93; Luschnig 5ff., 13ff.

6. Weil calls the humor "fort amusant et plein d'un enjouement delicieux" (2–3); Arrowsmith (28) refers to the "sportive, farcical element"; Nielsen (99) calls it a "hoax" meant "good-naturedly"; Beye (117) calls it a "cat and mouse game"; Grube (144) addresses the "comic spirit of the last scene."

Works Cited

Althusser, Louis. "Ideology and Ideological State Apparatuses." In *Lenin and Philosophy and Other Essays*, pp. 127–188. New York: Monthly Review Press, 1971.

Arripe, Marie-Laure. "Contribution à une critique de l'échange des femmes." In *La Dot: La Valeur des Femmes*, pp. 67–81. G.R.I.E.F. Toulouse: Travaux de L'Université de Toulouse-Le Mirail, 1982.

Arrowsmith, William. *Alcestis*. New York: Oxford University Press, 1974.

Barrett, W. S., ed. *Hippolytos*. Oxford: Oxford University Press, 1964.

Bernal, Martin. *Black Athena: The Afroasiatic Roots of Classical Civilization*. Vol. 1. New Brunswick, N.J.: Rutgers University Press, 1987.

Beye, Charles. "Alcestis and Her Critics." *Greek Roman and Byzantine Studies* 2 (1959): 109–127.

Burnett, Anne Pippin. "Hearth and Hunt in *Hippolytus*." In *Greek Tragedy and Its Legacy*, edited by Martin Cropp, Elaine Fantham, and S. E. Scully, pp. 167–286. Calgary: University of Calgary Press, 1986.

Calame, Claude. *Les choeurs de jeunes filles en grèce archaïque*. Rome: Ateneo et Bizzari, 1977.

Chronicle of Higher Education. "Bennett Calls Stanford's Curriculum Revision 'Capitulation to Pressure.'" Vol. 34, 33 (April 27, 1988): A2.

Conacher, D. J. *Euripidean Drama: Myth, Theme, and Structure*. Toronto: University of Toronto Press, 1967.

Culham, Phyllis. "Decentering the Text: The Case of Ovid." *Helios* 17 (1990): 161–170.

Dale, A.M., ed. *Euripides. Alcestis*. Oxford: Clarendon Press, 1954.

de Lauretis, Teresa. *Alice Doesn't: Feminism, Semiotics, Cinema*. Bloomington: Indiana University Press, 1984.

———. *Technologies of Gender*. Bloomington: Indiana University Press, 1987.

Delcourt, Marie. *Oreste et Alcméon*. Paris: Sociétè d'édition les Belles Lettres, 1959.

de Romilly, Jacqueline. *Thucydides and Athenian Imperialism*. Translated by Philip Thody. New York: Arno, 1979.

duBois, Page. "On Horse/Men, Amazons, and Endogamy." *Arethusa* 12 (1979): 35–49.

Foucault, Michel. *Power/Knowledge: Selected Interviews and Other Writings, 1972–1977*. Edited by Colin Gordon. Translated by Colin Gordon, Leo Marshall, John Mepham, and Kate Soper. New York: Pantheon Books, 1980.

Freud, Sigmund. *Jokes and Their Relation to the Unconscious*. Translated by James Strachey. New York: W. W. Norton, 1960.

Grube, G. M. A. *The Drama of Euripides*. London: Methuen, 1941.

Haley, Shelley. "Black Feminist Thought and Classics: Re-membering, Reclaiming, Re-empowering." In *Feminist Theory and the Classics*, edited by Nancy Sorkin Rabinowitz and Amy Richlin, pp. 23–43. New York: Routledge, 1993.

———. "Classics and Minorities." In *Classics: A Discipline and Profession in Crisis?*, edited by Lowell Edmunds and Phyllis Culham, pp. 333–338. Lanham, Md.: University Press of America, 1989.

Hallett, Judith. "Feminist Theory, Historical Periods, Literary Canons, and the Study of Greco-Roman Antiquity." In *Feminist Theory and the Classics*, edited by Nancy Sorkin Rabinowitz and Amy Richlin, pp. 44–72. New York: Routledge, 1993.

Hirschfeld, Charles, ed. *Classics of Western Thought*. New York: Harcourt, Brace, World, 1964.

Irigaray, Luce. *This Sex Which Is Not One*. Translated by Catherine Porter. Ithaca: Cornell University Press, 1985; French original, *Ce Sexe qui n'en est pas un*. Paris: Editions de Minuit, 1977.

Keuls, Eva. *The Water Carriers in Hades*. Amsterdam: Hakkert, 1974.

Knox, Bernard, ed. *Masterpieces of the Ancient World*. Series editor Maynard Mack. New York: W. W. Norton, 1987.

———. "The *Hippolytus* of Euripides." *Yale Classical Studies* 13 (1952): 3–31.

———. "The *Medea* of Euripides." *Yale Classical Studies* 25 (1977): 193–225.

Lévi-Strauss, Claude. *Elementary Structures of Kinship*. Edited by Rodney Needham. Translated by James Bell, John Sturmer, and Rodney Needham.

Boston: Beacon, 1969. French original, *Les Structures élémentaires de la parenté.* Mouton, 1949.

Luschnig, C. A. E. *Time Holds the Mirror: A Study of Knowledge in Euripides' "Hippolytos."* Mnemosyne Supplement, vol. 102. Leiden: Brill, 1988.

MacKinnon, Catharine. "Feminism, Marxism, and the State: An Agenda for Theory." In *Signs Reader: Women, Gender, and Scholarship,* edited by Elizabeth Abel and Emily Abel, pp. 227–256. Chicago: University of Chicago Press, 1982.

Nielsen, Rosemary. "Alcestis: A Paradox in Dying." *Ramus* 5 (1976): 92–102.

Padel, Ruth. *In and Out of the Mind: Greek Images of the Tragic Self.* Princeton: Princeton University Press, 1992.

———. "Reflections on Feminism and Classical Scholarship." *Gender and History* 2 (1990): 198–211.

Page, Denys, ed. *Euripides. Medea.* 2nd ed. Oxford: Clarendon, 1961.

Poovey, Mary. "Feminism and Deconstruction." *Feminist Studies* 14.1 (1988): 51–65.

Rabinowitz, Nancy Sorkin. *Anxiety Veiled: Euripides and the Traffic in Women.* Ithaca: Cornell University Press, 1993.

———. "Female Speech and Female Sexuality; Euripides' *Hippolytos* as Model." *Helios* 13 (1986): 127–140.

———. "Introduction." In *Feminist Theory and the Classics,* edited by Nancy Sorkin Rabinowitz and Amy Richlin, pp. 1–20. New York: Routledge, 1993.

Reckford, Kenneth. "Phaethon, Hippolytus, and Aphrodite." *Transactions and Proceedings of the American Philological Association* 103 (1972): 405–432.

Ridpath, John, ed. *Ridpath Library of Universal Literature.* New York: Globe, 1899.

Rubin, Gayle. "The Traffic in Women: Notes on a 'Political Economy' of Sex." In *Toward an Anthropology of Women,* edited by Rayna Reiter, pp. 175–210. New York: Free Press, 1975.

Sedgwick, Eve Kosofsky. *Between Men: English Literature and Male Homosocial Desire.* New York: Columbia University Press, 1985.

Segal, Charles. "Signs, Magic, and Letters in Euripides' *Hippolytus.*" In *Innovations of Antiquity,* edited by Ralph Hexter and Daniel Selden, pp. 410–455. New York: Routledge, 1992.

———. "The Tragedy of the *Hippolytus*: the Waters of Ocean and the Untouched Meadow." *Harvard Studies in Classical Philology* 70 (1965): 117–169.

Sissa, Giulia. *Greek Virginity.* Translated by Arthur Goldhammer. Cambridge, Mass.: Harvard University Press, 1990. French original *Le Corps virginal.* Paris: Librairie Philosophique J. Vrin, 1987.

Skinner, Marilyn. "Classical Studies, Patriarchy, and Feminism: The View from 1986." *Women's Studies International Forum* 10 (1987): 181–186.

————. "Expecting the Barbarians: Feminism, Nostalgia, and the 'Epistemic Shift' in Classical Studies." In *Classics: A Discipline and Profession in Crisis?*, edited by Lowell Edmunds and Phyllis Culham, pp. 199–210. Lanham, Md.: University Press of America, 1989.

————. "Greek Women and the Metronymic: A Note on an Epigram by Nossis." *Ancient History Bulletin* 1: 39–42.

————. "Nossis *Thēluglōssos*: The Private Text and the Public Book." In *Women's History and Ancient History*, edited by Sarah Pomeroy, pp. 20–47. Chapel Hill: University of North Carolina Press, 1991.

————. "Sapphic Nossis." *Arethusa* 22 (1989): 5–18.

Snyder, Jane. *The Woman and the Lyre: Women Writers in Classical Greece and Rome*. Carbondale: Southern Illinois University Press, 1989.

Webster, T. B. L. *The Tragedies of Euripides*. London: Methuen, 1967.

Weil, H. *Alceste*. Paris: Hachette, 1891.

Winnington-Ingram, R. P. "Hippolytus: A Study in Causation." In *Entretiens sur l'antiquité classique VI: Euripide*, pp. 169–197. Geneva: Foundation Hardt, 1958.

Zeitlin, Froma. "Playing the Other: Theater, Theatricality, and the Feminine in Greek Drama." *Representations* 11 (1985): 63–94.

————. "The Power of Aphrodite: Eros and the Boundaries of Self in the *Hippolytus*." In *Directions in Euripidean Criticism*, edited by Peter Burian, pp. 52–111. Durham: University of North Carolina Press, 1985.

————. "Travesties of Gender and Genre in Aristophanes' *Thesmophoriazeusae*." *Critical Inquiry* 8 (1981): 301–327.

Zweig, Bella. "The Primal Mind: Using Native American Models for the Study of Women in Ancient Greece." In *Feminist Theory and the Classics*, edited by Nancy Sorkin Rabinowitz and Amy Richlin, pp. 145–180. New York: Routledge, 1993.

4. Playing Caliban: Césaire's *Tempest*

Joan Dayan

> 'Ban
> Ban
> Cal-
> iban
> like to play
> pan
> at the Car-
> nival
>
> Edward Kamau Brathwaite, "Caliban"

In his 1939 epic *Cahier d'un retour au pays natal* (Notebook of a return to the native land), Aimé Césaire faced a terrible labor. To reclaim his identity and thereby gain a voice, he had to journey into a past revised as grotesque. Recognizing himself in the "ugly and comical nigger" on the tram in Martinique, Césaire attempted to find a voice by descending into what Fanon in *Peau noir, masques blancs* (Black skin, white masks) would call a "zone of non-being" out of which "an authentic upheaval can be born." The plight of recognition, set against the background of a history defined as negative, deformed, or null, was seized in the revisionary promise of the neologism *négritude*, which used the pejorative term *nègre* as basis for redefinition.

Césaire's challenge to remember is a call to language, to know again the duplicitous power of naming. After the Amerindians (Carib, Arawak, Taino, and Siboney), the original inhabitants of the Caribbean, were annihilated, and nothing remained but a blankness waiting to be filled by African slaves, a name would remain. The name would stand for what had been destroyed. "Cannibal" uttered by those who "civilized" the land would live on to justify the extirpation of a race and the conquest of a world. Black slaves, their names forgotten, their past obliterated, were renamed in the New World. But no matter their new names, they would, when it served the settler's purposes, embody the figure of the deformed and language-less savage. Caliban, now defined in most dictionaries as an anagram of Cannibal, or as something nasty, brutish, and short, specifically, the "grotesque and brutish slave in Shakespeare's *Tempest*" (*American Heritage*), evokes images of the fierce Caribs of the West Indies. It was Shakespeare who first used the term for his "lying slave" who spoke the most beautiful language in the play, when Prospero wasn't around.

I

In 1971 as I began my book on the Haitian poet-in-exile René Depestre, a professor asked me, "Why write about the Caribbean?" A question of propriety and tact. The problem of language, of speaking *to* or *for* another, is always a duplicitous business. If I, in my professional garb as critic, say, "A new history is now being written in the Caribbean by writers who, faced with an 'absence of ruins,' with the absence of written records, turn toward a past reviled or forgotten," who am I to articulate the turn?

The Caribbean is a hybrid world, somewhere in between Afrique Guinée and the Metropole, marked by the alternating nostalgia for "authenticity" and the desire for "assimilation": a society where ritual is shot through with TV and dinette sets, where the Haitian god of death Guédé Nibo can walk into a ceremony with a pack of Camels. In thinking about how to interpret literary production in the Caribbean in terms other than those of a "Mother Country," I want to examine the transits of Caliban. I will examine at length Césaire's adaptation of Shakespeare's *Tempest* in order to demonstrate how matters of terminology delimit authority, while dispossessing those not granted a special or privileged identity. In the permeable locale of academic criticism, the question remains: Who does the defining, and who possesses the goods, or gods, and when?

In the twentieth century, Caribbean writers reappropriated the name Caliban with all its negative connotations. Inheritors of a legacy of darkness, barbarism, and evil, those who bore the brunt of being the object of someone else's imagination used the name to signal reversal and revolt. René Depestre's "nègre-tempête" (tempest nigger), once possessed by the vodoun gods, strides to the "Dixie pit" of the American South in his *Arc-en-ciel pour l'occident chrétien* (A rainbow for the Christian West) to become the "Caliban determined—unashamed to assume his 'Caribbean blood,' his cannibalism, his fighting calibanité" (108–109).[1] This recognition marks yet another stage in the process begun by Aimé Césaire and the negritude poets in 1930s Paris: "Because we hate you, you and your reason, we appeal to the dementia praecox of flaming madness, of unrelenting cannibalism" (*Cahier d'un retour au pays natal*; my translation).[2]

As counter in an argument of extremes, the name Caliban tended to replay the debate between those fighting for a "new" language and those trapped in the illusion of assimilation. Roberto Retamar's Caliban ("we reclaim as a mark of glory the honor of considering ourselves descendents of the *mambi*, descendents of the rebel, runaway, *independentista* black, *never* descendents of slave holders" 16) tried to supplant José Enrique Rodo's mulatto Ariel (1900). The master/slave relationship so brilliantly given voice by the brash "Caliban dialectician" of Césaire's 1969 *Une tempête* (A tempest) asserted protest with a vengeance. And some poets, Derek Walcott, for example, sought to escape what he felt was the simplistic savagery of Caliban as "enraged pupil" by casting his lot with Prospero, by giving the howl to Crusoe.[3]

Caliban's force, like that of his name, lies in ambiguity. He occupies a space somewhere between the alternating fullness and vacancy of the colonial experience. Note that historians from Du Tertre and de Rochefort to Bryan Edwards found the Caribs a highly indeterminate and therefore fascinating race. Their unknowability made them a blank that could be filled by the intruder's projections. Alternately fierce and noble, the Caribs more than the Arawaks remain in most narratives the recipients of the colonizer's disdain or idealization. Even Baudelaire, in his "Salon of 1846," lamenting that *"the origin of sculpture is lost in the night of time,"* would describe it as a "Carib art" (187).

Once decimated, and annulled by history, the Caribs (before the name became synonymous with cannibal) could be treated as myth, a golden romance and a timeless response to the ever-present Africans. As Gordon Lewis writes in *Main Currents in Caribbean Thought*, making a fortune in a profit-oriented plantation world depended upon regarding the slave as a "nonperson" (the dehumanization Césaire called "thingification" in *Discours sur le colonialism* and what Depestre recognized as the needs of capital to convert color into commodity). Lewis explains:

It is suggestive that the romanticizing literature seized upon *le bon sauvage*, rather than *le bon nègre*, as its hero figure: it would have been difficult to have seen the detribalized and de-culturated African slave as the repository of Antillean innocence; that was a task left for the European abolitionist literature of the eighteenth century.

(89)

In its transit through texts and histories, the name Caliban merges Carib and African.[4] But the merger remains ambivalent in its effects. In praise of Caliban, Retamar declares, "What is our history, what is our culture, but the history, the culture of Caliban?" His injunction is mystifying, a tautological challenge that asks a question whose very terms—history and culture—resist definition.

Whether Shakespeare's Caliban is African, "this thing of darkness I acknowledge mine" (as Prospero says) or Caribbean, given the derivation of the name, or at any rate an inhabitant of the New World (since Shakespeare mates Sycorax with Setebos, a New World great devil), is not the issue here. What matters is how Shakespeare *unlocalizes* Caliban and confounds the origins so marked in contemporary, and often reductive assumptions of the name.

Let us take Caliban as a call to inquiry, and attempt to retrieve something of the magic and power of the name, its ability to disguise and to reveal. Given the haunting sublimity of *The Tempest*, its lurking ambivalences, its tough weave of beauty and defilement, we can imagine Shakespeare at work making his language. Familiar with Florio's translation of Montaigne's "Cannibales," Shakespeare might have formed an anagram of the name for the Carib nation. But we can go further. The word originates in some form of the name for the Caribs, *kallinago, kalliponam*; and several renderings of the name by New World explorers include as a first syllable, "Car-," "Cal-," and "Can-." Sounding out *Cali*, a non-etymological spelling of *Calli*, formed of the Greek word meaning beauty (κάλλος), Shakespeare commands the name into being. The name contains the contradictions so much a part of those first narratives of the Indies. *Cali-ban*: to proclaim Beauty/to curse or prohibit Beauty. In his first words to Caliban, Prospero talks as summoner:

> What, ho! Slave! Caliban!
> thou earth, thou! Speak!
> . . . .
> Come forth, I say!
> . . . .
> Thou poisonous slave, got by the devil
> himself
> Upon thy wicked dam, come forth!

(1.2.313–320)

In summoning Caliban as earth or slave, Shakespeare's Prospero suggests the duplicity of the figure. As both summoner and transgressor, Caliban sings, "'Ban, Ban, Ca-Caliban." Taking in the doubleness of *ban*, he, like Prospero, prohibits, curses, or forbids beauty. Thus, Caliban, inviting and forbidding, bears within him the oscillation that will become his destiny: a something to be either disdained or claimed, cursed or celebrated.

Shakespeare grasped the full irony of the colonial experience, and Césaire knew it. *The Tempest* begins with usurpation and exile. Extirpated from his native land by his brother Antonio and sent off to a strange island (as the Africans were exported to the Caribbean), Prospero enacts a second usurpation. He takes the island away from Caliban, an "inhabitant" who is so savage and inhuman that in his stage directions, Shakespeare describes the island only as "uninhabited." Shakespeare's play, like Césaire's, is shot through with a language of bondage, coercion, and liberation. The breaking of bounds, in Prospero's case especially, also implies a stripping away of masks, a removal of artifice that leaves Prospero weaker once his "charms are overthrown." And both plays interrogate history, call for origins, and summon remembrance. Asked by Miranda for her story, Shakespeare's Prospero wonders:

> But how is it
> That this lives in thy mind? What sees thou else
> In the dark backward and abysm of time?
> If thou remembrest aught ere thou cam'st there,
> How thou cam'st here thou mayst.
>
> (1.2.48–52)

The promise of knowing "How thou cam'st here" bears consideration in the context of the colonial drama. For Albert Memmi, the fact of the colonized is that he or she is outside "the game of history." Frantz Fanon gives colonialism that special talent (as George Lamming says of Prospero in *The Pleasures of Exile*) of "throwing the past in your face."[5] Prospero is wary of both Ariel and Caliban's search for origins, and the past he gives us is his interpretation of history. Yet Shakespeare decenters Prospero's position as sole historian by also giving us Caliban's account of his origination.

Shakespeare's subversive decentering of power and legitimacy also results from the indeterminacy of origins and locale throughout the play: "The blue-ey'd hag" Sycorax was exiled from Argier, Algiers in the Old World, to the magic island. By mating the hag with Setebos, a Patagonian divinity, he further merges contradictory details. And the course of the voyage is not to the New World, "the stil' vexed

Bermoothes," but from Tunis to Naples. Truly magical, the island is a center for conflation, misrepresentation, and reversal. The dual topography of Mediterranean and Atlantic, Old World and New, and the slippages between these places, allows Shakespeare both to demonstrate the fictive attributes of any so-called "history" of exploration and to question any single, privileged source of value, determined by any single race or nation. Gonzalo's natives, "mountaineers / Dew-lapp'd like bulls . . . / men whose heads stood in their breasts," are as much figments of his imagination as any of the strange shapes conjured by Prospero.

II

In writing *Une tempête* Césaire turns back to *The Tempest* in order to retrieve and sustain his voice in a context that defies easy dichotomy. The problem with the ongoing argument about the Caliban complex is the incarceration of the militant, heady Caliban as icon in the academy: a move as dangerous as Léopold Senghor's vague *"essence noire,"* what Depestre calls his "totalitarian négritude." Houston Baker, responding to the issue of *Critical Inquiry* entitled "'Race,' Writing, and Difference" (Autumn 1985), argues for an explosion of "the venerable Western trope of Prospero and Caliban . . . the rationalist and the debunker, the colonizer and the indigenous people" (190). In an attempt to break out of a cult of the *either/or*, leading to yet another canonization of Caliban, I want to consider how Césaire's *Tempest* demands a full politics and poetics of deformation and demystification. It seems to me that it is not so much naming, but remembering that matters: an act of naming that carries with it the burden of the past. The liberated Caliban in taking on his name drags the residue of bondage behind him; he sheds the name as he takes on and fully inhabits his history.

Yet in choosing to confront Shakespeare's *Tempest*, Césaire takes on a name and a history that might not be seen as his own. He makes no claims for originality. The title page presents *"Une tempête*: d'après la Tempête de Shakespeare. Adaptation for a black theater." As his list of characters he writes simply: "Ceux de Shakespeare," with *"Deux précisions supplémentaires"* (Two additional qualifications): *Ariel*, "a slave, ethnically a mulatto," and *Caliban*, "a black slave"; and *"Une Addition"* (One addition), Eshu, "a black devil-god."

Césaire's adamant refusal to give his work some illusion of primaryness is crucial to our understanding of what might first seem to be mere celebratory rebellion. Howling for an instrument of reconnection, Caliban/Césaire does not simply negate. Instead, he recognizes the force of mutuality, the knot of reciprocity between master and slave, between a prior "classic" and his response to it. This labor of reciprocity accounts for the complexities of Césaire's transformation: a labor that defies any simple opposition between black and white, master and slave, original and adaptation, authentic and fake.

In denying his text the status of original, Césaire teaches us how to return to the Shakespeare "original," to reread it and know the possibilities for reversal inherent in a drama too often treated as a dramatization of the opposing claims of nature vs. nurture, art vs. nature, or civilization vs. savagery. Although a discussion of "influence," of the anxiety of returning to the givens of a prior text, might be a means of approaching *Une tempête*, it oversimplifies the nature of Césaire's bold superimposition. If we take Césaire at his word and read his play as an adaptation, not as a disavowal or destruction of what preceded it, then we begin to understand how both texts are complicated through mutual adaptation or *convertibility*. What might have seemed to be a case of simple rebellion becomes instead an accommodation that puts the stuff of legend (the romantic gesture of rebel or conquerer) in a dialogue so powerful that it implicates both colonized and colonizer.

Césaire's *Tempest* is a difficult play to read. Not because of a complicated language (it lacks the hermeticism of much of Césaire's poetry), but because of an apparent acceptance of a Caliban shouting "Freedom," and a Prospero calling upon "civilization." Yet if the pulverization of facile dualism and false empowering constitutes the real drama of Shakespeare's play, I will argue that Césaire's adaptation asks questions that undermine any possible pleasure in revolt. Like most of Césaire's writings and his political career, Caliban's play is beset by contradictions that work beneath the surface polarities to undo, interrogate, and warn.

Césaire knows that it is as misleading and distorting to idealize the black nay-sayer as to praise the Eurocentric establishment. Dramatizing the dangers of any counter-mythology, *Une tempête* confronts the ambiguities already discussed. In his experimentation with different kinds of poetic and political rhetoric, whether Ariel's fanciful neo-symbolism or Caliban's bald negations, Césaire proves that the lapse of language into cliché threatens the black rebel, the mulatto lackey, and the white master. Césaire's "revision" of Shakespeare's *Tempest* must be dealt with not in terms of easy essentialism, but as a procedure of continuing complications. Correspondingly, I will analyze Césaire's play as an inquiry into power, viewed as a contagion capable of involving every character in a damning reciprocity.

Apart from technical changes, additions, or displacements as the gathering of five acts into three; the appearance of the African gods Eshu (the "player of tricks") and Shango (force of thunder and lightning); and the transformation of Ariel into accommodating lyricist, the real break with Shakespeare's text occurs in the continuing dialogue between Prospero and Caliban. Césaire's drama turns on their mutuality, their reciprocal recognition: their relationship is an exercise in whose language matters, who has the last word.

In stressing the labor of language in the play, Césaire demands that his readers consider claims other than literary. Dramatizing competing theories about the colonial encounter, he hopes to instruct people in the question of revolution and its possibility in the contemporary Caribbean. Works like Fanon's *Black Skin, White Masks* (1952), Césaire's own *Discourse on Colonialism* (1955), Mannoni's *Prospero and Caliban: The Psychology of Colonization* (1956), and Memmi's *The Colonizer and the Colonized* (1957) provide a ground for understanding Césaire's *Tempest*. These texts form a significant dialogue on the articulation of the self as subject, a formation that depends upon language, desire, and recognition.

The dialogue between the so-called colonizer and colonized is questioned and complicated when we note the reciprocal relations between writers from Metropolitan France and their colonial subjects. Mannoni had taught Césaire in Fort de France, Martinique, at the Lycée Schoelcher, where Césaire would later teach Fanon. In France during the fifties the discourse on dispossession, splitting (*dédoublement*), and mastery in psychoanalytic circles, especially Jacques Lacan's seminars, where Mannoni was a major interlocutor, was no doubt affected by moves toward decolonization in Africa and the Caribbean, as well as by France's brutal efforts to contain revolts in Madagascar and Algeria. For Césaire, a concrete *"prise de conscience,"* the activity of expression, is key to recognition. In *Une tempête* the task of awareness is shaped, however, by what denies or disallows recognition: the magus Prospero's words silence, distort, or ignore Caliban's attempt to devise speech. Yet Caliban initiates a new discourse and engages Prospero in a new text. Marx recognized that "Hegel . . . seizes Labor as essence, as what proves good the essence of man," and labor is the fact of Caliban's existence. To Prospero's words about teaching him language ("you should be able to bless me for having taught you how to speak"), Caliban simply responds: "You've taught me nothing at all. Except, of course, to jabber your language in order to understand your orders: cut the wood, wash the dishes, catch fish, plant vegetables, because you're too lazy to do it" (1.2.p.25).

Fundamentally, the conditions of the play show that given the limitations of a situation where everything seems stacked against you, there is still possibility of conversion. Césaire grounds that possibility in Hegel's delineation of the tense bond, the unerring reciprocity between the one who calls himself master and the one who responds as slave. What matters in Hegel's discussion in his *Phenomenology* is his analysis of convertibility: "Just as lordship showed its essential nature to be the reverse of what it wants to be, so, too, bondage will, when completed, pass into the opposite of what it immediately is: being a consciousness repressed within itself, it will enter into itself, and change round into real and true independence" (237). This "revolution" inspired Césaire's creation of Caliban, whom he describes as "a rebel—the positive hero, in a Hegelian sense. The slave is always more important than his master—for it is the slave who makes history" (quoted in Belhassen 176). Caliban makes history both by participating in a world of marvels and by articulating himself in a context inimical to him.

The force of the Hegelian dialectic is that by realizing the will of the master, cutting wood or washing dishes, Caliban generates a transformation of matter that allows him to succeed where Prospero fails. How does this happen? As early as his *Discourse on Colonialism*, Césaire knew how the colonial relationship chains both colonizer and colonized in implacable dependence. "First we must study how colonization works to *decivilize* the colonizer, to *brutalize* him in the true sense of the word . . . colonization, I repeat, dehumanizes even the most civilized man" (*Discourse* 13). If "colonization = thingification," then the *Tempest* will demonstrate how Prospero, the magus of Western art and civilization, turns into a thing—a reduction dramatized as a failure of language.

Caliban can claim a history and name himself because of Prospero's involvement in their discourse, an intimate dialogue that is not granted Ariel. Ariel's songs, unlike Caliban's, are not accompanied by labor. Prospero mocks their emptiness, their lyrical resistance to change and evasion of action. "It's always like that with intellectuals . . . what interests me are not your fears but your deeds" (1.2.p.23). Or later in the play, "Say here, you're not going to set fire to the world with your music" (3.5.p.84). Caliban's work songs are dedicated to Shango, the fiery storm-god who recalls and reconstitutes Shakespeare's stage direction for the first act of his *Tempest*: "A tempestuous noise of thunder and lightning heard" (1.2.p.23).

Nowhere do we get so full a sense of the necessity and the peril of a struggle that is also key to recognition as when Ariel warns Caliban, "you know that in that game [war] Prospero is unbeatable." Caliban answers:

> Better death than humiliation and injustice . . . Besides, the last word belongs absolutely to me . . . The day I feel all is lost, let me steal barrels of infernal powder, and this island, my possession, my work, from the heights of the empyrean where you like to soar, you'll see it explode in the air, I hope, with Prospero and me in the debris.

> (2.1.p.38)

The choice of death here is no empty rhetoric. In *Black Skin, White Masks* Fanon writes, "Man is human only to the extent to which he tries to impose his existence on another man in order to be recognized by him" (216–217). Finding his source in Hegel, he recognizes that the "double process of both self-consciousnesses" in the relationship between master and servant does not apply to the white master and the black slave. "One day the White master, *without conflict*, recognized the Negro slave" (216–217).[6] For Fanon, this recognition—coming without conflict—lacks the reciprocity necessary for full consciousness of self. The fear of death, not the longing for love, alone gives freedom. While Ariel is willing to say, "Yes, master," until Prospero fulfills his "promise" of freedom, Caliban will risk his life to become part of what Fanon describes as "a world of reciprocal recognitions."

Placed irrevocably on the outside of mutuality, Ariel remains lost in the position of grateful child, recipient of the good will and gifts of a master who continues to be master. But Césaire's Caliban answers such abstractions as "conscience," "patience, vitality, love" by denying an "easy freedom." He undermines Ariel's liberal cant (his "exalting dream" of "a marvelous world" of "brotherhood") by recognizing, not ignoring a history of outrage, violation, and loss. In the most critical addition to Shakespeare's text, Caliban remembers, and renames himself. When Caliban tells Prospero, "I will no longer be Caliban . . . I'm telling you that from now on I will not respond to the name of Caliban," Prospero falls automatically into the role of renamer. He cannot remain unengaged in the dialogue that Caliban initiates. How about *Cannibal*, Prospero mocks, re-anagramatizing Caliban, and thus inverting the move from Cannibal to Caliban. Or he tries again, *Hannibal*, adding, "They all love historic names" (collapsing Caliban's identity into the plural, anonymous "they"). Caliban will choose X—for the man without a name—a sign for what has been taken away. That fact, he says, is history. "You talk about history . . . well, that's history, and everyone knows it! Every time you call me it reminds me of the basic fact that you've stolen everything from me, even my identity!" (1.2.pp.27–28)[7]

Yet Caliban sees immense possibilities in what has been un-named, submerged, and violated. His attempt to recall, to summon forth a past that can convert nothing into a source of affirmation, is nowhere so effective as when he remembers his mother Sycorax. Prospero has warned, "There are some genealogies it would be better not to brag about. A hag! A witch from whom, thank God, death has delivered us!" Caliban resists this attempt to degrade his origins.

> Dead or living, she is my mother and I will not renounce her!
> Besides, you believe she's dead, because you believe the earth is a
> dead thing . . . It's so much more convenient! Dead, when you
> stamp on her, dirty her, trample her under your conquering foot!
> Me, I respect her, because I know that the earth lives
> and Sycorax lives.
> Sycorax my mother!
> Serpent! Rain! Lightning!
>
> (1.2.pp.25–26)

Prospero can only respond to his slave's recollection by attempting to persuade him that his words are nothing but "witchcraft," and he thus implicitly acknowledges their power.

Césaire intends that we understand the colonial situation, and he presents a Caliban who not only engages Prospero but somehow stops short of revolution. Act 3 represents a strangely thwarted con-frontation. Following the failed attempt to overthrow Prospero with the laughable Trinculo and Stephano, Caliban blames himself for thinking that "paunches and bloated faces could make a Revolu-tion!" He toasts Prospero: "Prospero, to the two of us!" Weapon in hand, he rushes at Prospero who has just appeared, and Prospero responds in a way that could be performed as farce: "Strike, well, strike then! Your master! Your benefactor! You're not even going to spare him!" But Caliban does spare him: he lifts his arm and then hesitates. How do we interpret this deliberate hiatus? The scene ends up being nothing but gesture. Prospero tells Caliban, "You're just an animal: you do not know how to kill," and Caliban answers Prospero, "Defend yourself! I'm not an assassin." Both have been trapped by language and implicated by it. As Prospero sends Caliban

to prison, he says, "Stupid like a slave! Now the comedy is complete" (3.4.p.79). But the comedy is not over, and that is Césaire's
point. There remains one scene to be played: a mutually willed con-
finement that leaves master and slave alone in a wash of words.

The ending of Césaire's play sustains the dialogue between Prospero and Caliban. In Shakespeare's *Tempest* we assume that Caliban
resumes control of the island as Prospero, having laid aside his book
and his staff, returns to Naples. But Césaire's Prospero chooses to
remain on the island. After ten years, he still *needs* to talk to Caliban. He wants to "make peace," urging "We've ended up being com-
patriots!" Caliban refuses, saying that he will continue the struggle.
But the fight can only be sustained through language, as Caliban
inquires into his past, activates his own history, and denounces
Prospero:

> Prospero, you are a great illusionist:
> you know deception well.
> And you've lied so much to me,
> lied about the world, about yourself,
> that you've ended up imposing on me,
> an image of myself:
> underdeveloped, as you put it,
> a sub-capable,
> that's how you made me see myself,
> and I hate this image! And it's false!
> and I know myself too!
>
> (3.5.p.88)

Prospero judges these words as evidence of Caliban's "inverted
world," suggesting that their relationship has been reversed, that the
tables have turned. Caliban lectures about the truth of the colonizer's "mission" or "vocation": "You've got a chance to make an end
of it: / You can beat it! / I'm sure you will not leave! / Your 'mission'
makes me laugh / your 'vocation!' / 'Your vocation is to give me
shit!' / And that's why you stay here, / like those sods who created
the colonies / and who now can't live anywhere else" (3.5.p.89).

Without Caliban's labor the island becomes protagonist: "dirty
nature" takes its revenge on the white magician. But only after Césaire has made sure we hear yet again the two competing voices.
Caliban sings a song to Shango, *"Shango marches powerfully /
across the sky, his path!"* as Prospero proclaims his transformative
powers:

> I've uprooted the oak, raised the seas,
> shook up mountains, and bared my chest to adversity,
> I've answered Jupiter thunderbolt for thunderbolt.
> Better yet! From the noise, from a monster, I have
> made man!
> But oh!
> To have failed to find the path to
> man's heart . . .

> (3.5.p.89)

Prospero then turns to Caliban: "Well, I hate you too! / Because you're the one who first made me doubt myself." The uncertain, troubled old man of Shakespeare's play here justifies himself to the departing nobles:

> Hear me well.
> I am not a master in the banal sense of the word,
> as this savage believes,
> but the conductor of a vast score:
> this island.
> I alone raise up voices,
> And chain them as I please,
> arranging out of confusion
> one intelligible line.
> Without me, who would know how to
> draw music from all that?
> This island is mute without me.
> My duty, then, is here.
> Here I will stay.

> (3.5.p.90)

And once left alone with Caliban, Prospero says, "Now, Caliban, to us both!" (3.5.p.91)

Césaire's final imaging of Prospero surrounded by the vermin, insects, and reptiles that have infested his cave, reveals his defeat by the material world that Caliban's labor had commanded, shaped, and controlled. By the end of the play, Prospero, in a stupor of self-coincidence, aged and weary, is reduced to automatic gestures, and his language fails.

> It's odd, but for some time now we've been invaded by
> possums . . . Some Mexican hogs, wild boars, all this dirty

nature! But mainly possums . . . Oh, those eyes! And that
base grin on their faces. It's as though the jungle wants
to beseige the cave. But I will defend myself . . . I will not let my
work perish!

(3.5.p.92)

He screams, "I will defend civilization!" to an unresponsive nature,
to an unanswering Caliban. The play ends with a powerless Prospero, suffering alone in his decrepitude, while Caliban gets the last
word. He proclaims his new-found freedom, with the sound of surf
and the chirping of birds as the background to his song, "FREEDOM
OHÉ, FREEDOM!"

Caliban's "Uhuru" (meaning "Independence" or "Freedom" in
Swahili) has punctuated Césaire's drama; indeed, the play turns on
the question: what constitutes freedom? Yet, Césaire leaves the
question unresolved. The end of his play remains ambiguous, Caliban and Prospero two voices shouting in the tempest. What is Caliban's future? Why in his final declaration of freedom does he change
from Swahili to French, "LA LIBERTÉ, OHÉ, LA LIBERTÉ!"? In the
context of Césaire's two earlier history plays (both fables and inquiries), *Une Saison au Congo* and *La Tragédie du Roi Christophe*, the
final shout of freedom becomes less than hopeful. He knows that
the struggle to sustain an ideal of freedom is far more difficult than
its mere proclamation.

We should not forget that Césaire wrote his *Tempest* not only as
a response to the upbeat spirit of black assertion in the sixties (the
moves toward independence in Africa and the Caribbean), but out of
the torpor that is contemporary Martinique, ever stagnant in its
ongoing role as accommodating child of France (an overseas *dé-
partement* of France since 1946). Indeed, in contemporary Africa
and the Caribbean, Caliban's call for "freedom" is a painful reminder
of what has *not* happened, a summons that once placed in the context of contemporary events sounds out its status as hollow cliché.
Césaire knows, even as he creates his militant Caliban, that his
"Uhuru" could be nothing more than a spurious affirmation: for the
question is not independence, but what follows. This crucial question Césaire leaves out of the *Tempest*, leaving a hollow at the center of his rhetorical celebration.

Césaire's *Tempest* makes us attend to failure, to what might be
an aberrant task. For how can Caliban define himself in a Caribbean
that now suffers under a neo-colonialism far more pernicious than
the old colonial situation, where the strategies of the oppressor have

been transmitted and internalized? Where the same coercive structures have been reproduced, this time by black functionaries, those
whom Walcott calls, "all o'dem big boys, so, dem ministers / ministers of culture, ministers of development, the green blacks, and
their old toms . . . / magicians of the New Vision" (*Another Life*
269).

Rob Nixon, in his superb essay, "Caribbean and African Appropriations of *The Tempest*," argues that "the value" of Césaire's play
"for African and Caribbean intellectuals faded once the plot ran out.
The play lacks a sixth act which might have been enlisted for representing relations among Caliban, Ariel, and Prospero once they
entered a postcolonial era" (576). Yet, that sixth act might well be
La Tragédie du Roi Christophe. Written six years before the *Tempest*, the "tragedy" bears witness to the drama of a decolonization
so failed that its first act must be presented as farce.

Christophe, a black Prospero, replies to vacancy (the loss of a
name and identity) by perpetuating a tradition of renaming that sti-
fles an effective voice under empty form. In the years following Haiti's amazing victory over the French in Vertières in 1803, Christophe
(who succeeded Dessalines) would combat French hegemony and
imperial power with his own orgy of naming.[8] It is the nature of
Christophe's reiteration that turns history into farce. Unlike the
Caliban who tries to cut through the false magic of Prospero's utterance, Christophe invents for Haiti a nobility, his "Grace the Duke
of Limonade, the Duke of Marmalade."

In this play on the perils of decolonization, Christophe passes
through two stages. The first is his recognition of a history of outrage and loss:

> In the past they stole our names
> Our pride
> Our nobility.
> . . .
> Pierre, Paul, Jacques, Toussaint! Those are the
> humiliating brand marks with which they obliterated
> our real names.
>
> (1.3.p.37)

The second is his mystifying renaming that covers over the fact of
Africa, the terrors of slavery. Believing that "we can't rescue our
names from the past," Christophe simply substitutes the semantic

traps of French mastery. The naming substitutes a convention of liberty, power, or redemption, for its actuality: "With names of glory I will cover your slave names / With names of pride our names of infamy" (1.3.p.37).

The French fragment of Caliban's song that ends the *Tempest* is thus terrible in its irony. Read in conjunction with Christophe's "rhetoric of honor," the song to the African god Shango is pulverized, leaving only the snatches of Prospero's language: a call to liberty shown to be as irresistible and as delusive as the "charms" of Shakespeare's "wronged Duke of Milan." Césaire's play on "revolution" fades into thin air, as baseless and finally, as insubstantial, as Prospero's gloriously ephemeral masque. For as Césaire demonstrates in *La Tragédie du Roi Christophe*—his most solemn meditation on the caprices of power—how slippery, how easily reversed is the divide between Caliban and Prospero, colonizer and colonized.

III

Negritude. Black Orpheus. Caliban. Names chosen for the labor of return, for the seizure of voice from the shadows of a past annihilated, reviled, and traduced. To remember, to reconstitute a self through language is not always a luxury of leisure, but as Toni Morrison demonstrates in *Beloved*, a descent into a past of broken words and empty names: "Was that it? Is that where the manhood lay? In the naming done by a whiteman who was supposed to know?" (125)

Morrison is talking about knowledge, and the surest proof of that gift: to speak, to name again in a world where everything seems to have been already named. Césaire confronts Shakespeare's play and takes on the burden of response. He is deliberate in his "adaptation," with all the complexities and failures such a refusal of originality or uniqueness implies. To see the formerly colonized as agents of knowledge remains the goal of Césaire's hybrid labor. Thus turning from *the one* way of approaching the relation between definers and defined to *the many*, he replaces the definite with an indefinite article: substituting *Une tempête* for *The Tempest*. Such a project of continuing re-definition warns against turning into fetish or commodity those cultures teachers hope to rescue from neglect, or those writers they attempt to bring into presence.

Césaire writes as late-coming chronicler of a place, any island in the Caribbean where history began with a complex violation: an orgy of naming by colonizers who acted as if nothing was there until they came to claim it. To teach Césaire's text as mere reaction to what is prior or canonical, without confronting the syncretic, oddly mixed nature of Shakespeare's play is to continue to marginalize the colonial subject outside the untouchable "master plots" of civilization and conquest.

What if we were to teach Shakespeare's *Tempest* by reading Césaire's adaptation first? We could then read what I have called the convertibility between classical and revisionary not in terms of a simple either/or dichotomy—with the two texts as counters in an argument of extremes—but through a process of continuing complications. The double and contradictory movement of claims to authority or nation-building are as much a part of Shakespeare's world as Césaire's. If we begin to understand the fertile collision and mutual abiding of these reciprocal worlds, we can combat the endless talk about *canons* that changes nothing in the academic hierarchies, but continues to mask the locus of authority by rhetoricizing a liberalism that legitimates by exclusion and categorization.

One of the most coercive strategies in the academy today is the categorization of something called "Western" and something called "non-Western," and the resulting fetishizing of the so-called third-world text. How in this imposition of terms, the academic sanction of generalities and the false assumptions they allow, do we teach Caribbean literatures? Or should we say "Postcolonial" literatures? These words do not *mean* in the context of the societies they claim to describe, but they do order. They make possible some very problematic reductions.

Mediated to his bones by the colonial myth, as well as learned in texts prized by those conservatives of "tradition," Fanon, for example, is not non-Western. What does it mean, then, if we put his *Black Skin, White Masks* in the second semester of a year course on "Great Books," "Global Studies," or "Cultural Studies?" Students might well see his work as a reaction to the so-called West, a kind of secondary gain. In the process, however, the "Great Tradition" remains unscathed, whole and sacred in its firstness, its status as primary, while the other texts on the margins get to negate or react against, and sometimes transform. But even so, these operations are always in the context of something constituted as original. Teachers and critics can keep the classics on one side, pure and pristine, while teaching the "new," multicultural tokens off on the other. The particulars of these reactive texts are then gobbled up by conceptual frameworks that have very little to do with the facts of their production.

Before the rage for "diversity," the West Indian poet and historian Edward Kamau Brathwaite intuited the problems inherent in liberal commands that masked the continued, coercive interests of the status quo. In *Contradictory Omens*, first delivered in Ife in December 1970 and then at the Johns Hopkins University in 1973, published in Jamaica in 1974 and reprinted in 1985 (still unavailable in the United States), Brathwaite warned that hegemony can be "achieved . . . largely by remote control." Chinua Achebe had once wished that the word "universal" could be banished from our language, for it perpetuated an instrumental myth of homogeneity. And in *Contradictory Omens*, Brathwaite describes the dangers in the "optimistic, universalistic" view:

> Integration and national understanding are far more likely to have real meaning if they are based upon the knowledge of difference rather than upon external stimuli from "world culture." . . . "World culture" can only create yet another client culture.
>
> (48)

In this essay, I have attempted to complicate the binaries, to make sure that a play like Shakespeare's *Tempest*, when read with Césaire's adaptation for a black theater, does not remain the same. Something happens to our claims to knowledge, or more specifically, *how we come to know*, when we read Shakespeare with and through Césaire: not as a "racist" authority text, but as a text itself riddled with ambivalence and equivocations that Césaire helps us to see. Concerns about legitimacy, mastery, or coercion, especially when trying to recover a voice or history distorted, ambiguous, or null, should be on our minds whenever we confront the domination of form and its ahistorical appeal. Incarcerating a "third world" writer in a place apart from the "classic," is to proffer the dead token of a hollow victory. Significantly, as many have recognized, the very concept of "third world" is questionable. If Naipaul wrote about the Caribbean as "the third world's third world," Sidney Mintz, the anthropologist who first demystified the generality of the place called the Caribbean, reminds us that the Caribbean "was being force-fit into the first world, the European world, before the third world ever existed" (916–944).

> It can probably be shown that the special distinctiveness of the Caribbean area within the sphere of the "underdeveloped world" inheres in its ambience as a cluster of colonies . . . only superficially "non-Western," taking on their particularity precisely because they are in some ways, and deceptively, among the

most "Western" of all countries outside the United States and
Western Europe.

(917)[9]

Any study of a text inside the Western cultural tradition must include a deconstruction of the very concept *Western*, just as I have
argued that an understanding of Prospero or Caliban must engage us
in disentangling the very terms of mastery and servitude. Whether
in the "center" or "periphery," claims of authenticity or threats of
fakery are inextricably mixed. Both Shakespeare and Césaire understood the false magic of benevolence, the cunning artifaces of
language.

Césaire's *Tempest* is as much a response to a prior Caribbean text
as it is to Shakespeare's play. Nine years before Césaire's play, the
Barbadian-in-exile George Lamming published his *Pleasures of Exile*. The problem he recognized as most vexing for the West Indian
exile was that of language. When he wrote his chapter, "a Monster,
a Child, a Slave," he concentrated on the moment when Caliban,
goaded by Prospero's demand for more work, curses Prospero's gift:
"I gave you language" (83–108). What is striking here is that Lamming's Caliban is not very distinct from Mannoni's "primitive" and
dependent *person of color* (specifically, the colonized Malagasy in
revolt) in *Prospero and Caliban: The Psychology of Colonization*.[10]
For Lamming, to have no language is equivalent to being a beast, or
as he put it, *de-formed*, but to have only the language of the oppressor is to be dependent, a child or monkey mimic of the master.
While Lamming recognized the colonial relation as the central drama
of Shakespeare's play, something odd (or too predictable) happens to
his presentation of Caliban.

> To be a child of Nature . . . is to be situated in Nature, to be iden-
> tified with Nature, to be eternally without the seed of a dialectic
> which makes possible some emergence from Nature.
> Such is Caliban, superfluous as the weight of the earth until
> Prospero arrives with the aid of the Word which might help
> him to clarify the chaos which shows its true colors all over
> his skin.
>
> (110)

Lamming, though writing about Shakespeare, seems to accept implicitly the stigma which slavery impressed upon the "African character": his Caliban possesses that earthy innocence that assumes he

did not exist in any important sense as a person until he was "discovered."

As I have emphasized, Césaire reads his Shakespeare differently, and brings out what might have remained latent in our readings of *The Tempest*. Shakespeare's Caliban had language, after all, for he taught the arrivants the names of things on the enchanted island. Césaire's Caliban, like Shakespeare's own, thus goes beyond the choice of mute, unaccommodated nature or mimic: George Lamming's "mute earth" or Derek Walcott's "enraged pupil." Given the choice of heroics or the rhetoric of revolt, Césaire writes a play that turns (in its persistent references back to the original) on the crisis of legitimacy. In the process, he breaks out of the trap of colonization and challenges his readers to de-platonize their understanding of reality. Césaire's exercise in syncretism, the absorptions and permeability of diverse histories and cultures, helps us break down and reconstitute such abstract and inevitably neutralizing distinctions as literate/illiterate, developed/underdeveloped, historic/prehistoric, all of which oversimplify the nature of the encounter between the West and the rest of the world.

IV

"Pluralism," Gayatri Spivak argues, "is the method employed by the *central* authorities to neutralize opposition by seeming to accept it. The gesture of pluralism on the part of the *marginal* can only mean capitulation to the center." I end with this quotation,[11] since I think the use of a term like "pluralism" to minimize difference or neutralize conflict is part of the now popular march toward the "global" or the "multicultural."

It is no accident that the commodification or celebration of "minority" literatures happens at a time when black communities, especially, are the most disfranchised, the most dispossessed. What is the relation between the multicultural enterprise in the academy—the call for diversity—and what is happening in those places in the United States that house those we are busy talking and writing about? What gets to be recognized as a *usable image* or a *popular text*? And when? As soon as the Caribs of the New World were decimated, they were praised and idealized in most natural histories of the Caribbean. And as the "third world" becomes what Maurice Bishop of Grenada had hoped would be nobody's "backyard," more and more people are writing about the Caribbean. Things tend to become favorite objects of study—literary themes—once their disappearance is assured.

Our real task in approaching the demands of complicated cultural histories should be to articulate a *method*, a way of teaching—and learning—that will not limit a "literary" text, in particular, to such "qualities" that allow us to wrench it out of less absolute, more contingent (historical and social) contexts. We need to question how texts and our responses to them are constituted by social realities too easily masked by something vague and grand called "literariness."

The academy has always been the privileged, if subtle arena for the perpetuation of a dominant, sanctified ideology. As Gramsci put it, we are "experts in legitimation." Wole Soyinka has warned of "a second epoch of colonization": "a universal-humanoid abstraction defined and conducted by individuals whose theories and prescriptions" have very little to do with the places and peoples out of which such studies gain strength. What is most valuable about current questions of canon formation is not the attack against an individual writer and the substitution of another (Shakespeare vs. Césaire, for example) but the attempt to reintroduce conflict and difference, to elicit questions and discomfort, instead of seeking accord. As Césaire expressed it in his early *Notebook of a Return to the Native Land*, true as always to his project of deconstruction, his battle against any iconic quest, whether for some phantom Africa or Léopold Senghor's celebrated *black essence*:

No, we've never been amazones of the King of Dahomey. . . .
And since I have sworn to leave nothing out of our history
(I who love nothing better than a sheep grazing his own
afternoon shadow), I may as well confess that we were at
all times pretty mediocre dishwashers.

No easy assumption of a glorious—and ultimately mystifying—negritude, but as in his *Tempest*, a re-appropriation, transmission, and questioning of the very *making of history*.

Notes

I thank Sarah Lawall for the invitation to participate in her NEH Institute for the Theory and Teaching of World Literature (1987), where many of the ideas in this paper were first developed. A shorter version of this essay appeared in the *Arizona Quarterly* (Winter 1993).
    1. See also his *Bonjour et adieu à la négritude* (153–160). All translations in this essay are my own, unless otherwise indicated.

2. The first version appeared in the Paris magazine *Volontés* in August 1939. The best translation of the *Cahier* to date is by Clayton Eshleman and Annette Smith.

3. Walcott's essay "The Muse of History" gives a stunning analysis of his poetics of Adamic naming in the New World, as opposed to what he condemns as "servitude to the muse of history" and "a literature of recrimination and despair."

4. For a discussion of the conversions of Caliban see Peter Hulme. As Hulme argues, Caliban is an icon for voice. He is discourse, a "Monster" constituted through words: "Caliban, as a compromise formation, can exist only within discourse: he is fundamentally and essentially beyond the bounds of representation" (108).

5. See Albert Memmi, *The Colonizer and the Colonized*: "He is in no way a subject of history any more. Of course, he carries its burden, often more cruelly than others, but always as an object" (91). The mechanism of colonization as elaborated by Memmi unfortunately perpetuates the myth of the colonized as lack. No longer agents, they remain in the world, but emptied of value: victims but never makers of history. George Lamming, in "A Monster, a Child, a Slave," also gives us a Caliban who "is never accorded the power *to see* . . . superfluous and dumb" (108). Colonized, yet privileged, Lamming here forgets the other history, those other ways of self-definition and *marronage* that sustained religions, languages, and traditions in spite of what the "master" race imposed: "he has no self which is not a reaction to circumstances imposed upon his life" (107).

6. Fanon claims that the master he describes differs from Hegel's. "For Hegel there is reciprocity; here the master laughs at the consciousness of the slave. What he wants from the slave is not recognition but work" (220).

7. In *X/Self* (1988), the final book of a trilogy that includes *Mother Poem* (1977) and *Sun Poem* (1982), Edward Kamau Brathwaite uses the *X* to signal the Caribbean self unselved: "who dat speaking / I is who / I-self / I was trying to say what my name." See Dayan, "The Beat and the Bawdy" (504–507).

8. Once the richest French colony in the New World, with a trade that outstripped that of the thirteen North American colonies throughout the eighteenth century, Saint-Domingue became the first independent black nation in 1804, after the only successful slave rebellion in history. For the complexities involved in working out personal identity in Haiti while making a nation, see Dayan, "Haiti, History, and the Gods."

9. See also Edward Said's sharp reflection in "Third World Intellectuals and Metropolitan Culture." Speaking of those writers once identified as colonial or native, he argues: "There is no sense in their work of men standing *outside* the Western cultural tradition, however much they think of themselves as articulating the adversarial experience of colonial and/or non-Western peoples" (36).

10. See Fanon's brilliant deconstruction of Mannoni's text—which should also be compared with Césaire's response in *Discourse on Colonialism*—in *Black Skin, White Masks* (83–108).

11. Neither Gayatri Spivak nor I recall the source of the quotation.

158   *Joan Dayan*

Works Cited

Baker, Houston. "Caliban's Triple Play." *Critical Inquiry* 13.1 (1986): 182–196.

Baudelaire, Charles. "Salon de 1846." In *Curiosités esthétiques, L'Art romantique, et autres oeuvres critiques*, edited by Henri LeMaitre, pp. 97–200. Paris: Garnier, 1962.

Belhassen, S. "Aimé Césaire's *A Tempest*." In *Radical Perspectives in the Arts*, compiled by Lee Baxandall, pp. 175–177. Harmondsworth: Penguin, 1972.

Brathwaite, Edward Kamau. *Contradictory Omens: Cultural Diversity and Integration in the Caribbean*. Mona, Jamaica: Savacou Publications, 1974.

———. *Mother Poem*. New York and Oxford: Oxford University Press, 1977.

———. *Sun Poem*. New York and Oxford: Oxford University Press, 1982.

———. *X/Self*. New York and Oxford: Oxford University Press, 1987.

Césaire, Aimé. *Cahier d'un retour au pays natal*. Paris: Bordas, 1946.

———. *Collected Poetry of Aimé Césaire*. Translated by Clayton Eshleman and Annette Smith. Berkeley: University of California Press, 1983.

———. *Discourse on Colonialism*. Translated by Joan Pinkham. New York and London: Monthly Review Press, 1972. *Discours sur le colonialisme*. Paris: Présence africaine, 1955.

———. *Une tempête*. Paris: Seuil, 1969.

———. *La Tragédie du Roi Christophe*. Paris: Seuil, 1963.

Dayan, Joan. "The Beat and the Bawdy." *The Nation* (April 9, 1988): 504–507.

———. "Haiti, History, and the Gods." In *After Colonialism: Imperial Histories and Postcolonial Displacements*, edited by Gyan Prakash. Princeton: Princeton University Press, forthcoming.

Depestre, René. *Bonjour et adieu à la négritude*. Paris: Robert Laffont, 1980.

———. *A Rainbow for the Christian West*. Translated with Introduction by Joan Dayan. Amherst: University of Massachusetts Press, 1977.

Fanon, Frantz. *Black Skin, White Masks*. Translated by Charles Lam Markmann. New York: Grove Press, 1952. *Peau Noire, Masques Blancs*. Paris: Seuil, 1952.

Hegel, Georg-Friederich. *Phenomenology of Mind*. Translated by J. B. Baillie. New York: Harper and Row, 1967.

Hulme, Peter. *Colonial Encounters: Europe and the Native Caribbean, 1492–1797*. London and New York: Methuen, 1986.

Lamming, George. "A Monster, a Child, a Slave." In *The Pleasures of Exile*, pp. 95–118. 1960. London: Allison & Busby, 1984.

Lewis, Gordon. *Main Currents in Caribbean Thought: The Historical Evolution of Caribbean Society in Its Ideological Aspects, 1492–1900*. Baltimore and London: Johns Hopkins University Press, 1983.

Mannoni, D. O. *Prospero and Caliban: The Psychology of Colonization*.

1956. Translated by P. Powesland. New York: Frederick A. Praeger, 1964. *Psychologie de la colonisation*. Paris: Seuil, 1950.

Memmi, Albert. *The Colonizer and the Colonized*. Introduction by J.-P. Sartre. Translated by Howard Greenfield. 1957. Boston: Beacon Press, 1967.

Mintz, Sidney. "The Caribbean as a Socio-Cultural Area." *Cahiers d'histoire mondiale*, 9 (1966): 916–944.

Morrison, Toni. *Beloved*. New York: New American Library, 1987.

Nixon, Rob. "Caribbean and African Appropriations of *The Tempest*." *Critical Inquiry*, 13 (1987): 557–578.

Retamar, Roberto. *Caliban and Other Essays*. Translated by Edward Baker. Foreword by Frederic Jameson. Berkeley: University of California Press, 1983. Originally "Notes toward a Discussion of Culture in Our America." *Casa de las Americas* 68 (1971).

Rodo, José Enrique. *Ariel*. Montevideo: Impr. de Dornaleche y Reyes, 1900.

Said, Edward. "Third World Intellectuals and Metropolitan Culture." *Raritan* (Winter 1990): 27–50.

Shakespeare, William. *The Tempest*. Edited by Stephen Orgel. Oxford: Clarendon Press, 1987.

Walcott, Derek. *Another Life: Collected Poems, 1948–1984*. New York: Farrar, Straus and Giroux, 1986.

———. "The Muse of History." In *Carifesta Forum: An Anthology of Twenty Caribbean Voices*, edited with Introduction by John Hearne, pp. 111–128. Kingston: Institute of Jamaica and *Jamaica Journal*, 1976.

5. Celtic Literature and the European Canon

Maria Tymoczko

The fascination of Celtic literature to other European cultures and literary traditions can be documented for well over a millennium, traced through direct references as well as borrowings of genre, theme and motif, character and plot. Yet it is a paradox that Celtic literature has entered the European canon principally through adaptation and refraction rather than translation. The purpose of my work is to explore the factors that influence reception of materials from other literary systems as they intersect with canon formation; Celtic literature is an ideal test case for this investigation because of its close association with European letters but its limited entry into most literary canons.[1]

Even a brief review of the borrowing and adaptation of Celtic literature into other European traditions must begin with early medieval literature. The Celtic genres of voyage and vision literature were adapted into medieval Latin, where they began an independent literary development, leading ultimately to Dante's *Divine Comedy*, a work that is at once vision and voyage (Boswell). At the same time, specific adaptations of the voyage and vision literature such as *Navigatio Sancti Brendani* (The voyage of Saint Brendan) or *Purgatorio Sancti Patricii* (Saint Patrick's purgatory) circulated and ultimately came to enjoy wide popularity through translation from the Latin texts into many of the medieval vernacular literatures. There were also more general poetic influences on medieval Latin literature stemming from Celtic lands. The similarities between the poems of Sedulius Scottus and the functions, forms, and repertory of Old Irish poetry, for example, show that Sedulius was functioning in a Carolingian context as an Irish *fili* (the Irish seer-poet); such poetic forms and functions became one model for medieval Latin occasional poetry, blending with the models inherited from Rome. While Celtic material was being absorbed into medieval Latin literature, it was also making an impact on Germanic traditions. The pro-simetrum form of Old Icelandic sagas (the mixture of prose and po-etry), the forms and functions of skaldic poetry, and various motifs and tale types are all elements of the Old Norse tradition that have been ascribed in part to Irish influence (Turville-Petre). Still others have argued that the particular collocation of elements associated with Grendel and his mother betrays motival influence from Celtic literature on Old English literature as well (Puhvel).

It is no wonder that such borrowings and extensions of Celtic literature occurred in the early Middle Ages, for while most of Europe was struggling to maintain the rudiments of learning and culture, Celtic culture, particularly Irish culture, was flourishing. The Irish missionaries to England, Scotland, and the Continent came from a vigorous cultural ambiance that produced stunning manuscript and metal works of art, that kept literature at the center of cultural life, and that had the first literate secular class of Europe. They became the models for and teachers of Northern Europe; and their influence reached across the Alps, with Irish pilgrims traveling to Rome and Irish foundations being established as far south as Bobbio.[2]

The literature of the Brythonic Celts (rather than Irish literature) was most influential in the twelfth century and the later Middle Ages during the second major period of the European absorption of Celtic literature. During that period Old French culture, the domi-nant vernacular culture of Europe, came into close contact with Bry-thonic cultures (the Celts of Wales, Cornwall, Devon, and Brittany) as a result of conquest and other forms of cultural interchange. Fol-lowing the Norman conquest of England and Wales, there was a bur-geoning of Arthurian literature in the several genres of chronicle, romance, and *lai* in most of the vernaculars of Europe, as well as in medieval Latin. While the genre of romance itself is not Celtic, some of the content of Arthurian literature clearly is Celtic, be-cause Arthur and many of the characters in his entourage had been traditional heroes of all the Brythonic Celts long before the Norman invasion of Britain. Geoffrey of Monmouth's seminal work, *Historia Regum Britanniae* (The history of the kings of Britain), is a refrac-tion of native Welsh heroic literature—and of the Celtic genres of king tale and pseudo-history—conditioned by Latin historiography and Latin epic; the work served as the historicized grounding for more imaginative treatments of the same characters in later medi-eval European literature. Geoffrey was also responsible for popular-izing the British seer and poet Myrddin, adapted as Geoffrey's Mer-linus, the Merlin of vernacular literature. Other Celtic plots and characters were also borrowed into the larger European tradition at the time, including the important and influential material associated with the British hero Tristan.[3]

The most important Celtic genres for the development of European literature in the later Middle Ages were vaticination poetry (prophetic poetry) and the *lai*. Though prophecy exists in most cultures, the specific form of secular vaticination poetry which flourished in Wales from the tenth century onward was adapted in Geoffrey's *Prophetiae Merlini* (The prophecies of Merlin), a text that continued to be popular virtually to the present and that influenced subsequent European prophecies. The origin of the *lai* is obviously Celtic, coming as the term does from the Celtic word for "song, poem" (cf. Old Irish *láid*, "poem, song"); it was a productive genre from the twelfth century onward in several European languages, although the meaning of the word and of the genre changed over time, moving steadily away from the Celtic form (Bullock-Davies). It is impossible to survey in detail all the European indebtedness to Celtic literature during the later Middle Ages, but even the few examples mentioned indicate engagement with Celtic literary content and form and illustrate the wide variety of adaptations and refractions made of Celtic material.

The Tudor period in England was another era which took up various tales from Celtic literature, in part because the English crown had hereditary ties to Wales and Welsh culture. The interest in Britain's Celtic past is reflected in the revival of Arthurian material in Spenser, for example, and in the use of other materials from Celtic sources (by way of Geoffrey of Monmouth and Holinshed's *Chronicles*) in Shakespeare's plays, notably the character Lear. Celtic fairy lore is also reflected in Spenser's texts. Scholars have argued that aspects of Celtic fairy lore surface in Shakespeare's treatments of the fairies, and it is possible that his Queen Mab owes something to the medieval Irish queen Medb (Nutt). During the period there was a revival of interest in Merlin's prophecies and in vaticination poetry as well.

Since the eighteenth century there has been a steady use of Celtic material in European literature. Within the framework of the travelogue which was popular at the time, Swift's *Gulliver's Travels* incorporates realms of giant and miniature human beings, materials which seem in some respects indebted to Celtic motifs; like Spenser, Swift apparently became acquainted with some Irish literary elements during his residence in Ireland. Swift's satire also can be situated in the Irish comic tradition (Mercier Chapter 7). The epic works of James Macpherson, presented as translations of Ossian, constitute a more deliberate, if erratic, eighteenth-century refraction of Celtic literary materials within English tradition. Although Macpherson's works have been neither sufficiently representative of their Gaelic originals nor sufficiently interesting as literary works in their own right to have been admitted into twentieth-century literary canons, he achieved tremendous success with his contemporaries. Macpherson's works, and the controversy surrounding them, led to the collection, translation, and adaptation of Celtic materials in all Celtic countries—Scotland, Ireland, Wales, Brittany; his writings are precursors of nineteenth-century Romantic efforts to incorporate Celtic material into English and French literature in the form of both adaptations and translations. Following Macpherson, Hersart de la Villemarqué published popular French ballads representing the songs and poems of Breton tradition, and numerous other nineteenth-century adaptations of Breton popular tales were made, among which the adaptations of the story of Ys are conspicuous for inspiring treatments in French literature, art, and music.

The Anglo-Irish literary revival represents still another literary movement that adapted and refracted Irish literature into English. The writers of the movement—including Yeats, Synge, A. E., and Gregory—reused a great number of Irish motifs, plots, and characters within the framework of English poetics; they also incorporated Irish mythopoeic imagery into English discourse. Through the works of these authors many of the stories and mythic figures of Irish literary tradition found their way into English literature and thence into the mainstream of Western literature. Through Yeats the Irish characters of CúChulainn and Oengus and the Irish plots of *The Death of Aife's Only Son* and *The Only Jealousy of Emer*, for example, have entered the canon; through Synge the Irish-speaking peasantry has become known; through the final work of Joyce the Irish hero Finn mac Cumaill and other elements of Irish literary tradition have found an international audience.

Finally, the fantasy writers of the twentieth century have turned to Celtic literature for inspiration and materials. J. R. R. Tolkien, for example, drew on the Irish *síd*, the Irish otherworld and its residents, for his stately portrait of the elves, and he is indebted to Celtic material for other linguistic elements and motifs as well. C. S. Lewis also used Celtic literary motifs in his Narnia series. Since Tolkien and Lewis, numerous other fantasy writers have turned to Celtic literary traditions for source material. The Welsh *Mabinogi* has provided a foundation for such writers as Evangeline

Walton and Lloyd Alexander, while the Arthurian legend has been "re-Celticized" by such authors as Mary Stewart and Marion Zimmer Bradley.

This brief survey of the borrowing and adaptation of Celtic literature in Western literary tradition shows the perennial appeal of Celtic literature, particularly the appeal of Irish and Welsh literature. It is all the more astonishing, then, that Irish and Welsh literary works are so rarely included in canons of Western literature. Whether we measure canons by the contents of anthologies, syllabi of surveys, recommended reading lists for graduate students in comparative literature, or frequency of discussion in general critical publications, Celtic literature is conspicuously absent. Even allowing for the minority status of Celtic languages, this is remarkable. How do we explain the neglect of such early Irish stories as *Fingal Rónáin* (How Ronan slew his son), a concise and powerful—if brutal—short prose tale with lyric insets? Why are the Four Branches of the Welsh *Mabinogi* not universally known, composed as they are in some of the most supple medieval prose preserved in any language and blending in a marvelous way ancient mythic material and elegant courtly themes? Why do we not read *Culhwch ac Olwen, Culhwch and Olwen*, the earliest preserved Arthurian narrative in any language, a tour-de-force of humorous exaggeration, alongside with Chrétien de Troyes? Why are not Irish and Welsh nature poems, which surpass other European vernacular poems in the range and acuteness of natural observation despite their formal complexity and grace, not included in every anthology of European poetry?[4] Why is there no place of honor for *Aislinge Meic Conglinne* (The vision of Mac Conglinne), the most sophisticated medieval satire in any language? Celtic literature has been formative for Western tradition, but it has only entered canons of world literature in such refractions as Arthurian romance or Yeats's Cuchulain plays, where Celtic material is processed in languages and formal structures other than those native to Celtic cultures.

There are many ways to approach this paradox that I have raised; indeed it risks becoming an unwieldy question. We may gain a purchase by considering the reception of the archaic features of Celtic literature, since the archaism of Celtic literature has been an important factor governing the reception of Celtic literature outside Celtic areas. The archaism has made the literature irresistible and fascinating at the same time that it has limited the extension and translation (in the etymological sense as well as the literal sense) of the literature to a wider world. The interplay of aspects of Celtic literary archaism as positive yet negative factors—attracting interest yet disrupting acceptance—in the integration of Celtic literature within world literature, thus, bears examination as an epitome of the entire question.

Celtic literature is archaic in virtually every respect. The archaism is manifest in the function of literature and the status of literary practitioners in Celtic cultures. It is well known that Celtic poets were as much prophets as entertainers; they were shamanistic figures—seers, shapers, satirists whose art could maim or kill. The Celtic terms for poets and poetry link the practitioners with vision, sight, shaping, smithing, as, for example, the Irish words for "poet" (*fili* and *éices*, both meaning "seer") illustrate. On both sides of the Irish sea, Celtic poets impressed non-Celtic observers with their second sight and the extravagant ways that second sight was manifest—trances, ravings, extempore poetic utterances, and dream visions, often induced by ritual and cultic practices.[5] In its formal structures Celtic literature is equally archaic. Narrative poetry was seemingly not part of Celtic tradition; where there are narrative poems they betray a foreign influence in their content, as do, for example, early poetic treatments of biblical material. The archaism of Celtic narrative is also reflected in the narrative mode of early Irish literature where the narrative line is carried in prose, but the prose is interspersed with poetic inserts.[6]

The importance of sound in Celtic poetics may also represent an archaism. In his discussion of Welsh poetry, Thomas Parry has observed:

> It is important here to recall the critical standpoint which determined Welsh poetry down to the end of the eighteenth century, that is to say, so long as the least element remained of what can properly be called the Welsh tradition. *That standpoint is that sound is as important as sense; that metre and* cynghanedd, *the whole framework of verse, are as much a part of the aesthetic effect as what is said.*
>
> (48–49)

Poetry in Celtic lands was, thus, like charms and incantations, efficacious as much for the meter and sound structure as for its "content." It is no surprise that Irish *filidecht*, "the art of the poet," should have involved learning various sorts of incantatory practices.

The archaism of Celtic literature is apparent in other aspects of Celtic literary systems such as generic types, characters and character types, and narrative building blocks including ancient motifs and tale types. Thus, for example, literary satire in Irish tradition is never far from personal invective, ridicule, and lampooning, genres which are in turn related to the magical practice of cursing (Robinson, Mercier Chapter 5). The archaism of Celtic hero tale as a genre is seen, too, in the mixed tone of such tales as the Welsh *Culhwch and Olwen* or most of the Irish tales in the Ulster Cycle—tales that include humor and burlesque as well as elements more characteristic of the elevated tone of epic.[7] As for characters, the elegant and courtly Four Branches of the *Mabinogi*, for example, feature characters whose names are etymologically related to those of Gaulish deities, thus indicating that the characters and narrative material descend from ancient mythos.

The value system, the ethics, and the material culture reflected in much of early Celtic literature is also ancient. An extreme form of the heroic ethic motivates Old Welsh poems such as *Y Gododdin* (The Gododdin), and there is a similar value system represented in the Irish Ulster Cycle, which also represents a milieu reminiscent of that of the Gauls as described by classical writers (see Jackson *The Oldest Irish Tradition*). Christianity has made little ostensible impact on the Ulster Cycle; the result is that the Irish hero tale is closer to classical epic than to any other medieval epic tradition, and the pre-Christian gods of Ireland play an active role in the events of the tales. A pre-courtly outlook is seen in the grotesque and macabre elements permeating the literature—scatological, sexual, and gory materials are found in narratives and poems of the most heroic sort. Other aspects of the belief structure underlying Celtic literature are also archaic. The Celtic belief in two space-time continua, one the world of mortals coexisting with a second supernatural realm, the otherworld, stands as an example.[8]

Two periods of borrowing and adaptation of Celtic literature into European letters can serve as test cases for the reception of Celtic archaism—the borrowing and refraction of Brythonic traditions by Latin and French letters in the twelfth century and the adaptation of Irish literature by the Anglo-Irish literary revival. Both periods and movements are complex, and no consensus has been reached on the extent to which either literary development depends on Celtic materials, the means by which material was adapted from Celtic literature, and the meaning of the Celtic substratum in the overall achievement of the literary movement. Thus, the observations below are to be understood as schematic in some important ways.

During the twelfth century, a major adaptation of Celtic literature is represented by the transposition of Welsh historical and pseudohistorical material in Geoffrey of Monmouth's *History of the Kings of Britain* and the subsequent proliferation of chronicles and romances based on Geoffrey's adaptations of these Celtic subjects. Why Geoffrey would have adapted Welsh historical subjects for a Norman audience has been debated in the critical literature, and it has been suggested that Geoffrey was attempting to provide for its Norman conquerors a history of the newly conquered island that could stand alongside the history of France; he may also have hoped to forge a Welsh-Norman bond against their common enemy, the English. Of all the Celtic heroes in his narrative, Geoffrey most develops Arthur, and Arthur achieved the greatest success in later romances and chronicles as well. Part of the appeal of this material was probably that Arthur provided a counterweight to the pull of Rome; he was credited with being the civilizing center of a culture.

But the archaic aspects of Welsh tradition were also part of the appeal of these materials to the French and thence to the rest of Europe. Geoffrey's history foregrounds the archaic role of the poet as seer and prophet, a role which had been institutionalized in the vaticination poetry popular in Wales from the tenth century onward and which was associated with several traditional poetic characters, Myrddin in particular. The initial inclusion of such prophecies in Geoffrey's work, attributed to a seer whom he called Merlinus, was greeted with so much success that Geoffrey went on to do a second work, *Vita Merlini* (The life of Merlin), about the same figure. In adapting the archaic function of prophecy associated with the Celtic poet, Geoffrey was also transposing certain archaic Celtic poetic and formal values as well: the focus on sound and imagery in poetry, rather than rationally penetrable content.

Another archaism of Celtic literature was adapted in the so-called Breton *lais* of twelfth-century French tradition, which reveal a fascination with the supernatural ambiance of Celtic literature, an ambiance connected in native Celtic tradition with the archaic belief in the otherworld that has already been examined. In some of the *lais*, specific markers of the Celtic otherworld are obvious—in *Graelant*, for example, the underwater location of the supernatural woman's abode seems telling.[9] The appeal of the Celtic otherworld is traced in Arthurian romances, as well, in which various motifs, characters, and environments typical of the Celtic otherworld surface (Loomis passim).

Francophone literature of the twelfth and thirteenth centuries is marked by its interest in a great deal of nontraditional material, and the rise of romance at the period is related to a more general interest in translation of material of all sorts into Old French. Arthur was enthusiastically taken up in innovative cultural centers along with other Celtic material such as the Tristan story and the character of Merlin; but Old French audiences and patrons were also interested in adaptations of classical narratives, in material from Byzantium and the east, and in hagiographic literature from a variety of areas, to name but a few of the many nontraditional materials absorbed into French literature at the period. The influx of new subject matter is related to formal changes; it appears to be correlated as well with changes in the literary establishment, marking the transition from an oral traditional literature to an authored non-traditional literature (Tymoczko "Translation as a Force"). All the nontraditional materials absorbed into Old French literature, including the Celtic material, can be seen as a form of alterity. They reflect an interest in "the other," and they appealed to a large extent because they were exotic; the exotic qualities were harnessed in the molding of new literary forms and functions, and new social ideals and values.

Celtic material was attractive at the period in part because its archaism was read as other, as exotic. For example, although the function of poetry and the role of poets in Celtic culture derive from common Indo-European roots, by the Middle Ages most of the rest of Europe had turned away from this ancient common heritage and had evolved a very different place for its literature and its literary practitioners. As a consequence, Celtic poets and poetry exerted a kind of atavistic appeal from the early medieval period when Irish visions were borrowed into Latin, through the period of Geoffrey of Monmouth, to the time of the Anglo-Irish literary revival. Similar arguments might be made about the appeal of Celtic concepts of the otherworld to a wider European audience, for despite certain culturally specific aspects, Celtic concepts of the otherworld show great similarity to ideas found in many cultures worldwide, and they blend easily with European fairy lore and the otherworld of European wondertales. But these beliefs were less dominant in the French culture area than in Celtic lands.[10] Thus, in many respects Celtic archaism contributed to the absorption of the literature by other European cultures during the period.

On the other hand, not all of the archaic features of Celtic literature promoted the reception of the literature, nor could all archaic features be translated or transposed easily. Geoffrey's originals have not survived, largely perhaps because they were oral, but internal evidence in Geoffrey's own text indicates that his Celtic materials are molded by the generic framework of Latin historiography and Latin epic. In the process of adapting Welsh tales to Medieval Latin text, Geoffrey used classical mythology as the dynamic equivalent for Celtic pagan deities, the Roman rhetorical tradition as a basis of oratory and direct discourse, and Latinate models for the management of battle scenes in the *The History of the Kings of Britain*. Geoffrey also recast the Celtic socio-cultural substratum of his sources into a social, legal, and cultural framework which would be familiar to his audience.[11]

When Geoffrey's texts are compared with surviving Welsh Arthurian materials, it is also clear that he rejected the humor, burlesque, exaggeration, gigantism, and fantasy that characterize both *Culhwch and Olwen* and *Breuddwyd Rhonabwy* (The dream of Rhonabwy), and that are likely to have characterized Welsh Arthurian tradition overall.[12] Moreover, he uses narrative prose rather than the mixture of verse and prose which may have characterized his Welsh sources. Some of the archaism of Geoffrey's Celtic originals was, thus, disruptive to the transfer of the material and could not be transferred directly. Moreover, at a period when Francophone culture was turning away from a warrior ethos to a new courtly ethic, the archaic heroic ethic found in Welsh Arthurian literature would not have been well received. A simple translation of this material was thus impossible. Part of Geoffrey's genius was to have been able to adapt untranslatable material to forms that could be received by his readers and his patrons. His success is attested not only by the rewards he received in his lifetime but also by the number of extant manuscripts of *The History of the Kings of Britain* and the number of its translations into the vernacular languages of Europe (Loomis 88–89).

Similar features are apparent in the textual configuration of the *lais*. As already noted, the *lais* reflect an interest in Celtic concepts of the otherworld, yet it is significant that most of the stories told by Marie de France use supernatural phenomena—like the motif of the bird skin or the motif of the werewolf—that are pan-European. The exotic otherworld of the Celts is absorbed in limited ways; it provides ambiance in these stories more than concrete motifs or plot sequences. The Celtic otherworldly ambiance is filled out with motifs already familiar to a Francophone audience.

In general, material from one culture is taken up most easily by another when there are cognates or correlates in the receptor system; when there are not, the source material is usually processed in some way to conform to the receptor context. Such bounds on the reception of the exotic qualities of Celtic literature underlie the medieval French reception and refraction of Celtic literature. Alterity is in dynamic tension with familiarity. Moreover, it is clear that Celtic material is used as a means of projecting the self and remaking the self for Francophone audiences. Arthur is interesting to European literature neither because he is a Celtic tribal prince nor because he instantiates the Celtic ideal of Roman emperor—his two chief roles in Brythonic literature; in European refractions he becomes both king and feudal lord, assuming the social roles of greatest interest to the audience. The exoticism of Celtic literature is socially useful in Francophone culture only if it can be used to reflect viable alternatives for the society. Alterity serves as a means here for projection of the self and hence can be admitted only insofar as it remains within bounds that are acceptable for the self. These limitations on alterity affecting the uptake of Celtic Arthurian material into French literature in the Middle Ages also condition response to the formal aspects of the literature; as noted above, both the generic shape and the tonality of Welsh hero tale, as well as various motifs and tale types, are modified and processed in transmission across cultures.

Similar configurations in the use of early Irish material by the Anglo-Irish literary revival can be charted, and again the parameters of alterity can be related to self-image. The political climate for the reception of early Irish literature by the Anglo-Irish revival is more clear than is the ideological environment of the twelfth-century use of Celtic materials largely because the documentation is more extensive. In Ireland at the turn of the century there were ideological reasons for putting the native Irish heritage at the center of the Anglo-Irish literary system when Ireland was struggling for political independence from Britain; it was important in the political struggle, for example, to show that Ireland had a native cultural heritage equal in antiquity and weight to that of England. Such a cultural heritage could be used to justify Ireland's self-governance and could be used to counter British stigmatization of the Irish. Thus, the interest in Irish literature at the time was motivated partly by questions of national image; and it was, accordingly, essential that national image not be jeopardized by either the formal or thematic aspects of early Irish literature in the process of the absorption of the native literary tradition.

Early Irish literature, however, posed formidable problems to an English literary aesthetic and a Victorian system of values. The result was that adaptations and refractions of early Irish literature predominated over translations; retellings such as those of Standish O'Grady and Aubrey DeVere proliferated even as the translation program of the same literature was circumscribed in notable ways. The ideological environment conditioned the translation of the main early Irish epic, *Táin Bó Cúailnge*, for example, with the result that the tale was not translated in its entirety into English until 1976, seventy-one years after a full German translation appeared. Because the *Táin* presented problems of form, tone, and content that threatened to undermine the nationalist image, the *Táin* was partially suppressed in English translation (Tymoczko "Strategies"; "Translating the Old Irish Epic").

When the reception of early Irish literature at the period is assessed with respect to archaism, patterns emerge that are similar to those discussed with reference to the reception of Celtic literature in the twelfth century. In the case of the Anglo-Irish literary revival, the antiquity and archaism of early Irish literature was per se appealing, for reasons already mentioned. In addition, specific archaic features of early Irish literature attracted key writers, not surprisingly some of the same features that appealed to twelfth-century adaptors of Celtic tradition. The ideas of poet-as-seer and poet-as-priest were useful to Irish writers for they lent a sacral quality to a role that had become a butt in English culture, and they presented an alternative to the Catholic hierarchy in the priest-ridden context of Ireland itself. These notions were also useful in general in a modernist context as a means of repositioning poetry in a secularized world. It is thus no wonder that such authors as Yeats, A. E., and Joyce all draw on these archaic concepts regarding poetry and the poet.

Irish belief in the otherworld and Irish tales about the otherworld also appealed to most writers of the Anglo-Irish literary revival, and otherworld imagery is pervasive in the literature of the period. It was particularly congenial to the mystic interests of such writers as Yeats and A. E. It is no accident that three of Yeats's Cuchulain plays foreground encounters with the *síd* (*At the Hawk's Well, The Green Helmet, The Only Jealousy of Emer*), and each of the remaining two plays in the series features elements pertaining to the supernatural as well. Both the elevation of the poet in Celtic culture and the important role of the otherworld in the literature were elements that served the writers in their ideological opposition to the stark rationalism and practicality of Western industrialized life.[13] Still other archaic aspects of early Irish literature also appealed at the period. The rather uncompromising quality of the heroic ethic—the dominant ideology of the Ulster Cycle stories, for example—was put to ideological uses equally by revivalist translators, by other processors of the material such as Padraic Pearse, and by authors such as Yeats. The archaic heroic ethic was used to spur militant Irish nationalism, and literary refractions of the early Irish hero tales played a part in the eventual heroic posturing of the 1916 Easter Rising.[14]

At the same time other aspects of Irish literary archaism were extremely disruptive to the assimilation of early Irish literature by the literary revival. The generic problems caused by the form of the early Irish stories were severe, in particular the framework of prose narrative interspersed with various decorative elements, including verse insets (Tymoczko "Strategies"). Both ideological and generic interference was caused by the humorous and tonal aspects of early Irish literature as well, and the suppression of comic heroic tales in the translation record was at times the result (Tymoczko "Translating the Humour"). Moreover, scatological and sexual material in the early hero tales was unacceptable to Victorian, bourgeois propriety and to Catholic morality; because of the ideological and political purposes to which early Irish literature was put by the Irish literary revival, such cultural norms resulted in interference in the acceptance of these archaic aspects of Irish hero tales.

The twelfth-century period of adapting Celtic literature and the Anglo-Irish literary revival were each initiated by an important adaptor who was able to present the Celtic material in a radically processed form to his contemporaries and successors. The role of Geoffrey of Monmouth in refracting material related to Arthur and Myrddin has been considered; Standish O'Grady stands in much the same role with respect to the Anglo-Irish revival. Both of these writers undertook the task of defining which elements of Celtic literature were significant for their times. Moreover, each was instrumental in eliminating features of Celtic tradition that would have been troublesome to contemporaries among the receptor audience. It is perhaps not surprising to discover that Geoffrey of Monmouth in many ways anticipates the strategies and procedures of Standish O'Grady. O'Grady, like Geoffrey, integrated into his Celtic adaptations aspects of the values, customs, and material culture of his society, the rhetorical tradition of his language, and the generic conventions of his own period. The (in some ways brilliant) processed versions of Celtic literature produced by Geoffrey of Monmouth and Standish O'Grady served in turn as source texts for entire literary movements. Just as Standish O'Grady is father of the Anglo-Irish literary revival, Geoffrey of Monmouth is father of Arthurian romance.

The entire history of the relationship of Celtic literature to mainline Western tradition could be analyzed in terms similar to those I have used. The fascination with Celtic literature and its continual influence on Western literature traced over the past millennium as well as the puzzling absence of Celtic texts from most canons of world literature can be seen as a dialectical result of both the attraction and the disruptive influence of Celtic literary archaism in the reception of Celtic literature. Only in severely processed versions of Celtic literary texts are those countercurrents reconciled.

The case of Celtic literature is instructive regarding the role of alterity in the reception of foreign literary traditions. A source text may be attractive because of its perceived otherliness and perceived exotic qualities. Yet at the same time a receptor culture may project its own image onto a text or a literary movement of a source culture, setting bounds on the degree of alterity tolerated. I have examined these complexities at work in the European assimilation of Celtic literature in the twelfth century and the twentieth century. In the case of the Celtic otherworld this tendency can be characterized neatly. Where early medieval Ireland preserved a vision of pagan paradise, Christian Europe saw Christian heaven; where the Brythonic Celts saw a cosmology, Old French literature presented a world of *avanture*; where early Irish literature had alternate realms, the Anglo-Irish literary revival saw a confirmation of mysticism; where the Celts had a belief system, contemporary writers find fantastic alternate worlds. Receptor cultures often respond to source texts by projecting their own cultural experience into the source, and recognizing in the source only those things that are substantially related to the receptor system. The other becomes a mirror for the self, the encounter with the other a confirmation of the self.

In teaching world literature these considerations are germane. Canon formation is only one factor in the reception of world literature, and expansion of canons may be valuable but not sufficient for an expanded sense of world literature. Literatures are often received by receptor systems or incorporated into canons only after processing and refraction; processing may take a dramatic form such as those discussed here, or it may take as simple a form as excerpting and condensing. The ways in which literatures become processed are in turn affected by alterity—the complex result of an interest in the other in relation to the self. Teachers can expose the workings of these processes for their students, or they can perpetuate them, engaging in the same processes recursively: limiting their assignments to the offerings of a single anthology, choosing shorter selections from already excerpted works, picking readings for their "relevance."

Notes

1. For an introduction to the works of Celtic literature discussed below see the literary histories of Parry and of Williams and Ford. MacCana pro-

vides a good overview of Celtic mythology. Translations of the texts discussed are found in Jones and Jones and in Cross and Slover, unless otherwise noted. Bibliographies and critical apparatus in these sources provide suggestions for further reading.

2. See Dillon and Chadwick Chapter 8 on this period of Irish culture.

3. See Loomis Chapters 8, 11–13, for an overview of these developments.

4. Jackson, *Early Celtic Nature Poetry* and sources cited offer an overview of Irish nature poetry.

5. In the twelfth century Giraldus Cambrensis described the possession of the *awenyddion*, the poets, who answered questions and delivered prophecies in ecstatic trances or dreams (I. Williams 8). As late as the sixteenth century, Irish poets were known to be masters of prophecy, and they were famous for their ability to rhyme rats to death (Robinson 95–97). These archaic functions of poetry and the archaic nature of the poets' role are deeply rooted, going back to a common Indo-European heritage as Calvert Watkins and others have demonstrated. See also Williams and Ford (30–49) and sources cited there for information about the *fili*.

6. Dillon (9 ff.) has argued that this type of narrative may reflect the earliest Indo-European narrative form. It has also been suggested (though by no means is it universally accepted) that Welsh narrative was originally a mixture of prose and verse; for this argument see I. Williams.

7. For the archaism of the comic elements and the place of the comic elements in the overall archaism of Irish tradition see Mercier.

8. MacCana 123–129 gives a brief overview of the topic. The Celtic otherworld is central to many works of Welsh literature, particularly the First and Third Branches of the *Mabinogi*, and the Welsh Arthurian poem *Preiddeu Annwfn* (The spoils of Annwn), where Arthur and his comrades undertake a raid upon the otherworld. The otherworld also plays a large role in Irish literature, being prominent in most of the narrative cycles; and it is Irish literature that offers the most evidence about the nature of the Celtic belief in the otherworld. The nature of the Celtic otherworld is too complex to be considered in detail here, but it should be noted that the otherworld is penetrable by mortals, particularly at the time of the Celtic new year's festival, and visitors from the otherworld are able to reach the world of men as well. Frequently the otherworld is reached by boat, for it is often conceptualized as located on islands to the west. Fragmentary evidence suggests that Celtic belief in the otherworld is old, since there are traces of otherworld motifs in evidence about the Gauls; and belief in the otherworld remained strong in Celtic lands up to modern times.

9. A translation of *Graelant* is found in Mason.

10. The attraction of Celtic literature was not limited to its archaism—in a Francophone context, Arthur, for example, was appealing because he was a nontraditional leader who could be used freely for the projection of the desires and ideals of French culture.

11. E.g., primogeniture replaces Celtic models of inheritance, fosterage is deemphasized, and so forth.

12. One could also argue that the sexual and scatological elements of Welsh narrative would have been equally problematic.

13. It was for such qualities, too, that Matthew Arnold had valorized Celtic literature in his important critical essay, "On the Study of Celtic Literature"; the terms of that valorization in turn influenced the reception of early Irish literature by the Irish literary revival.

14. In "The Man and the Echo" Yeats later pondered about his *Cathleen ni Houlihan*, the play that in 1902 had made a strong nationalist appeal in terms of early Irish heroism, "Did that play of mine send out / Certain men the English shot?" The answer is almost surely yes.

Works Cited

Boswell, C. S. *An Irish Precursor of Dante: A Study on the Vision of Heaven and Hell Ascribed to the Eighth-Century Irish Saint Adamnán, with Translation of the Irish Text.* London: David Nutt, 1908.

Bullock-Davies, Constance. "The Form of the Breton Lay." *Medium Aevum* 42 (1973): 18–31.

Cross, Tom Peete, and Clark Harris Slover, eds. *Ancient Irish Tales.* 1936. New York: Barnes and Noble, 1969.

Dillon, Myles. "The Archaism of Irish Tradition." *Proceedings of the British Academy* 33 (1947): 1–20.

Dillon, Myles, and Nora K. Chadwick. *The Celtic Realms.* London: Weidenfeld and Nicolson, 1967.

Jackson, Kenneth. *The Oldest Irish Tradition: A Window on the Iron Age.* Cambridge: Cambridge University Press, 1964.

———. *Studies in Early Celtic Nature Poetry.* Cambridge: Cambridge University Press, 1935.

Jones, Gwyn, and Thomas Jones, trans. *The Mabinogion.* 1949. New York: Dutton, 1963.

Loomis, Roger Sherman, ed. *Arthurian Literature in the Middle Ages.* Oxford: Oxford University Press, 1959.

MacCana, Proinsias. *Celtic Mythology.* London: Hamlyn, 1970.

Mason, Eugene, trans. "The Lay of Graelent." In *French Medieval Romances from the Lays of Marie de France,* pp. 148–162. 1911. New York: Dutton, 1924.

Mercier, Vivian. *The Irish Comic Tradition.* Oxford: Oxford University Press, 1962.

Nutt, Alfred. *The Fairy Mythology of Shakespeare.* London: David Nutt, 1900.

Parry, Thomas. *A History of Welsh Literature.* Translated by H. Idris Bell. Oxford: Oxford University Press, 1955.

Puhvel, Martin. *"Beowulf* and Celtic Tradition." Waterloo, Ont.: Wilfred Laurier University Press, 1979.

Robinson, Fred Norris. "Satirists and Enchanters in Early Irish Literature." In *Studies in the History of Religions,* edited by David Gordon Lyon and George Foot Moore, pp. 95–130. New York: Macmillan, 1912.

Turville-Petre, G. "On the Poetry of the Scalds and of the Filid." *Ériu* 22 (1971): 1–22.

Tymoczko, Maria. "Strategies for Integrating Irish Epics into European Literature." *Dispositio* 7 (1982): 123–140.

———. "Translating the Humour in Early Irish Hero Tales. A Polysystems Approach." *New Comparison* 3 (1987): 83–103.

———. "Translating the Old Irish Epic *Táin Bó Cúailnge*: Political Aspects." *Pacific Quarterly Moana* 8 (1983): 2.6–21.

———. "Translation as a Force for Literary Revolution in the Twelfth-Century Shift from Epic to Romance." *New Comparison* 1 (1986): 7–27.

Watkins, Calvert. "Indo-European Metrics and Archaic Irish Verse." *Celtica* 6 (1963): 194–249.

Williams, Ifor. *Lectures on Early Welsh Poetry*. Dublin: Dublin Institute for Advanced Studies, 1944.

Williams, J. E. Caerwyn, and Patrick K. Ford. *The Irish Literary Tradition*. Cardiff: University of Wales Press, 1992.

6. Love and Country: Allegorical Romance in Latin America

Doris Sommer

In Latin America, as elsewhere, the project of building modern nations went hand in hand with another productive engagement. Simultaneous with political desiderata for free republics were other, apparently more intimate desires to establish modern families founded on love. And while the political programs assumed their own legitimacy because they could set conditions for "natural" unfettered economic and social intercourse, bourgeois family life achieved unprecedented importance as the model of republican virtue. The significance of historical romances, published throughout the nineteenth century, is more than merely to provide material for a retrospective view from which to read a past world of politics through fictional texts. Romances were significantly programmatic in their own time; they provided contemporary blueprints for modernity, drafted by nation builders for the select citizenry who could read them. Historical fiction supplied sentimental training for appropriate desires, desires for domestic consolidations at the level of the nation and the household. Some of the historical romances published in Latin America from the middle to the end of the nineteenth century are stunning examples of the genre, familiar to readers of European literature through Walter Scott and Alessandro Manzoni. In almost every Latin American country, a particular romance has become the "national novel." It is a term that refers not so much to their market popularity, although to be sure many were immediately popular, but to the fact that they were officially institutionalized as required reading, a stable of civic education, in the newly (re)constituted states. They desperately needed to legitimate themselves after years of parricidal Wars of Independence from Spain followed by the fratricide of recurring civil wars that lasted at least until the conciliatory efforts in which these novels participate. The states, in other words, tacitly accepted the novels as their founding fictions, fictions which produced a desire for (usually bourgeois and liberal) states from the apparently natural sentimental love that characterizes romance. By romance I mean a cross between our contemporary use of the word as a love story and a nineteenth-century use that distinguished romance as more boldly allegorical than the novel.[1] Latin American romances are almost inevitably stories of star-crossed lovers who represent particular regions, races, parties, economic interests, and the like. Their passion for conjugal and sexual union spills over to a sentimental readership in a move that apparently hopes to win partisan minds along with hearts. I will be suggesting that romantic passion provided a rhetoric for the hegemonic political project, in Gramsci's sense of subduing the antagonist through "love" rather than coercion.[2] This intimacy between the novel and hegemony, and more generally between the discourses of sexuality and nationalism, is a configuration that allows us to reconsider what allegory means in terms of these novels and so to re-read Latin American novels, both the nineteenth century canon and the new novels that tried so hard to bury that canon. If allusions to European novels suggest that this configuration is hardly foreign to them, it may be an indication of what there is to learn by reading Europe from the margins. The programmatic brand of Latin American novels seemed obsolete for the new Latin American novelists of the 1960s and 1970s and for many of their readers. But the continuing appeal of national romance for the literary "Boom" (dominated by García Márquez, Fuentes, Cortázar, and Vargas Llosa) can be measured by the obsessive efforts of the new novelists to free themselves of this positivist tradition. The Boom's parodies of the romance, its fine ironies and playfulness, can be read as a rejection of developmentalist assumptions and a capitulation to the apparent chaos of Latin American history. It is a giddiness that comes from reaching a premature end of history and finding that the word *end* ceases to be synonymous with purpose. Instead it is a looking back without being able to distinguish any process to the movement. Since Fuentes's essay *The New Latin American Novel*, readers of Latin American criticism have been accustomed to thinking of these revisions of history as describing circles in which original tragedies repeat themselves as farce. But the image I prefer is one that Mario Vargas Llosa builds up to in *Aunt Julia and the Scriptwriter*: an earthquake that levels the most baroque architectural and literary construction imaginable. The construction helplessly confuses Vargas Llosa's autobiographical romance with the scriptwriter's stereotypic, everescalating, and mutually invading soap operas until it is impossible to distinguish one story, character, or moral from the others, until the poor scriptwriter cracks under the once multiple but now cumulative and mangled project that falls on his, their, our, heads.

For those who survived the Boom, it evidently could not have been the end of history. Time passes and pendulums swing. Even some writers who had written circles around history in the sixties and seventies began to experiment with new versions of more traditional forms.[3] This is also true of film, as Fredric Jameson shows by measuring the "enfeebled" post-modern history of glossy nostalgia films in America against the historically dense Latin American cinema he calls "magic realist."[4] The return of a repressed historical tradition in Latin American narrative may make us wonder why the Boom's playfully pessimistic terms were largely accepted as literarily mature, which is perhaps to say consistent with the First World's taste for the post-modern. The echoes of (self-) congratulation, the almost narcissistic pleasure of having one's ideal notions of literature mirrored back, should make us ask what had eluded readers of the fictions that the Boom deliberately left behind. The question, moreover, forces itself on Latin Americanists now that history is back in style. This post-Boom period of the 1980s may therefore make it easier to understand and to *feel* the passionately political quality of Latin America's earlier great novels.

The attraction is practically visceral. It owes, I believe, to a feature that I hinted at previously, although until now it has evidently gone unremarked: the erotic and romantic rhetoric that organizes the apparently historical novels. This language of love, specifically of productive sexuality at home, is remarkably coherent despite the programmatic differences among the nation-building novels. Through what we may call an erotics of politics, various and competing social ideals are all ostensibly grounded in the "natural" romance that legitimates the nation-family through love. This natural and familial grounding provides a model for apparently nonviolent national consolidation during periods of internecine conflict. To paraphrase another foundational text, after the creation of the new nations, the domestic romance is an exhortation to be fruitful and multiply.

By assuming a certain kind of translatability between love stories and national conciliation, writers and readers have in fact been assuming what amounts to an "allegorical" relationship between personal and political narratives, a relationship that my reading is bound to repeat. I call this relationship allegorical because I find no other term to describe how one apparently autonomous discourse consistently represents the other and invites a double reading of narrative events. Lovers represent traditionally antagonistic sectors, while their parents or rivals are often the political obstacles that love should, and sometimes does, overcome. The title heroine of *Amalia* (José Mármol, 1855) is more than a particular heroine. She is also her native interior province of Tucumán, as her lover, Eduardo, is the commercial port of Buenos Aires. And throughout the book their courtship is the possible alliance which would found a new liberal Argentina. The romance between Mr. Buenos Aires and Ms. Tucumán takes very little space in this almost six hundred-page novel. But it does occupy the center of the book. And it is precisely at the center in Buenos Aires, somewhat decentered in Amalia's suburban house, that they could have hoped to make their love last. The bulk of the novel is a wonderfully unorthodox jumble of intrigues, drawing room dialogues, detailed descriptions of interiors and clothing worthy of the "fashion" journals that opposition intellectuals used as a screen (in both senses—as Lefebvre says—of hiding and showing), historical documents, and character studies of historically identifiable agents. All this is loosely coordinated by a contest of strategy against the agents of dictator Rosas. The tension builds toward an unbearable pitch that irresistibly quickens the pulse. Or is the throbbing a function of the love song that Mármol has been playing in harmony with the life-and-death theme? In fact we want much more than survival for the heroes. We want them to survive because we increasingly desire their union. Similarly, the hero of *Martín Rivas* (Alberto Blest Gana, 1862) is Chile's northern mining interests, determined to convince Santiago's banking families (Leonor) that their characteristic disdain for the "radical" mining bourgeoisie has been less pleasant and profitable than fiscal cooperation would be. The provincial secretary who had left the mines falls in love with the banker's daughter, and finally wins her through proofs of prudence and ingenuity. Everything ends well in the main plot, just as everything had come out all right for Chile's ruling elite in the political struggles of the preceding decade. In this bourgeois revision of Stendhal's *The Red and the Black*, personal heroism is reasonable, not sacrificial; it is also practically indistinguishable from public virtue.

The conciliation that Brazil's national novel provided crossed racial rather than regional lines. But to do so, José de Alencar had to whiten and customize Brazil's dark population, displacing the masses of blacks and mulattoes for noble, indigenous Indians. A native prince subjects himself to the service of a conqueror's daughter and then saves her from the father's ambushed fort. The survivors then melt into one another's eyes and arms. The title hero of *The Guaraní* (1857) is the entire redeemable dark-skinned population, enlightened and sentimental enough to submit to his adored white mistress, just as the Dominican national hero (thanks to Manuel de Jesús Galván's 1882 *Enriquillo*) woos his half Spanish bride and finally submits to the conciliatory paternalism of Spain's empire. As a rhetorical solution to the crises in these novels/countries, miscegenation (an unfortunate translation for *mestizaje*, or blending, which is practically a slogan for many projects of national consolidation) is often the figure for pacification of the "primitive" or "barbarous" races, so that the productive alliances announced by the term are usually between sectors of the national elite. This is true also for *Cumandá* (Juan León Mera, Ecuador, 1887) and *Tabaré* (Juan Zorrilla de San Martín, Uruguay, 1888). Other novels recognize that elite alliances need a broad, multicolored base. Failure to bring the racial (love) affairs to a happy ending accounts for the tragedies of *Sab* (Gertrudis Gómez de Avellaneda, Cuba, 1841), *Cecilia Valdés* (Cirilo Villaverde, Cuba, 1882), *María* (Jorge Isaacs, Colombia, 1867, where the originally Jewish heroine is a figure both for the exclusive plantocracy *and* the inassimilable blacks), and *Birds without a Nest* (Clorinda Matto de Turner, Peru, 1889, in which the mestiza heroine and her white lover cannot marry because a lecherous priest had fathered them both). Nevertheless, *El Zarco* (Manuel Altamirano, Mexico, 1901) marries the mestiza to her Indian hero and celebrates the indigenous leadership that seemed possible since the Indian Benito Juárez's presidency.

From these brief references it should be clear that if I shuttle back and forth from reading romantic intrigues to considering political designs, it is because everyone else was doing the same. Fredric Jameson recently joined this readership, or its putative descendants, when he considered the possible charms of contemporary "third-world literature," charms that the first-world reader apparently keeps missing. "All third-world texts are necessarily, I want to argue, allegorical, and in a very specific way: they are to be read as what I will call *national allegories*."[5] We will miss the interest of third-world literature, Jameson says, by missing the allegory, "a form long discredited in the west and the specific target of the Romantic revolution of Wordsworth and Coleridge, yet a linguistic structure which also seems to be experiencing a remarkable reawakening of interest in contemporary literary theory" ("Third-World Literature" 73). With this gesture, Jameson also joined a number of critics who bemoan allegory's fall from favor and who individually attempt to redeem and appropriate the term, as if there were a "repressive hypothesis" about allegory that ensures it as the topic of our critical discourse.[6] If we would but learn how, Jameson exhorts us, we could get beyond the rather unremarkable surface narrative to "an unveiling or deconcealment of the nightmarish reality of things, a stripping away of our conventional illusions or rationalizations about daily life" ("Third-World Literature" 70). This reading lesson is a gratifying acknowledgment for some of us and a welcome reminder for others about the way many people still read and write, so that it will not do to simply dismiss the relationship between nation and allegory.[7] But Jameson both affirms too much by it (since clearly some "third-world" texts are not "national allegories") and too little (since "national allegories" are still written in the first-world, by Pynchon and Grass, among others). I also wonder if Jameson's assumption that these allegories "reveal" truth in an apparently transparent way, rather than construct it with all the epistemological messiness that using language implies, doesn't already prepare him to distinguish too clearly between third- and first-world literatures. Even he strains at the borders by including Dostoyevsky with Proust and Joyce as a purveyor of first-world literary satisfactions.

In any case, the texts that concern me here date from a period before that vexed geo-literary breakdown, before Jameson's guilt-ridden worry over readerly disappointments with "underdeveloped" literature.[8] When Latin America's national novels were being written, there were no first and third worlds, but only an old world that was producing model texts and a new world where those texts were grist for the nation-making mill. Perhaps this choice of novels accounts for my admittedly unorthodox but not wholly original appropriation of the term *allegory*. I take it to mean a dialectical structure in which one page of the narrative is a trace of the other, in fact where each helps to write the other. A more standard interpretation describes allegory as a narrative with two parallel levels of signification. These are temporally differentiated, with one revealing or "repeating" the anterior level of meaning (either trying desperately to become the other or looking on from a meta-narrative distance at the futility of any desire for stable meaning). Jameson's sense that the personal level reveals the priority of the political seems safely within this interpretation. Nevertheless, he observes that the static structure could be "set in motion and complexified were we willing to entertain the more alarming notion that such equivalences are themselves in constant change and transformation at each perpetual present of the text" (73). Had Jameson wanted to trace the change from one moment to the next, he might well have taken Walter Benjamin's lead in identifying allegory as the vehicle for time and dialectics. My working definition tries to take that lead and to define the allegory in Latin America's national novels as a narrative in which erotics is coterminous with politics in an interlocking, rather than parallel, relationship.[9] The combination of allegory and dialectic will no doubt be oxymoronic for readers who begin with standard definitions, but it was the basis for Benjamin's effort to salvage allegory for historical narrative, and probably to salvage historicity itself from the late Romantic love of immediacy so dear to Nazi culture.

Benjamin's essay on "Allegory and Trauerspiel," in *The Origin of German Tragic Drama* (1928), is a polemic against the Romantic critics who preferred symbol over allegory. This was the same as preferring a "resplendent but ultimately non-committal knowledge of an absolute" over the consciousness that language, like allegory, functions in time as a system of conventions (159–160). The self-alienation of allegory was then seen as a defect, not as a virtue, while symbol was celebrated as the more organic, less artificial, figure that worked by an apparently synecdochal extension of the referent itself. By sacrificing the distance between sign and referent, which allegory respectfully acknowledges, symbols resist critical thinking and invite responses more akin to awe and ecstasy than to philosophical irony. Allegory works through narrative duration, but symbol is felt like an epiphany.

Benjamin was apparently impatient with the Romantics' philosophical laziness. With the symbol they had short-circuited the apotheosis of the beautiful, even sacred, individual. "In contrast the baroque apotheosis is a dialectical one," because its subject could not stop at the individual but had to include a politico-religious dimension (160). This speculative counterpart to the symbol Benjamin calls allegory. It was where the undervalued dialectic survived as the drab backdrop for symbols. "That worldly, historical breadth," which identifies allegory as a figure of narrative duration, is "dialectical in character" (166). So instead of remapping the contour that the Romantics drew between the figures, Benjamin reassigns values to the allegorical constant and to the symbolic flash.

His prime example of the allegorical dialectic is the relationship between human history and nature, which was of course the Romantics' favorite instance of symbolic correspondences. But Benjamin takes care to point out a strategic difference between the figures: "Whereas in the symbol destruction is idealized and the transfigured face of nature is fleetingly revealed in the light of redemption, in allegory the observer is confronted with the *facies hippocratica* of history as a petrified, primordial landscape." In one, nature is a hint of eternity; in the other it is a record of decay. In one, nature seems independent of culture; in the other nature and human history mark one another (167). And the dialectic is what distinguishes modern secular allegory, initiated with baroque literature, from the medieval variety in which nature is the immutable background for the history it contains (171). Yet Benjamin evidently had difficulty maintaining the distinction by 1938 when he wrote notes for an essay on "Baudelaire as Allegorist." Benjamin identified the poet as a straggler of the seventeenth-century "allegorical way of thinking"; but he explicitly adds that Baudelaire had excluded dialectics from this notion of history.[10] Despite Baudelaire's rage against the system of commodity production, his allegory was a record of decay as strangely alienated from process as were the (other) commodities produced.[11]

Benjamin's distinction between medieval and baroque allegories may therefore have seemed negligible to Paul de Man, or he may have found the respect for dialectics to be embarrassingly naive. In either case, de Man maintains what amounts to an agnostic reading of the medieval, theological version. If I pause to consider de Man's notion of allegory (which is not directly relevant to my own appropriation of the term), it is to clear some space, because his version has become so general as to practically cancel Benjamin's more promising dialectical model.[12] In its strictly parallel structure de Man's allegory is surprisingly conventional; and in its agnostic and static "pseudo-knowledge" it produces a mirror image of Romanticism's omniscient symbol, ironically reproducing the same enchantment of timelessness. But for this post-Romantic to reach stasis, he has to detour around his own glosses on Benjamin's laconic (or inconsistent) meaning for allegory, glosses that we can read as new leads.

Years after publication of Benjamin's *Trauerspiel* book, de Man would begin "The Rhetoric of Temporality" (1969) by citing Benjamin in a way that seemed to revive his critique of the Romantics.[13] But Benjamin had insisted on distinguishing between allegory and symbol through the concept of time, the Romantics' real contribution to philosophy (*Trauerspiel* 166), while de Man cannibalizes unstable symbols into the fissured structure of allegory in which time is revealed as the Romantics' most ingenious fiction (*Blindness* 204), the fragile construct upon which the nervous habit of dialectical thinking is bound to fail. And the failure, the incommensurability of the temporal and the essential levels, is what he calls allegory. De Man in fact declares his polemic against Benjamin from the very title of his essay, which makes temporality a function of rhetoric. The battle cry is time, but the stakes are the dialectic. For de Man allegory is where the dialectical buck stops passing; it achieves a kind of static wisdom that knows nothing for sure. Allegory may pretend to reveal a stable meaning, but it does so with a peculiar kind of Christian "bad faith," hoping to fail and thereby to achieve the enlightenment of self-conscious ignorance. This is the gist of "Pascal's Allegory of Persuasion" ("Pascal's Allegory" 23). Rousseau's *Julie* provides de Man with a more secular version of allegory, a type of double vision akin to irony in which one level throws doubt on the validity of the other ("Allegory: [Julie]" 205). Those who try to read "individual passions such as love" in *Julie* as figures for "the collective and social dimensions of the state" are embarrassed, or should be in de Man's judgment, because "the dialectics of love and of politics are finally superseded by a religious experience that is no longer dialectical in any sense and simply obliterates the entire experience that precedes it" (192).

Whether de Man interprets allegory as the highroad for wise fools or the intersection where skeptics can waver, he privileges the term because it cannot arrive at the exhaustive translations of meaning that others thought they saw along the way. Yet curiously for one so determined to dissolve the illusion of temporality, de Man insists on the temporal (and ontological) priority of one level of allegory "repeated" in the other, as if we must all assume the possibility of a stable knowledge that we know to be impossible (*Blindness* 207). And just as curiously, Benjamin never manages to make temporality count for anything constructive. His dialectic goes only downward and backward into an infinite regression in which "history does not assume the form of the process of an eternal life so much as that of irresistible decay . . . Allegories are, in the realm of thoughts, what ruins are in the realm of things" (*Trauerspiel*, 177–178). Irresistible, too, would be the corollary tragic sense of life for those of us who tend to suffer more from allegorical double vision than from symbolic ex(im)plosions. But before we are overcome by comforting pessimism, we should keep in mind that it depends on Benjamin's backsliding into a theological definition of allegory, namely, that human, historical time is only an opportunity for distance from nature, for decay. In Benjamin's essay, as well as de Man's, allegory is the trajectory of a philosophically felicitous failure, the recurrent waking from an endless dream of absolute presence.

If, however, we can take a lead from Benjamin (and from the dialectical moments in de Man's Pascal and Rousseau) to sustain the idea of mutually constructing terms without dragging ourselves down to reach for true grounding, we may get a sense of how the foundational fictions work. My understanding of their allegorical structure consciously delays the ultimate questions of meaning, because I am more concerned to suggest how these books achieved their persuasive power than to determine whether they had any right to do so. The foundational fictions are philosophically modest, even sloppy. Lacking the rigor that would either keep levels of meaning discrete or show how that was impossible, these novels hypostatize desire as truth and then slide easily from one level of signification to the other. They practice deconstruction of binary oppositions, but they do not stop to speculate self-critically on the slips of meaning. With the exception, perhaps, of *María*, these novels are not trapped in unproductive impasses. They do not actively worry about overstepping "truth" and justice, because they know themselves to be performing and seducing. Their object is to win at love and at politics, not to anchor the narrative in an absolute truth. And they are content to set a dialectical relationship in motion that will construct personal and public discourses "upon each other in a circle without end," as Pascal had put it. With no stable philosophical ground to either violate or lament when it falls apart, foundational novels are precisely those fictions that try to pass for truth and to become the ground of political association.

If the novelists had closely followed a popular model such as Rousseau, they might have worried about what they were doing. Rousseau had fretted over the "referential error" of the word *love*. He sensed that rather than being the cause of desire, love was desire's effect. "Love is a mere illusion: it fashions, so to speak, another Universe for itself; it surrounds itself with objects that do not exist or that have received their being from love alone; and since it states all its feelings by means of images, its language is always figural" (Second Preface). And figure masquerades as reality once "pathos is hypostatized as a blind power . . . , it stabilizes the semantics of the figure by making it 'mean' the pathos of its undoing . . . the figurality of the language of love implies that pathos is itself no longer a figure but a substance" (*Allegories* 198–199). But the novelists who wrote nation-building fictions didn't fret. The possibility that hypostatized passion would be taken for empirical reality was hardly a "danger" at all but precisely their opportunity to construct a legitimating national culture. Whereas Rousseau's heroine counterpoises passion with piety in a way that must have seemed too classical and anachronistic to Latin American writers from the middle of the nineteenth century on, they were making a virtue of love. For Rousseau erotic passion is pathological (*Allegories* 209); for them it was the cure to the pathology of social sterility.

Despite their almost sycophantic admiration of French and English novelists, the Latin Americans dared to improve on, or to correct, the tragic, extramarital, and unproductive love affairs of the masters. Argentina's then future general and president Bartolomé Mitre wrote *Soledad* in 1845, a novel prefaced with a manifesto for producing national history as/in fiction. His own contribution is named after the young heroine who spends her time reading Rousseau's *Julie* (the scene of reading European fiction is a stock element in the Latin American genre) to avoid contact with her aged unpleasant husband. And presumably titillated by the novel, she is also preparing to launch an affair with an unworthy young man. She is saved, though, when her cousin and childhood sweetheart comes home from the War of Independence and stays to marry her, after the repentant old husband blesses the couple and conveniently dies. Julie's impossible and incestuous dream to combine propriety with passion[14] comes true for Soledad. *Martín Rivas*, as I mentioned, also sets the romance right. It rewrites Stendhal's *The Red and the Black* by having the provincial secretary, Martín, actually marry his boss's daughter, Leonor. I should note that in the American version, love is sentimental and not romantic in the sense of unrequitable and non-mutual that describes European literary affairs of the same period. René Girard writes that "Romantic passion is . . . exactly the reverse of what it pretends to be. It is not abandonment to the Other but an implacable war waged by two rival vanities" (108). When, for example, Stendhal's Mathilde de la Mole finally admits her passion for Julien, when she considers herself his slave, the struggle for recognition between them ends and his passion cools. Before this scene he had temporarily made her indifferent by revealing his love. This kind of erotic power play is decidedly un-American. Leonor's adorably foppish brother gets the moral of the corrected story right when he quips, "The French . . . say: l'amour fait rage et l'argent fait mariage; but here love makes both: rage et mariage" (Blest Gana 249).

This "improvement" does not mean that the national novels represent any literary advance over *Julie*; on the contrary, they are far more conventional. The genre has all "the stock characters in a situation of sentimental tragedy, persecuted by the social inequities of wealth and class and by the caprices of a tyrannical father" that have been carelessly identified in *Julie*. They are closer in spirit to what de Man says about "*Werther* or the Mignon chapter in *Wilhelm Meister* or *Sylvie*," than to *La Nouvelle Héloïse*, which "would be a very different (and a much shorter) text . . . if the narrative had been allowed to stabilize" (*Allegories* 215). More predictable, and understandably less challenging to read for de Man, these novels set up a dialectic between love and the state—as does *Julie* in the first part—but never stop, as Julie does, to turn around (in the

Augustinian sense of converting; Burke 51) and look back. They look relentlessly forward, and so do not draw desire into the infinite regress of loss and nostalgia that seems inevitable in allegory (Fineman in Greenblatt 46). Instead, they set desire into a spiral or zigzagging motion inside a double narrative structure that keeps projecting the narrative into the future. Rather than rue their artificiality, I read these novels as celebrating their own handiwork as revolutionary departures. There is no crisis associated with the loss/ castration that triggers the telling. Instead, the loss opens a space because it is the father who has been castrated, not the hero of the piece. I am suggesting that some allegories, such as the ones considered here, may have no preexisting and eternal level of referentiality, but—like Nietzsche's point about the fiction of empirical moorings—make themselves up, all the while attempting to produce an illusion of stability.

Calling these novels *romances* is hardly meant to understate their public function. In the United States, at least, this label has traditionally underscored the ethico-political character of our most celebrated narrative. And given the erotic coding for political factors in Latin American romance, there is no need here to distinguish between epic and romance, even in our contemporary meaning as love story, between nation-building and refined sensibility. In Spanish America the two are one, Walter Scott and Chateaubriand in the same potboilers, *pace* Georg Lukács. In *The Historical Novel* (1937; 70), Lukács set Scott apart from Chateaubriand by an unbreachable esthetic and political distance. During the Popular Front, Lukács was reducing his own 1915 distinction between epic and novel[15] in order to defend the novel's construction of social coherence as no less binding than the epic. Novels, he now maintained, could be just as objective and historical. And Scott came closest to the "great historical objectivity of the true epic writer" (34) who respects and even celebrates historical necessity (58) as progress. Chateaubriand, by contrast, "chopped and changed his material at will" (290), "tr(ying) hard to revise classical history in order to depreciate historically the old revolutionary ideal of the Jacobin and Napoleonic period" (27). Like other sentimentalists, he was writing what we now call *romance* when, Lukács implies, he should have been writing novels. Scott looks ahead; Chateaubriand looks back; Scott's heroes are average participants in historical change; Chateaubriand's are uniquely sensitive victims of history. How could the two possibly be reconciled?

The possibility seems even more remote when we remember that Anglo-American criticism traditionally opposed novel to romance in terms that now appear to be inverted. Novel was the domestic genre of surface detail and intricate personal relationships, while romance was the genre of boldly symbolic events. The tradition probably originated with Dr. Johnson's definition of romance as "a military fable of the middle ages; a tale of wild adventures in love and chivalry." The novel, on the other hand, was "a smooth tale, generally of love." But Walter Scott adjusted Johnson's definitions in his own article on romance (1823) for the Encyclopaedia Britannica, stressing the novel's "ordinary train of human events (in) the modern state of society." That is to say, or imply, that it is a lesser genre, fit more for lady writers and readers than for robust men. Scott claims, and is largely granted, significance as a historian because he is a "romancer," concerned not only with the "marvelous and uncommon" but also with the extra-personal and social dimensions of a collective past.

In the United States writers like Hawthorne and his admirer Melville picked up this distinction and insisted they were writing romance as opposed to novels because of their dedication to America's mission. In his preface to *The House of Seven Gables* (1851), Hawthorne wrote that "when a writer calls his work a Romance, it need hardly be observed that he wishes to claim a certain latitude, both as to its fashion and material, which he would not have felt himself entitled to assume, had he professed to be writing a Novel" (Chase 18).[16] Undoubtedly, Hawthorne was hereby distinguishing his ambitious and broadly social projects from those sentimental novels of the "female scribblers." And Perry Miller was convinced in retrospect that American romances were precisely not novels because they were not love stories. "[T]he true burden of Romance in America, . . . was not at all the love story. What all of them were basically concerned with was the continent, the heritage of America, the wilderness" (252). The distinction, though, misses one of the most salient points of the allegory to which Miller refers; the wilderness was woman, the object of man's desire, and thus the source of his guilt as a conqueror. Cooper, at least, suggested the connection between the public good and private desire when he boasted that the distinguishing characteristic of romance was that it aimed to deal poetic justice all around and thus achieve a higher truth than any available from chronicles, where too many heroes marry the wrong girls (Miller 250).[17] North American critics have also noticed that the apparently male romance and female novels keep very close company.[18] For Meyra Jehlin, in fact, any distinction would be moot, since all U.S. fiction of the nineteenth century was some variety of romance.[19]

But even Lukács, who in the service of the Popular Front[20] theo-
rized the opposition between "heroic" narratives of historical events
and romantic tales of lachrymose longing, showed, despite himself,
how the genres can combine in practice to produce the very same
conventional genre of European political romance that de Man
counterpoises with *Julie*. Lukács admitted that novels of "underdeveloped" European countries could portray neither Scott's middle-
of-the-road modernity nor his celebration of past events. It was possible for Scott, of course, only because England had already achieved
its "progressive" bourgeois formation. And the happy outcome of
her history produced an entire class of heroes; that is to say, win-
ners. But for countries such as Germany or Italy, where the unifica-
tion of a modern bourgeois state was frustrated, so too was the project of writing celebratory Scott-like novels. As in Latin America,
European foundational fictions sought to overcome political and historical fragmentation through love. Lukács points to the strategy
but doesn't call attention to the recurring allegorical pattern or to
its relevance, even for Scott. "Thus, while Manzoni's immediate
story [in *The Betrothed*] is simply a concrete episode taken from
Italian popular life—the love, separation, and reunion of a young
peasant boy and girl—his presentation transforms it into a general
tragedy of the Italian people in a state of national degradation and
fragmentation [into] *the* tragedy of the Italian people as a whole"
(70). "Gogol, too, concentrates the downfall of the Cossacks in the
romance of *Taras Bulba*. It is the tragedy of one of the principal
hero's sons who, in love with a Polish aristocratic girl, becomes a
traitor to his people." (74)

Latin American "historical novelists" found themselves in a similarly pre-modern situation, although, to follow Benedict Anderson,
I should add that they did so before many Europeans, and became
models in prose as well as politics.[21] Therefore, Latin American histories during the foundational period tend to be more projective than
retrospective, more erotic than data driven. Their genre is romance,
which is itself a marriage of historical allegory and sentimentality.
The capital marries, and even moves close to the provinces in
Amalia, still only an ideal for some Argentines; Tupis and Portuguese parent a nation of tropicalized gentlemen in Brazil's national
dreamwork; and autochthonous husbands succeed imported bandits
in Mexico's prescription for happiness. Viewed from the margins,
then, Scott's "middle-brow" exemplarity becomes questionable.
Still, Scott was a model of what a fully integrated national culture
could be, just as the extraordinary heroes of Latin American romance were. But to work for his willing heirs in many cases Scott

first had to wed Chateaubriand, or Rousseau, or Stendhal. It was their passionate (and especially in Chateaubriand's exoticizing case) sentimentalism that helped to *supplement* the histories which lacked usable, that is, constructive and flattering, data.

Romance, then, is not only the generic brand of nineteenth century American fiction, as Jehlin points out. In Latin America, at least, it is also the supplement or the correction for a history of nonproductive events. Otherwise, why would the familiar form seem adequate to the task of nation building? Why else would Latin American political and military leaders cultivate and promote the romantic novel as perhaps the most significant discursive medium for national development? Evidently, they assumed an analogy, commonplace in political philosophy, between the nation and the family, and by extension, between ideal history and (domestic) romance. To marry national destiny to personal sentimentalism was precisely what made these books peculiarly American. On the one hand, little seemed to determine the direction of historical discourse from the middle to the end of the nineteenth century, since, as the Venezuelan statesman and cultural arbiter Andrés Bello seemed to complain, basic data were lacking (48–49). But on the other hand, and this is my point, not just any narrative filler would have done. The glee I surmise in Bello's exhortation to supplement history surely owes to the opportunity he perceives for projecting an ideal history through that most basic and satisfying genre of romance. What better way to argue the polemic for civilization than to make desire the relentless motivation for a literary/political project? To read on, to suffer and tremble with the lovers' drive toward marriage, family, and prosperity, and then to be either devastated or transported in the end is already to become a partisan.

If I read a double and corresponding structure between personal romance and political desiderata, in which the lovers are also particular classes, regions, or races, it is not, as I said, because any priority of the personal or the political register is assumed. I read each register as the effect of the other's performance, something like the Marquis de Sade's explanation of sexual desire as the effect of another's commotion (although the analogy would certainly have scandalized the Latin American founders).[22] The erotic interest of the novels is heightened by the fact that the lovers are also previously antagonistic sectors; the very prohibitions against their union add excitement to the courtship. And political projects seem transparent and inevitable as a result of the "natural" erotic desire between lovers who need an ideal state in order to be united. In historical accounts, the political characterization of Juan Manuel Rosas, for

example, is still debated. Was he a bloodthirsty and vindictive barbarian who singled out Argentina's intelligentsia for terror and tor-
ture? Or was he a sophisticated defender of Argentine cultural and
economic autonomy, no more bloody than his equally extravagant
opponents who wanted to Europeanize the country as soon as possible? If we "know" from reading *Amalia* that Rosas was an un-
scrupulous dictator, our knowledge is to a considerable degree a political articulation of the erotic frustration we share with Amalia
and Eduardo. And we feel the intensity of their frustration because
we know that their obstacle is the horrible dictator.

What I find ingenious, indeed brilliant, about this novel produc-
tivity is that one libidinal investment ups the ante for the other.
And every obstacle that the lovers encounter heightens more than
their mutual desire to (be a) couple, more than our voyeuristic but
keenly felt passion; it also heightens their/our love for the possible
nation in which the affair could be consummated. The two levels of
desire are different, which allows us to remark on an allegorical
structure; but they are not discrete. Desire weaves between the individual and the public family in a way that shows the terms to be
contiguous, co-extensive as opposed to merely analogous. And the
desire keeps weaving, or simply doubling itself at personal and political levels, because the obstacles it encounters threaten both levels of happiness. These obstacles are almost always a social convention or a political impasse; that is, they are public and interpersonal
rather than some intimate and particular differences between the
lovers. The fact that the lovers almost never quarrel probably has
something to do with the vestigial epic character of these romances;
its heroes and heroines appear on the scene full blown, immutable,
and easily distinguished from the masses of servants and supporters.
When this bourgeois genre was imported by Latin Americans it suf-
fered some sea changes, along with its companion ideology of liberal
democracy (see Schwarz). The Latin American elite wanted to mod-
ernize and to prosper, yes; but it wanted at the same time to retain
the practically feudal privilege it had inherited from colonial times.
Logically, a functioning aristocracy by any name might prefer to represent itself in immutably ideal terms. Therefore, its heroes need
not be the self-reflexive, naive, and developing protagonists that European theorists expect in the novel.

To mention the "aristocratic" quality of Latin America's bourgeois heroes is meant to reinforce an observation about a particular
narrative lack in their stories. It is the lack of personal antagonism
or intimate arguments between lovers, the stuff that sentimental
romance is apparently made of. The only problems here seem exter-

nal to the couple; yet they can thwart the romance, which of course underlines the desire to see it flourish. So it is not only desire that doubles itself on public and private levels here; it is also the public obstacle that deters (and goads) the erotic and national projects. If Amalia and Eduardo need Argentina's consolidation to consolidate their personal relationship, dictator Rosas is the infuriating (and inspiring) impediment to intimacy. Once the couple confronts the enemy, desire is reinforced, as is the need to overcome the obstacle and to consolidate the nation. That promise of consolidation constitutes another level of desire and underscores the erotic goal, which is also a microcosmic expression of nationhood. This zigzagging movement describes a kind of allegory that works primarily through metonymy rather than metaphor, unlike the standard definition.[23] There is no insistence here on translating from one discourse to another, say from the Good Shepherd in standard Christian allegory to God himself. In these sentimental epics, the romantic couple *is* the nation in microcosm. The lovers' frustrations *are* obstacles to national development, in the same way that requited love already *is* the foundational moment.

One level represents the other and also fuels it, which is to say that both are unstable. The unrequited passion of the love story produces a surplus of energy, just as Rousseau said it would,[24] that is then directed against the political interference between the lovers. And on the other hand, the enormity of the social abuse, the unethical power of the obstacle, invests the love story with an almost sublime sense of transcendent purpose. As the narrative progresses, the pitch of sentiment rises along with the ardor of commitment, so that the din makes it ever more difficult to distinguish between erotic and political fantasies for an ideal ending.

Of course the allegories will appeal rhetorically to some legitimating a priori principle. Being a justification for modern and antiauthoritarian projects, that principle is often Nature, which has been conveniently redefined since the days of Enlightened Independence as interactive rather than hierarchical. If erotic desire seemed to be the natural and therefore eternal grounding for happy and productive marriages (including national families by extension), it was thanks to these redefinitions. Nature was no longer the classical realm of predictable law but the realm of flux, where energy could meet obstacles and turn frustration into excess. It was a world that produced angels and monsters, not clockwork. The allegories will strain at points against these redefinitions. For one thing, the writing elite was loath to give up its hierarchical privilege, and for another, characters may exceed or somehow miss an ideally assigned meaning. But the observation I am making is far more fundamental than any demonstration of the allegory's partial failures. I am simply observing the incredible measure of its success in promoting national projects and constructing an inclusive national identity.

From our historical distance as the heirs of national romances we may be mistaking both romantic love and patriotism as natural givens, when in fact we know them to be constructed, perhaps by the very novels that seem merely to represent them. When we remember this possibility, it seems reasonable to ask whether what may have passed for effects of the greater culture in the novel (i.e., the representation of romantic love or of conciliatory nationalism) may indeed be causes of that culture. After all, there is no historical basis for imagining that romantic love or love of country are constants. If heroes and heroines in mid-nineteenth-century Latin America were passionately desiring one another across traditional barriers that a new state would erase, they were also learning how to desire by reading European novels.[25] The irresistible way that novels constructed sexual desire as the most natural social bond, and the double dealing of the allegorical form that slides from sexuality into politics, helped to marry politics to nature. It constructed imaginary and loving national communities that were horizontal and democratic rather than hierarchical. The novels, in other words, were teaching future republicans to be passionate in a rational and seductively horizontal way.

Notes

1. "Character itself becomes, then, somewhat abstract and ideal, so much so in some romances that it seems to be merely a function of plot. The plot we may expect to be highly colored. Astonishing events may occur, and these are likely to have a symbolic or ideological, rather than a realistic, plausibility. Being less committed to the immediate rendition of reality than the novel, the romance will more freely veer toward mythic, allegorical, and symbolistic forms" (Chase 13).

2. For a succinct definition, see Mouffe (181): "[A] hegemonic class has been able to articulate the interests of the other social groups to its own by means of ideological struggle. This, according to Gramsci, is only possible if this class renounces a strictly corporatist conception . . . also presupposes a certain equilibrium, that is to say that the hegemonic groups will make some sacrifices of a corporate nature."

3. In some cases, the masters of the Boom themselves moved away from the canon. Both Cortázar and Vargas Llosa, for example, abandoned the extravagant formal experimentation of *Rayuela* (Hopscotch) and *La casa verde* (The green house) and drifted toward certain modes of "realism": *El*

libro de Manuel (A manual for Manuel) and *La guerra del fin del mundo* (War of the end of the world). Even García Márquez left behind the radical "marvelous realism" and self-referential écriture of *Cien años de soledad* (One hundred years of solitude) and moved on to the overflowing orality of *El otoño del patriarca* (Autumn of the patriarch). Furthermore, the "dictator novels" which appeared in 1974–1975, García Márquez's *El otoño del patriarca*, Carpentier's *El recurso del método* (Reasons of state), and Roa Bastos's *Yo el supremo* (I the supreme)—Donoso's *Casa de campo* (A house in the country) is later but could be included—recuperate a representational topic which had a certain ascendancy much before the heyday of the Boom (e.g., Miguel Angel Asturias's *El Señor Presidente,* 1946) but only to deconstruct the centralizing power that underlies the concept of dictatorship. See Yúdice and Sommer.

4. The label "magic realism" is evidently borrowed from an earlier period, which Jameson acknowledges by referring to Carpentier's definition (311). That style spills over to García Márquez's prose in *One Hundred Years of Solitude* and also into the recent novel by his compatriot Gustavo Alvarez Gardeazábal, *Condores no entierran todos los días* (1984), the book on which the exemplary "magic realist" film is based. And Jameson is right to sharply distinguish it from post-modern nostalgia films. But it is not the only cinematic style that could offer a contrast with the "historically enfeebled" post-modernism of the industrial West. Another way of pointing out the difference is to say that the subject is not dead in Latin American film and literature. If the Boom problematized the authority and knowledge, it did not kill the subject off. That might be too great a luxury, or merely redundant, for those already marginalized by history. Instead, Latin American narrative is busy constructing multiple selves from the margins of post-modern cynicism.

5. ". . . third-world texts, even those which are seemingly private and invested with a properly libidinal dynamic—necessarily project a political dimension in the form of national allegory: *the story of the private individual destiny is always an allegory of the embattled situation of the public third-world culture and society.* Need I add that it is precisely this very different ratio of the political to the personal which makes such texts alien to us at first approach, and consequently, resistant to our conventional western habits of reading?" (Jameson "On Magic Realism" 69).

6. See Melville, "Notes on the Reemergence of Allegory," for a response to a series of essays published in *October* by Douglas Crimp, Joel Fineman, and Craig Owens.

7. This is what Aijaz Ahmad does in his otherwise stunning response, "Jameson's Rhetoric of Otherness and the 'National Allegory.'" My own earlier work on this relationship, *One Master for Another: Populism as Patriarchal Rhetoric in Dominican Novels,* received Jameson's flattering attention in early draft stages.

8. A "particularly self-defeating" strategy for arguing the importance and interest of third-world literature is "trying to prove that these texts are as 'great' as those of the canon itself . . . This is to attempt dutifully to wish

away all traces of that 'pulp' format which is constitutive of sub-genres, and it invites immediate failure insofar as any passionate reader of Dostoyevsky will know at once, after a few pages, that those kinds of satisfactions are not present. . . . The third-world novel will not offer the satisfactions of Proust or Joyce; what is more damaging, perhaps, is its tendency to remind us of outmoded stages of our own first-world cultural development . . ." ("Third-World Literature" 65). We should ask, I think, whether Dostoyevsky comes from the same place (not the same league) as Proust.

9. For a more developed discussion, see my "Allegory and Dialectics: A Match Made in Romance."

10. "The correspondence between antiquity and the modern is the only constructive conception of history to be found in Baudelaire. It excluded a dialectical conception rather than contained it" (47).

11. "Tearing things out of the context of their usual interrelations—which is quite normal where commodities are being exhibited—is a procedure very characteristic of Baudelaire. It is related to the destruction of the organic interrelations in this allegorical intention" (41). Baudelaire is also likened to medieval clerics throughout where his differences from baroque procedure are noted (48).

12. A visible example is Lloyd Spencer, the translator and commentator of "Central Park," who doesn't mention the question of dialectics. He may simply have overlooked the difference between medieval and baroque allegory, although he refers at several points to Benjamin's work on *Trauerspiel*. More likely, he read Benjamin back from the use de Man would make of him. "Allegories, even those which proclaim the stability and fullness of meaning in the (hierarchised) universe can thus be seen as deconstructing themselves, as revealing the opposite of that which they seek to imply. In the allegorists which he chose to study most closely, this has only become a more conscious and therefore in both senses a more critical process" (63). And Stephen Melville's "Notes on the Reemergence of Allegory" begins with an explicit reference to de Man as the most important figure for the reemergence in literary criticism.

13. (*Blindness* 188–189). He criticizes them for finding allegory to be "dryly rational and dogmatic" and for preferring the almost ineffable "infinity of a totality" available through the symbol. He also complains that the custom of favoring the emotional rush of symbol over the intellectual speculation of allegory has led readers to overlook allegorical structures or to mistake them for something else. Characteristically, however, de Man introduces this opposition to show that the distinction has been drawn too sharply. Symbols may pretend to obliterate time and distance, to *be* what they refer to, but this is the impossible dream of language. They decompose under de Man's stare, and the fault line between language and essence is the same line that identifies allegory's double structure. De Man's "deconstruction" here is a curiously one-way affair. Rather than locating a mutually productive tension between the terms, he subsumes symbol into allegory, perhaps because it is already a schizophrenic, fissured, and undecidable structure. It is the figure of all rhetorical figures for de Man, his shorthand

for describing how language works (as it was for Benjamin, whom de Man does not mention here).

14. See Tony Tanner on Rousseau in his *Adultery in the Novel* (113–178).

15. "The epic gives form to a totality of life that is rounded from within; the novel seeks, by giving form, to uncover and construct the concealed totality of life . . . [T]he search, which is only a way of expressing the subject's recognition that neither objective life nor its relationship to the subject is spontaneously harmonious in itself, supplies an indication of the form-giving intention" (60).

16. Chase uses this distinction to announce his own version of the generic differences, especially as they distinguish the English narrative tradition from the American. He cites, for example, F. R. Leavis's comment that Emily Brontë's *Wuthering Heights* is a sport and adds that it would fit rather well in the bolder American tradition that purposefully neglects to offer coherent resolutions to contradictions (3–4). Chase illustrates through his choices that the great American romances of Cooper, Hawthorne, Melville, and Simms constitute the center of our tradition, whereas Scott is the sole great representative of romance in England. One reason for romance in America is that it accommodates the "Manichaean quality of New England Protestantism" (10–11).

17. And Scott, in his late musings, seemed not to care about the gen(d)eric differences. In 1829, when he reissued the *Waverley* novels under his proper name, Scott made little if any distinction between romance and novel in his "Advertisement," "General Preface," or his "Preface to the Third Edition." The terms seem interchangeable, despite the fact that a distinction had been brewing in England for decades before Scott wrote. Perhaps that critical difference owes to Scott's strategic denial of a penchant for the newer, bourgeois, and sentimental novel. Certainly his stories qualify as love stories despite their historical detail. He, in fact, helped to domesticate romance, to bring the adventurous hero back to earth and back home. And home was Rowena, not Rebecca; it was the legitimate, prescribed family.

18. Leslie Fiedler points out that only a few years before Cooper wrote his great romances, he was training himself as a writer by imitating, not the manly historical romancer Walter Scott, but that English gentlewoman and mistress of the domestic psychological novel, Ms. Jane Austen. Cooper's earliest novel, titled like one of hers, *Persuasion* (1820), was no parody, but a serious attempt to study the problem of marriage; and this "first maker of America's myths" continued to impersonate a female with the pseudonym of Jane Morgan until 1823 (Fiedler 186, 190). In general Fiedler shows how the genres bleed into one another even in their own nineteenth-century terms. The idealizing "new-comic" plot of the historical romance (boy gets, loses, and regains girl) is evidently a love story; while the sentimental tales of seduction, repentance, and female triumph are in America quite as allegorical and morally ideal as the patriotic romances.

19. Myra Jehlin argues that, in the terms of our contemporary criticism,

the difference between romance and novel becomes even more blurred, because today's theories of the novel tend to distinguish it from nineteenth-century American works in general. If novels resist or self-consciously construct a narrative closure, neither the high-minded adventure stories nor the sentimental tales of this hemisphere qualify as examples. Their desire is ultimately contained in the lap of family life. The strict and abstract moral code that organizes American "romances," through often equally abstract characters, makes Billy Budd bless his executioner for defending social stability; it also makes Henry James typically bring his heroines to the point of recognizing their error and choosing to be good and to fit into an established bourgeois society, while Flaubert's Emma Bovary can learn only that she has no good choices. It's not that American heroes expect to win, but that their losing is a martyrdom to the unquestioned values of a status quo. For the novelist Flaubert, the rise of capital was a historical catastrophe; for the romancer James, capital was simply a fact of life, because America offered a way of transcending class and history. Jehlen further suggests that the core of America's stable and transcendent ethics is the bourgeois family which has "inspired the strident masculinity, even the celibacy of its heroes." We can say, in other words, that the domestication, or "bourgeoisification," of romance in the Americas assumes either that the hero is a lover turned husband or that he should be. Whether one fixes on a notion of romance as an erotic quest for stable love or as the quest for freedom that apparently gives up stability, the North American examples finally bring their heroes home or watch them self-destruct.

20. Georgi Dimitroff, probably the main cultural theorist for the Third International of the Communist Party in 1935, defended a similar popular front position. When announced that it was a mistake for communists to abandon national heroes and traditions to the manipulations of fascists, it became legitimate and desirable to address the masses in a familiar rhetoric of soil and blood (nation and family) despite the political ambiguity in the Party's desperate appeal for mass support. And long after World War II, the nationalist/"communist" culture persists, perhaps because that very culture makes alternatives so hard to formulate (Dimitroff 78).

21. About the American states Anderson writes, "For not only were they historically the first such states to emerge, and therefore inevitably provided the first real models of what such states should 'look like' but their numbers and contemporary births offer fruitful ground for comparative enquiry" (49).

22. Leo Bersani describes the " . . . Sadean view of sexual excitement as a shared commotion . . . we do not have sex with others *because* they excite us; excitement is the consequence of sex rather than its motive . . . Sexual excitement must be represented before it can be felt; or, more exactly, it *is* the representation of an alienated commotion" (145). I find it suggestive that this essay appears in a book called *Allegory and Representation*. One reason may be that it deals with only one term, representation; but the more provocative reason for me is that sadism works in a dialectic of mutually constructing subjects, as does allegory.

23. In his review of the scholarship on allegory, Joel Fineman says it works in two possible ways: perpendicularly, in which case metaphor organizes it (like the great chain of being and other visual, hardly narrative, models) and horizontally, organized by metonymy which produces narrative (understood to function within each of the particular levels, discretely). He says, though, that Jakobson sees metaphor as central in either case: "it is always the structure of metaphor that is projected onto the sequence of metonymy, not the other way around, which is why allegory is always a hierarchizing mode, indicative of timeless order, however subversively intended its contents might be . . . an *inherently political and therefore religious* trope, not because it flatters tactfully, but because in deferring to structure it insinuates the power of structure, giving off what we can call the structural effect" (32; my emphasis).

From my vantage point, this seems to be arguing tautologically. Why does the political level necessarily look sacred?

24. I owe this observation to Professor Jean Bethke Elshtain.

25. In *Foundational Fictions* I develop some speculations about the mutual construction of patriotism and sexuality from the end of the eighteenth century on by juxtaposing Michel Foucault's *History of Sexuality* with Benedict Anderson's *Imagined Communities.*

Works Cited

Ahmad, Aijaz. "Jameson's Rhetoric of Otherness and the 'National Allegory.'" *Social Text* 17: 3–25.

Alencar, José Martiniano de. *Iracema, The Honey-Lips: A Legend of Brazil.* Translated by Isabel Burton. 1886. New York: F. Howard Fertig, 1976. Originally published as *Iracema: Lenda do Ceara* (Sao Paulo: Atica, 1984).

Alvarez Gardeazábal, Gustavo. *Condores no entierran todos los días.* Barcelona: Destino, 1972.

Anderson, Benedict. *Imagined Communities: Reflections on the Origin and Spread of Nationalism.* London: Verso, 1983.

Asturias, Miguel Angel. *El Señor Presidente.* Buenos Aires: Losada, 1946.

Bello, Andrés. "Autonomía cultural de América." 1848. In *Conciencia intelectual de América*, edited by Carlos Ripoll, pp. 48–54. New York: Eliseo Torres, 1966.

Benjamin, Walter. "Central Park." Translated by Lloyd Spencer. *New German Critique* 34 (1985): 32–58.

———. *The Origin of German Tragic Drama.* Translated by John Osborne. London: New Left Books, 1977. Originally published as *Ursprung des deutschen Trauerspiels* (Frankfurt: suhrkamp, 1963).

Bersani, Leo. "Representation and Its Discontents." In *Allegory and Representation*, edited by Stephen Greenblatt, pp. 145–162. Baltimore: Johns Hopkins University Press, 1981.

Blest Gana, Alberto. *Martín Rivas.* Translated by Mrs. Charles Whitman.

New York: Alfred Knopf, 1918. Originally published as *Martín Rivas* *(Novela de costumbres político-sociales)*. Prólogo, Notas y Cronología por Jaime Concha (Caracas: Biblioteca Ayacucho, 1977).

Burke, Kenneth. *The Rhetoric of Religion: Studies in Logology*. Boston: Beacon Press, 1961.

Carpentier, Alejio. *Reasons of State*. Translated by Frances Partridge. New York: Knopf, 1976. Originally published as *El recurso del método* (Mexico: Siglo Veintiuno, 1974).

Chase, Richard. *The American Novel and Its Tradition*. 1957. Baltimore: The Johns Hopkins University Press, 1983.

Cortázar, Julio. *A Manual for Manuel*. Translated by Gregory Rabassa. New York: Pantheon, 1978. Originally published as *El libro de Manuel* (Buenos Aires: Sudamericana, 1973).

———. *Hopscotch*. Translated by Gregory Rabassa. New York: New American Library, 1967. Originally published as *Rayuela* (Buenos Aires: Sudamericana, 1966).

Crimp, Douglas. "On the Museum's Ruins." *October* 13 (1980): 41–57.

———. "Pictures." *October* 8 (1979): 75–88.

de Man, Paul. "Allegory: (Julie)." In *Allegories of Reading*, by de Man, pp. 188–220. New Haven, Conn.: Harvard University Press, 1979.

———. *Blindness and Insight: Essays in the Rhetoric of Contemporary Criticism*. Oxford: Oxford University Press, 1971.

———. "Pascal's Allegory of Persuasion." In *Allegory and Representation*, edited by Stephen J. Greenblatt, pp. 1–25. Baltimore, Johns Hopkins University Press, 1981.

———. "The Rhetoric of Temporality." In *Interpretation: Theory and Practice*, edited by Charles S. Singleton, pp. 173–210. Baltimore: Johns Hopkins, 1969.

Dimitroff, Georgi. *The United Front*. San Francisco: Proletarian Publishers, 1975.

Donoso, José. *A House in the Country*. Translated by David Pritchard with Suzanne Jill Levine. New York: Knopf, 1984. Originally published as *Casa de campo* (Barcelona: Seix Barral, 1978).

Fiedler, Leslie A. *Love and Death in the American Novel*. Rev. ed. New York: Stein and Day, 1966.

Fineman, Joel. "The Structure of Allegorical Desire." *October* 12 (1980): 47–66.

———. "The Structure of Allegorical Desire." In *Allegory and Representation*, edited by Stephen J. Greenblatt, pp. 26–60. Baltimore: Johns Hopkins University Press, 1981.

Fuentes, Carlos. *La nueva novela latinoamericana*. Mexico: Joaquín Mortiz, 1969.

Gallegos, Rómulo. *Doña Bárbara*. Translated by Robert Malloy. New York: Peter Smith, 1948. Originally published as *Doña Bárbara* (Santiago de Chile: Ercilla, 1984).

Galván, Manuel de Jesús. *Manuel de Jesus Galvan's Enriquillo: The Cross and the Sword*. Translated by Robert Graves. New York: AMS Press,

1975. Originally published as *Enriquillo: leyenda histórica dominicana: 1503–1538*. Prologo de José Marti (Santo Domingo: Taller, 1976).

García Márquez, Gabriel. *The Autumn of the Patriarch*. Translated by Gregory Rabassa. New York: Harper and Row, 1976. Originally published as *El otoño del patriarca* (Buenos Aires: Sudamericana, 1975).

———. *One Hundred Years of Solitude*. Translated by Gregory Rabassa. New York: Harper and Row, 1970. Originally published as *Cien años de soledad* (Buenos Aires: Sudamericana, 1967).

Girard, René. *Deceit, Desire, and the Novel*. Translated by Yvonne Freccero. Baltimore: Johns Hopkins University Press, 1965.

Gómez de Avellaneda, Gertrudis. *Sab*. Translated by Nina Scott. Austin: University of Texas Press, 1993. Originally published as *Sab* (Paris: Agencia general de librería, 1920).

Isaacs, Jorge. *María, a South American Romance*. Translated by Rollo Ogden. New York: Harper and Brothers, 1890. Originally published in 1867 as *María*. 4th ed. Prologue by Roberto F. Giusti. Buenos Aires: Losada, 1971.

Jameson, Fredric. "On Magic Realism in Film." *Critical Inquiry* 12.2 (1986): 301–325.

———. "Third-World Literature in the Era of Multinational Capitalism." *Social Text* 15 (1986): 65–88.

Jehlen, Myra. "New World Epics: The Novel and the Middle-Class in America." *Salmagundi, a Quarterly of the Humanities and Social Sciences* 36 (1977): 49–68.

Lefebvre, Henri. "Toward a Leftist Cultural Politics: Remarks Occasioned by the Centenary of Marx's Death." Translated by David Reifman. In *Marxism and the Interpretation of Culture*, edited by Cary Nelson and Lawrence Grossberg, pp. 75–88. Urbana and Chicago: University of Illinois Press, 1988.

Lukács, Georg. *The Historical Novel*. Translated by Hannah Mitchell and Stanley Mitchell. Boston: Beacon Press, 1963.

Mármol, José. *Amalia: A Romance of the Argentine*. Translated by Mary Serrano. New York: E. P. Dutton, 1919.

Melville, Stephen. "Notes on the Reemergence of Allegory, the Forgetting of Modernism, the Necessity of Rhetoric, and the Conditions of Publicity in Art and Criticism." *October* 19 (1981): 55–92.

Miller, Perry. *Nature's Nation*. Cambridge, Mass.: Belknap Press, 1958.

Mouffe, Chantal, ed. *Gramsci and Marxist Theory*. London: Routledge and Kegan Paul, 1979.

Owens, Craig. "*Einstein on the Beach*: The Primacy of Metaphor." *October* 4 (1977): 21–32.

———. "The Allegorical Impulse: Toward a Theory of Postmodernism." *October* 12 (1980): 67–86, 13 (1980): 61–80.

Parra, Teresa de la. *Mama Blanca's Souvenirs*. Translated by Harriet de Onís. Revised by Frederick H. Fornoff. Pittsburgh: University of Pittsburgh Press, 1993. Originally published as *Las memorias de Mama Blanca* (Buenos Aires: Universitaria, 1966).

Rivera, José Eustasio. *The Vortex.* Translated by Earle K. James. New York: G. P. Putnam, 1935. Originally published as *La voragine.* Edited and with Intro. by Fernando Curiel. (Mexico: Dirección General de Publicaciones, 1972).

Roa Bastos, Augusto. *I the Supreme.* Translated by Helen Lane. New York: Knopf, 1986. Originally published as *Yo el supremo* (Caracas, Venezuela: Ayacucho, 1986).

Schwarz, Roberto. "Misplaced Ideas: Literature and Society in Late Nineteenth-Century Brazil." *Comparative Civilizations Review* 5 (1979): 33–51.

Scott, Walter. "Essay on Romance." In *Essays on Chivalry, Romance, and the Drama,* pp. 65–108. London: Frederick Warne, 1887.

Sommer, Doris. "Allegory and Dialectics: A Match Made in Romance." *Boundary* 2 18:1 (1991): 60–82.

———. *Foundational Fictions: The National Romances of Latin America.* Berkeley: University of California Press, 1991.

———. *One Master For Another: Populism as Patriarchal Rhetoric in Dominican Novels.* Lanham, Md.: University Presses of America, 1984.

Spencer, Lloyd. "Allegory in the World of the Commodity: The Importance of *Central Park.*" *New German Critique* 34 (1985): 59–77.

Tanner, Tony. "Rousseau's *La Nouvelle Héloise.*" In *Adultery in the Novel: Contract and Transgression,* 113–178. Baltimore: Johns Hopkins University Press, 1979.

Vargas Llosa, Mario. *The Green House.* Translated by Gregory Rabassa. New York: Harper and Row, 1968. Originally published as *La casa verde* (Barcelona: Seix Barral, 1965).

———. *The War of the End of the World.* Translated by Helen Lane. New York: Farrar, Straus, Giroux, 1984. Originally published as *La guerra del fin del mundo* (Barcelona: Seix Barral, 1981).

Villaverde, Cirilo. *Cecilia Valdés or Angel's Hill: A Novel of Cuban Customs.* Translated by Sydney G. Gest. New York: Vantage, 1962. Originally published as *Cecilia Valdés o La Loma del Angel: novela de costumbres cubanos.* Edited by Olga Blondet Tudisco and Antonio Tudisco. (New York: Las Américas, 1964).

Yúdice, George, and Doris Sommer. "Latin American Literature from the 'Boom' On." In *Post-Modern Literature,* 189–214. Edited by Larry McCaffery. Westport, Conn.: Greenwood, 1987.

7. Reading Genres across Cultures: The Example of Autobiography

Janet A. Walker

The study of literary genres has long been one of the major approaches to literature of comparative literary study in the West. Western critics, and readers, have grown accustomed to considering that the literature of the Western world belongs to genres established in classical literature as well as to genres that achieved recognition as the various European vernacular literatures developed—in any case, as belonging to various forms ". . . present[ing] and represent[ing] human action and vision" (Hernadi 9) and linked by common linguistic and philosophical bonds. A challenging situation confronts the Western critic and reader at this point in the late twentieth century, however: the growing awareness in the West of the existence of literary traditions unrelated to Western literature linguistically, philosophically, and historically. As A. Owen Aldridge suggests, the West has entered once again into a period of intense international contact similar to the period of increased contact among European countries after the Napoleonic wars that brought forth Goethe's ideal of *Weltliteratur* (9)—only now the contact is largely with literatures of the non-Western world. Once there exists an awareness of this body of literature, several questions clearly need to be asked: First, are there recognizable literary forms in non-Western traditions? Second, how are they similar to Western genres, and how do they, in their differences, urge a revision of Western generic classifications and descriptions, both of the literary system that includes the various genres and of individual genres themselves?

Goethe, when he became aware, near the end of his life, of a non-Western literary work, reacted to the challenge posed by it by finding ways to include it in the Western literary system. Referring, in the conversation with Eckermann of January 31, 1827, to a Chinese work of lengthy fiction that he had read, as a Chinese "novel" (*Roman*), Goethe drew the alien work into the tripartite generic system of lyric, epic-novel, and drama that was becoming dominant in his country at the time. He was able to classify the Chinese work using the German generic term *Roman* because he felt that its formal characteristics and its preoccupations were close to what he understood to be those of a European novel, in particular, the novels of Richardson. But Goethe was able to include the Chinese "novel" in the German/European genre of the novel also on the basis of a philosophy, derived from his countryman Herder, that saw universal human qualities in literary creations of the most diverse peoples. This sort of universalizing view is visible in his remark, later in the same conversation, to the effect that, based on his reading of the Chinese work he had realized that the Chinese people depicted in it "think, act, and feel almost exactly as we do . . ." (Eckermann 223). In the present-day climate of a multiculturalism that stresses difference, not similarity, between distant literatures, Goethe's remark (to use Masao Miyoshi's term) "domesticates or neutralizes the exoticism of the [foreign] text" with its tendency to "exaggerate the familiar aspects" (9), the so-called universal human aspects that, Miyoshi suggests, often turn out, on closer examination, to be Western (16). But I feel that it is more fair to view Goethe's comment as anchored in its time and place, which represented for the West an unusual spirit of inclusivity.

Goethe was no systematic theoretician of literary genres—in fact, he made his remark about the "Chinese novel" not to identify the existence of a genre of the novel in China, though his remark certainly implied a recognition of that sort, but rather to express his belief in the universality of human artistic expression and to stress the validity of aesthetic creations from the most diverse parts of the world, even those areas of the world relatively unknown to Europeans of his time. But contemporary systematic theoreticians of genre show no similar awareness of the existence of literary creations, and genres, outside of the West. Three authors of recent book-length theoretical studies of genre, Paul Hernadi, Alastair Fowler, and Adena Rosmarin, for example, base their arguments entirely on Western literature and orient themselves exclusively towards Western genres, thus not taking up the challenge posed to Western genre study that Goethe began to be aware of when he read his "Chinese novel." It has remained for those Western critics with expertise in a non-Western language or languages to consider the problem of literary genres in an intercultural context. In 1963, for instance, the French comparatist Etiemble, himself possessing a knowledge of Chinese and Japanese as well as several European languages, urged that genres of all literatures be studied whether they were linked by historical contact or had arisen independently of one another (62), and suggested, as an example of such a study, a "comparative poetics of *Noh* and of tragedy" (57).

Contemporaneously with Etiemble's directive for a new orientation toward comparative genre study, Robert H. Brower and Earl Miner and James J. Y. Liu exposed the classical traditions of Japanese and Chinese lyric poetry, respectively, to the Western reader, explicitly comparing their conceptions of the lyric genre with those of the West and implicitly challenging Western readers and critics to revise their ideas of the nature of the lyric. More recently, André Lefevere has briefly treated the problem of literary genres in truly global terms; and Earl Miner, after challenging the universality of Western assumptions about the nature of specific literary genres and modes in several articles,[1] has recently published a book, *Comparative Poetics*, in which he considers genres of the literary systems of the West and Asia (China, Japan, and India) in an intercultural context. In a sense Miner universalizes these distant poetic systems by arguing for the existence of a tripartite schema of lyric-narrative-drama, yet he allows for major differences of emphasis, contrasting the lyric-based poetics of Asia with the more drama-based poetics of the West. In addition, several articles have appeared that attempt to juxtapose a Western genre with a non-Western genre that appears to have similar formal characteristics as well as a similar conception of "human action or vision," to return to Hernadi's formulation.[2] Finally, two book-length studies comparing individual genres in Japan and the West have appeared: Marilyn J. Miller's study of autobiographical literature, to which I shall have occasion to refer, and Mae J. Smethurst's study of tragic or serious drama. The results of such studies suggest that genres long assumed by Western critics to be an inalienable part of the Western literary tradition are found indigenously in non-Western literary traditions as well.

That this is true also of the genre of autobiography has been slow to be acknowledged by Western critics. In fact, the typical position of Western critics and theorists on autobiography has been that this genre is a quintessentially Western one. Georges Gusdorf, for example, in a 1956 essay that helped to spark the ensuing lively theoretical discussion of autobiography in the West, considered the question of whether autobiography was an intercultural genre,[3] and gave a firm negative reply:

> . . . it would seem that autobiography is not to be found outside of our cultural area; one would say that it expresses a concern peculiar to Western man, a concern that has been of good use in

his systematic conquest of the universe and that he has communicated to men of other cultures; but those men will thereby have been annexed by a sort of intellectual colonizing to a mentality that was not their own. When Gandhi tells his own story, he is using Western means to defend the East. . . .

(29)

Gusdorf's references in the essay itself to autobiography in two non-Western literary traditions—the Indian and the African—prove that he tried to examine non-Western traditions for evidence of an autobiographical genre, but his argument that non-Western literatures have no indigenous forms of autobiography was invalidated by the fact that he did not consider evidence from non-Western traditions in the long period before Western influence.

Among other Western critics writing on autobiography, James Olney showed himself to be the most open to the possibility of the existence of autobiography in non-Western literatures, yet he referred, as had Gusdorf, only to modern forms of autobiography that had been influenced by Western philosophical assumptions and literary forms: to the autobiography of the modern Indian statesman Sarvepalli Radhakrishnan (*Metaphors of Self* 20–21) and, in his *Tell Me Africa* (1973), to autobiographies of twentieth-century African writers. Furthermore, theoretical studies of autobiography by Philippe Lejeune and Elizabeth Bruss discussed only Western autobiography, not even raising the question of whether autobiography exists elsewhere in the world. Finally, the only study of autobiography in general after Gusdorf's that considered the question of the intercultural nature of autobiography, that of Georges May, followed Gusdorf's position. That May took the question seriously is evident from his remark that he consulted specialists in Chinese literature on the question of whether autobiography existed in China. Yet his statement that he was assured by the Chinese specialists that two writers of autobiography, Shen Fu (1763–1809?) and Shen Congwen (1902–1988), were exceptions in a tradition otherwise lacking in autobiography, seems strange given evidence to the contrary that existed at the time May wrote his study and that has accumulated since.[4]

Indeed, evidence has been around for a long time that autobiography exists indigenously in several non-Western literary traditions. At the time May was writing his book on autobiography, Yves Hervouet was publishing an article delineating a tradition of autobiography in China going back to the pre-Christian era, and Franz Rosenthal had described an indigenous Arabic tradition as early as 1937. In 1985 Marilyn J. Miller published the only book-length study so far that juxtaposes a non-Western genre of autobiography—this is her structuralist analysis of classical Japanese *nikkibungaku*[5] (literally, *diary literature*)—to Western autobiographical writings. In the same year a brief essay by a noted Japanese comparatist, Saeki Shōichi, appeared which delineated the Japanese tradition of autobiography. And in 1989 Donald Keene published his introduction to Japanese diaries written between A.D. 847 and 1854: *Travelers of a Hundred Ages*. It is worth noting that, as in the case of the intercultural study of genres, the intercultural study of autobiography has been done by specialists in non-Western literature or by comparatists with an expertise in one or more non-Western literatures. A refreshing exception to this general truth, however, is the near eighty-page essay tracing the course of autobiography from its beginnings in all world traditions up to the present, by the sociologist Vytautas Kavolis. Approaching the study of intercultural autobiography with the assumption that all civilizations, not just the Western, are attentive and have been attentive throughout their history to what he calls "individual self-understanding" (59), Kavolis discusses the "designs of self-comprehension" (76) of Western as well as Chinese, Japanese, Indian, Arabic, and even less major non-Western traditions.

Kavolis, from his perspective as a student of comparative civilizations, has made a strong case for the existence of indigenous forms of autobiography worldwide, and Miller has defined the existence of a Japanese tradition of autobiography and compared it to Western autobiography through a juxtaposition of several types of Japanese autobiographical writing with their structurally and thematically closest equivalents in the Western tradition.[6] My aim will therefore not be to prove the existence of autobiography outside of the Western world, or to duplicate Miller's efforts in juxtaposing Japanese to Western autobiography, but rather to provide a brief descriptive overview of autobiography as the Japanese have considered it and classified it, then to compare and contrast aspects of it with those of Western autobiography, pointing out the particular Japanese features that challenge the Western view of autobiography. Finally, I use Japanese autobiography as a test case to speculate on the implications of the existence of Japanese, and other non-Western indigenous genres of autobiography, for the reading and teaching of autobiography in the West.

Descriptive Overview of Japanese Autobiography

In the West, works with an autobiographical intent were written from very early times, as Georg Misch, in particular, has shown, but it was only from around 1763 (Spengemann 176) or 1826 (Olney "Autobiography" 6) that the term "autobiography" was used. And it was only in the later decades of the nineteenth century that autobiographical works written up to that time were classified as autobiographies or autobiographical works—that is, that the genre of autobiography as such became recognizable (Spengemann 177) and therefore subject to theoretical examination. In Japan, works that seem, from a Western point of view, to have a clearly autobiographical intent appear at the beginning of the Japanese literary tradition. Unlike Western tradition, however, which has marginalized autobiography to a no-man's land of "fact" where "fictional," in the sense of created, imaginative works were privileged, the Japanese tradition considers autobiographical works as central to its classical canon. This is due to Japan's early development of a poetics that is based on its most esteemed genre: lyric (Miner *Comparative Poetics* 7–8). In Japan as well as in China, the fact of oral delivery brought about an emphasis on the poet as the actual speaker of the poem (Miner, *Comparative Poetics* 112–113), on the poet expressing his or her intent through the poem, and on the poem as having a factual existence through the existence of its speaker. Thus, when the first autobiographical form, the prose *nikki* (personal memoir) evolved around the middle of the tenth century, the presence in it of numerous poems by the author gave by extension a lyrical factuality to the events narrated in it, guaranteeing the presence in the work of a historical person who could be seen, through the writing of the poems, as having an autobiographical intent, from the Western point of view—though no such conception existed in the Japanese tradition. The fact that the poems expressed the intent of this real person did not, however, preclude the assumption that the poems, and the prose, expressed a stylized and fictionalized self.

The classical lyric-based poetic system, then, enabled the emergence of and validated the existence and flourishing of autobiographical writings of various sorts. *The Princeton Companion to Classical Japanese Literature*, in a sub-section of Part Six entitled "Kinds," lists three categories of literature written before contact with the West that can be viewed as autobiographical (Miner et al. 344–345, 347–348)—the term taken both in the Japanese sense and from the Western point of view. These are the *nikki*, often misleadingly translated as "diary" but more accurately translated as "fictionalized memoir" or "poetic memoir," which emerged in the mid-tenth century, during the Heian period (795–1185), and declined in the fourteenth century; the *kikō*, or travel record, a fictionalized autobiographical account of a journey, a form that evolved from the Heian-period *nikki* form and came into its own during the Kamakura (1185–1336), Nambokuchō (1336–1392), and Muromachi (1392–1573) periods, and achieved a brilliant flowering in the late seventeenth century (Edo or Tokugawa Period, 1603–1868); and the *zuihitsu*, or random jottings, which brought forth outstanding examples in the Kamakura period and is still practiced today.

The *Companion* characterizes the *nikki* and the *kikō* as "being taken to be about their author rather than someone else . . . " (345), thus defining an aspect of autobiography agreed upon also by all Western critics.[7] Both of the terms *nikki* and *kikō* were used to designate those forms during the periods when they were flourishing, but the other term used to designate classical Japanese autobiographical writings, *zuihitsu*, is described in the *Companion* as a name applied only in the modern period to a small number of earlier works miscellaneous in structure and in prose that "set down observations, reflections, and feelings in an apparently casual way" (305). That the "observations, reflections, and feelings" are those of the author makes the genre autobiographical in a broad sense. The *Companion* lists fifty-two titles under the joint heading *nikki* and *kikō*, the titles ranging chronologically from 935 to 1821, and the list is not exhaustive. Of these, at least six, the *Tosa Nikki*, the *Kagerō Nikki*, the *Makura no Sōshi*, the *Murasaki Shikibu Nikki*, the *Sarashina Nikki*, and *Oku no Hosomichi*, are considered major works of Japanese literature. For the *zuihitsu* only nine works are entered, but one of them, *Tsurezuregusa*, is also ranked among the major works of the Japanese literary tradition.

Among the works classified as *nikki* in the *Companion*, one type is the first- or third-person account of the author's life over a lengthy period of time, a type that is similar to the familiar Western autobiographies listed by Gusdorf as typical autobiographies: Rousseau's *Confessions* and Goethe's *Dichtung und Wahrheit*, for example (28).[8] These range from about one hundred to about three hundred pages in length—brief in comparison with Gusdorf's typical Western autobiography.[9] The earliest of these, the *Kagerō Nikki* (194 pages), narrated in a mixed first- and third-person point of view by Michitsuna no Haha (The Mother of Michitsuna), translated as *The Gossamer Years* (974), covers a period of more than twenty years in the author's life.[10] The *Sarashina Nikki* (112 pages) by Sugawara no Takasue no Musume (The Daughter of Sugawara Takasue), narrated also in a mixed first- and third-person point of view and translated as *As I Crossed a Bridge of Dreams* (ca. 1060), treats the author's life from age thirteen to at least fifty. A third work of this kind is the *Kenrei Mon'In Ukyō no Daibu Shū*, by a court lady with the title Kenrei Mon'In Ukyō no Daibu (96 pages), translated as *The Poetic Memoirs of Lady Daibu* (1232?). It treats several periods of the author's life chronologically from 1174 to 1232. Sometimes classified as a *nikki* and sometimes as a *shikashū* (personal poetry collection), due to the prominence of its poems,[11] the work is quite different from others in this category, conveying more the sense of a collection of poems from various periods of a life grouped together and presented chronologically than the chronological narrative of a life. And the *Towazugatari* (271 pages) by Gofukakusa In Nijō (ca. 1313) translated as *The Confessions of Lady Nijō*, covers the author's life over a span of thirty-six years, from 1271 to 1307.

A second type of *nikki* is the account, often but not always briefer than the preceding type of autobiography, of a limited period of the author's life. An example of this type is the *Sanuki no Suke Nikki* (184 pages) by a court lady whose title was Sanuki no Suke, translated as *The Emperor Horikawa Diary* (ca. 1127). This work treats events over a two-year period of the author's life and focuses on the death of the author's lover, Emperor Horikawa, and the grief it aroused in her. A third variety of *nikki* is one that reveals strong links with the traditions of history and biography and gives as well a sense of the author's personality. Whereas the previously mentioned *nikki* concentrate on the author's life alone, this third type conveys the author's feelings about events and people but also describes public events in an objective manner. The major example is the *Murasaki Shikibu Nikki* (123 pages) by Murasaki Shikibu, a court lady who was also the author of the great fictional work, *Genji Monogatari* (*The Tale of Genji*). Translated as *The Diary of Murasaki Shikibu* (ca. 1010), the work describes and comments on events and people at the imperial court over parts of the two years 1008 and 1009. Marilyn J. Miller rightly discusses this work in juxtaposition to Saint-Simon's *Mémoires*, as a kind of court memoir (197–218). Another example is the *Ben no Naishi Nikki* (Shirley Yumiko Hulvey translated eighty-two pages out of a total of about three hundred), a court memoir covering the years 1246–1252, by the court lady-poet Ben no Naishi. Intended as a near official account of the major events of the reign of Emperor Gofukakusa, this *nikki* is typical of thirteenth-century public *nikki* in that it allows little room for the author's emotions.

It should be pointed out that a consideration of Japanese *nikki* in terms of a definition of autobiography that requires identity of author with narrator has resulted in the omission of at least two works considered major ones in the Japanese canon of *nikki*. These are the *Tosa Nikki* (thirty-three pages) by Ki no Tsurayuki, translated as *The Tosa Diary* (ca. 935), chronologically the first work in the *nikki* genre, and the *Izumi Shikibu Nikki* (eighty pages), a poetic memoir attributed to the noted woman poet, Izumi Shikibu, translated as *The Izumi Shikibu Diary* (ca. 1008). There are reasons why each of these is a borderline case of autobiography when viewed by a Westerner. The *Tosa Nikki*, which, like the *Sanuki no Suke Nikki*, treats a single major episode in the author's life, a journey taking several months, is difficult to consider as an autobiographical work since the author, the famous male poet of his time, Ki no Tsurayuki, conceals his personality under the persona of a court lady who purports to write about *her* life. Even though the work makes the decided impression of being by a male writer,[12] the blurring of the narrator's identity, through the fluctuation back and forth between a male and a female narrator, puts into question the identity between author and narrator that is a requirement of Western autobiography.

The other borderline case, the *Izumi Shikibu Nikki*, similarly treats one major episode in the life of the heroine, a famous poet of her time: her love affair with a prince that developed in the course of about a year. In this case it is not clear that Izumi Shikibu is the author of the work, and the work takes a somewhat omniscient point of view that is foreign to other *nikki*. It is evident, then, that the term *nikki* does not coincide with the Western notion of autobiography. Miner's cautious statement that the *nikki* are "taken to be about their author" (*Princeton Companion* 345), and Jin'ichi Konishi's failure even to mention the identity of author and narrator as a defining characteristic of the *nikki*—for Konishi the *nikki* is merely about a historical rather than a fictional person (II 253, 256)—indicate that the emphasis of the *nikki* is not chiefly on the identity of author and narrator but rather on its narration of the "'real event,' the life and experiences of a historical individual" (Konishi II 252). Some *nikki*, even most *nikki*, then, are autobiographical in the Western sense, but some are not.

A fourth kind of *nikki*, of which there is only one example, is the *Makura no Sōshi* (345 pages) by the court lady Sei Shōnagon; it is translated as *The Pillow Book of Sei Shōnagon* (1000?). The most beloved and revered of the *nikki* through ten centuries, the work is a "loosely ordered" (Konishi III, 492) *nikki*[13] consisting of such diverse elements as anecdotes, sketches for fictional works, reflective passages, and lists, all of them conveying the author's opinions and judgments. Whereas the other kinds of *nikki* all ordered themselves according to the passing of time, whether the private time of an epoch or epochs of a life or the public time of the court, the author of this work left the sections in no particular order. As the most revered Japanese autobiography, it challenges the Western hegemonic life-trajectory, much as Montaigne's *Essais* continue to challenge the Rousseauian linear autobiography so favored by Western theorists of autobiography.

The *kikō*, or travel account, is a *nikki* that focuses on the life of a particular historical person in the context of a journey that he or she has taken. Works of this genre vary greatly in their communication of a sense of the author's self, some subordinating it almost entirely to an account of the journey, and others revealing it, at times intensely, in the midst of an evocation of visited places. According to Herbert Plutschow, about seventy travel records were written between the twelfth and sixteenth centuries.[14] He divides these travel records about evenly into two kinds, those written on command by poets for the emperor or some other high-ranking person linked to the imperial court, as a kind of official record of a journey, and those written voluntarily by hermits and lay-priests recording a journey undertaken for personal, often spiritual reasons (7). Most of these are fewer than thirty pages long and focus on a limited journey over a short period of time.

The official travel accounts combine a dry, factual, court-memoir style with a diary orientation, frequently noting the date, the time of day, and the weather as well as the place visited. By contrast, the travel records composed by hermits and lay-priests pay more attention to the places and their spiritual significance, and they are more personal, expressing religious and other emotions. *Kikō* that reveal an evolving spiritual self are the series of five *kikō* by the great *haikai* poet Matsuo Bashō written between 1685 and 1692. A late, and lengthy example of a *nikki* and *kikō* combined, one that expresses a more modern kind of feeling, is the *haiku* poet Kobayashi Issa's *Oraga Haru* (1819; 110 pages in translation), translated as *The Year of My Life*. On the whole, the works in this genre convey much less of a sense of self than do the *nikki*, the interest being more in recording visits to places famous for their poetic associations or spiritual significance, as well as in the almost ritualized composing of poetry on these places.[15] The *kikō* of Bashō and the hybrid *nikki-kikō* of Issa are surely among the few great works in this form, though a number of others, including the *Izayoi Nikki*, translated as *The Journal of the Sixteenth-Night Moon* (1279–1280; thirty-five pages in translation), by the Nun Abutsu, are popular due to the high quality of their poetry.[16]

The third autobiographical form in classical Japanese literature, the *zuihitsu*, is a miscellaneous genre that "sets down observations, reflections, or feelings (of the author) in an apparently casual way" (Miner, et al. 305). The form derived from the Chinese genre, and the Japanese generic term is a translation of the Chinese term *sui-bi* (literally, following the brush); it came to Japan along with other aspects of learning from Song Dynasty (960–1279) China. One work now classified in the genre, *Hōjōki* (twenty-one pages), translated as *An Account of My Hut* (ca. 1212), by Kamo no Chōmei, has the "interest in intellectual matters" typical of the Chinese *sui-bi* and the later *zuihitsu* (Konishi III, 492), but it seems to fall formally more into the briefly popular *ji* (*ki* in Japanese) or record form, a Chinese-derived short form that included an "objective exposition of facts" as well as the "personal opinions of the author" (Konishi III, 297).[17] The *Hōjōki* in its structure and content is a miniature *Pilgrim's Progress* in a Buddhist vein by a courtier-turned-hermit. The first true *zuihitsu*, according to Jin'ichi Konishi, is the *Tsure-zuregusa* (169 pages), by Kenkō (Yoshida Kaneyoshi), translated as *Essays in Idleness* (1330–1331). A collection of miscellaneous sections not in chronological order, some of them essays, some of them anecdotes, the work gains its high popularity in the Japanese literary tradition from its presentation of the author's intelligent, learned, and opinionated encounter with the past, in the form of customs and attitudes, poetry, and events.

Finally, Saeki Shōichi (1985) describes a fourth type of autobiographical writing, one that emerged only in the late sixteenth century and one that is similar to Western autobiographies from the Renaissance period on, that attempt to give a portrayal of a whole life. Retrospectively called *jiden* (self-narrative) only in the modern period,[18] works in this form were written not only by the samurai elite but also by "Buddhist priests, provincial merchant-scholars, . . . Kabuki actors, [and] indigent shogunal vassals . . ." (366). Of the *jiden* written in the Edo period (1603–1868), the most famous is the *Oritaku Shiba no Ki* (277 pages) by Arai Hakuseki, member of the samurai elite and advisor to the shogun Tokugawa Ienobu. The work has been translated as *Told around a Brushwood Fire* (1716–1717). Longer than any of the earlier autobiographical works except the *Makura no Sōshi*, the work is similar to Rousseau's *Confessions* in its quality as the autobiography of a public figure that nevertheless takes into account the personal, and in its function as an apologia.

Another example of the *jiden* is the colorful, slangy *Musui Dokugen* (1843), by the low-ranking samurai Katsu Kokichi, translated as *Musui's Story* (157 pages in translation).[19] An example of an autobiographical writing by a Buddhist priest is that by the famous Zen master Hakuin Zenji (1686–1769).[20]

Characteristics of Japanese Autobiography

Autobiography arose early in Japanese literary history—indeed, two of the first important works of Japanese prose, the *Tosa Nikki* (ca. 935) and the *Kagerō Nikki* (974), were both in the *nikki* form, the seminal Japanese autobiographical form and the one, besides the *zuihitsu*, which is still written now, that has had the longest history. And autobiography continued as an important contribution to Japanese literature throughout its history, at the point of Japanese literature's contact with the West in the 1870s coming together with Western autobiographical forms to create new forms of autobiographical writing.[21] Of the various autobiographical forms in the Japanese tradition, some of the *nikki* resemble Western autobiographies in their intention to "turn back on one's own past, to recollect one's life in order to narrate it," to use Gusdorf's description of the autobiographical impulse that he identifies only with the West (29). The *jiden* that emerged in the Edo period, in particular, are similar to standard Western autobiographies in their intentions and concerns, as well as in their relative length.

But the *nikki* that narrate part of a life and the *kikō* that narrate the self in the scope of a brief journey, and the essay-like, fragmentary *sōshi* and *zuihitsu* that encapsulate a self in perceptions and events, are by far the more highly esteemed forms. In contrast to the equivalently fragmentary or brief forms of autobiography in the West—the diary, the essay, and the brief autobiographical sketch— that have not traditionally been held in high esteem by Western theorists of autobiography,[22] these enjoy a central, privileged status among Japanese readers and literary critics. It seems, then, that Gusdorf's and May's conception of autobiography as only the retrospective narrative of a full life was the form of autobiography they were seeking when they looked at non-Western literary traditions for evidence of autobiography, and that this preference for the full-life autobiography may have kept them from seeing the other forms in which autobiography occurred in those traditions.[23]

How is one to explain the rise of autobiography in Japan? Gusdorf had argued that autobiography could not exist in other literary traditions than the Western because he thought that only in the West did there exist the two major "metaphysical preconditions" for the rise of autobiography. One of these is humanity's emergence from the "mythic framework of traditional teachings" and its "entrance into the perilous domain of history" (30). But it can be argued that the Japanese tradition possessed this precondition for the rise of autobiography, though it was shaped by Japan's own particular circumstances. Japanese culture had by the eighth century moved out of the realm of myth into the world of history, as is evidenced by the appearance of the first history of Japan, the *Nihon Shoki* (Chronicles of Japan, 720). And Konishi sees the ordinary, history-bound man emerging in literature, as opposed to the mythic or fantastic man of earlier literature, precisely in the *nikki*, the first Japanese genre to show autobiographical concerns (II, 265–266).

The awareness of history is most evident in the sub-genre of the *nikki* that I have labeled the *court memoir*, in which, for authors at the court writing semi-official court history such as Murasaki Shikibu and, later, Ben no Naishi, history is what the emperor, the empress, and the courtiers do, expressed in their authors' strong consciousness of daily events and festivities in the reign of a particular emperor. Authors of the *nikki*, whether court memoirs or more personal accounts, do not mention historical events in their works, but this is due not to a lack of awareness of these events but rather to their adherence to conventions that prohibit their mentioning such events in literature. Insofar as all of the writers of *nikki* and *zuihitsu* were members of the ruling class, however, their works were informed by an awareness of the links between their private lives and the important political events of the day. Kamo no Chōmei in his *Hōjōki* (ca. 1212) was quite aware of the battles of the disastrous civil war between the ruling Taira and rising Minamoto clans in the mid-1180s, events which resulted in the fires in the capital that he narrates in his work and which were one of the causes of his decision to leave the turbulent capital to become a hermit in the countryside. And the author of the *Kenrei Mon'In Ukyō no Daibu Shū* (1232?) was also painfully aware of the battle between these two clans in 1185, one that decided the future in favor of the Minamoto clan but also incidentally took the life of her lover. The author's awareness of her life in historical time was expressed, then, in the attentiveness to, though not the mention of historical events, and in the recounting of events at the emperor's court—but also in the sensitivity to customs, poetry, and clothing of the past and present.

Gusdorf's idea of the self that is narrated in Western autobiography is one that sees itself as independent of other selves, in a culture that has broken away from an earlier stage of civilization in which the individual felt himself to exist "*with* others in an interdependent existence that asserts its rhythms everywhere in the community" (29). He sees Western humanity as having emerged from this situation to a point where "the important unit . . . is the isolated being" (30), and he seems to privilege this state of being as a prerequisite for writing the self in the Western way. But Dorinne Kondo is only one of a number of recent scholars who are pointing out the existence, in the past and the present, of different kinds of selves, and this in turn suggests that there are different kinds of autobiographies.[24] She argues that the Japanese self is not an isolated being or a "whole, bounded subject" (32), as in Gusdorf's and others' formulations, but, instead, is "contextually constructed, relationally defined . . ." (26). In the Japanese autobiography, then, the awareness of the "singularity of each individual life . . ." (Gusdorf 29) typical of Western autobiography is accompanied by a sense of the individual involved in the cycles of nature, and in relations with other people and with the past. Especially in the longer *nikki* that have more prose and fewer poems, and attempt to come to terms with a longish period of the writer's life, such as the *Kagerō Nikki*, the *Sarashina Nikki*, and the *Towazugatari*, one has the feeling that the author's self is constructed and, in the last work, "negotiated with others" (Kondo 42) in a complex play of power relations.

Gusdorf emphasizes as the second metaphysical precondition for the emergence of autobiography the "curiosity of the individual about himself," the sense of a self engaged in an "autonomous adventure" (31). The "sense of curiosity" implies the presence, in the Western autobiography, of self-writing, of the Socratic imperative "Know Thyself." This involves a turning toward the past, and the rigorous use of memory as a kind of knowledge to uncover experiences that are then organized into a story from the viewpoint of the present-day self, leading up to the present in time. In the Japanese autobiography, by contrast, the impetus to write a life is often lyrical, which is why poems are an important element, in *nikki* such as the *Kenrei Mon'In Ukyō no Daibu Shū* the main element.[25] The Japanese *nikki* and *kikō* intensify the self of the work through lyrics; and the often short narrative sections intensify the self through the narration of a "real event" (Konishi II 252)—not a story—that is presented in the present tense, and often with minimal retrospective shaping, to give the highest sense of immediacy. In the *kikō* the self is "imbedded in the poetic tradition"; the self on its journey seems to exist only to "recognize the beauty of previous poems written about specific *meisho*, or places made famous through poetry, that it sees."[26]

Both the Western and the Japanese traditions of autobiography rest on the assumption that "the materials in the text have *some* basis in verifiable biographical fact . . ."[27]—though it may be impossible to verify the materials in the text through recourse to sources outside the text. According to Albert E. Stone, "modern societies like the United States accord legal status to the truth value of autobiographies" (Stone 104), thereby forcing a distinction between fact and fiction (104) and, in the process, making it difficult to see the fictional aspects of an autobiography without having to consider them untrue or, at the worst, legally fraudulent or libelous. But in Japanese autobiography, once the work was seen to be factual, both through its poems, which were viewed as facts of the poet, and its "real events," to use Konishi's term, the author could freely fictionalize the work in various ways.[28] The self in the lyric poetry was always a fictive one, expressing emotions (*kokoro*) and using imagery and allusions in conventional ways; this self as inscribed in poetic tradition dominated in the *nikki* and *kikō* that had large amounts of poetry. Authors of the more exclusively narrative *nikki* used the literary techniques that Albert E. Stone sees "deployed in virtually all autobiographical texts. . . .": techniques such as "description, reflection, . . . and meditation; and other common literary features including characterization, dialogue, . . . [and] dramatic scenes . . ." (Stone 104). In the *Hōjōki* and the *Tsurezuregusa* the authors utilized fictionalized personae of the hermit or recluse (*inja*) and connoisseur, respectively. Furthermore, some authors of *nikki* shaped their lives into a plot loosely organized according to a theme or pattern: in the *Kagerō Nikki*, the stages the author saw her marriage undergoing, from disillusionment to bitterness ending in calm resignation; in the *Towazugatari*, the passage from a passionate worldly life to a religious life. Authors of *nikki* treating a briefer period of life might shape the work according to a dominant emotion or experience: in the *Sanuki no Suke Nikki* grief over the loss of a loved one, and memories of happier days; in the *Izumi Shikibu Nikki* the development of a love affair.[29]

The presence of fictionalization is what makes it impossible to consider the *nikki* as a *record of days*, which was the term's original meaning—though the sense of days passing is almost always present in the *nikki*, whether in the literal reference to dates in chronological order or in the imbedding of "real events" in courtly festivities or natural time. The existence of fictional patterning in *nikki* should not encourage one to view them as autobiographical fiction either, for the main focus is the "real events" in the life of an historical individual, over which the aesthetic blanket of fictionalization is thrown. Until recently Western theorists of autobiography have had a difficult time accepting that the self of autobiography is a "fictive structure," as Paul John Eakin puts it (3), or that the writing of autobiography is a process of self-discovery and self-creation involving imagination as well as memory. Japanese autobiographers, by contrast, and especially the authors of *nikki*, have assumed the mixed factuality-fictionality of the self from the beginning of their tradition and have freely stylized their lives in the service of art.

Looking at the relative status of autobiography in Japan and in the West, it is clear that autobiography occupies very different positions in the hierarchy of genres. In the West, up until the relatively recent critical and theoretical attention to it as a literary genre, autobiography was considered a "marginal, generically inferior" form of literature (Stanton 3); or it was not viewed as literature at all, but rather as a sub-species of historical writing. In the Japanese tradition, however, autobiographical works, though of course they were not called that, were classed among the major prose works of their time—the *Makura no Sōshi* was viewed as the greatest *nikki*—and they have maintained a high degree of authority in the Japanese literary canon since then, though they were never able to compete with the most prestigious form, lyric poetry. Another obvious and significant difference between the status of the genre of autobiography in the West and in Japan is that while men initiated the tradition of factual personal records, usually written in Chinese, and a male poet was the first to write a *nikki*, or poetic memoir, in Japanese (the *Tosa Nikki*, ca. 935), it was women writers who greatly expanded the scope of the *nikki* as a literary form.[30] It was women writers who dominated the field of autobiographical writing from the late tenth to the late eleventh century, and the field of fictional prose in general. After this time, however, women were gradually displaced from the field of literature, and from autobiographical writing, as they were from public life as a whole. The last female writer of a *nikki* is Gofukakusa In Nijō, author of the *Towazugatari* in the early fourteenth century, and only one important *kikō*, the *Izayoi Nikki*, is by a woman. Women writers did not enter the field of literature again in a significant way until the 1890s.

In the West, by contrast, autobiography defined traditionally as the lengthy retrospective account of a whole life, was largely a male genre. Until recently historical and theoretical studies of autobiography either omitted a discussion of women autobiographers or relegated them to the periphery of the subject. But recent studies of female autobiography, among them one edited by Domna C. Stanton and another written by Sidonie Smith, have begun the immense task of recovering women's autobiography from virtual oblivion, providing a history of women's autobiography and speculating on how the feminine practice of autobiography relates to—or against—what has been identified as the canonical male tradition. Janel M. Mueller, in an essay in the Stanton volume, notes that *The Book of Margery Kempe* (1438)—that is, an autobiography by a woman—was the first autobiography in English (57); and other essays in the volume uncover traces of women's autobiography in other European traditions. But much more study needs to be done before it can be adequately clarified what women writers contributed to the genre of autobiography as it emerged in the Renaissance West. In any case, a comparison with the Western tradition reveals that the Japanese literary tradition presents a case, possibly unique in literary history, of a literary tradition in which autobiographical literature appears very early, is a dominant genre or an important current in the literature throughout its history, and furthermore is shaped from its beginnings, and dominated for a crucial time, by women.[31]

The Japanese tradition of autobiography is an important one, then, worthy of attention by Western theorists of autobiography and readers of autobiography. But Vytautas Kavolis points out that not only the Japanese tradition is an important one for autobiography, but also the Chinese, Islamic, and Indian ones, all of which have "histories of at least a thousand years old" (59). Kavolis goes even further to underline the significance of these non-Western indigenous traditions of autobiographical writing when he notes that

> . . . East Asia before the eighteenth century rivals the West in the range and depth of attention to individual self-understanding, and is radically surpassed in numbers only since the Puritan revolution, more precisely after 1648.
>
> (59)

The existence of all of these important indigenous traditions of autobiography outside of the sphere of Western culture poses challenges to the Western theoretical and critical establishment, for if autobiography is now known to exist in the non-Western world, it must from now on be considered in its intercultural dimension. This will entail a willingness on the part of the Western critic to take into account forms of autobiography that differ from those of the West, and to allow for the existence of other kinds of selves than those familiar from Western autobiography. It will involve an acceptance of the non-Western challenge to the generic assumptions and definitions of Western autobiography.

Concluding Pedagogical Postscript

The existence of indigenous non-Western traditions of autobiography poses a challenge also to what Arnold Krupat has called the "institutional or pedagogical canon," or literature as it is taught in the schools (*For Those* 24). For if autobiography exists outside the Western world, the genre can no longer be taught as if it were solely a Western genre. Thus, alongside of the familiar classics of autobiography such as Augustine's and Rousseau's *Confessions*, one might expect to see works such as the pre-modern Chinese autobiography *Fou Sheng Liu Ji* (*Six Records of a Floating Life*, 1809), and the pre-modern Japanese *Makura no Sōshi* or *Towazugatari*. Furthermore, autobiography exists as well in the modern literatures of Africa, in modern Arabic literature, in the above-named Asian literatures and in other Asian literatures, and in Native American literature, to name only a few, in culturally hybrid forms spawned by the meeting of these literatures with European-American literature.[32] Such bicultural forms must be included in the institutional canon as well, and examined for the light they shed on autobiography as a whole.

In conclusion, I would like to offer some remarks on my experiences teaching a Japanese autobiography in an introductory course in literary genres. In the unit on autobiography, I would typically start with the supposedly but actually not so familiar *Confessions* of Augustine (ca. 400), then work chronologically through the *Kagerō Nikki* (974) to *Mountain Wolf Woman, Sister of Crashing Thunder: The Autobiography of a Winnebago Indian* (taken down by Nancy Oestreich Lurie, 1958). But here I shall make the *Kagerō Nikki* the focus of my reading, bringing in the other two works to make comparisons and contrasts. I start out with the Western term *autobiography*, dividing it into *auto* (self) and *biography* (life-writing). I pose the questions "How is the self constructed? Who Writes? and For Whom?" Finally, "What form does the autobiography take," and "How is it linked to the self that is constructed?" I impress upon the students the fact that the three texts belong together generically, though I am careful to ground each text in its historical circumstances.

The Mother of Michitsuna, known only in relation to her son, Michitsuna, began her personal narrative, destined only for a small audience of fewer than one hundred people (Konishi II 269–271), in 974. Due to the fact that her audience knew her, her husband, and her son (the main three people mentioned in her narrative), she did not have to mention their names and details of their lives. There was no precedent for a self-narrative covering a large portion of a life when she began to write, only the *Tosa Nikki*, which covers several months of a journey. The work covers the years 954–974, and achieves its unity through its concentration on her marriage, which began in 954 and was still going, in its own way, when the author concluded her narrative at age thirty-six in 974. Her motive for telling her story, as she indicated in her opening phrases, was to offer an account of a noblewoman's life that was more realistic than those fantasy lives provided by the romances of the day. But realism often means "the unpleasant side of life," and the author may have been moved to communicate this side, in the form of the suffering of her marriage, in Part 2 of the work. In a way typical of earlier and later writers of *nikki*, the author relied heavily on poems (*waka*) she had written earlier, inserting them in her work to give the authenticity of her poetic voice (Konishi II, 291). In particular, Parts 1 and 3 are heavy with poems: 124 in Part 1, and eighty in Part 3 (Konishi II, 291). Part 1, which covers the years 954–968, recounts her marriage from its beginning to her disillusionment with her husband, for whom she is only one woman among a number waiting for his attentions. The narrative here has the tenor of a *shū*,[33] or string of poems connected by brief narrative sections, and the self at times is subsumed under the poetic tradition and its delineation of a typical love affair.

Part 3, treating only three years, 972–974, likewise has the flavor of a *shū*, concerned as it is with narrating the author's son's courtship of women through poetic exchanges. Under the burden of the delineation of a conventionalized development of love, the author often uses the third person. It is in the second part, covering the years 969–971, that the author gives the sense of the life of a real noblewoman that she intended. In this section, with fewer poems (fifty-five), the author makes the narrative her focus, treating her negotiations with her husband over visits, her taking refuge in pilgrimages to escape the misery of her loneliness and anger. Here the first person dominates, and the poems express a more personal self than those in the other two parts (Konishi II 291). The author uses the fictional technique of suspense, as the marriage goes toward an angry confrontation, and the narrator toward extreme mental instability; introspection occurs at two or three points in this part; and there are descriptions of what the author saw on her pilgrimages that are vivid and realistic, similar to those in the *Makura no Sōshi* but antedating them by twenty or thirty years. One can say that this work deals in some way with past, present, and future, as does Augustine's *Confessions* in its recounting first his past life up to and including his conversion (the first nine books), his present (Book 10),

and his future (Books 11–13), as seen in his reflections on the meaning of religion. Part 1 treats the past, Part 2 the painful present, or at
least the feelings aroused by the marriage as it goes on day by day,
and Part 3 the future marriage of the author's son and her involvement with another member of the future generation, her adopted
daughter. There is also a sense in which the author attains a state of
relative peace in Part 3, in which she, like Augustine, finds satisfaction in a collective purpose and future, though hers is the family and
to a lesser extent religion, and his is religion and the church. One
can see why Kavolis would have singled this autobiography out as
an autobiography showing similarities to the Western ones he knew.
Yet to impose this structure on the work is to neglect the sense of
the self as relational and subsumed in poetry that is a hallmark of
the Japanese autobiography.

I include an autobiography by a Native American in the course on
literary genres to further relativize the notion of Western autobiography, and to alert students to the phenomenon of autobiography as
linked to collective political circumstance, namely the unequal
power relationship between Native Americans and the whites who
came to live on their land. For the Native American autobiography
is what Arnold Krupat (1985) calls a "bicultural composite composition," a text often requested by a white anthropologist or linguist,
for scientific purposes, from a Native American, to be read by a
largely white, and non-literary, audience. Krupat points out how the
Native American informant negotiates some power for himself and
his culture by telling his story, though it is shaped by the anthropologist to fit the requirements of a Western-style narrative. Thus,
when Nancy Lurie first asked Mountain Wolf Woman to narrate her
life, she ended up with "less than half a reel of tape" (Lurie xiv)—not
nearly long enough for a full-length narration of the self by Western
standards. What emerged, through the coaxing and later, under the
editorial hands of Lurie, was an approximately eighty-page narrative, organized roughly chronologically but also according to topics.
One wonders what this narrative could have in common with
American autobiography, autobiography by white Americans whose
literary lineage is European, other than the basic narration of a self.
But there is a major way in which Mountain Wolf Woman's self-
narrative is similar to that of the tenth-century Japanese female autobiographer. Both of them construct the self relationally, the Japanese author in negotiation with her husband and with the poetic
tradition, the Native American autobiographer in relation to her
tribe and its history and customs, in relation to her family, including

her descendants, and in relation to her adopted niece, the anthropologist Nancy Lurie, who asked her to tell her story.

Reading Japanese autobiography, then, leads the student to realize, first, that there are forms recognizably autobiographical in other parts of the world, and to see that the claims that the genre is unique to the West are false. Second, it relativizes major Western assumptions about autobiography: for example, that the autobiographer is an *I* isolated from society and unified in his or her selfhood who recollects and "reconstitutes himself [herself] in the focus of his [her] special unity and identity across time" (Gusdorf 35). Reading Japanese autobiography substitutes another hypothesis for this assumption: that a self imbedded in the poetic tradition and the human community recollects and narrates the "real events" of his or her life, usually in the present tense. I have only had space to give one example of how reading a non-Western genre and understanding its differing assumptions can challenge Western generic assumptions. The reading of other traditions of autobiography will further relativize Western assumptions, making it possible to recognize and validate other forms and other selves within them. The intercultural study of literary genres such as autobiography has the effect of placing the Western student of literature squarely in a global literary context appropriate to the political situation of a world united in familiar ways—through trade, warfare, and individual contacts. It enables, as well, a realization of Goethe's ideal of *Weltliteratur* to an extent that was not possible in the nineteenth century.

Notes

I would like to express my gratitude to Earl Miner, Lynne K. Miyake, and the two anonymous reviewers of this collection for their helpful suggestions on how to improve this essay.

1. For articles that challenge Western notions of narrative by juxtaposing very different Japanese notions of narrative to them, see Miner, "Some Theoretical Implications of Japanese Linked Poetry" and "Some Issues for Study of Integrated Collections." For an essay that questions the universality of Western mimesis, see his "The Grounds of Mimetic and Nonmimetic Art: The Western Sister Arts in a Japanese Mirror."

2. Examples of such articles are one on heroic poetry and epic in China and the West by Marie Chan, one on Chinese and Western nature poetry by J. D. Frodsham, one on full-length Chinese *hsiao-shuo* and Western novels by Andrew H. Plaks, and one on the Chinese *shih* and Western lyric by Pauline Yu. All of these studies treat both similarities and differences be-

tween Western and Chinese forms, and do not attempt to make the Western genre the standard. See also the book-length study of various intercultural genres in Japan and the West by Armando Martins Janeira, which, while it sets out to find Japanese genres that are the most comparable to Western ones in their presentation of a certain type of human action and vision, does not attempt to domesticate the Japanese genres.

3. Georg Misch had already considered this question, and had included Islamic autobiography in his monumental *Geschichte der Autobiographie* (962-1006). For this information I am indebted to Vytautas Kavolis (93). Yet, as was typical for Western students of autobiography, Misch omitted Asian traditions.

4. It is probable that Gusdorf, Olney, and May were all looking in other traditions for the lengthy retrospective narrative of a life that became dominant in the West after the Renaissance and was considered the norm by theorists of autobiography such as Lejeune (14), while other autobiographical forms such as diaries, personal essays, briefer accounts of a life or part of a life, and letters were seen as marginal. May's certainty that there were only two Chinese autobiographies turns out to reflect the same prejudice in favor of the full-length life-narrative—but this time on the part of the Chinese specialists he consulted. Interestingly, in 1976 the French sinologist Yves Hervouet published an article surveying autobiography in China. He found that Chinese autobiography, like Western, showed a "consciousness of personality" and the "entrance into the domain of history"; furthermore, it has the "will to make an apologia and [has] the goal of creating a work of art . . . " (108). The major difference between Chinese and Western autobiography was the Chinese tradition's preference for short forms such as the autobiographical preface to a longer work, *biji* (random personal notes), *riji* (diaries), and travel narratives. Hervouet characterizes Shen Fu's *Fou Sheng Liu Ji* as the only "true autobiography," the only "complete autobiography" (127) of pre-modern China, thus demonstrating his preference for the full-length narrative of the self. The other autobiography mentioned by May is Shen Congwen's *Congwen Zizhuan* (Autobiography of Congwen, ca. 1932); it remains untranslated into a European language. For a translation of Shen Fu's "autobiography"—actually, more a series of sketches, as its title indicates, though it does give the sense of a whole life—see the reference in Works Cited. Jaroslav Průšek referred as early as 1957 to this work as "the first Chinese autobiography of any length" (24). For studies of Chinese autobiography and the autobiographical impulse, see also Rodney L. Taylor, Wendy Larson, and Wu Pei-yi.

5. Marilyn Miller applies the term *nikkibungaku* (*nikki* or poetic memoir literature) to all pre-modern Japanese autobiographical forms, using the term more broadly than Japanese critics, who generally limit the use of the term to the Heian and Kamakura autobiographical forms. Helen Mc-Cullough (1990) uses the term *nikki*, translating it *memoir*, in reference to autobiographical forms of these periods, and distinguishing it from the *kikō* or travel memoir, of the Kamakura, Muromachi, and Edo periods.

6. Miller's study pursues structural analogies between the *nikki* and Western "autobiography, confession or apology"; the *"jirekishi-monogatari"* (historical chronicle) and the "memoir"; the *"monogatari-nikki"* (talediary) and "confessional novels or new non-fiction"; the *"sōshi"* (personal notes) and the "notebook or personal essay miscellany"; and *"kashū nikki"* (personal poetry collection-poetic diaries) and "poetic manuals" or *"kikō* and lyrical autobiographical writing" (Table of Contents, n.p.). Miller's analysis and comparison of these "equivalent" forms is insightful, but her need to find such exact equivalents to the Japanese forms among Western autobiographical forms has made her skew somewhat her description of the Japanese autobiographical system, dividing the three or four categories used by Japanese critics into five so that they fit the Western forms. Her effort makes one realize how hard it is to avoid subjecting the literature of another culture to one's own patterns of thought.

7. But Jin'ichi Konishi, in his discussion of the Heian-period conception of the *nikki*, argues that "the content of a *nikki* need not be the author's personal experiences" (II, 253). In fact, the practice of calling works of the Heian period *nikki* that were not actually about their authors suggests that a more basic definition of a *nikki* is a work in prose that deals with the "life and experiences of a historical individual" (Konishi II, 252). Konishi underscores two things: the fact that most Heian prose works were not given a generic classification or titled by the author, and the extent to which the words *nikki, monogatari* (tale) and *shū* (collection) were applied indiscriminately to the same work. Modern Japanese genre theory tends to see *nikki* as "about their author."

8. The fact that I begin with this form, the full-length autobiography, shows my Western preference.

9. I have provided the length of the Japanese works in the original, based on consultation of major editions of classical Japanese literature, or in translation, if I could not locate the Japanese text. All of the Japanese lengths are those of the works in the *Nihon Koten Zensho* series except those of the *Kenrei Mon'In Ukyō no Daibu Shū* and the *Oritaku Shiba no Ki*, which are those of the *Nihon Kotenbungaku Taikei* series.

10. The finest *nikki*, and most of the best *zuihitsu* and *kikō*, have been translated into English. Translations of these are marked with an asterisk in Works Cited. A bibliography of translations of "memoirs," the term that Helen Craig McCullough uses loosely to cover all three genres of Japanese autobiography, is found in her *Classical Japanese Prose* (577–578). McCullough also provides descriptions and critical comments on the various works, as well as on the tradition of autobiographical writing in pre-modern Japan (15–26). For other useful discussions of the *nikki*, in particular, see Edwin A. Cranston's Introduction to *The Izumi Shikibu Diary* (under Izumi Shikibu 90–125); Earl Miner (*Japanese Poetic Diaries* 3–20); Phillip Tudor Harries' Introduction to *The Poetic Memoirs of Lady Daibu* (under Kenrei Mon'In Ukyō no Daibu 28–47); and Shirley Yumiko Hulvey's "The Nocturnal Muse" (210–220). Donald Keene makes some valuable general observa-

tions on the nature of Japanese diary-writing in his Introduction to *Travelers of a Hundred Ages*, pp. 1–13. But his histories of pre-modern Japanese literature provide more detailed discussions of the Japanese autobiographical genres, and of specific works in those genres. See his *Seeds in the Heart*, which covers the period up to the late sixteenth century, for discussions of *nikki*, *kikō*, and *zuihitsu*, especially Chapters 9, 10, 21, 22, and 25. His *World within Walls* treats the *kikō* of the late seventeenth-century poet Bashō; see Chapter 5, especially pp. 80–86 and 90–107.

11. For a discussion of the differences between the *nikki* and the *shikashū* that focuses on the two genres as personal forms of expression, see Phillip Harries' Introduction to his translation of *Kenrei Mon'In Ukyō no Daibu Shū* (28–47).

12. In a forthcoming essay entitled "*The Tosa Diary:* In the Interstices of Gender and Criticism," Lynne K. Miyake argues that the use of the diary form (a form used publicly only by males), the diction, and the objective view of public events in *The Tosa Nikki* reveal the presence of a male author despite the conveniently assumed female persona, resulting in a text that blends genders.

13. Many Japanese critics, and *The Princeton Companion*, classify this work as a *zuihitsu* because of its fragmentariness, but I agree with Helen McCullough and Jin'ichi Konishi in classifying it as a *nikki*, largely because of its historical contiguity with the *nikki* genre.

14. Plutschow and Hideichi Futuda have translated four *kikō* that Plutschow judges to be among the best of those extant, and that represent the two kinds of diaries that he discusses. These are the *Takakura-in Itsukushima Gokō Ki* (*Account of the Journey of the Ex-Emperor Takakura to Itsukushima*, 1180), the *Shinshō Hōshi Nikki* (*Diary of Priest Shinshō*, 1223), the *Miyako no Tsuto* (*Souvenir for the Capital*, 1370–1372), and the *Zenkōji Kikō* (*Account of a Journey to the Zenkōji Temple*, 1465). The first is an official travel diary, written for political as well as poetic purposes; the other three are by hermit-priests and were written for religious and poetic purposes. Plutschow lists six other *kikō* written between the twelfth and the sixteenth centuries that he rates as outstanding. These are the *Tōkan Kikō* (*An Account of a Journey to the East*, 1242?), translated by Helen Craig McCullough (421–446); the *Izayoi Nikki* (*Journal of the Sixteenth-Night Moon*, 1279–1280) (McCullough 340–376); the *Tosa Nikki* (*A Tosa Journal*) (McCullough 73–102); the *Towazugatari* (*The Confessions of Lady Nijō*, ca. 1310), translation under Gofukakusa In Nijō; the *Ise Daijingū Sankeiki* (*Diary of a Pilgrim to Ise*, date not given), translated by Arthur Sadler, *Meiji Japan Society* (Tokyo, 1940); and the *Tsukushi Michi no Ki* (*Pilgrimage to Dazaifu*, 1480), by the noted poet Sōgi, translation under Eileen Kato. (Note that Plutschow considers the *Tosa Nikki* and the *Towazugatari*, which I have described as *nikki*, as *kikō* due to the journey element.) Another fine *kikō* that has been translated by Steven D. Carter is Sōgi's *Shirakawa Kikō* (Record of a journey to Shirakawa, 1468). The *kikō* was an important genre in its time; Konishi notes that besides the fifty

some texts that Plutschow mentions for those years, texts that have been edited, there are many others existing in "woodblock-printed texts or manuscripts" (Konishi III, 483).

15. Konishi writes that the *kikō* were extremely interesting for the contemporary audience (III, 483) who were aware of the political intrigues behind the official travel accounts, the Buddhist practices underlying the religious pilgrimages, the famous places (*meisho*) mentioned in the works, and the *waka* tradition which is obvious everywhere in them. For an account of the political situation underlying the *Takakura-in Itsukushima Gokō Ki*, see Plutschow (8–9). See also McCullough (289–290) and Konishi (III 294–296) for background information necessary for the modern reader to begin to understand the *Izayoi Nikki*. This discussion reveals the extremely close relationship that was assumed between the author and the reader of the *kikō*, especially, but also of the *nikki*. A modern audience, whether Japanese or foreign, would have difficulty enjoying these works because of the lack of sense of the historical, as well as the literary context.

16. The Nun Abutsu was a fine poet, as was Sōgi, the author of two *kikō* mentioned in footnote 14.

17. Jin'ichi Konishi classifies the work as a *nikki* (III 297–298), but I, along with most Japanese critics, prefer to view it as a *zuihitsu*.

18. The term *jiden* was used from the Meiji period (1868–1912) on, at first to designate Western autobiographies and then later in reference to Edo-period works such as that by Arai Hakuseki that were seen as similar to them. For a famous Meiji-period example of a *jiden* see that by Fukuzawa Yukichi.

19. This work is 126 pages in the Tōyō Bunko edition, No. 138 (Tokyo: Heibonsha, 1969).

20. Philip B. Yampolsky, in his collection of translations of Hakuin's writings entitled *The Zen Master Hakuin*, notes that Hakuin's work entitled *Itsumadegusa* (Ivy, 1765–1766) is "largely autobiographical," with two out of three sections dealing chronologically with his experiences as a Zen aspirant and then as a monk (Yampolsky 230–231). But there is another work that has brief autobiographical sections, dealing chronologically with Hakuin's spiritual development. This is the *Orategama* (published in 1749) and *Orategama Zokushū* (Continuation of *Orategama*, published with it in 1751). The first of the three letters in *Orategama* contains a one-and-a-half-page account of Hakuin's spiritual development (Yampolsky 31–32), but the *Zokushū* has a longer passage that reads like a spiritual autobiography (115–122).

21. The *shishōsetsu*, or *I*-story, which emerged in the late Meiji period, certainly owes something both to Western fiction, fictional autobiography, and autobiography, and to the indigenous forms of autobiography. For a discussion of this important genre in modern Japanese literature see studies by Irmela Hijiya-Kirschnereit and Edward Fowler.

22. For example, Karl Joachim Weintraub, in his account of Western au-

tobiography, faithfully treats the fragmentary autobiographical forms of Petrarch (letters and other personal writings), Jerome Cardano, Giambattista Vico (essays and autobiographical sketches), and Montaigne (essays), but his preference for the full-length self-narrative is seen in his presentation of Montaigne as a figure for whom "the models fail," who had "difficulty in orienting his self" in narrative (Weintraub 166), and whose work is "hardly a genuine autobiography" (167). That was in 1978. The tendency now is to view autobiography as, each one, "a *sui generis* artifact . . ." (Stone 96). Stone goes on to insist on the need for ". . . grounding . . . an individual text in its manifold cultural conditions . . ." (96). Thus, the ground is laid for a consideration of autobiography in all its Western forms, as well as in cultures other than the Western.

23. I do not know whether Gusdorf actually looked at other literary traditions of the pre-modern era for evidence of autobiography; May looked and found a form that was long enough to give the sense of a full life (Shen Fu). Kavolis, in looking at the Japanese tradition, describes the Japanese type of autobiographical text as in a "modality of drifting through time" (37) and mentions, besides the public autobiography of Arai Hakuseki, the tenth-century *Kagerō Nikki* and the seventeenth-century *Oku no Hosomichi* of Bashō as major texts, omitting the more fragmentary, and more typically Japanese forms, from consideration. And he integrates the *Kagerō Nikki* into the Western tradition of full-length autobiography by putting it under the heading of the "psychological framing of self-interpretation of an individual's life" that Rousseau pioneered in his *Confessions*; "the Japanese poetic diarist of the tenth century has anticipated . . . [this, but] in a more passive tonality" (52). But Kavolis is generally very sensitive to the many different modes of selfhood and self-writing existing in a number of cultures.

24. Arnold Krupat writes of the "collective" model for the self and the "dialogic" model for the text in Native American autobiography (*Voice* 196). In a later essay he speaks of the "synecdochic self" that narrates the Native American autobiography, a self that says: "I understand myself as a self only in relation to the coherent and bounded whole of which I am a part" (Krupat "Native American Autobiography" 174). And Stephen Butterfield argues that the "self" of black autobiography is ". . . not an individual with a private career, but . . . is conceived as a member of an oppressed social group, with ties and responsibilities to the other members" (Butterfield 3). For both Native Americans and African-Americans, autobiography has had a collective purpose quite unlike the individualistic purpose of traditional Western autobiography.

25. The composition of poems, and the inclusion of poems, often exchanges of poems between the author and another party, in a *nikki*, was erotic and relational; on a daily basis, the ritual of writing poetry to another fulfilled a desire to communicate. As Richard Bowring notes, ". . . the ability to express oneself in poetry becomes a necessary part of being desirable for either sex" (Bowring 53). When an author inserted poems into her

text, it was to enter into a relational dialogue with other parties in the text, as well as with the reader, the latter viewed as a person aware of poetic conventions and endowed with the same desire to communicate.

26. Lynne K. Miyake, letter to the author, December 29, 1992.

27. Paul John Eakin, letter to the author, March 9, 1988. See also Bruss' Rule 2 (11).

28. Hijiya-Kirschnereit notes in this context: "The Japanese understanding of art ties artistic value . . . never only to particular strategies of structuring and encoding, but presupposes always a particular relationship of the work of art to reality, which . . . [is] the principle of truth [*jitsu*] or genuineness [*makoto*] and which contains strong ethical-moral components" (128). Thus, factuality, the truth of real events, brings with it the notion of sincerity.

29. For an analysis of the way the *Izumi Shikibu Nikki* fictionalizes the poet's love affair according to the stylized pattern of a love affair as found in poetry collections, see Walker "Poetic Ideal and Fictional Reality in the *Izumi Shikibu Nikki.*"

30. For a brief account of the politics of gender in diary-writing, see H. Richard Okada, *Figures of Resistance* (160–162).

31. The gender domination within the genre of autobiography has in turn influenced the way female authors of autobiography approach the act of writing in the two cultures. In the West, where the genre was defined as male, women seeking to write what Domna C. Stanton calls "autogynographies" had to "constitute the female subject" in a system that essentially "defined women as the object" (14). In Japan, by contrast, women had constituted the female subject over the centuries in lyric poetry, which they wrote as did men. The requirement that men shun the unprestigious territory of prose in the native language, Japanese, in order to distinguish themselves in Chinese poetry and prose, left Japanese prose open to women to explore, and to shape as female subjects. In their hands, then, Japanese prose developed into the prestigious genre of the *nikki* and the less prestigious genre of the *monogatari*, though a work that eventually came to be seen as a masterpiece, the *Genji Monogatari* (*Tale of Genji*, ca. 1010), was written in that genre, and by a woman.

32. For studies of modern non-Western traditions of autobiography see, besides Kavolis, the studies of Fedwa Malti-Douglas (Arabic), and Arnold Krupat and H. David Brumble III (Native American).

33. For the idea that Parts 1 and 3 of the *Kagerō Nikki* are structured like a *shū* and the Part 2 more like a *nikki*, I am indebted to Jin'ichi Konishi (II 291, 293).

Works Cited

(Asterisks indicate that the work is a translation of a Japanese autobiographical work.)

*Abutsu Ni (The Nun Abutsu). *Izayoi Nikki* (*Journal of the Sixteenth-

Night Moon). In *Classical Japanese Prose*, pp. 340–376. See McCullough, 1990.

Aldridge, A. Owen. *The Reemergence of World Literature: A Study of Asia and the West.* Newark: University of Delaware Press, 1986.

*Arai Hakuseki. *Oritaku Shiba no Ki (Told Around a Brushwood Fire: The Autobiography of Arai Hakuseki).* Translated by Joyce Ackroyd. Princeton: Princeton University Press; Tokyo: University of Tokyo Press, 1979.

Blanchard, Marc Eli. "The Critique of Autobiography." *Comparative Literature* 34 (1982): 97–115.

Bowring, Richard. "The Female Hand in Heian Japan: A First Reading." In *The Female Autograph*, pp. 49–56. See Stanton, ed., 1984.

———. trans. *Murasaki Shikibu: Her Diary and Poetic Memoirs (Murasaki Shikibu Nikki).* Princeton: Princeton University Press, 1982.

Brower, Robert H., and Earl Miner. *Japanese Court Poetry.* Stanford: Stanford University Press, 1961.

Brumble, H. David III. *American Indian Autobiography.* Berkeley, Los Angeles, and London: University of California Press, 1988.

Bruss, Elizabeth W. *Autobiographical Acts: The Changing Situation of a Literary Genre.* Baltimore and London: The Johns Hopkins University Press, 1976.

Butterfield, Stephen. *Black Autobiography in America.* Amherst: University of Massachusetts Press, 1974.

*Carter, Steven D. "Sōgi in the East Country: *Shirakawa Kikō.*" *Monumenta Nipponica* 42 (1987): 167–209.

Chan, Marie. "Chinese Heroic Poems and European Epic." *Comparative Literature* 26 (1974): 142–168.

Cranston, Edwin A., trans. *The Izumi Shikibu Diary: A Romance of the Heian Court.* With an introduction by Cranston. Cambridge, Mass.: Harvard University Press, 1969.

Eakin, Paul John. *Fictions in Autobiography: Studies in the Art of Self-Invention.* Princeton: Princeton University Press, 1985.

Eakin, Paul John, ed. *American Autobiography: Retrospect and Prospect.* Madison: The University of Wisconsin Press, 1991.

Eckermann, Johann Peter. *Conversations of Goethe with Eckermann and Soret.* Translated by John Oxenford, pp. 211–215. London: George Bell and Sons, 1882. Originally published as *Gespräche mit Goethe in den letzten Jahren seines Lebens*, pp. 222–227 (Leipzig: Brockhaus, 1868).

Etiemble, René. *The Crisis in Comparative Literature.* Translated by Herbert Weisinger and Georges Joyaux. East Lansing: Michigan State University Press, 1966.

Fowler, Alastair. *Kinds of Literature: An Introduction to the Theory of Genres and Modes.* Cambridge, Mass.: Harvard University Press, 1982.

Fowler, Edward. *The Rhetoric of Confession: Shishōsetsu in Early Twentieth-Century Japanese Fiction.* Berkeley: University of California Press, 1988.

Frodsham, J. D. "Landscape Poetry in China and Europe." *Comparative Literature* 19 (1967): 193–215.

*Fukuzawa Yukichi. *The Autobiography of Yukichi Fukuzawa* (*Fukuō Jiden*). Translated by Umeyo Hirano. New York: Columbia University Press, 1966.

*Gofukakusa In Nijō (Lady Nijō). See under Brazell, Karen.

Gusdorf, Georges. "Conditions and Limits of Autobiography." In *Autobiography: Essays Theoretical and Critical*, edited by James Olney, pp. 28–48. Princeton: Princeton University Press, 1980.

Harries, Phillip Tudor, trans. *The Poetic Memoirs of Lady Daibu* (*Kenrei Mon'In Ukyō no Daibu Shū*). With an introduction by Harries. Stanford, Calif.: Stanford University Press, 1980.

Hernadi, Paul. *Beyond Genre: New Directions in Literary Classification*. Ithaca: Cornell University Press, 1972.

Hervouet, Yves. "L'Autobiographie dans la Chine traditionelle." In *Etudes d'histoire et de littérature chinoise offertes au Professeur Jaroslav Průšek*, pp. 107–141. Paris: Bibliothèque de l'Institut des Hautes Etudes Chinoises, 1976.

Hijiya-Kirschnereit, Irmela. *Selbstentblössungsrituale: Zur Theorie und Geschichte der autobiographischen Gattung 'Shishōsetsu' in der modernen japanischen Literatur*. Wiesbaden: Franz Steiner Verlag, 1981.

*Hulvey, Shirley Yumiko. "The Nocturnal Muse: A Study and Partial Translation of 'Ben no Naishi Nikki,' A Thirteenth-Century Poetic Diary." Ph.D. Diss. University of California, Berkeley, 1989.

*Izumi Shikibu (?). *The Diary of Izumi Shikibu* (*Izumi Shikibu Nikki*). Translated by Earl Miner. In *Japanese Poetic Diaries*, pp. 30–39, 93–153. See Miner, 1969.

Janeira, Armando Martins. *Japanese and Western Literature: A Comparative Study*. Rutland, Vt.: Tuttle, 1970.

*Kamo no Chōmei. *An Account of My Hut* (*Hōjōki*). Translated by Donald Keene. In *Anthology of Japanese Literature: Earliest Era to Mid-Nineteenth Century*, edited by Donald Keene, pp. 197–212. New York: Grove Press, 1955.

*Kato, Eileen. "Pilgrimage to Dazaifu: Sōgi's *Tsukushi no Michi no Ki*." *Monumenta Nipponica* 34 (1979): 333–367.

*Katsu, Kokichi. *Musui's Story: The Autobiography of a Tokugawa Samurai* (*Musui Dokugen*). Translated with Introduction and notes by Teruko Craig. Tucson: The University of Arizona Press, 1988.

Kavolis, Vytautas. "Histories of Selfhood, Maps of Sociability." In *Designs of Selfhood*, edited by Kavolis, pp. 15–103. Rutherford, Madison, Teaneck: Fairleigh Dickinson University Press, 1984.

Keene, Donald, trans. *Essays in Idleness: The Tsurezuregusa of Kenkō*. New York: Columbia University Press, 1967.

———. *Seeds in the Heart: Japanese Literature from Earliest Times to the Late-Sixteenth Century*. New York: Henry Holt and Co., 1993.

———. *Travelers of a Hundred Ages*. New York: Henry Holt and Co., 1989.

————. *World within Walls: Japanese Literature of the Pre-Modern Era, 1600–1867*. New York: Holt, Rinehart and Winston, 1976.

*Kenkō (Yoshida Kaneyoshi). See under Keene.

*Kenrei Mon'In Ukyō no Daibu. See under Harries.

*Ki no Tsurayuki. *A Tosa Journal (Tosa Nikki)*. Translated by Helen Craig McCullough. See McCullough, pp. 73–102.

————. *The Tosa Diary*. Translated by Earl Miner. In *Japanese Poetic Diaries*, pp. 20–30, 57–91. See Miner, 1969.

*Kobayashi, Issa. *Oraga Haru: The Year of My Life: A Translation of Issa's Oraga Haru*. Translated by Nobuyuki Yuasa. 2nd ed. Berkeley, Los Angeles, and London: University of California Press, 1972.

Kondo, Dorinne K. *Crafting Selves: Power, Gender, and Discourses of Identity in a Japanese Workplace*. Chicago and London: The University of Chicago Press, 1990.

Konishi, Jin'ichi. *A History of Japanese Literature*. Vol. 2, *The Early Middle Ages*. Translated by Aileen Gatten. Edited by Earl Miner. Princeton: Princeton University Press, 1986.

————. *A History of Japanese Literature*. Vol. 3, *The High Middle Ages*. Translated by Aileen Gatten and Mark Harbison. Edited by Earl Miner. Princeton: Princeton University Press, 1991.

Krupat, Arnold. *For Those Who Come After: A Study of Native American Autobiography*. Berkeley, Los Angeles, and London: University of California Press, 1985.

————. "Monologue and Dialogue in Native American Autobiography." In *The Voice in the Margin: Native American Literature and the Canon*, by Krupat, pp. 132–201. Berkeley, Los Angeles, Oxford: University of California Press, 1989.

————. "Native American Autobiography and the Synecdochic Self." In *American Autobiography*, pp. 171–194. See Eakin, ed., 1991.

Larson, Wendy. *Literary Authority and the Modern Chinese Writer: Ambivalence and Authority*. Durham and London: Duke University Press, 1991.

Lefevere, André. "Systems in Evolution: Historical Relativism and the Study of Genre." *Poetics Today* 6 (1985): 665–679.

Lejeune, Philippe. *Le pacte autobiographique*. Paris: Seuil, 1975.

Liu, James J. Y. *The Art of Chinese Poetry*. Chicago: University of Chicago Press, 1962.

Lurie, Nancy Oestreich, ed. *Mountain Wolf Woman, Sister of Crashing Thunder: The Autobiography of a Winnebago Indian*. Ann Arbor: The University of Michigan Press, 1961.

McCullough, Helen Craig, ed. *Classical Japanese Prose: An Anthology*. Stanford: Stanford University Press, 1990.

Malti-Douglas, Fedwa. *Blindness and Autobiography: "Al-Ayyām" of Ṭāhā Ḥusayn*. Princeton: Princeton University Press, 1988.

*Matsuo Bashō. *The Narrow Road to the Deep North and Other Travel Sketches*. Translated by Nobuyuki Yuasa. Baltimore: Penguin, 1966.

———. *The Narrow Road through the Provinces* (*Okumo Hosomichi*). Translated by Earl Miner. In *Japanese Poetic Diaries*, pp. 39–47, 155–197. See Miner, 1969.

May, Georges. *L'Autobiographie*. Paris: Presses Universitaires de France, 1979.

Miller, Marilyn Jeanne. *The Poetics of "Nikki Bungaku": A Comparison of the Traditions, Conventions, and Structure of Heian Japan's Literary Diaries with Western Autobiographical Writings*. New York and London: Garland, 1985.

Miner, Earl. *Comparative Poetics: An Intercultural Essay on Theories of Literature*. Princeton: Princeton University Press, 1990.

———, trans. *Japanese Poetic Diaries*. Berkeley and Los Angeles: University of California Press, 1969.

———. "On the Genesis and Development of Literary Systems." Part 1. *Critical Inquiry* 5 (1978): 339–353; Part 2. *Critical Inquiry* 5 (1979): 553–568.

———. "Some Issues for Study of Integrated Collections." In *Poems in Their Place: The Intertextuality and Order of Poetic Collections*, edited by Neil Fraistat, pp. 18–43. Chapel Hill and London: University of North Carolina Press, 1986.

———. "Some Theoretical Implications of Japanese Linked Poetry." *Comparative Literature Studies* 18 (1981): 368–378.

———. "The Grounds of Mimetic and Nonmimetic Art: The Western Sister Arts in a Japanese Mirror." In *Articulate Images: The Sister Arts from Hogarth to Tennyson*, edited by Richard Wendorf, pp. 70–98. Minneapolis: University of Minnesota Press, 1983.

Miner, Earl, Hiroko Odagiri, and Robert E. Morrell. *The Princeton Companion to Classical Japanese Literature*. Princeton: Princeton University Press, 1985.

Misch, Georg. *Geschichte der Autobiographie*. Vol. 3, *Das Mittelalter*. Part 2, "Hochmittelalter in Anfang." Frankfurt am Main: Schulte-Bulmke, 1962.

Miyoshi, Masao. "Against the Native Grain: The Japanese Novel and the 'Postmodern' West." In *Off Center: Power and Culture Relations between Japan and the United States*, by Masao Miyoshi, pp. 9–36. Cambridge, Mass. and London: Harvard University Press, 1991.

Morris, Ivan, trans. *As I Crossed a Bridge of Dreams: Recollections of a Woman in Eleventh-Century Japan* (*Sarashima Nikki*). New York: Harper and Row, 1971.

———, trans. *The Pillow Book of Sei Shōmagon* (*Makura no Sōshi*). New York: Columbia University Press, 1991.

Mueller, Janel M. "Autobiography of a New 'Creatur': Female Spirituality, Selfhood, and Authorship in *The Book of Margery Kempe*. In *The Female Autograph*, pp. 57–69. See Stanton, ed., 1984.

*Murasaki Shikibu (Lady Murasaki). See under Bowring.

Okada, H. Richard. *Figures of Resistance: Language, Poetry, and Narrating* in *"The Tale of Genji" and Other Mid-Heian Texts.* Durham and London: Duke University Press, 1991.

Olney, James, ed. *Autobiography: Essays Theoretical and Critical.* Princeton: Princeton University Press, 1980.

————. "Autobiography and the Cultural Moment: A Thematic, Historical, and Bibliographical Introduction." In *Autobiography,* pp. 3–27. See Olney, ed., 1980.

————. *Metaphors of Self: The Meaning of Autobiography.* Princeton: Princeton University Press, 1972.

————. *Tell Me Africa: An Approach to African Literature.* Princeton: Princeton University Press, 1973.

Plaks, Andrew H. "Full-length *Hsiao-shuo* and the Western Novel: A Generic Reappraisal." In *China and the West: Comparative Literature Studies,* edited by William Tay, Ying-hsiung Chou, and Heh-hsiang Yuan, pp. 163–176. Hong Kong: The Chinese University Press, 1980.

Plutschow, Herbert, and Hideichi Fukuda, trans. *Four Japanese Travel Diaries of the Middle Ages.* Introduction by Herbert Plutschow. Cornell University East Asia Papers 25. Ithaca: China-Japan Program, Cornell University Press, 1981.

Průšek, Jaroslav. "Subjectivism and Individualism in Modern Chinese Literature." In *The Lyrical and the Epic: Studies of Modern Chinese Literature,* by Průšek. Edited by Leo Ou-fan Lee, pp. 1–28. Bloomington: Indiana University Press, 1980.

Rosenthal, Franz. "Die arabische Autobiographie." *Studia Arabica.* Rome: Pontificium Institutum Biblicum (1937): 1–40.

Rosmarin, Adena. *The Power of Genre.* Minneapolis: University of Minnesota Press, 1985.

Saeki Shōichi. "The Autobiography in Japan." Translated by Teruko Craig. *Journal of Japanese Studies* 11 (1985): 357–368.

————. *Jidenbungaku no Sekai* (The World of autobiographical literature). Tokyo: Asahi Shuppansha, 1983.

————. *Kindai Nihon no Jiden* (Modern Japanese autobiography). Tokyo: Kodansha, 1981.

*Sanuki no Suke. *The Emperor Horikawa Diary: Sanuki no Suke Nikki.* Translated by Jennifer Brewster. Honolulu: University of Hawaii Press, 1977.

Seidensticker, Edward, trans. *The Gossamer Years: A Diary by a Noblewoman of Heian Japan (Kagerō Nikki).* Rutland, Vt.: Tuttle, 1964.

*Sei Shōnagon. See under Morris.

*Shen Fu. *Six Records of a Floating Life.* Translated by Leonard Pratt and Chiang Su-hui. Baltimore: Penguin, 1983.

Smethurst, Mae J. *The Artistry of Aeschylus and Zeami: A Comparative Study of Greek Tragedy and Nō.* Princeton: Princeton University Press, 1989.

Smith, Sidonie. *A Poetics of Women's Autobiography: Marginality and the Fictions of Self-Representation.* Bloomington and Indianapolis: Indiana University Press, 1987.

Spengemann, William C. *The Forms of Autobiography: Episodes in the History of a Literary Genre.* New Haven and London: Yale University Press, 1980.

Stanton, Domna C. "Autogynography: Is the Subject Different?" In *The Female Autograph*, pp. 3–20. See Stanton, ed., 1984.

Stanton, Domna C., ed. *The Female Autograph: Theory and Practice of Autobiography from the Tenth to the Twentieth Century.* Chicago and London: The University of Chicago Press, 1984.

Stone, Albert E. "Modern American Autobiography: Texts and Transactions." In *American Autobiography*, pp. 95–120. See Eakin, ed., 1991.

*Sugawara no Takasue no Musume. See under Morris.

Taylor, Rodney L. "The Centered Self: Religious Autobiography in the Neo-Confucian Tradition." *History of Religions* 17 (1978): 266–284.

Walker, Janet A. "Poetic Ideal and Fictional Reality in the *Izumi Shikibu Nikki.*" *Harvard Journal of Asiatic Studies* 37 (1977): 135–182.

Weintraub, Karl Joachim. *The Value of the Individual: Self and Circumstance in Autobiography.* Chicago and London: The University of Chicago Press, 1978.

Wu, Pei-yi. *The Confucian's Progress: Autobiographical Writings in Traditional China.* Princeton: Princeton University Press, 1990.

Yampolsky, Philip B., trans. *The Zen Master Hakuin: Selected Writings.* With Introduction by Yampolsky. New York and London: Columbia University Press, 1971.

Yu, Pauline. "Alienation Effects: Comparative Literature and the Chinese Tradition." In *The Comparative Perspective on Literature: Approaches to Theory and Practice*, edited and with Introduction by Clayton Koelb and Susan Noakes, pp. 162–175. Ithaca and London: Cornell University Press, 1988.

Part 3.

LANGUAGES OF COMMUNITY

READING THE LANGUAGE(S) OF THE TEXT

Introduction

Sarah Lawall

Essays in this section move from considering larger textual patterns to a closer focus on specific language *use*: here, language as the instrument of translation, and literary language as overlapping layers of linguistic culture.

Translation itself is a familiar issue in academic discussions of world literature. Purists find it an embarrassment that world literature courses must be taught in translation: how can we vicariously experience another world view when the words embodying that view have been transmuted into *our* words, stemming from *our* experience? They are not reassured by Goethe's dictum (in discussing the exchange of national images he called "world literature") that the best translations preserve a foreign essence and are "identical with the original in form and content." Such texts have not yet come on the market. In some cases teachers will have read the original work and can point out nuances to the class, but few know all the languages in the usual world literature course. If translation is inevitable—and if, moreover, a great deal of literary and cultural influence is *attributable* to translated texts—the important thing may be to analyze what happens in translation and how it affects our understanding of a work and its world.

Eugene Eoyang discusses translation as a problematics of linguistic and cultural assumptions. To translate is first of all to *read* a work and it is that reading, colored by preconceptions and personal experience, which is communicated. The intended audience—bilingual or monolingual, student or casual reader, coming from one or another cultural background—is also a factor, and Eoyang proposes an ontological grid of translation categories to distinguish between their diverse functions and scope. Comparing translations by Arthur Waley and Ezra Pound of poems from the *Shih Ching* (the ancient Chinese *Book of Songs*), he demonstrates how differing aims and expectations produce quite different English versions of the

same text. A translator's selection of larger rhetorical frames dis-
closes cultural attitudes even more clearly than do individual words.
Homey or formal vocabulary; eroticism brought out or blurred; gender attributions when none are stated: each decision contributes to
an implied world view. When readers (and teachers) choose between
translations, Eoyang observes, they are choosing one or another version of reality, and revealing their own frames of reference.

Translation studies generally work between different national languages considered as homogeneous or at least standardized wholes,
with dialects relegated to a separate, contributing position. English
is English, and French is French: at least until one thinks of the
enormous variety of Anglophone and Francophone literatures that
have created a new area of scholarly specialization complete with
its own journals (*World Literature Written in English; Francogra-
phies*), dictionaries, and professional organizations. Who "owns" the
mother tongue? American English is not British English; Anglo-
Irish and Anglo-Indian (or Indo-Anglian) literatures exist as separate
categories; French Canadian writers no longer look to Paris for linguistic purity; the Spanish of Latin America is distinct from that of
Spain; and so on wherever one linguistic culture has left its mark on
another (Augustine's Latin is not that of Cicero . . .). In brief, the
supposedly standardized European languages have been dispersed
throughout their former colonial empires and have evolved as different forms, each reflecting the history and culture of its new setting. The political implications of this dispersal are still debated.
Whereas conservative critics try to preserve the purity of European
English or French (criticizing "nonstandard" English in African novels, or marveling that writers like Césaire have such mastery of
"their" French), some African writers have asked whether it is appropriate to use the colonizer's language at all, burdened as it is with
concepts and vocabulary inherited from an imperialist past. The
Kenyan Ngugi wa Thiong'o, in *Decolonising the Mind: The Politics
of Language in African Literature* (1986), urged that African writers
should write in their own maternal languages; conversely, the Nigerian writers Chinua Achebe and Wole Soyinka argued that English
was already "their" language (in addition, respectively, to the Ibo
and Yoruba tongues), and that they had a right to develop it as they
chose.

The decision by several Nigerian writers to write in a special *African* English is the topic of Chantal Zabus's essay. Discussing linguistic usage in novels written between 1952 and 1985 by Amos
Tutuola, Gabriel Okara, Cyprian Ekwensi, and Ken Saro-Wiwa,
Zabus examines the relative weight given to English and African

speech patterns. She outlines an increasing use of African elements that points towards the development of a new, hybrid literary language—a process she calls relexification. In her first example, English is a dominant literary language broken by African words or semantic patterns; it subsequently appears as an equal partner in a mixed style that simulates African language inside English narrative. Finally, standard English is absorbed into a totally different form: experimental novels written in the "Pidgin English" language common to different tribal cultures of modern Nigerian society. Zabus does not claim that future Nigerian literature must be written in Pidgin English, but she makes a strong argument for a logical evolution towards an indigenous and polyphonic style. Forcing English to take a minor or contributing role in the creation of a new lexicon clearly has both aesthetic and ideological significance. As her analysis uncovers different layers of cultural identity in these texts of mixed African-English language, she demonstrates the need to examine the technical processes of everyday language—as well as image chains, or the interaction of characters—in the cross-cultural readings of world literature.

8. The Many "Worlds" in World Literature: Pound and Waley as Translators of Chinese

Eugene Chen Eoyang

Any concern with world literature, dependent as it is on translation, cannot ignore the role that translation and translators play in our encounter with foreign works in our native language.[1] The language through which we read the literature of the world—which by definition means literature partly, or mostly, in languages other than the one we are native in—will doubtless affect our view of the world. But it would be an ethnocentricity—familiar in Anglophone, Francophone, Sinophone, or Japanophone mindsets—to think that the only worthwhile works in other languages are those that have been translated into our own. Nor are we as aware as we should be that works available in unique translations present both a blessing and a dilemma. As they provide the only access to an otherwise inaccessible work for the monolingual, they take the place, *faute de mieux*, of the original: to all intents and purposes, they *become* the original work in the target language. Their access is, however, a mitigated blessing, because the reader in the target language can hardly be aware of the interlingual transformations that occur in any act of translation. For years, Constance Garnett was the late Victorian voice of Dostoyevsky in English, although recently new translations have been issued, which show both her limitations and her genius; a late Victorian Dostoyevsky is an imposture at the same time as it is a remarkable, and undoubtedly historicized, creation. The translations of Ibsen's plays for a generation or more were transmitted through the voice of William Archer; now, of course, we have the option of several versions. In our own time, the work of Gabriel García Márquez is available only in Gregory Rabassa's (fortunately) excellent versions. For more than a generation, the Japanese classic, *The Tale of Genji*, was presented to English-reading audiences in the definitive translation by Arthur Waley, published in six volumes from 1925 to 1936. Then, forty years later, in 1976, Edward Seidensticker published his equally definitive, but very different, version, in two volumes. How, one might ask, can there be two definitive versions? And which version should a student of world literature choose? And why? Even when multiple translations of the same work exist in one language, the original is usually represented solely by one version: for example, to many readers of English not trained to read the ancient Hebrew of the Old Testament or the *koine* Greek or Aramaic of the New Testament, the Authorized Version, published in 1611, is the "standard" by which all other translations are measured—whatever its inaccuracies and lapses may be. Yet the premises for these choices, to say nothing of their implications, have gone largely unexamined. But with the increasing availability of translations, particularly of works in the public domain, not protected by copyright, the student of world literature must ask, not only what is lost (or gained) in translation, but also what is lost (or gained) in *each* available translation. The analysis presented here is an attempt to arrive at certain principles in choosing different versions of the same work, using two key figures in the translation of traditional Chinese poetry: Ezra Pound and Arthur Waley. Both are major conduits through which students of world literature will approach Chinese literature; and both were major influences on subsequent translators.

One of the most frequently posed questions by world literature teachers innocent of Chinese is "Who is the better translator? Arthur Waley or Ezra Pound?" Like so many interesting questions, it is unanswerable, not because there are no answers (partisans can be found on both sides), but because as a question, it is—as the philosophers would say—ill-phrased. There is the obvious but necessary need to ask first: on which poem is Waley's or Pound's version to be preferred? There are also the prior questions: what does one mean by "translation"? What criteria are assumed in a judgment of value in translation? What can be learned from these versions and by their comparison, either about the original or about the process of translating? These are the questions that must first be addressed, before one can ask meaningfully the question: Who is the better translator? Waley or Pound?

These prior questions—on the ontology of translation (what is it?), on its criteria of canonicity (how does one judge it?), and on what might be called its heuristics (how does one teach from it? what can be learned by studying them?)—are by no means settled, nor can they be definitively resolved. Yet, these questions are worth exploring, for by asking them, we will be able to see the larger issues implicit in the Waley or Pound choice, which illuminate not only the generics of translation but the dynamics of language and culture, the methodology of cross-cultural comparison, and the many "worlds" in world literature.

The text that attracted both Waley and Pound is, of course, the *Shih Ching* 詩經, the ancient Chinese classic which is itself surrounded by complex and interesting questions of historicity, genre, and canonicity. Important hermeneutical questions about this work can be asked, and voluminously answered, but I will resist the temptation to rehearse that scholarly scenario.[2] For the purposes of this discussion, one posits the original existence of these works, not as texts, but as songs, paeans, celebrations, laments, memorials "composed"—either orally or in writing—by ancient peoples or persons unknown, who lived sometime before the reputed lifetime of Confucius, whose dates are 551–479 B.C.[3]

The typologies of translation are numerous. Distinctions have been drawn between translations and imitations, and between translations and "versions"; these distinctions have also been denied: some argue that all translations are, in some ways, imitations, and that a translation is inevitably a version.[4] But these are author-determined classifications and do not take into account the factor so often neglected in translation studies: the audience. Just as with the assumption that the original is one and inviolate, so also it has been assumed—but with far less warrant—that the audience for translations of a work is and should be one and the same. A look at literal translations, imitations, adaptations, etc., will show that their ontological differences can be adduced only if one examines the intended, or implied, audience. A literal version, for example, is not intended for a bilingual reader who has no need of word-for-word equivalents and would not grasp the meaning of the original work in such a mechanical way.[5] Nor is a literal version intended for the general reader who does not know the original and is not likely to appreciate the "accuracy" of the rendering or the clumsiness of word-for-word versions since it disappoints expectations of reading literature. Literal versions—or "trots" in academic parlance—are actually aids to the student of the language in which the original is transmitted. Imitations, on the other hand, are the more appreciated when the reader is thoroughly familiar with the original. Pope's imitation of Juvenal and of Homer, Dryden's of Ovid and Virgil, and Pound's of Propertius are to be savored by a reader who is assumed to be conversant with the originals in Greek and Latin. The translations by Edward Fitzgerald of the *Rubaiyat* of Omar Khayyam, the renderings of the *Confucian Classics* by James Legge, and the

English versions of the Bible dating from at least the Tyndale-Coverdale rendering, on the other hand, were directed at audiences who were *not* expected to know the original: readers who—with only negligible exceptions—could not, and were not expected to read, Persian, Chinese, Aramaic, or *koine* Greek. Indeed, these audiences comprise distinct and identifiable hermeneutical *ecumene*; there are worlds in the audiences for world literature.

The differences in intended audience seem crucial in creating a useful, and historically accurate, genealogy of translation. In another study, I characterized the first type of translation as "co-eval," that is, designating works that subsume the original as a reference in the "imitation";[6] the second type I have called "surrogate" translations; with these the reader is expected to be innocent of the language in which the original was written.[7] The third type, which includes literal versions, and "trots," is directed at a reader who is assumed to be neither wholly innocent of the original nor entirely familiar with it. I have characterized these translations as "contingent" because they are neither self-sufficient, *faute de mieux*, because the original is effectively absent, or nonexistent, as in "surrogate" translations, nor self-sufficient, because the spirit and meaning of the original is effectively present, as in "co-eval" translations. The reader of "contingent" translations is the student of the language, who is not always—alas!—a student of literature. Texts and editions for this readership have proliferated in recent generations. These versions, with their accompanying linguistic apparatus and the density of their annotation and exegesis will often bewilder the general reader.[8] They are sometimes presented in a "metalanguage" comprehensible neither to the speaker of the original language nor to the native speaker of the target language untrained in the specialized discourse. In the case of translations from the Chinese, these may be familiar as "sinological" translations. Transliterations are but one example of this "metalanguage," particularly obvious in non-alphabetic languages, where native speakers are often an unreliable source, since they are spared the burden of "romanizing" words they know in non-transliterated orthography.[9]

To clarify the differences between the three categories of translation, I propose the "ontological grid" shown in Table 1. The characterization of untranslated works as both explicitly absent and implicitly absent might seem a banal insight, but it reflects an important lesson of epistemology, for it underlines the difference between realizing and not realizing that something is missing, and it reminds us of the crucial importance between self-conscious

Table 1.

Target Text	Source Text	
untranslated works	explicitly absent	implicitly absent
surrogate translations	explicitly present	implicitly absent
contingent translations	explicitly absent	implicitly present
co-eval translations	explicitly present	implicitly present

and blithe ignorance. In translation, it represents the difference between *knowing* about the existence of an important work in another language that is as yet untranslated, and *not knowing* about it.[10]

"Surrogate" translations presuppose the inaccessibility of the original for its readers, and the effective nonexistence of the source text. In this perspective, there is the possibility of a certain linguistic chauvinism: a work does not exist until it is translated in the significant target language. The practice, alas, of a number of departments of English that teach "continental" works in their English versions without any consideration of their preexistence in the source language is a lamentable confusion of cultural as well as literary identities and stems from a dangerously ignorant linguistic provinciality, akin to the ardent belief of many Southern Baptists in America that the Bible was written in English.[11]

On the other hand, "contingent" translations show by their very impenetrability and cumbersomeness that *only* the original exists. If "surrogate" translations are often misused by the language provincial, "contingent" translations are as often abused by the language snob. Translations will be denigrated as impostures and impossibilities. Anything less than the *ipsissima verbum* in the original tongue is viewed as at best an irrelevancy, and at worst a desecration. But ironically, there is a language provinciality here as well, for language snobs fail to realize the importance of translations for the very source culture they admire: where would Buddhism in China be without translations from the Sanskrit and the Pali? where would Christianity be without the translations from the semitic languages and from ancient Greek? Since Babel, presumably, few if any languages have developed *ex nihilo*, but rather as variants and translations from other languages. The hoariness of ancient tongues, whether Sanskrit, Chinese, Hebrew, Greek, or Latin, should not blind us to their crucially derivative character.

"Co-eval" translations are the presage of what might be called the ultimate post-Babelian future, where everyone knows everyone else's language. The paradigm of the future is not so much the "melting pot" model, where all languages and cultures become one bland pabulum, but a pluralistic "harmony of flavors" where each ethnic ingredient retains its character yet contributes to a delectable whole. "Co-eval" translations might start with the self-translations of Vladimir Nabokov of Russian into English (and a few works written in English into Russian) and of Samuel Beckett from French into English and English into French. Certainly, both versions "co-exist" in these translations; in some cases it might be hard to discern which is artistically the more original, however easy it might be to determine originality in terms of chronological priority.

These generic characterizations are not meant to be rigidly categorical: one should not expect in every instance to determine unequivocally whether a given translation is "surrogate," "contingent," or "co-eval," though in most instances these distinctions will prove useful.[12] These three categories are not to be thought of as equally exclusionary: a "surrogate" translation and a "co-eval" translation will address mutually exclusive classes of readers: one cannot be both ignorant of an original *and* familiar with it. But the "contingent" category is more fluid: students of the original work and of the original language can read with profit both a "surrogate" version and a "co-eval" one, though the works are less relevant to their interests. All three classes of translation are, of course, relevant to the student of translation; they also represent three distinct audiences, three distinct worlds, in world literature. We might characterize these worlds as: monolingual (surrogate), metalingual (contingent), and bilingual (co-eval).

With these categorical and generic classifications in place, I can now address the Waley-Pound question. In judging value for each of these "genres" of translation, different criteria will be applied. "Surrogate" translations will be judged solely according to their impact on the target language reader: whether it piques sufficient interest to ensure the survival of the work in a new language. Fitzgerald's *Rubaiyat* and the King James Version of the Bible are prime examples of successful "surrogate" translations. Accuracy or fidelity to the original text is not a crucial factor.[13] "Contingent" translations are to be judged by the degree of usefulness to the student: their purpose is to ease access for the non-native reader to the original. Readability is not a desideratum for these versions: Nabokov's version of Pushkin's *Eugene Onegin* falls in this category, along with the almost impenetrable translations, with their brackets, extended footnotes, and linguistic mutations that characterize many academic renderings. Co-eval translations answer to perhaps the most stringent requirements: they must succeed as literary works in their own right, and—in some measure—satisfy those who are familiar with the original. The remarkable translations of Gabriel García Márquez by Gregory Rabassa, and both Arthur Waley's and Edward Seidensticker's versions of *The Tale of Genji*, each in its own way, measure up to the target as well as the source-language audience.[14]

From this perspective, let us examine songs from the *Shih Ching* in the Pound and Waley versions. Let us start with *Shih Ching* no. 40. Here is Pound:

> North gate, sorrow's edge,
> purse kaput, nothing to pledge.
>
> I'll say I'm broke
> none knows how, heaven's stroke.
>
> Government work piled up on me
>
> When I go back where I lived before,
> my dear relatives slam the door.
> This is the job put up on me,
> Sky's "which and how"?
> or say: destiny.
>
> Government work piled up on me.
>
> When I come in from being out
> my home-folk don't want me about;
> concrete fruit of heaven's tree
> not to be changed by verbosity.

It would be easy to dismiss this version as a strained attempt to create a "literary" poem where none existed. Pound's eclectic diction, mixing the intellectual slang of "purse kaput" with the homey "my home-folk don't want me about" and the abstract nominalizations, "Sky's 'which and how' " and "concrete fruit of heaven's tree," presents a pastiche that is awkward and unnatural. The version is obviously an attempt at a "surrogate" version, for Pound ignores the student learning the source language and the reader familiar with the original. Pound makes no effort to accommodate the original meaning: the translation reads like a poetic exercise verging toward, but failing to achieve, originality. The vestiges of the refrain in the original, which consists of three lines, occurring at the end of each of the three stanzas, is conflated by Pound into one line—"Government work piled up on me."

What Pound has tried to do is to compose a successful poem to be read, rather than a lyric to be sung; the texture of his language is contrived and cerebral, whereas the original is closer to visceral utterance. Pound makes only a token attempt to preserve the balladic form of the Chinese (the conflated refrain is repeated only once), and there is no attempt to preserve the theme and variation pattern in the original.

Arthur Waley's version preserves more of the original structure; there is, at least, a line-for-line correspondence to the original:

I go out at the northern gate:
Deep is my grief.
I am utterly poverty-stricken and destitute;
Yet no one heeds my misfortunes.
Well, all is over now,
No doubt it was Heaven's doing.
So what's the good of talking about it?

The king's business came my way;
Government business of every sort was put on me.
When I came in from outside,
The people of the house all turned on me and scolded me.
Well, it's over now.
No doubt it was Heaven's doing,
So what's the good of talking about it?

The king's business was all piled up on me;
Government business of every sort was laid upon me;
When I came in from outside,
The people of the house all turned upon me and abused me.
Well, it's all over now.
No doubt it was Heaven's doing,
So what's the good of talking about it?

In this version, the formulaic structure of the original is manifest: each variation on the line is preserved; each verbatim repetition carefully duplicated. Clearly, Waley had the original in mind, not merely as a catalyst for poetic inspiration, but as a form, a content, to be preserved as much as possible in English. The student of the language, and of the *Shih Ching*, finds these renderings useful as an aid to the original text. Yet, there is something awry here. The Waley version is verbose and tedious in a way that the original, with its basically four-word, four-syllable lines, is not in Chinese. (Each stanza has seven lines; most of the lines contain four word-syllables in Chinese, except for line four, which has only three characters, and line two in the second two stanzas, which has six characters: see Appendix A.)

Clearly there are no gross inaccuracies in the Waley, at least at the level of the individual line, though the result would be hard to recognize as poetry. Waley's version tries neither to replace the original nor to vie with it; it is a serviceable "contingent" translation that can be relied upon to render at least the sense of the original plaint. Yet, "contingent" translations, when they are successful, are also calculatedly *un*successful; they create a void which can be filled only by reading the original.[15] They are accurate without being satisfying; their value is contingent, and only in the access they provide to the original.

If these versions by Pound and Waley were to be evaluated, one could say defensively that Pound attempted a "surrogate" translation but did not succeed; Waley provided a "contingent" translation, which succeeded within its generic limitations. Notice the failure adduced in the one case is not the same as the failure adduced in the other; Pound's translation fails because it is an inept piece of poetic writing, not because it is inaccurate. Waley's succeeds despite its slack verbosity because it effectively evokes the original; indeed, it almost compels the reader to consult the original. But the two are being judged on different criteria, because they proceed from entirely different premises.

Yet both versions are equally unsatisfactory in one respect: neither captures the vocative immediacy of the original expression which even two millennia of scholarly exegesis in Chinese have not quite managed to erase. These are intensely commonplace sentiments, with a universality which the song does not try to hide; the diction is simple, almost visceral in its directness. There is nothing in the poem that smacks of the studio, of belles-lettres, or of scholarship. At the risk of self-exposure, I will share a version which I've developed to render some of the disarming accessibility of the original. The title of this version might be, and has been, used as the title of a popular song:

THAT'S LIFE

> Can't work there any more—
> Now I'll be poor.
> No one knows
> All my woes.
> What's the use—

> That's life!
> What's the point?
>
> Working in a bureaucracy—
> All kinds of work piled up on me.
> They played fast and loose,
> And really cooked my goose.
> What's the use—
> That's life!
> What's the point?
>
> Slaving in a bureaucracy—
> All kinds of work were dumped on me.
> They found every excuse
> To cook my goose.
> What's the use—
> That's life!
> What's the point?

I make no brief for this version as anything more than an illustration of the direct sentiments, disarmingly expressed, in the original. What this version lacks, of course, is the "hoariness" that the original text has acquired: twenty-five centuries of scholarly commentary cannot help but leave their mark. Yet, few would deny the original folkloric provenance of these words; few would refute the fact, even if they occasionally forget it, that this is a poem from the section of the *Shih Ching* entitled "Airs of the States," a section traditionally regarded as a collection of songs from the people reflecting their complaints, miseries, joys, and sorrows, which was intended to serve as a "mirror for magistrates."

Pound's version of *Shih Ching* no. 75 is nothing short of an embarrassment: one would never have guessed from it that a simple lovelorn lyric was the inspiration (see Appendix B). Even allowing for the traditional allegory, commonplace in Confucian commentaries, of reading the neglected and unrequited girl as the minister neglected by the emperor, Pound's version is far-fetched:

> Live up to your clothes,
>   we'll see that you get new ones.
> You do your job,
>   we'll bring our best food to you 'uns.
>
> If you're good as your robes are good
> We'll bring you your pay and our best food.

Nothing too good, bigosh and bigob
For a bureaucrat who will really attend to his job.

The jazzy colloquialisms, the brash diction, the inflated rhetoric represent Pound's inventiveness out of control; it is creativity without a critical conscience, fecundity without discrimination. How far this departs from the poetry in the original can be seen in a comparison with Waley's version:

> How well your black coat fits!
> Where it is torn I will turn it for you.
> Let us go to where you lodge,
> And there I will hand your food to you.
>
> How nice your black coat looks!
> Where it is worn I will mend it for you.
> Let us go to where you lodge,
> And there I will hand your food to you.
>
> How broad your black coat is!
> Where it is worn I will alter it for you.
> Let us go to where you lodge,
> And there I will hand your food to you.

Waley leaves out the line-ending vocalizer— 兮 *hsi*—which marks the ballad, a "heigh ho," "tra-la-la" insertion to fill out the line or to end with emphasis, but, on the whole, his version reflects the simplicity and poignancy of the original. There are many such lyrics in the *Shih Ching*, the pure and unadorned expression of folk sentiment, originally sung communally, perhaps antiphonally.[16] Pound's version smacks of false rhetoric, the sophisticated condescension of a wordsmith mimicking the sounds of the populace. Waley's rendering is more modest, and given the modest posture of the persona in the song, more appropriate in tone. Pound's "surrogate" version misfires; Waley's "contingent" version is prosaic, but it preserves some of the spare abjectness of the original. Note also the strident, imperative tone of Pound's rendering, so at odds with the deferential elegance of most traditional Chinese poetry.

Shih Ching no. 90 is a perfect instance of the theme-and-variation ballad form (see Appendix C). There are three stanzas of four lines each, and four words (thus four syllables) in each line. In the first line, the first two words are the same in every stanza; in the second, again, the first two words are the same; the third line in each stanza is identical; and in the last line, only the last word is changed from stanza to stanza. The song is an almost abstract design, with no internal progression, and what appears to be random variation. It conforms to a common ballad formula, where limited demands are put on the invention of the singers. The repetitions are the heart of the poem, an obvious vestige of its oral origins. One of the problems, so often glossed over in discussions of translation, is not merely the difficulty of translating from one language to another, but of translating from oral to written discourse. The difference between script as phonetic transcription—the case with Indo-European languages—and script as ideogram—the case with Chinese—further exacerbates the difficulties. Repetition in an oral mode has a different value from repetition in a written or printed mode (which is why refrains of songs in printed texts are not repeated verbatim, but are abbreviated in one way or another). The same words in the same positions read in a text, without the accompaniment of music, are boring; as lyrics in a song, in a refrain, the same words elicit an incremental pleasure. The differences become obvious when we see Waley's "contingent" version, for—faithful as it tries to be—the result is boring and lifeless:

> Wind and rain, chill, chill!
> But the cock crowed kikeriki.
> Now that I have seen my lord,
> How can I fail to be at peace?
>
> Wind and rain, oh, the storm!
> But the cock crowed kukeriku
> Now that I have seen my lord,
> How can I fail to rejoice?
>
> Wind and rain, dark as night,
> The cock crowed and would not stop.
> Now that I have seen my lord,
> How can I any more be sad?

The first line includes an error common among translators of Chinese: the term *ch'i-ch'i* 淒淒 is an onomatopoeic compound, connoting cold and chill, like the shivering sound, created by the doubled frontal spirant; in connotation it is comparable to English "Brrr!" Waley wrongly translates each member of the compound as a separate word, yielding " . . . chill, chill." He preserves the phonetics of the doubled frontal spirant, but he violates the phonemic unity of the onomatopoeic compound. And he resorts to an interesting device to render the onomatopoeia of the *chieh-chieh* 喈喈

(archaic *ts'ier*) and the *chiao-chiao* 膠膠 (archaic *klôg*) in the second line of the first two stanzas respectively: he borrows from Japanese, and provides Japanese onomatopoeia—*kikeriki/kukeriku*—in an English translation of a Chinese poem![17]

Pound is sensitive to the preponderance of repetition in the text, and sensitive to its potential dullness on the page, so his version is a free-wheeling re-creation that preserves the repetition in more palatable ways—at the level of imagery rather than at the lexical level, but even here he varies the lexical form: "wind and rain," *feng-yü* 風雨 he renders alternatively: " . . . wind, and the rain," " . . . wind and the rain," "Wind, rain . . ."; "cock crows," *chi-ming* 雞鳴 he renders: "cock crow," "the cock crows and crows," "the cock's never-ending cry." Pound adapts an oral lyric into a readable text, converting its verbatim repetitions to phonemic variants.

> Cold wind, and the rain,
> cock crow, he is come again,
> > my ease.
>
> Shrill wind and the rain
> and the cock crows and crows,
> I have seen him, shall it suffice
> > as the wind blows?
>
> Wind, rain and the dark
> as it were dark of the moon,
> What of the wind, and the cock's never-ending cry;
>
> Together
> again
> he and I.

Pound has composed a version that "sits" better on the page than either the original or its more literal translations, as a text to be read rather than as a song to be sung. It replaces the ancient oral Chinese song with a modern American poetic text; one is surrogate for the other.

A more successful surrogate version, which relates to the original *Shih Ching* poem not as a copy, nor as counterpart and correlative, but as variant to theme, is no. 143 (see Appendix D). The original folk song is a love-plaint, full of longing and almost inarticulate desire; it is pure lyric, with the emotion repeated and intensified with every stanza, but with no narrative progression. Waley gives a fair attempt at a faithful rendering:

A moon rising white
Is the beauty of my lovely one,
Ah, the tenderness, the grace!
Heart's pain consumes me.

A moon rising bright
Is the fairness of my lovely one.
Ah, the gentle softness!
Heart's pain wounds me.

A moon rising in splendour
Is the beauty of my lovely one.
Ah, the delicate yielding!
Heart's pain torments me.

As an example of a simple folk expression, these versions are valuable, yet from a literary point of view, there is not much interest. One sees clearly enough the persona in the poem: a girl addressing her swain in his absence, and probably without his knowledge (modern adolescents might recognize this condition as a "crush"!). Pound transforms this simple lyric into a not-so-simple piece of romantic rhetoric, replete with bookish imagery ("erudite," "colleague," "enquiring," "undurable"), paranomasia ("my heart is tinder"), and syncopated rhyme:

The erudite moon is up, less fair than she
who hath tied silk cords about
                              a heart in agony,
She at such ease
                    so all my work is vain.

My heart is tinder, and steel plucks at my pain
so all my work is vain,
                    she at such ease
                    as is the enquiring moon.

A glittering moon comes out
less bright than she the moon's colleague
that is so fair,
          of yet such transient grace,
at ease, undurable, so all my work is vain
                    torn with this pain.

Pound notes, more in satisfaction than in apologia, "A few transpositions, but I think the words are all in the text." Yet, a reader familiar with the original poem is not likely to recognize the original in this rendering. Several important aspects of the original are missing in Pound's version. First, he chooses an implicitly male "I" persona whose object of desire is female; the Chinese, by leaving the subject unstated, is ambiguous on this point. Second, his tone is leisurely, contemplative, studied, and discriminating ("less fair than she," "of yet such transient grace," "at ease, undurable"); his syntax is contorted and complex ("less bright than she the moon's colleague"); the tone in the original is urgent, breathless, scarcely articulate, an utterance whose aspirations (in both senses) are reinforced by the repetition of the balladic line-ending *hsi* 兮 . The original is pure evocation, simple apostrophe, with little or no predication.

On another occasion, I have considered several of Pound's versions of the *Shih Ching* which, though different from the original in significant ways, yet bear comparison with them. Indeed, they succeed not only with the reader innocent of the original; those familiar with the original have reason to marvel as well.[18] His version of *Shih Ching* no. 23 ("Lies a dead deer on yonder plain") ranks with his "River Merchant's Wife: A Letter," his translation of a ballad by Li Po, published almost forty years earlier, as an instance of a successful "co-eval" translation, one that can be appreciated not only for its own literary value, but also as an adjunct to the original. Waley's version conveys some of the chaste simplicity in the original lyric: an expression of feral innocence, of virginity both proud and vulnerable:

> In the wild there is a dead doe;
> With white rushes we cover her.
> There was a lady longing for the spring;
> A fair knight seduced her.
>
> In the wood there is a clump of oaks,
> And in the wilds a dead deer
> With white rushes well bound;
> There was a lady fair as jade.
>
> "Heigh, not so hasty, not so rough;
> Heigh, do not touch my handkerchief.
> Take care, or the dog will bark."

Waley's rendering of "longing for the spring" is perfect for the Chinese expression, *huai ch'un* 懷春, which suggests the stirrings of sexual desire. In this connection, Waley's choice of "lady" is perhaps not so felicitous, since that word suggests someone more experi-

enced than the virgin in the poem (the original is *nü* 女 "girl")—
"maiden" would have been better. Nor is Waley's rendering of *yu*
誘 (to entice, seduce, tempt) in the past tense very well judged.
For it is clear from the poem that the seduction is in process; it is
potential, not yet achieved; the action involved is indicative, not
perfective. The brilliance of the imagery is the conjunction of the
image of the dead doe, and the imminent loss of the girl's virginity.
Waley's penultimate line is disastrously irrelevant and non-sensical:
"Heigh, do not touch my handkerchief"; the word in question is
shui 悦 , which is the sash women use to wrap their robes around
them, and therefore an extremely crucial and functional article of
clothing.

Pound's rendering captures both the imagery and the dramatic
situation with flawless resourcefulness:

> Lies a dead deer on yonder plain
> whom white grass covers,
> A melancholy maid in spring
> > is luck
> > for
> > lovers.
>
> Where the scrub elm skirts the wood,
> be it not in white mat bound,
> as a jewel flawless found,
> > dead as doe is maidenhood.
>
> Hark!
> Unhand my girdle-knot,
> > stay, stay, stay
> > or the dog
> > may
> > bark.

The insistent "stay, stay, stay" at the close is a trouvaille, for it suc-
cinctly preserves the ambivalent tone of entreaty and protest in the
poem. Good as the poem may be in Chinese, a reader of the original
can only delight at Pound's rendering, for he now has access to two
poems that—"co-evally"—interpret the same experience; each of
them creates its own voice, and preserves a memorable moment.

We can now attempt an answer to the question "Who is the better
translator, Waley or Pound?" by rephrasing it into another question:
"For whom is Pound or Waley the better translator?" The student of
Chinese will find Waley generally the more reliable; the student of

poetry will often find Pound the more interesting. Waley may be limp and laborious, but he never falls into the meretricious or the bombastic. Pound, on the other hand, may be uneven, but some of his versions achieve poetry in a way that Waley's never do. Where Waley is safe, Pound is inspired. In contemplating the comparison, one is reminded of a more famous comparison, the one Johnson made of Dryden and Pope. The parallels between the two comparisons are not exact, but there are similarities. Of Pound, it could be said, as Johnson did of Dryden: "Pound's performances were always hasty . . . he composed without consideration, and published without correction. What his mind could supply at call, or gather in one excursion, was all that he sought, and all that he gave." It might be said of Pound and Waley that "of Pound's fire the blaze is brighter, of Waley's the heat is more regular and constant. Pound often surpasses expectation, and Waley never falls below it." However, one must be careful not to force a false equivalence of comparisons: if we can characterize Pound, as Johnson did of Dryden, that he "is read with frequent astonishment," we cannot with equal justice characterize Waley, as Johnson did of Pope, that he may be read "with perpetual delight."

Waley produces "contingent" translations of unerring if often bland good taste. Pound produces "surrogate" translations of variable quality, ranging from misjudged exercises in failed rhetoric to superlative re-creations with a life of their own. Pound invariably attempted "surrogate" translations, versions that addressed an audience that would be content with his view of the original.[19] Waley's posture was somewhat ambivalent; he often spared the reader the scholarly apparatus that he was familiar with, yet he was modest about the literary character of his translations, going to such lengths as renumbering the *Shih Ching* poems according to subject matter to facilitate reference by the student interested in anthropology and content analysis. In the preface to the Second Edition (1960), Waley indicated as his intended audience "Anyone using my book for documentary purposes, that is to say, for the study of comparative literature, folklore, or the like. . . . "[20] Waley translated to show the intrinsic or extrinsic value of the originals: hence, his versions were "contingent" on their value. Where Pound translated for an audience of general readers, Waley addressed an audience of students and scholars.

I have categorized the audiences for translation as: the monolingual, the "metalingual" (or the incipiently bilingual), and the bilingual. "Surrogate" translations accommodate the first, "contingent" translations the second, and "co-eval" translations attract the third.

Most teachers of world literature (Waley would have called them teachers of comparative literature) depend on "surrogate" translations. An intelligent response to the question "Who is the better translator? Waley or Pound?"—like many questions in many fields in the modern period, from relativity theory to narratology—reverses the focus of inquiry, turns both telescope and microscope back at the viewer. Instead of determining what the object of study is, these disciplines ask, "Who is the subject of inquiry?"[21] "What is the vantage point in a field of study?" "Whose point of view is being subsumed by the question?" Translating these concerns to the current theory and practice of world literature, one must convert the question "What is world literature?" to "Which worlds are in us, who study world literature?" "Is there really any such thing as 'non-Western' literature, or is that denomination merely a reflection of Western ethnocentricity?" When we ask the question, "Waley or Pound?" we are—whether we realize it or not—asking a profoundly relevant question about ourselves.[22]

Appendix A

Shih Ching # 40

Pound's version

North gate, sorrow's edge,
purse kaput, nothing to pledge.

I'll say I'm broke
none knows how, heaven's stroke.

Government work piled up on me

When I go back where I lived before,
my dear relatives slam the door.
This is the job put up on me,
Sky's "which and how"?
or say: destiny.

Government work piled up on me.

When I come in from being out
my home-folk don't want me about;
concrete fruit of heaven's tree
not to be changed by verbosity.

Waley's version

I go out at the northern gate;
Deep is my grief.
I am utterly poverty-stricken and destitute;
Yet no one heeds my misfortunes.
Well, all is over now,
No doubt it was Heaven's doing.
So what's the good of talking about it?

The king's business came my way;
Government business of every sort was put
    on me.
When I came in from outside,
The people of the house all turned on me
    and scolded me.
Well, it's over now.
No doubt it was Heaven's doing,
So what's the good of talking about it?

The king's business was all piled up on me;
Government business of every sort was
    laid upon me;
When I came in from outside,
The people of the house all turned upon
    me and abused me.
Well, it's all over now.
No doubt it was Heaven's doing,
So what's the good of talking about it?

出自北門，
憂心殷殷。
終窶且貧，
莫知我艱。
已焉哉！
天實為之，
謂之何哉！

王事適我，
政事一埤益我。
我入自外，
室人交徧讁我。
已焉哉！
天實為之，
謂之何哉！

王事敦我，
政事一埤遺我。
我入自外，
室人交徧摧我。
已焉哉！
天實為之，
謂之何哉！

Appendix B

Pound's version

Live up to your clothes,
  we'll see that you get new ones.
You do your job,
  we'll bring our best food to you 'uns.

If you're good as your robes are good
We'll bring you your pay and our best food.

Nothing too good, bigosh and bigob
For a bureaucrat who will really attend to
  his job.

Shih Ching # 75

緇衣之宜兮，敝予又改為兮。適子之館兮，還予授子之粲兮

緇衣之好兮，敝予又改造兮。適子之館兮，還予授子之粲兮

緇衣之席兮，敝予又改作兮，適子之館兮，還予授子之粲兮

Waley's version

How well your black coat fits!
Where it is torn I will turn it for you.
Let us go to where you lodge,
And there I will hand your food to you.

How nice your black coat looks!
Where it is worn I will mend it for you.
Let us go to where you lodge,
And there I will hand your food to you.

How broad your black coat is!
Where it is worn I will alter it for you.
Let us go to where you lodge,
And there I will hand your food to you.

Appendix C

<table>
<tr><td>

Pound's version

Cold wind, and the rain,
cock crow, he is come again,
    my ease.

Shrill wind and the rain
and the cock crows and crows,
I have seen him, shall it suffice
    as the wind blows?

Wind, rain and the dark
as it were dark of the moon,
What of the wind, and the cock's never-
    ending cry;

Together
again
he and I.

</td><td>

Shih Ching # 90

風雨淒淒，雞鳴喈喈。既見君子，云胡不夷。

風雨瀟瀟，雞鳴膠膠。既見君子，云胡不瘳。

風雨如晦，雞鳴不已。既見君子，云胡不喜。

</td><td>

Waley's version

Wind and rain, chill, chill!
But the cock crowed kikeriki.
Now that I have seen my lord,
How can I fail to be at peace?

Wind and rain, oh, the storm!
But the cock crowed kukeriku.
Now that I have seen my lord,
How can I fail to rejoice?

Wind and rain, dark as night,
The cock crowed and would not stop.
Now that I have seen my lord,
How can I any more be sad?

</td></tr>
</table>

Appendix D

Pound's version

The erudite moon is up, less fair than she
who hath tied silk cords about
      a heart in agony,

She at such ease
      so all my work is vain.

My heart is tinder, and steel plucks at my pain
So all my work is vain,
      she at such ease
      as is the enquiring moon.

A glittering moon comes out
less bright than she the moon's colleague
that is so fair,
      of yet such transient grace,
at ease, undurable, so all my work is vain
      torn with this pain.

(Pound's note: "A few transpositions, but I
    think the words are all in the text.")

月出皎兮，佼人僚兮，舒窈糾兮，勞心悄兮
月出皓兮，佼人懰兮，舒懮受兮，勞心慅兮
月出照兮，佼人燎兮，舒夭紹兮，勞心慘兮

Waley's version

A moon rising white
Is the beauty of my lovely one,
Ah, the tenderness, the grace!
Heart's pain consumes me.

A moon rising bright
Is the fairness of my lovely one.
Ah, the gentle softness!
Heart's pain wounds me.

A moon rising in splendour
Is the beauty of my lovely one.
Ah, the delicate yielding!
Heart's pain torments me.

Notes

This paper was prepared originally for presentation at a Summer Humanities Institute on The Theory and Teaching of World Literature held in 1987 at the University of Massachusetts, Amherst. A slightly altered version appears in my *The Transparent Eye: Reflections on Translation, Chinese Literature, and Comparative Poetics* (Honolulu: University of Hawaii Press, 1993).

1. As this is written in English, English is assumed in the following pages to be the "native language." However, it should not be assumed that English is the only language in which the world's literature can be subsumed. The Gorky Institute of World Literature has been in existence in Russia for more than half a century, and the concept of "world literature" has been familiar in Russian for at least that long; Japanese remains the language into which more foreign works are translated more quickly than any other, so Japanese may be regarded as a language particularly hospitable to world literature. An interesting project would be to compare the different notions of world literature in different languages.

2. For a survey of these issues, see Yu (44–83).

3. The Confucian character of the traditional interpretation of these texts is reflected in Pound's title for his versions: *The Confucian Odes: The Classic Anthology*. Waley's version, *The Book of Songs*, is more anthropological and emphasizes the folkloric character of the original.

4. See John Hollander's "Versions, Interpretations, and Performances" for an analysis of the distinctions and, for the argument against the distinctions, Susan Bassnett-McGuire, "Ways through the Labyrinth: Strategies and Methods for Translating Theatre Texts" (101).

5. Vladimir Nabokov might be cited as a perverse and eccentric exception, but his insistence of literal renderings no matter how awkward was a strategy calculated to remind the reader of the ultimate futility of translation, not to render the essence of the work through translations.

6. This genre has been a staple in traditonal Western literature, when the reader could be expected to know the classical languages at least as well as his own; and it is no accident that imitations should have flourished during the Neo-Classic period, when classical virtues were emphasized.

7. These terms were developed in my essay, "Translation as Excommunication: Notes toward an Intraworldly Poetics," presented before the first Sino-American Symposium on Comparative Literature, held in Beijing, China, August 31 to September 2, 1983.

8. Bilingual editions fall into this category, as does Stanley Burnshaw's widely used *The Poem Itself*. David Hawkes's *A Little Primer of Tu Fu*, addresses a student audience and provides the original text, a transliteration, a paraphrase, and a line-for-line translation.

9. Chinese is particularly burdened in this respect: the speaker of English learning Chinese must be familiar with at least half a dozen transliteration systems (Wade-Giles, pin-yin, Guoyuu Romatzy, postal system, Yale, p'o-p'o-mo-ph'or).

10. Part of Japan's success in recent years may be attributed to the fact that Japanese scholars lead the world in translating into their native tongue works of all sorts from other languages.

11. These instances proliferate as more translations become available: a recent Ph.D thesis, vaunted by its department as one of its best, addressed the topic "Confucianism and Ezra Pound," yet no one conversant with Chinese, or knowledgeable in the voluminous Confucian tradition, or capable of examining Pound's understanding or misunderstandings of Chinese, was on the dissertation committee.

12. These categorizations seem to me more helpful with literary translations than other typologies that have been proposed. Katharina Reiss's ternary divisions—informative, expressive, or operative—are based on the source text, and cover a wider scope, distinguishing between, for example, text-books, belles-lettres, and advertisements. Juliane House's distinction between "overt" translations, where the reader is aware that what is being read is a translation, and "covert" translations, where the translation is "almost accidentally in a language other than the original," distinguishes between culturally sensitive productions (literature) and culturally less-sensitive communications (mathematics, scientific documents) but doesn't sufficiently recognize reader-based conceptions of genre implicit in every literary translation. See Marilyn Gaddis Rose, "Translation Types and Conventions" (32).

13. The voluminous scholarship since the discovery of the Dead Sea Scrolls (conveniently accessible in the multi-volume Anchor Bible) makes the King James Version of the Bible no longer a reliable textual resource, but its literary value as a "surrogate" translation remains undiminished. Robert Graves, similarly, has exposed the linguistic errors in Fitzgerald's version of *Rubaiyat* and has supplied a more "accurate" version, yet he has not managed to replace Fitzgerald in providing a better "surrogate" rendering.

14. The two versions of the *Genji* pose a somewhat special case, however, since the original is not in contemporary Japanese, but in a language that few in Japan can read. Indeed, what makes Heian Japanese difficult is its use of Chinese calligraphs sometimes as semantemes and sometimes as phonemes—i.e., as indicators of either meaning or sound. Hence, there are no living source-language speakers, and hence no truly bilingual readers of the *Genji*. It has often been observed that the Japanese resort to Waley's translation (and now doubtless, Seidensticker's) more often even than to the "translations" of the *Genji* into modern Japanese in the versions by, among others, Yosano Akiko or Tanizaki Junichiro.

15. Renato Poggioli's dictum is: "Artistic translation presupposes . . . both the ideal presence of the original, and its physical absence."

16. Marcel Granet, in his *Fêtes et chansons de la Chine* (1919) two generations ago, cited parallels in contemporary folk singing in southeast Asia, which he considered—from an anthropological perspective—offshoots of the original folk tradition that produced many of the songs in the *Shih Ching*.

17. One could also argue that *Kikeriki* is German for cock's crow; in any case, the language is neither English nor Chinese.

18. Eoyang, "The Confucian Odes: Ezra Pound's Translations of the *Shih Ching*."

19. In addition to the consultation, somewhat permissive, of Achilles Fang at Harvard, Pound had resort to at least three previously published translations: James Legge's (1893), Waley's (1937), and Bernhard Karlgren's (1950).

20. The implicit view of comparative literature as a field of study that precludes any interest in the original, or the original language, is now not as much in fashion as in Waley's day.

21. The ambivalence of the word *subject* is apposite here, for present in any field of inquiry is not only the agent, the central intelligence (subject) conducting the inquiry, but also the field of study (subject) as reflecting subjective biases.

22. At the Tamkang Conference, an interlocutor pointed out that I really hadn't answered the question posed at the outset of the paper. I agreed, pointing out that I turned the question back on itself. To which his response was that I had begged the question. My retort was that, on the contrary, far from begging the question, I had clarified it so that a meaningfully specific question could first be asked, and then, just as meaningfully, answered. Contemporary logic and rhetoric provide pseudo-logical formulations as "begging the question" to contradict an assertion. But few are aware of the complexities of "begging the question." There are times when, logically, we should be nothing short of importunate toward a question.

Works Cited

Bassnett-McGuire, Susan. "Ways through the Labyrinth: Strategies and Methods for Translating Theatre Texts." In *The Manipulation of Literature: Studies in Literary Translation*, edited by Theo Hermans, pp. 87–102. New York: St. Martin's Press, 1985.

Burnshaw, Stanley. *The Poem Itself*. New York: Holt, Rinehart and Winston, 1960; Thomas Crowell, 1976.

Eoyang, Eugene. "The Confucian Odes: Ezra Pound's Translations of the *Shih Ching*." *Paideuma* 3:1 (Spring 1974): 33–42.

———. *The Transparent Eye: Reflections on Translation, Chinese Literature, and Comparative Poetics*. Honolulu: University of Hawaii Press, 1993.

Granet, Marcel. *Fêtes et chansons de la Chine*. 1919. Translated by Evangeline Edwards as *Festivals and Songs of Ancient China*. New York: E. P. Dutton, 1932.

Graves, Robert, and Omar Ali-Shah. *The Original Rubaiyyat of Omar Khayaam, A New Translation with Critical Commentaries*. Garden City: Doubleday and Company, 1968.

Hawkes, David. *A Little Primer of Tu Fu*. Oxford: The Clarendon Press, 1967.

Hollander, John. "Versions, Interpretations, and Performances." In *On Translation*, edited by Reuben Brower. Cambridge, Mass.: Harvard University Press, 1959; New York: Oxford University Press, 1966.

Pound, Ezra. *The Confucian Odes: The Classic Anthology*. Cambridge, Mass.: Harvard University Press, 1954; New York: New Directions, 1959.

Rose, Marilyn Gaddis. "Translation Types and Conventions." In *Translation Spectrum: Essays in Theory and Practice*, edited by Rose, pp. 31–40. Albany: State University of New York Press, 1981.

Waley, Arthur. *The Book of Songs*. London: Allen and Unwin, 1937; New York: Grove Press, 1960.

Yu, Pauline. "Imagery in the Classic of Poetry." In *The Reading of Imagery in the Chinese Poetic Tradition*, pp. 44–83. Princeton: Princeton University Press, 1987.

9. Under the Palimpsest and Beyond: The World, the Reader, and the Text in the Nigerian Novel in English

Chantal Zabus

The Anglophone reader of world literature cannot in all fairness claim to know the three thousand or more languages spoken today as well as their literary corollaries.[1] Such a reader thus reads works in translation, that is, not the original-language texts. When reading original English-language texts, that same Anglophone reader may expect, with reason, to read about his or her familiar *Umwelt* (Jameson 42). Yet such a reader is bound to be jolted by the various uses to which English has been put from the moment it stopped being the sole monopoly of England and its settler colonies.

To take only one example, the British writer David Lodge does not use English in the same way as does the recent Booker prize winner, Nigerian Ben Okri. Lodge and Okri (or John Fowles and Wole Soyinka) are admittedly "apples and oranges," but they are both fruit that sell equally well on the world market. It is up to the consumers of world literature to peel the orange in a different way than they would the apple. Any reader concerned with the interplay of meanings and intentions in mixed texts is invited to uncover the cultural layers and contesting worlds in ferment behind the apparently homogeneous English of many texts.

Such texts belong to the vast corpus of the non-Western, postcolonial literatures written in English, an English which has become, in the wake of the collapse of the British Empire, the ex-colonizer's language. Now that the Empire is busy "writing back to the centre," using the postcolonial techniques of abrogation,[2] the very notions of canonicity and the "familiar" are on the verge of dismantlement. The post-colonial act of reading will therefore require the world literature reader to revise his or her positioning vis-à-vis not only canonicity but also the cultural difference that is more or less felicitously conveyed by such a seemingly familiar language as English.

My paradigm will be the Nigerian novel in English, which was born only a few decades before Nigeria came to independence in

1960, as a result of a long process of colonization which involved, among other things, the imposition of English as a prestige language triumphing over the Nigerian languages which were artfully demoted to the status of "dialects." By the same token, literature in Nigerian languages (e.g., D. O. Fagunwa's Yoruba writings) was supplanted by an English-language body of literature which, ironically, was going to become instrumental in conveying Nigerian culture to the world literature reader, who is made to realize that it is English, but not quite—that it is "other" while being the same.

In order to come to terms with the "otherness" of such a language as English, I will be using the governing metaphor of the palimpsest. As a writing material, on which an original writing has been effaced to make room for a second, the palimpsest relates to the practice of reading for the "world" of an original text hidden behind translation. However, one may not always realize that this original-language text itself may be a palimpsest that translation can scarcely uncover. It is not by chance that the image of the palimpsest is also central to the late twentieth-century ideologies of deconstruction (in the person of Jacques Derrida) and decolonization, for both movements herald the palimpsest as the ideal synecdoche for the simultaneous undoing of a given order of priorities in language and meaning, and the embedding of the new order in the text. Thus what is at work in the Nigerian novel in English is, with a "difference," the same "linguistic guerilla warfare" that the Moroccan Abdelkebir Khatibi has observed in the so-called bilingual Maghrebian (Moroccan, Algerian, Tunisian) novels in French (Khatibi 47–48n.; Meddeb 16; Zabus "Linguistic Guerilla").

The texts that I will consider here are palimpsests in that, behind the scriptural authority of the European language, the earlier, imperfectly erased remnants of the source language, e.g., the African language, are still visible. I distinguish two palimpsestic modes. In the first mode, one could liken the critics' task to that of the chemist, in that the critics make use of critical reagents whereby, in Derrida's words, they can "make the effaced writing of papyrus or a parchment visible again" (Derrida 8). Derrida's numismatic notion of the "ef-face-ment" of the original figure behind the metaphoric Western philosophical discourse sheds light on the impossibility of recovering the original in the European-language or Europhone text, more generally, because its invisibility is also its invincibility. What is recovered thus in deciphering the West African, e.g., the Nigerian, palimpsest is not so much the source language in filigree in that text as its scriptural trace. As will be explained later, the second palimpsestic mode goes beyond the trace, beyond the palimpsest.

I have singled out the works of three Nigerian writers who have pushed linguistic experimentation in both palimpsestic modes to its limits: (1) Gabriel Okara's *The Voice* (1964), which I will contrast with Amos Tutuola's *The Palm-Wine Drinkard* (1952) and (2), beyond the first mode, Ken Saro-Wiwa's *Sozaboy* (1986).

Under the Palimpsest

One may indeed wonder what really happens when a West African writer simulates the African language in the Europhone narrative. Against the extant unsatisfactory nomenclature,[3] I propose to identify this phenomenon as that of relexification,[4] a term which I have borrowed from linguistics but which can be transfered to literary stylistics and redefined as the forging of a new literary-aesthetic medium out of the elements of an alien, dominant lexicon. As a method, relexification stems from a need to solve an immediate artistic problem: that of rendering African concepts, thought-patterns, and linguistic features in the European language. As a strategy *in potentia*, it seeks to subvert the linguistically codified and to affirm a historically repressed language and a specific ethnicity via the imposed medium.

Whether lexico-semantic or morpho-syntactic, the relexified medium may not reflect variations in current oral or written usage in West Africa, i.e., Nigeria. For instance, Igbo people use "eleven" instead of "ten and one" (*iri na otu*), which Achebe used in *Things Fall Apart* to render the traditional Igbo counting system (Achebe 37).[5] Also, no Fanti-speaking person greets another with the words "I give you the dawn" (*me ma wo akye*), a formula used by the character Naana in Ghanaian Ayi Kwei Armah's *Fragments*. As a world-creating, essentially literary and diachronic practice, relexification differs from mother-tongue interference, inadvertent calquing or loan-translation. (The main difference between calquing and relexification is that the former is inadvertent while the latter is deliberate.) I will consider calquing in Amos Tutuola, whose work I consider the precursor of relexification in its earlier, synchronic form.

Tutuola's first published novel, *The Palm-Wine Drinkard*, is the "written telling" of a Yoruba composite folk-tale which attempts to simulate in writing the live performance of the competent raconteur, with the obvious difficulty that arises not only from a mediocre command of English but also from the imposition of a literary organization over oral narrative material. Although I do not intend to take in my purview questions related to orality, let it suffice to say that Tutuola reminds us, through the essential weaknesses of his tale, that the central document in oral literature or orature is the live performance. Kola Ogunmola and Hubert Ogunde first provided an operatic version (1963 and 1967) of the tale, *Ọmútí*. The operatic performance was based not on *The Palm-Wine Drinkard* but on a translation of Tutuola's folk novel into Yoruba because it was found that "it would be very difficult to set Tutuola's lyrics in English to truly African rhythms. In any case no orchestra employing African instruments existed which could perform from a written score" (Axworthy). In light of our approach, the translation from English to Yoruba to remedy the technical impossibility of adapting English prose to "truly African rhythms" may here be read as the uncovering of the original Yoruba substratum in Tutuola's botched palimpsest. The Yoruba translation is also, possibly, the text that could have come into being, had Tutuola written the tale originally in Yoruba or had he translated his own text.

What received the most attention in early reviews and later reassessments of *The Palm-Wine Drinkard* is its language, which has been described as a young, ungrammatical, incomprehensible, imperfectly acquired second language.[6] Most of Tutuola's stylistic unorthodoxy is attributable to direct or semi-direct calquing (also called transliteration and loan-translation) from his mother tongue, Yoruba.[7] It results in the transfer of grammatical relations, lexico-semantic transplants, shifts, extensions, analogical constructions, and morpho-syntactic innovations. Some of these transplants can be observed:

(1) in the use of tenses, as in the negated preterit of "to be" (kan):

```
. . . even    a pond        did not be   near     there . . . (75)
> kódà    adágún omi   kan kò sí   níẹgbẹ ibẹ
```

instead of "even a pond was not to be found . . ."

(2) in the use of verbs:

```
. . . it   remained   me     alone (28)
>    ó   ku           èmí   nìkan
```

instead of ". . . I was left alone / I was the only one left."

(3) in the indirect clause structure, calqued on the Yoruba interrogative clause:

```
He (Death) asked me from where did I come? (13)
> Ikeé     bi     me   nibo     ni   mo(ti)   wá?
    Death   ask   me   at-place   be   I   from   come
```

instead of "Death asked me where I came from";
or in

(4) the nominalization of adjectives (a) or the use of the adverbial form of the adjective (b):

(a) . . . we met *uncountable* of them at the gate (59)
        àìmọye
        > à-ì-mọ-iye
        prefix-not-know-number > that you do not know
        the number of instead of "we met an uncountable
        number of them / countless / numerous people";

(b)	this	old	man	was not	a	really	man . . .
>	ọkùnrin	arúgbó	yìí	kì í		sẹ	ènìyàn lásán.

Calquing from Yoruba is also observable in the occurrence of certain redundancies as in the duplication of adverbs, a characteristic of the Kwa languages of West Africa which gave rise to the same feature in Pidgin English; in the non-standard behaviour of prepositions; in the awkwardly repetitive use of pronouns due to the lack of gender in the Yoruba third person singular subject and direct object pronoun—ò—and the third person singular possessive adjective—rẹ̀. The calque of a Yoruba phrase is sometimes used to explain a culturally bound notion like the common reference in Yoruba folklore to the dead "walking backward or with our back" (97) from the Yoruba *fi ẹhin rìn* (use-back-walk) as opposed to the living "walking forward or with our face" (96) from the Yoruba *fi orí rìn* (use-head-walk) or *fi ojú wa rìn* (use-eye-our-walk). Tutuola's innovations thus range from stylistic cul-de-sacs to felicitous, delightfully bizarre, and even poetic coinages such as "two o'clock in the mid-night," (14) from *aago mèjí ọgànjọ́ ònu* (clock-two-deep-night), and in "unreturnable-heaven's town," from *ilú àjò àrèmabò* (town-journey-not return).

The semantics, syntax, and general morphology of the Yoruba language, as well as devices found in Yoruba prose narratives such as the real need for *copia*, or the continual flow of discourse, are not the only source of Tutuola's innovations. The other recognizable source is the English language. These coinages are derived analogically from existing English rules as in "shareful" derived via suffixation of "-ful" after "mindful" or in "ghostess" after "princess." Some of these innovations stick indelibly in the record of literary history, like "drinkard," as in the title, *The Palm-Wine Drinkard*, which resists compulsive assaults of correction.

Tutuola's inventiveness, however, does not fully account for his abandonment of obligatory categories in English. His idiosyncrasies are indeed overshadowed by the stylistic unorthodoxies resulting from inadvertent calquing and by the inconsistent and haphazard occurrence of such innovations. These leave little room for intentionality, that is, the glottopolitical will to do violence to the dominant language. When Tutuola's conscious will to resort to the Yoruba language as a source of inspiration surfaces, his unwitting calquing has the potential of developing into deliberate relexification. Calquing thus antedates and evolves to become relexification when the Europhone writer has at his command the appropriate tools and a subversive will to deconstruct the colonial pattern of dominance.

I now propose to examine how this will manifests itself in the workings of relexification as in Gabriel Okara's *The Voice*, which is thus far the most deliberate experiment in syntactical relexification in West African literature of English expression. The will to do violence is here to be understood as the appetence "to violate" (OED), that is, "to disregard, fail to comply with, act against the dictates or requirements of" the European prose narrative. Textual violence therefore does not preclude the gentleness of Okara's linguistic experimentation in his poetry, about which he said: "So I write naturally. I do not want to outdo the British" (Okara Interview 44).

Unlike Tutuola, Okara has expounded his beliefs about language manipulation. Okara's explanation of his creative strategy in an interview provides an excellent description of "relexification," although he does not use the word:

> As a writer who believes in the utilisation of African ideas, African philosophy, and African folk-lore and imagery to the fullest extent possible, I am of the opinion the only way to use them effectively is to translate them almost literally from the African language native to the writer into whatever European language he is using as his medium of expression.
>
> ("African Speech" 15)

Okara does not translate, as he contends in this interview, in that he does not seek equivalency and does not aim at recoding the original according to the norms of the target language. Unlike translation, relexification lets his native Ijo tongue speak. I shall further distinguish between relexification and translation.

Every page of *The Voice* is saturated with lexico-semantic inno-

vations strangely reminiscent of the double- or triple-barreled coinages in Gerard Manley Hopkins's "sprung rhythm" poetry, which
held a great fascination for Okara.[8] These coinages are relexified
from Ijo:[9]

"wrong-doing-filled inside" (*Voice* 31)
>búlóù sè kìríghà-yè-mìè kùmò bèinnìmì
inside all wrong-thing-do only filled

"a fear-and-surprise-mixed voice" (66)
>yé   òwèì má tàmàmáa mò gùánìmì ókólo
thing fear and surprise with mixed voice;

"making-people-handsome day" (70)
>kémé mìé èbimò èréin
person make handsome day.

Morpho-syntactic innovations such as the postponement of the verb
or of the negative can be traced to Ijo syntactical patterns:

"To every person's said thing listen not" (7)
>Kémé gbá yémó sè pòù kúmó
Man say things all listen not,

"Shuffling feet turned Okolo's head to the door" (26)
>Sísírí sìsìrì wèníbùòàmò Okòló tèbè wàimò wáríbùò dìamè
Shuffling moving-feet Okolo's head turned door faced.

The syntax is here so altered that a counter-value system is created
that jeopardizes the English logocentric relation between word and
referent. It also erodes the dominant language's syntax, that which
sustains linguistic imperialism.[10]

In its frequent, conscious departures from orthodox English semantics, syntax, and narrative stylistics, *The Voice* constitutes an
unprecedented experiment in textual violence. It most pointedly
epitomizes the West African palimpsest in that the sedimentary Ijo
etymons gnaw linguistically at the European language and thematically at Western primitive accumulation. The repressed African language struggles to surface in and inhabit—at times parasitically—
the European language.

Conversely, it may be argued that the repressed Ijo tongue falls
prey to a textual "glottophagia"[11] by which English "devours" the
African etymons and morphemes which now function as the linguistic debris of a nearly extinct language. By an analogous pro-

cess, the Ijo worldview becomes a decaying ethno-text, or a text conveying a moribund ethnicity. In that respect, Alain Ricard has referred to the risk of "folklorization" in objectifying the dominated language:

> If the language used by "minor" writers is made of devices and stylistic idiosyncrasies and is based on a static vision of the cultural situation, it then becomes obvious that the dominated language, the "other" language, will appear as an object.
>
> (42, my translation)

By exhibiting the dominant language's protean possibilities of adaptation, relexification can thus help revitalize and recirculate the target language in a perversely neo-colonial fashion at the expense of the source language.

This mutual cannibalism may be due to the fact that textual violence is directed against *and* via the dominant language. This double-edged subversiveness is endemic in relexification (although it varies in proportion), as it is in all acts of indigenization and, more generally, in all strategies of literary decolonization and revanchism. What is thus recovered in deciphering *The Voice* is the Ijo trace, a trace which suggests both the unadulterated parchment of Ijo culture and the spurious papyrus crimped by the European discursive mode.

The (in)visibility of the Ijo original further demarcates relexification from translation. Unlike translation, which operates from the language of one text to the other—the original and the translated version—relexification operates from one language to the other within the same text. Although no consensus has been reached about the process of ideation behind relexification, some writers[12] have admitted to the possibility of an African language original which, under the guise of carelessly jotted notes or elaborate literary fragments, is not visible in the record of literary history. Since the African language is latent and the European language manifest, the palimpsest is also by the same token a schizotext which further splits textual cohesion.

Beyond the Palimpsest

Beyond the first palimpsestic mode, the African language and the European language do not interact as dominant vs. dominated languages and are not tiered in layers, the trace of one inhabiting the other. The two unrelated registers are amalgamated into a pidgin-ized medium which refracts the sociolinguistic West African language contact situation.

Whereas Okara's literary experiment rests on an almost Manichean opposition or power relation between the mother tongue and the other tongue, the Pidgin medium dissolves the infernal "binarity" between target and source language. The pidginized medium thus moves closer to the West African sociolinguistic situation and, by the same token, to its ontological status.[13] It moves beyond the notion of an original to be recovered by accounting for the pidginization and increased creolization of English and the mother tongue. The critic is here the observer of a textual alchemy whereby baser or demoted registers are transmuted into an increasingly creolized medium, potentially the higher or upgraded language of first-person narratives. The critic thus moves away from papyrology, beyond the first palimpsestic mode, to gauge this new amalgamation of registers.

It is impossible here even to sketch a brief outline of the history of Pidgin as a literary medium but let it suffice to say that Pidgin English has been both underrepresented and, most notably, misrepresented. At first an embellishment and slot-filler, Pidgin (e.g., Nigerian Pidgin English or ẸnPi) was then rehabilitated. Its earlier monolithic functions (as baby-talk and bush-talk) were then revised and expanded to include other functions as the medium of urban prestige and integration (and disidentification with tradition), as a mode of inter- and intra-ethnic communication, and eventually as "the language ever more suited to the times" (Achebe *Man* 167).[14] Yet, because it is first and foremost an auxiliary language and therefore nobody's mother tongue,[15] Pidgin is restricted to dialogues in third-person narratives and it remains in the Anglophone novel a medium into which the character often slides, slips, or lapses, as in a fall from a higher register.

Ken Saro-Wiwa's *Sozaboy* originated or, perhaps, inchoated as a riposte to O. R. Dathorne's verdict about a short story titled "High Life": "While the style [Saro-Wiwa] had used might be successful in a short story, he doubted that it could be sustained in a novel." Dathorne further diagnosed that ". . . the piece is not in true 'Pidgin' which would have made it practically incomprehensible to the European reader. The language is that of a barely educated primary school boy exulting in the new words he is discovering and the new world he is beginning to know" (quoted in Saro-Wiwa Author's Note i). I have to concur with Dathorne that "High Life" is not in Pidgin. It is written in a Standard English which occasionally turns into the *précieux* and hypercorrect lingo of popular pamphleteering. This pseudo-Onitsha Market chapbook might be warning young men that every "bundle of sophistication . . . perambulating lackadaisically along the road may not necessarily be a woman" (Saro-Wiwa "High Life" 20). More importantly, "High Life" is the result, as Saro-Wiwa puts it, "of my fascination with the adaptability of the English language and of my closely observing the speech and writings of a certain segment of Nigerian society" (i). As a deliberate attempt at representing non-standard speech, "High Life" is the necessary prequel to *Sozaboy*, which is thus far the most conscious linguistic experiment with non-standard speech in the West African first-person narrative.

Already a glimpse becomes visible of Nigerian Pidgin's potential to be a first language in Cyprian Ekwensi's *Jagua Nana* (1961). Had Jagua Nana, Ekwensi's full-fledged "Pidgin personality," told her own story, she would have used an Igbo- and Yoruba-informed Pidgin and, had she had children, Pidgin would have been their native tongue. Jagua's rival, Nancy Oll, whose parents originally come from Sierra Leone, consistently communicates with her Igbo-speaking husband in Pidgin, even after she has completed her studies in England. Their children will probably speak Pidgin at home. In that respect, Bonneau contends that "it is in this type of situation that one can observe the triggering of the creolization or even nativization process" (my translation), basing her prophecy on Hall's definition: "A Creole language arises when a Pidgin becomes the native language of a speech-community" (Bonneau 19).

Ken Saro-Wiwa's protagonist, "Sozaboy," speaks a strange, lawless lingo on the verge of creolization. In this textual alchemy, the three transmutable registers are not yet blended into a creolized medium. These three registers are Nigerian Pidgin English, which borrows freely from the mother tongue, Kana; "broken English," that is, the unsystematic use of strings of English words; and standard idiomatic English. Saro-Wiwa has juxtaposed them and occasionally amalgamated the three codes into a "third code," or what he calls "rotten English." This variant is here meant to be the discordant "voice" of post–Civil War Nigerian society:

So now, I come reach the African Upwine Bar. Nobody inside at all at all. And no light sef. I come knock on the door. On all the doors. No answer. Even the whole street or even the whole Diobu. Nobody. I know say tory don wor wor.
    That night I was thinking and thinking what I will do to find

my mama. I prayed to God. I was begging him to show me the way in the name of our Lord Jesus Christ Amen. . . .

(*Sozaboy* 141)

Saro-Wiwa provides a glossary covering non-standard use of English in the twenty-one "Lombers" (numbers) that make up the book: Pidgin words and phrases such as "this girl na waya-oh" (this girl is something else), "na je-je" (it's stylish), "abi the girl no dey shame?" (or is the girl not shy?), "water don pass gari" (matters have come to a head); phoneticized mispronunciations of Standard English such as "Tan Papa dere" (Stand properly there), "Hopen udad mas" (Open order march), "terprita" (interpreter); words and designations presumably of Kana origin such as "Sarogua" (Ancestral spirit, guardian of Dukana); "wuruwuru" (chicanery; cheating); "ugbalugba" (problem), "tombo" (palm-wine). At times, Saro-Wiwa conveys only the "feel" of Pidgin by retaining some of its signal features like the reduplication of the adjective for emphasis and the non-inverted question. This method, however, makes Pidgin English look like an impoverished variant of the standard norm. At other times, Saro-Wiwa delves into the deep structure of Pidgin, causing the unwary, non-Pidgin reader to infer—perhaps wrongly—the meaning of such phrases as "simple defence" (civil defence); "man" (penis); "some time" (perhaps); "whether-whether" (no matter what); "as some thing used to be" (maybe); "does not get mouth" (has no rights); "country" (ethnic group).

As the author himself admits, "whether [this medium] throbs vibrantly enough and communicates effectively is my experiment" (Saro-Wiwa, i). As an experiment, the novel seems to be pointing in two directions: it may be seen as an attempt to capture a state of hybridization or bilateral *métissage* of languages in Nigerian society. The second direction points toward a dead end: Pidgin is here part of a post–Civil War linguistic "stew." Saro-Wiwa has entrapped the dancing, quicksilver quality of an essentially spoken language in the discursive mode of the novel before it is creolized in the social arena. In its scriptural rendition in Standard English (e.g., *Sozaboy* 39), the mother tongue seems to stand outside of this textual alchemy, untouched by the "baser" discordant registers. Yet, Kana *qua* Kana has been effaced and eclipsed by this "rotten English," which persistently rots away. It disembodies the tiers of the palimpsest into an as yet unrecognizable (or unrecognized) medium in the making in the West African text and context.

In the Nigerian context of broadcasting, a quasi-creolized Pidgin has indeed already been fashioned to meet the needs of the Nigerian Television Authority Network. For instance, the television drama, "Samanja," which was originally transmitted in Hausa on the Kaduna station, was "changed to a variety of Pidgin" once it was elevated to network status (Saro-Wiwa "A Television Drama" 6). Most Nigerian comedy on television is being written in Pidgin English but Saro-Wiwa himself is now contributing to English language television comedy to show that "Nigerians do not only 'laugh in Pidgin' and through slapstick" ("A Television Drama" 14). With *Sozaboy*, however, Achebe's cherished notion of the "levity of Pidgin" has been ousted by a new seriousness that can capture social unrest and the dislocation of the individual consciousness.

Whether we look under or beyond the West African palimpsest, we witness the gradual minorization of English and the subversion of its hegemony as a literary medium. In Tutuola's calquing, the Yoruba language and narrative stylistics do not dominate the English language to the extent of relexifying it because English is not inscribed in a pattern of dominance. Because Tutuola does not master English, he cannot subvert it. With Okara, English no longer has the traditional authority of a major written language. With Saro-Wiwa, English, in its non-standard use, has almost ceased to be a glottopolitical instrument of domination.

The potential minorization of the European language in the West African novel is very much akin to the concept of "minor literature" that Deleuze and Guattari articulated in approaching Kafka's work. Just as Kafka shunned the hyper-cultural usage of German and an oral, popular Yiddish to embrace the deterritorialized German of Prague,[16] the West African novelist of English expression has rejected the dominant European discursive mode and Pidgin *qua sermo vulgaris* for a new medium. Incidentally, Yiddish has functionally a great deal in common with Pidgin, which is grafted onto English in the same way (although to a lesser extent) than Yiddish, according to Deleuze and Guattari, "is grafted onto Middle-High German and . . . so reworks the German language from within so that one cannot translate it into German without destroying it; one can understand Yiddish only by 'feeling it' in the heart" (25). Like Prague German with its interferences of Czech and Yiddish, this new deterritorialized medium finds its place, away from its ancestral home, on African soil and in the novelist's literary imagination. By creating "linguistic third world zones" (27), the relexified text and the botched third code constitute a "minor literature," that is, a literature "which a minority constructs with a major language" (16).

This "new and unexpected modification" (25) that Kafka brought to Prague German recalls the textual violence (in the form of morpho-syntactic relexification) that occasionally breaks through palimpsestic layers. What is said of Kafka's syntactic experimentation could be said of Okara's: "He will turn syntax into a cry that will embrace the rigid syntax of this dried-up German [read: English]" (26). The "cry" has also quenched the "laugh[s] in Pidgin" which, in its creolization, has become the serious medium of first-person narratives.

The novelist's deterritorialization is simultaneous with his reterritorialization through relexification and reciprocal creolization. This dual movement, also inherent in the double-edged subversiveness discussed earlier, shows that the relexified or quasi-creolized medium is at a linguistic interface. The producer of that medium exists therefore also at a psycholinguistic interface between two systems of patronage. The reader may be at still another similar interface, reading the space in-between the original world that such mixed texts host, and the original-language text which is itself a "translation" of the original that the practice of translation should attempt to bring forth.

To adapt Said's useful phrase, we may be witnessing "a transfer of legitimacy from filiation to affiliation"; from the writer's filial bond to the mother tongue to his or her affiliation with a communally owned Creole, the hallmark of languages in contact. The two palimpsestic modes may indeed be stages which move the writer and the critic from papyrological stylistics to alchemic sociolinguistics, from underneath the palimpsest to beyond.

The world literature reader is thereby invited to join the writer and critic in an initiatory rite during which all three are expected to forego the monolithic world of linguistic and cultural innocence, and embrace the fertile interface of postcolonial hybridized poetics. Reading will never be the same again in a world that is expanding its metes and bounds to accommodate increased interbreeding, plurality, syncreticity, and the fragmentation of world literature into world literatures.

Notes

An earlier version of this paper was delivered at the Eleventh Annual Conference on Commonwealth Literature and Language Studies in German-Speaking Countries, and published in the Proceedings, *Crisis and Creativity in the New Literatures in English* (103–121); I have dealt with the topic at length in my book, *The African Palimpsest*.

1. Walter J. Ong claims that only seventy-eight of these three thousand languages have a literature. This claim is, however, highly controversial.

2. Salman Rushdie's words. On postcolonial abrogation, see Ashcroft et al., *The Empire Writes Back* (38–51).

3. Such terms as (psychic)translation, transference, and "transmutation" have permeated linguistic studies with particular reference to West African novels. (See Braj B. Kachru, Emmanuel Ngara, and James Booth.)

4. Loreto Todd describes the relexification of one's mother tongue using English vocabulary but indigenous structures and rhythms.

5. See Claudia Zaslavsky (44).

6. Criticism of Tutuola's use of English is polarized. At the end of the spectrum is a mawkish heralding of Tutuola's limitations. For instance, Geoffrey Parrinder contends that Tutuola's license makes the Europhone literature produced by more highly educated Africans a monolith of "rather stiff essays" (10). At the other end of the critical spectrum, Yoruba A. Afolayan categorized Tutuola's English as being that of a user "with post-primary education at approximately the level of present-day Secondary Class Four" (68).

7. In examining the following Yoruba samples from Tutuola's *The Palm-Wine Drinkard*, I consulted Prof. Yiwola Awoyale from the Department of Linguistics, University of Ilorin, Nigeria.

8. See Vincent (xii). One could argue that Ijo is to Okara what Latin was to Hopkins, but what rules the dynamics of Hopkins's "sprung rhythm" exists within the borders of the English language and, to some readers, never suggests another language, as it does in Okara's prose and poetry.

9. In order to ascertain the degree of relexification from Ijo, I consulted Mr. Gabriel Okara. They have been recently revised by Professor Kay Williamson of the University of Port Harcourt, Nigeria.

10. J. V. Stalin contends that the Balkan languages survived the Turkish assimilators' attempts at stultifying them because their syntax and grammar were in the main preserved (24). See also R. Budagov (7).

11. Adapted from the French sociolinguistic term *glottophagie* coined by Louis-Jean Calvet to refer to the linguistic colonization of Africa.

12. Olympe Bhêly-Quenum from Benin confesses that he writes in Fon or Yoruba, then translates his thoughts and develops the original idea in the target language (Chevrier 42–50).

13. Polygenetic theories of origin for Pidgins hold that each Pidgin is genetically related to the corresponding standard language, from which it diverged under the influence of a similar sociolinguistic situation. The monogenetic theory posits a general Pidgin (Creole) as a common ancestor which has developed distinct and mutually unintelligible varieties. For further detail, see Hymes.

14. See also Barbag-Stoll.

15. This needs to be qualified, for an estimated eight million people in Nigeria now speak ẸnPi or Nigerian Pidgin.

16. For the distribution of the European registers—Czech, Yiddish, Ger-

man, Prague German—Deleuze and Guattari have made judicious use of Henri Gobard's tetraglossic model (Gobard 34–38).

Works Cited

Achebe, Chinua. *A Man of the People*. London: Heinemann, 1964.
———. *Things Fall Apart*. London: Heinemann, 1958.
Afolayan, Yoruba A. "Language and Sources of Amos Tutuola." In *Critical Perspectives on Amos Tutuola*, edited by Bernth Lindfors, pp. 66–93. Washington, D.C.: Three Continents Press, 1975.
Armah, Ayi Kwei. *Fragments*. Boston: Houghton Mifflin, 1970.
Ashcroft, Bill, Gareth Griffiths, and Helen Tiffin. *The Empire Writes Back*. London: Routledge, 1989.
Axworthy, G. J. "The Stage Version of *The Palm-Wine Drinkard*." *Òmútí*, an opera by Kola Ogunmola, transcribed and translated by R. G. Armstrong, Robert L. Awujoola, and Val Olayemi from a tape recording by R. G. Armstrong and Samson Amali. Ibadan: University of Ibadan Institute of African Studies, 1972.
Barbag-Stoll, Ann. *Social and Linguistic History of Nigerian Pidgin English*. Tubingen: Stauffenberg-Verlag, 1983.
Bonneau, Danielle. "Le Pidgin English comme moyen d'expression littéraire chez les romanciers du Nigeria." *Annales de l'Université d'Abidjan* 5D (1972): 5–29. Revised in *Littérature-Linguistique-Civilisation-Pédagogie: Etudes anglaises N° 65*. Paris: Didier, 1973.
Booth, James. "Literature and the Politics of Language." *Writers and Politics in Nigeria*. New York: Africana, 1981.
Budagov, R. "K teorii sintaksiee skix otmosenij" (For a theory of syntactical relations). *Voprosy Jazkoznanija* 1 (1973).
Calvet, Louis-Jean. *Linguistique et colonialisme*. Paris: Payot, 1974.
Chevrier, Jacques. "Interview avec cinq écrivains africains." *Notre librairie* 78 (Oct.–Dec. 1984): 42–50.
Davis, Geoffrey, and Hena Maes-Jelinek, eds. *Crisis and Creativity in the New Literatures in English: Proceedings of the Eleventh Annual Conference on Commonwealth Literature and Language Studies in German-Speaking Countries*. Amsterdam: Rodopi, 1990.
Deleuze, Gilles, and Felix Guattari. *Kafka: Toward a Minor Literature*. 1975. Translated by Dana Polan. Minneapolis: University of Minnesota Press, 1986.
Derrida, Jacques. "White Mythology: Metaphor in the Text of Philosophy." *New Literary History* 6.1 (1974): 5–74.
Ekwensi, Cyprian. *Jagua Nana*. London: Hutchinson, 1961.
Gobard, Henri. *L'Aliénation linguistique*. Preface by Gilles Deleuze. Paris: Flammarion, 1976.
Hymes, Dell, ed. *Pidginization and Creolization of Languages*. Cambridge, England: Cambridge University Press, 1971.

Jameson, Fredric. *The Political Unconscious: Narrative as a Socially Symbolic Act.* London: Methuen, 1981.

Kachru, Braj B., ed. *The Other Tongue: English across Cultures.* Chicago: University of Illinois Press, 1982.

Khatibi, Abdelkebir. *Maghreb Pluriel.* Paris: Denoël, 1983.

Meddeb, Abdelwahab. "Le Palimpseste bilingue." *Du Bilinguisme* (collectif). Paris: Denoël, 1985.

Ngara, Emmanuel. *Stylistic Criticism and the African Novel.* London: Heinemann, 1982.

Okara, Gabriel. "African Speech . . . English Words." *Transition* 3.10 (1963): 15–16. Reprinted from *Dialogue*, Paris, 1962.

———. Interview. In *Walasema: Conversations with African Writers*, edited by Don Burness. Ohio University Monographs in International Studies. *Africa*, Series 46 (1985).

———. *The Voice.* London: Andre Deutsch, 1964.

Ong, Walter J. "Orality, Literacy, and Medieval Textualization." *New Literary History* 16.1 (1984): 1–11.

Parrinder, Geoffrey. Foreword. In *Life in the Bush of Ghosts*, by Amos Tutuola, pp. 9–15. New York: Grove Press, 1954.

Ricard, Alain. *Texte moyen et texte vulgaire. Essai sur l'écriture en situation de diglossie.* Doctorat d'Etat. Bordeaux III, 1981. Lille-Theses.

Said, Edward. "Introduction: Secular Criticism." In *The World, the Text and the Critic*, by Said, pp. 1–30. Cambridge, Mass.: Harvard University Press, 1983.

Saro-Wiwa, Ken. Author's Note. In *Sozaboy: A Novel in Rotten English*, by Saro-Wiwa, p. i. Port Harcourt: Saros International Publishers, 1985.

———. "High Life." In *A Forest of Flowers*, by Saro-Wiwa, pp. 65–73. Port Harcourt: Saros International Publishers, 1986.

———. "A Television Drama in Nigeria: A Personal Experience." African Literature Association Conference. Pittsburgh, Penn.: April 1988. Unpublished essay.

Stalin, J. V. *Marxism and Problems of Linguistics.* Peking: Foreign Languages Press, 1976.

Todd, Loreto. "The English Language in West Africa." In *English as a World Language*, edited by R. W. Bailey and M. Görlach, pp. 303–322n. Ann Arbor: University of Michigan Press, 1982.

Tutuola, Amos. *The Palm-Wine Drinkard.* London: Faber and Faber, 1952.

Vincent, Theo. "Introduction." In *The Fisherman's Invocation*, by Gabriel Okara, pp. ix–xv. London: Heinemann, 1978.

Zabus, Chantal. *The African Palimpsest.* Amsterdam and Atlanta: Rodopi, 1991.

———. "Linguistic Guerilla in the Maghrebian and West African Europhone Novel." *Africana Journal* 15 (1990): 276–292.

Zaslavsky, Claudia. *Africa Counts.* Westport, Conn.: Lawrence Hill, 1973.

Part 4.

LITERACIES

PATTERNS OF UNDERSTANDING

Introduction

Sarah Lawall

Previous sections have examined various texts and employed different approaches to reading the world of world literature. Interrogating aesthetic structures and structures of cultural representation, they analyze the different worldviews constituted by the text. These readings negotiate relationships between familiar and unfamiliar worlds. They depend on a process of comparison and contrast to grasp the interplay of cultural identities, literary-historical concepts, competing images of self, merged linguistic horizons, and reciprocal perceptions of otherness. In addition, they try to suggest general patterns of understanding, and they propose various strategies to comprehend textual and linguistic structures or to theorize the relationship of real and implied readers. Such reading practice implies a new *literacy* directed toward the concept of world literature; it also corresponds to recent definitions of literacy itself.

This is literacy understood as a dynamic process of understanding, not as the sheer memorization that characterized nineteenth-century tests of reading skill. Acknowledging the existence of diverse speech communities, print cultures, and conventions of discourse, it is clearly a literacy based on cultural expression. At the same time, it is not a passive "cultural literacy" to be represented by a dictionary of inert information. Instead, these readings are closer to the concept of literacy as *skills:* as the "functional" or "survival" literacy that involves not only knowledge but an active processing of written codes.

Recent studies of literacy have documented a wide variety of linguistic communities and conventions of discourse, suggesting that literacy must be understood not as reproduction of a particular content but rather as the ability to *process* information (potentially from a variety of sources) so as to take part in common discourse. Analogously, the closely related field of composition has been seen, in the words of one scholar, as "the mind studying its own operations in the peculiar realm of reading." Overall, this "literacy" is *proficiency*; it is *skill*; it is a self-conscious cognitive process. Usually associated with written language, such literacy cannot be confined to one set of codes and primarily concerns processes of understanding.

For this reason, we conclude the sections of *Reading World Literature* with three essays on processes of reading. The essay by Peter Rabinowitz and Jay Reise takes an interdisciplinary approach, comparing the ways listeners and readers process their respective musical and literary texts. The act of listening, the authors assert, is analogous to the act of reading in that both are dynamic, context-dependent processes. The most common questions in academic world literature—whether to extend the canon (coverage) or select a few representative works—fail to address the crucial topic of literacy or how we read in the first place. Only when we recognize our own reading and listening habits, influenced as they are by cultural (and technological) expectations, will we fully begin to read. Proposing a theoretical framework of technical, attributive, and synthetic components, Rabinowitz and Reise create a model of musical literacy that is directly applicable to other arts, including the art of literature. In its insistence on diverse frames of reference for reading, their model is particularly relevant to the study of world literature.

William Moebius turns his attention to the earliest period of a reader's experience of literature, children's literature, and explores the emotional impact and ambiguous lesson of these early readings in shaping adult views of the world. Children's literature establishes the initial framework in which readers understand words and images; it has its own canon of popular works, which are not necessarily approved by adult critics. Children's picture books are especially interesting, Moebius suggests, because they link written and visual language and thus draw on two interpretive domains whose messages occasionally clash. Moebius examines two classics of modern children's literature, *Curious George* and *Charlie and the Chocolate Factory*. Both are enormously popular with children, but one meets widespread adult disapproval and is suppressed in many bibliographies. Both works, fantastic narratives inside realistic settings, use interrelated verbal and visual clues to raise touchy issues of power and desire, alienation and suffering, pleasure and the sources of pleasure in everyday life. Like many works of children's literature, they are submerged and ultimately ambiguous morality tales that disturb adult readers who, revisiting their own childhood, encounter the beginnings of a problematic, multidimensional self.

Finally, Margaret Meek Spencer examines the very beginnings of literacy in the acquisition of language skills and the simultaneous development of multiple points of reference. Like Rabinowitz, she understands reading not as mere word-recognition but primarily as an interactive process involving text, reader, and social rules of discourse. Reading, therefore, can only be analyzed in relation to cultural frames and expectations. For Spencer, literacy (and the reading of literature) is an interaction with texts that takes place inside a larger game of producing meaning; it is "deep play" that draws its players into a game of metatextuality shared with other readers. Beginning readers learn the rules of the reading game, and that it *has* rules, as they thread their way through narratives that link familiar knowledge to surprises and new perspectives at every turn. From different local starting points—ethnic, gendered, geographic, privileged, or not privileged—children learn to recognize others' tales and to compose new stories themselves, exchanging narratives inside a gradually broadening community of meaning. Spencer's own narrative takes the form of another tale, the autobiographical account of her journey from being a narrowly trained canonical reader to a teacher of multicultural children and concurrently a researcher studying knowledge acquisition and the diverse forms of learning to read. Interestingly enough, her description of reciprocal community narratives and broadening circles of comprehension recalls an earlier image: Goethe's vision of the exchange of cultural identities through new literary works that would constitute a coming "world literature."

10. The Phonograph behind the Door: Some Thoughts on Musical Literacy

Peter J. Rabinowitz and Jay Reise

I

During the 1920s, at least two widely read detective novels (we won't spoil them by telling you which ones) took off from the assumption that Person A could be tricked into thinking that Person B was still alive by hearing a recording of B's voice after B had in fact been murdered. Reading these books three quarters of a century later, that premise seems naive, even preposterous: after all, everyone knows that even when it is placed behind a door in an adjoining room, a 1920s recording (with its boxed sound, lack of overtones, and inevitable surface noise) could hardly be mistaken for a real voice. How could this obvious flaw have passed by the authors (and original readers) of these novels?

What at first seems an authorial blunder, however, turns out to provide an important clue to understanding how people listen to music. For the success of these novels suggests that while 1920s recordings *no longer* sound realistic, that was not always the case. Indeed, these phonographic killings turn out to represent an instance of what we call the Latest Fidelity Syndrome, a phenomenon evidenced by nearly a century of testimonials about the high inherent quality of whatever happen to be the latest recording techniques, and by experiments that show how hard it can be, in the right context, to distinguish live from recorded sound.[1] This documentation suggests that human ears—or, to be more accurate, the ways human brains process what they hear—really *do* change with technology. Listeners deal with the "same" stimuli in different ways, depending on the context in which that information is received; and at any given time in the twentieth century, listeners appear to dwell less on the differences between live sound and up-to-date recordings than on their areas of overlap. Thus, in 1941, Irving Kolodin heard the sonorities of the Feuermann/Ormandy recording of Strauss's *Don Quixote* as "immaculately pure and beautifully rounded" and "the distinction of detail" as "extraordinary and unremitting"; but a decade later, he processed the same information in a different way, and came to criticize the same discs because "such integral matters of Strauss' orchestration as the sighing bass tuba and the frisky piccolo" were "quite indistinct" (*Guide* xii; *New Guide* 411).

An important part of the context which determines how sound is received is the predisposition (the knowledge, the presuppositions, and the expectations) of the audience. Thus, for instance, we have demonstrated in informal experiments with a variety of listeners that someone coming unprepared to the infamous 1889 Brahms cylinder is apt to hear nothing but indistinct sounds—random plunks without identifiable tune, rhythm, or harmony—hardly discernible behind a wall of surface noise. But a person who knows what he or she is listening *for*—a person with a score or previous familiarity with the First Hungarian Dance *plus* knowledge that Brahms is in fact playing part of that piece—can hear the music clearly over the din.

The Latest Fidelity Syndrome is, in turn, part of a larger phenomenon of listening. It is not simply perception of the physical sounds that is influenced by the listener's foreknowledge. Indeed, a listener's sense of all the parameters of a work of music depends to a greater or lesser extent on context. It is for this reason that any serious discussion of what might constitute musical "literacy" has to begin with an exploration of the act of listening. In saying this, we are assuming a somewhat different notion of literacy from that recently made popular by E. D. Hirsch. Hirsch centers on the "basic information needed to thrive in the modern world" (xiii). We certainly admit the importance of that kind of literacy (it is hard to "thrive" in the contemporary United States if the words "Beethoven" and "Michael Jackson" mean nothing at all to you), but such informational literacy would, if one extrapolates from what Hirsch says about literature, not require the actual hearing of any music whatsoever.[2] We are concerned here with a very different kind of literacy—the ability to listen intelligently and with pleasure. And study of that kind of literacy requires close examination of what is going on as musical sounds are processed.

Musicians have been slow to take this step in a serious and systematic way, even though the parallel focus on readers has for some time been a dominant interest of literary studies. In particular, music scholars tend to use the word *interpretation*, with its connotations of active involvement with the meaning of a work of art, quite differently from the way it is used by literary critics. In literature, the concept of "interpretation" generally includes the activities of the reader (including the critic) or the audience (even in discussions of drama, where it applies to actors as well). In musical circles, in contrast, interpretation is generally limited to the decisions made by the performer. Listening, in other words, has been treated as a fairly passive process, one that can perhaps be made "more accurate" with training, but one that is essentially non-interpretive. This view is profoundly mistaken: listening requires active participation by the audience in both perception and construction, and all who hear the music—audience as well as performers—interpret what they hear and react according to who they are. And it is precisely because different listeners (and even the same listener under different circumstances) listen and interpret differently that the musical experience has been and is so difficult to describe with any degree of conviction. Such differences in listening do not line up neatly along an objective continuum, and they make the problems of analysis considerably more complex than deciding between matters of "right" and "wrong," or of more or less accurate. Instead, they engage all the complexities that any interpretive difference does. And rather than being undesirable, these differences seem to us to reveal more of the nature of art than those aspects that can be objectively summarized.

What we would like to do here is set up the groundwork for talking about those differences—a preliminary model for studying the act of listening as an active, context-dependent process. Before we continue, however, it might be useful to address the question of why an essay on the act of listening is pushing its way into a book on world literature. There are, we believe, three interconnected reasons. First is what might be called the historical justification. At this moment, for a variety of reasons, the distinction between literature and music—or, at least between the studies of the two arts—is becoming more porous. We are not, of course, suggesting that there are no differences between musicology and literary theory. But much academic scholarship on music is increasingly broad in its theoretical reach. Narrative models, for instance, are increasingly important, as the provocative work of Anthony Newcomb makes clear; indeed, more generally, the work of such diverse thinkers as Susan McClary, Lawrence Kramer, and Jean-Jacques Nattiez increasingly blurs the lines between musical and literary theory.[3] It seems odd for literary scholars, long more flexible than their musical counterparts in the academy, to be shoring up the distinction just as musicians are finally starting to ask questions about it. In particular, a collection devoted in principle, as this one is, to breaking down barriers cannot afford the provincial gesture of declaring *this* border—a border already widely questioned elsewhere—beyond the limits of inquiry.

Second, there is a theoretical reason for introducing a musical argument into this book: the historical shift in the shape of musical studies is not based merely on loose analogies between the two arts but rests firmly on a significant theoretical pivot around which *all* the arts swing—music, literature, cinema, dance, painting. Specifically, we would argue, any act of cultural interpretation, whether it be reading, listening, or viewing, depends on cultural presuppositions that shape aesthetic experiences in significant ways. In this regard, what we say about music is intended as exemplary—for we believe that parallel arguments could be made for any of the other arts as well. This theoretical pivot, furthermore, is of particular importance to the concerns of this volume. If one wants to take seriously the question of how readers in one culture make sense of texts in another culture (a question at least implicitly at the center of any attempt to think about "reading world literature" these days), consideration of how culturally specific presuppositions influence the process of meaning-making becomes a high theoretical priority. The very point of intersection between the study of music and literature which we are exploring here is, therefore, central to any serious exploration of the most important questions of intercultural literary exchange. And by raising the matter of listening, we hope to provide a convenient way to shift some longstanding arguments about literary interpretation to a more explicitly conceptual plane.

Third, we have what might be called a pragmatic reason for pursuing music in this volume. In order to consider the ways in which presupposition influences interpretation, it is necessary to *get outside* one's own meaning-making practices so they can be scrutinized. Such getting outside involves, to some extent, shaking loose from the theoretical frameworks that guide one's investigations—or, at the very least, looking at those frameworks from a fresh angle. There are, of course, any number of ways to get a new perspective on one's theory and practice. But one of the most effective is to look at parallel problems of meaning-making as they appear in a different medium, for this procedure often foregrounds interpretive procedures that might otherwise be taken for granted. Our goal in this essay, to be sure, is not to chart a new theoretical framework for literary analysis (although we believe that the distinction we make among technical, attributive, and synthetic components is potentially useful for literary scholarship), or even to specify the particular consequences that might result from stepping back from familiar literary procedures. But we do believe that our study of listening can be useful to literary scholars by providing one alternative position from which to look back on literary practices, and we hope our essay will provide grounds on which some of the claims made elsewhere in the volume can be tested.

II

According to our model, the total act of listening involves the combination of three distinct elements, the braiding together of three separate strands; and the failure to recognize the distinctions (and interactions) among them is a source of consistent confusion in thinking about music.[4] The first component is what we call the "technical," the strand that consists of only those elements that are specifically represented in the musical notation on the page—or, in the case of un-notated music, those elements that would be notated were the music to be transcribed. Statements about the technical level would include the following: "The first note of Mozart's Piano Sonata in G, K. 283 is a D" or "The first chord of Beethoven's *Eroica* is a quarter note on the first beat of a measure."

It should be emphasized that the technical includes everything relevant to performance that is notated, even if its meaning is not absolute and is thus subject to discretion. The statement "Mahler's tempo indication of 'Adagissimo' at measure 159 of the last movement of his Ninth Symphony means that the piece should be played very slowly" is a technical statement, even though it is less precise than "Bartók's metronome marking at the beginning of his Fourth Quartet indicates that it should be played 110 quarter notes per minute." But "notated" does not mean the same as "written": titles (*La Mer*), written programs, the unsung texts in Liszt (for instance, the warning "Lasciate ogni speranza, voi ch'entrate" over the horns and trumpets near the beginning of the *Dante Symphony*), since they provide no direct instructions for performance, do not belong among the technical elements.[5]

To a large extent, traditional academic analysis has treated the technical component as if it were all there were to the music. It is for this reason, for instance, that Eduard Hanslick—who had such an enormous influence on those who followed him—could compare music to a kaleidoscope, claiming that the beautiful in music "is not contingent upon nor in need of any subject introduced from without, but that it consists wholly of sounds artistically combined"—that is, that "the essence of music is sound and motion" (47–48). Or, as Alan Walker puts it, "A musical communication is complete; it refers to nothing outside itself" (4).[6] A similar position is represented even more starkly by Milton Babbitt's formulation: "a composition can [manifestly] be regarded— . . . completely and accurately—as events occurring at time points" (14).[7]

In fact, though, the technical is only the raw material of the music. In and of itself, for instance, it has no hierarchy of importance among its details; it hence has no shape. Nor (as will be clearer later on) does it have content or symbolic resonance. Standing alone, the technical is in a significant way "meaningless"—which is why listeners are so often perplexed when they encounter music from a culture—or even in a style—with which they are unfamiliar. Despite a long history of theory and analysis to the contrary, listeners in fact come to meaningful terms with the technical only in combination with what we call the "attributive," a second component of the listening process that assigns or recommends meanings (in the broadest sense of "meanings"), a component that, *pace* Hanslick, is "introduced from without" (not only extra-compositional but sometimes, as we shall show, even "extra-musical"), and a component that is always more or less in place before the act of listening begins. To put it in different terms, listeners always experience the sounds of the music *through* an attributive screen that contextualizes it and gives it meaning. Indeed, to the extent that listeners do think that they "understand" music from other cultures, it is often simply that they have managed to cram the sounds into familiar categories. Thus, for instance, Gunther Schuller argues that Africans and early American slaves performed music that might well have been heard, by Western-trained ears, as bitonal—even though the performers themselves "did not think of it in those diatonic terms" (48). A similar process takes place when Western readers assimilate Asian dramas by processing them through such European categories as "tragedy."

Many types of information contribute to the attributive strand, but they can be usefully sorted into two primary categories: codes and mythologies. At least for Western musical academics, codes are less controversial. They consist of "regulations" of conventional behavior, and are often arrived at through statistical analysis. Thus, for instance, Walter Piston, near the beginning of his widely used book on harmony, orders a series of progressions "based on observations of usage"—that is, in terms of their relative frequency in tonal music of the Western common practice period (17).[8] Similarly, many writers, such as W. J. Henderson, codify formal aspects of sonata form ("it is accepted that the first theme is to be vigorous, or, at least, animated, and the second fluent and melodious") (47). Attributive codes, of course, do not involve what John R. Searle calls "constitutive" rules—rules (like those for football or chess) that "create or define new forms of behavior" and that "do not merely regulate playing . . . , but, as it were, create the very possibility of playing such games" (33). That is partly because musical codes are, for the most part, probabilistic rather than absolute, and hence less rigidly formulated than the rules of games. But more important, it is because breaking the rules of music does not mean that you are no longer playing the game: when you slide your rook diagonally you are no longer involved in a game of chess; but when you break the rule against writing parallel fifths, or introduce a note out of order in a twelve-tone row, or miss the *sam* in Karnatak music, you are still writing or performing music.

Indeed, many musical effects, like many literary effects, come precisely from breaking the rules. But the impact of such instances—the "failure," for instance, of Liszt's "Bagatelle sans tonalité" to resolve at the end—shows one of the primary ways in which musical codes function. The surprise of a broken rule requires prior knowledge of the rule broken: the codes help set up a frame of expectations within which the piece operates.

All musical parameters are subject to codification, either explicit or implicit. But the degree of codification differs, and the nature of those differences themselves varies according to cultural context. Indeed, styles can be defined in part by the differing degrees to which the musical elements are codified. Thus, in Western common practice music, rules of harmony are codified in more detail than rules of orchestration. (Still, Henry Edward Krehbiel's late nineteenth-century strictures against Handel's original orchestration remind us both that orchestration is coded too and that, like all codes, it is historically grounded: "To our ears, accustomed to the myriad-hued orchestra of today, the effect would seem opaque, heavy, unbalanced, and without charm were a band of oboes to play in unison with the violins, another of bassoons to double the 'cellos, and half a dozen trumpets to come flaring and crashing into the musical mass at intervals" [84]. In the eighteenth century, too, operatic trombones were reserved for circumscribed situations, and the surprise engendered by the string quartet in the Beatles' "Eleanor Rigby" suggests that certain expectations, and hence certain attributive codes, are in effect for rock instrumentation as well.) In many serial works, in contrast, there is no harmonic code as such. As composer Ernst Krenek puts it, once such parameters as pitch, rhythm, and density are strictly determined by serial principles, "it is no longer possible to decide freely . . . which tones should sound simultaneously at any given point." Harmony thus becomes the equivalent of "a chance occurrence" (90).[9]

Traditional analysis, of course, has always taken such codes into account; but for the most part, analysts have tended to treat them *as if they were technical*—that is, either as if they were derivable from the notes of a particular work, or as if they were more or less universal and hence unchanging from piece to piece. Thus, for instance, Alan Walker claims that the correct ordering of themes is "one which generates *maximum tension compatible with maximum comprehensibility*"—a rule that allows him to claim that given the material of a masterpiece, there is, as in a jigsaw puzzle, "only one assembly which is right" (54, 61).[10] Such an absolute rule allows for no contextual variation. In fact, however, while there is a sense in which there can be fairly uniform agreement about what is "there" on the technical level (at least in Western pieces using modern notation),[11] there are always conflicting codes through which a piece can be interpreted by a listener: V does not lead to I with quite the same pressure in Brahms as it does in Mozart; the codes for appropriate piano-writing differ (only partly because of technological changes in the instrument) as we move from Mozart to Beethoven to Liszt to Debussy to Godowsky to Crumb. As we shall show, listening to a particular piece of music always requires judgment about what codes to invoke. Application of codes is thus always an act of attribution, rather than description, and is always subject to legitimate dispute. The same applies to reading: the decision to read Shakespeare's *Measure for Measure* through the rules of "comedy" is an act of attribution that, in part, helps determine how a reader will interpret the play.

The second type of attributive information—what we call the mythological—has a more precarious hold in musical scholarship. The mythological consists of the discourse and the other cultural apparatus that surrounds the music in question—the historical "fact" that Liszt dedicated his Sonata to Robert Schumann, the stories about Charlie Parker's drug addiction, the cultural commonplaces that connect the period after sunset with the *chhayanata* raga, or the influential Disney-fabricated connections between Stravinsky's *Le Sacre du printemps* and *Fantasia*'s dinosaurs. It also includes what Susan McClary calls "the common semiotic codes of European classical music"—for instance, "the gestures that stereotypically signify 'masculine' or 'feminine,' placidity or violence"— although we, of course, are reserving the term *codes* for more explicitly articulated information (68). Performance history, too, is a crucial part of the mythological—as are the philosophical or aesthetic systems, such as Hanslick's or Leonard Meyer's, that ground the claims of validity made for particular analyses or particular analytic techniques.

Especially in its more conspicuous forms, the mythological makes many contemporary musicians uneasy. Krenek, for instance, is clearly addressing the mythological component of the attributive when he questions the innocence of artistic inspiration on the grounds that it is "conditioned by a tremendous body of recollection, tradition, training, and experience"; and his sweeping assertion that "the composer has come to distrust his inspiration" and to seek out "an impersonal mechanism" that will allow him "to avoid the dictations of such ghosts" expresses an urge to purify music of any mythological dimension (90). Babbitt's disdain is even more fierce: a "verbal act" such as the sentence (unattributed but taken in fact from Paul Henry Lang) "'There can be no question that in many of Mendelssohn's works there is missing that real depth that opens wide perspectives, the mysticism of the unutterable'" simply should not "be allowed," nor can "a book containing a sentence such as this [be saved] from the flames" (11).[12]

Even allowing for his irony and well-known wit, Babbitt's unmoderated rationalism shows a common but fundamental misunderstanding of such critical declarations. He poses as a hit man out to terminate all utterances in which there is "virtually nothing to be communicated"—a program hard to resist. But his purge hinges on a precarious equation between "responsible normative discourse" and what he calls "cognitive communication"—which in turn seems to be equivalent to empirically verifiable statements (11). To put it in other terms, Babbitt presumes that the only tenable class of utterances is the class of speech acts that J. L. Austin dubbed "constatives," "'statement[s]' [that] 'describe' some state of affairs, or . . . 'state some fact,' which [they] must do either truly or falsely" (1).[13] In fact, however, whatever its grammatical surface (and Austin, as much as anyone, taught the deceptive nature of such formal features), Lang's statement about Mendelssohn is most profitably considered, not as a constative, but rather as a performative, an utterance that performs an action—in this case, an utterance that advances a particular form of conduct. More particularly, Lang proposes a set of terms within which to listen to, and make sense of, Mendelssohn's art. Babbitt tries to shoot down such statements on the grounds that they are non-falsifiable; but that criticism misses the target when aimed at a sentence in which utility, rather than truth, is the motivating force. We are not suggesting, of course, that Lang's statement cannot be judged. Rather, we are urging that it be judged not on whether it matches up with some abstract, context-free truth but on whether the framework it proposes can be used to attribute meaning (or alternatively a lack of meaning) in the music at hand.[14]

Even statements that appear to be descriptions of what is "objectively there" often turn out to be advisories in disguise. Julian Haylock's claim that each of Rachmaninov's Op. 39 *Etudes-Tableaux* "contains an oblique (occasionally explicit) reference" to the *Dies Irae* (the Gregorian plainchant melody) does not really describe a unity within the set, but rather *attributes* unity to it, in order to persuade us to hear it in the same way he does.[15] And we are further suggesting that many apparently "objective" literary statements can be most profitably understood as performative recommendations as well. When critics point out, for instance, that Gabriel Conroy and Michael Furey in James Joyce's "The Dead" both take their names from archangels, they are not so much describing a "fact" of the text as proposing to their readers that a particular cultural commonplace serves as a useful and productive grid against which to make sense of the story.

In much the same way, every performance listeners hear becomes advisory to other, ensuing performances. Thus, for instance, James Parakilas distinguishes "classical," "early," and "new" music not in terms of repertoire or audience, but rather "as ways of thinking about performance," as "distinct attitudes toward musical style. . . . The classical style of playing Beethoven is not Beethoven's style of playing, but a style about Beethoven" (6–7). One might even say that each moment of performance becomes advisory and therefore immediately attributive to the rest of the performance, and even retrospectively attributive to the listener's interpretation of the portion of the piece already completed. Thus, in Leonard Bernstein's CBS recording of the Mahler Eighth, the controversial ritard at the recapitulation of the first movement offers a "way" of reconsidering the music, of reordering the elements, in the exposition and development.

One major aspect of the attributive level is the attribution of intention. This is not the place to discuss the extent to which composers really have intentions or know what they are (although most certainly believe that they do); nor is it the place to discuss the epistemological questions of whether intentions can ever be accurately recovered. Rather, our point is that the hypothetical *attribution* of intention inevitably contributes (even if implicitly) to most acts of listening or analysis. Intentionality is an example of what Susan Suleiman, in a discussion of implied authors and implied readers (variants of the notion of intention) in literature, calls "necessary fictions" (11). Without some notion of intentionality, for instance, there is no way to distinguish the "accidental" in a work—or to distinguish what is crucial from what is secondary—and hence no way to edit texts or to judge performances. Even most chance music places *some* limitations on the operations of chance: Boulez's Third Sonata is not without its imperatives from the composer.

Different listeners and different listening contexts call different attributive screens into play—Babbitt, for instance, obviously does not listen exclusively through that statement about Mendelssohn, although many other listeners do. And even Babbitt probably cannot avoid Lang's perspective entirely, even if it exists only as a negative term against which he defines his own listening practices. It is important to realize, too, that each person's attributive baggage can include false items, and even foolish items, as well as true ones. Thus, for instance, most American teenagers in the 1960s had an attributive screen through which they associated Indian music—regardless of its original social intentions—with marijuana and a generally anti-establishment attitude. But even though one can shift musical attributions, it is impossible to avoid them. Some attributive information is always in effect: no act of listening ever involves a direct, unmediated linking up of the listener and the notes on the page.[16]

Although listeners can shift attributions (even while listening), the various available attributive screens always precede any particular act of listening. Likewise, the technical always precedes the act of listening; even in improvised music the performer decides and plays before the listener hears. Where does the activity of the listener him- or herself enter the process? Listening, as we have said, involves active participation: although it requires both the technical and the attributive, the mere existence of those components only provides the possibility for music. It is up to the listener to actualize that potential, to *apply* particular attributive screens to the particular notes at hand in order to come up with a particular experience. We call this the synthetic component of listening. The technical, attributive, and synthetic can be exemplified as follows: "The next-to-last chord of the first movement of the Beethoven Fifth is a G major chord" is a statement about the technical; "A G major chord in C minor [the key of the Fifth Symphony] is a dominant" and "The Beethoven Fifth is a late-Classical, early Romantic piece and in that idiom dominant chords are most frequently followed by tonics" are attributive statements; "On hearing that G major chord, I expect a C minor chord to follow" is synthetic: that is, it is the conclusion drawn from the application of attributive information to technical facts.

One primary synthetic activity, as Leonard Meyer and Eugene Narmour have demonstrated, is the creation of expectations, the frustration and fulfillment of which are crucial to our musical experience. But synthetic activities also include the creation of hierarchies (that is, they focus the listener's attention). Thus, for instance, the synthetic result of confronting the Mahler First for the first time through the general attributive advice offered by Ethel Peyser ("the best advice I can give you [in a piece you have never heard before] is to listen intently to the first melody, phrase, pattern, tune, or theme") (12) will be to foreground the (rather slim) melodic material and to background the orchestration. But with a different attributive screen ("The Symphony's opening is the most evocative in the orchestral repertoire, creating an unforgettable sense of space and stillness") (Banks) the synthetic result might well be the opposite. Similarly, much as Krenek would have us try to escape from them, the synthetic also calls up associations and traditions. A listener's knowledge of seventeenth-century musical conventions may intersect with a hearing of Strauss's *Le Bourgeois Gentilhomme* to produce a whole set of associations about the time, class, even locale that the music represents.

There is an even more important aspect of the synthetic level. To understand how it operates, let us return to the first movement of the Beethoven Fifth. Even for a listener with the attributive screens we have described already (and most Western listeners have been well trained into the primacy of the V–I progression), expecting that final C minor chord—and experiencing the fulfillment of that expectation—does not exhaust the listening experience. The music also seems to "mean" something else which can only be described metaphorically. Indeed, the very word "fulfillment" is metaphorical. What does a listener really feel here? Finality? Closure? Fulfillment? Triumph? Exultation? Here we are talking about what we call, for lack of a better term, the symbolic aspect of the synthetic strand. It is one of the hardest qualities of music to describe, largely because its experiential nature rests on a paradox: to each listener it seems to be self-evident and hence undisputable; but it often varies so much from one listener to another that it seems impossible to share. Then too, it often seems metaphoric, in that it is connected to other, apparently "non-musical" realms of experience. Partly for this reason, it has the distinction of being almost universally misunderstood and scorned in academic musical circles. Indeed, harmony books tend to blush when they approach it; even a chapter on scales is apt to skirt the obvious, but crucial, fact that through three hundred years of tonal music, there has been a convention using the major mode to symbolize such things as nobility, happiness, and love, and the minor scales to represent death, sadness, and anxiety.

Yet the symbolic is not only the musical aspect that is most consciously grasped by the general public; more important, it provides the motivating force behind the acts of composition, performance, and listening. Although many music students, young composers, and even music professionals seem to talk as if technical ordering itself were the essence of music (at the least, contemporary Western classical music), in fact, to audiences music has seemed best to succeed as a series of mood symbols often conveying apparently direct and simple meanings. One can think here of the responses brought about (even intended) even by the untouchable "classics" (Bach, Mozart, Beethoven, Brahms), let alone the more obvious "mood composers" (Rimsky-Korsakoff, Debussy, Ellington, Messiaen) and rock artists. Thus, for instance, the listener who claims to experience a Werther-like mood when listening to Brahms's Piano Quartet No. 3 in C minor, Op. 60, is not responding in some foolish and irrelevant way, foreign to the "true" meaning of the music. On the contrary, Brahms precisely intended this effect, and even (slightly tongue-in-cheek) suggested adding an explicit attributive layer to the score in order to encourage it. When he gave the manuscript to his publisher, he wrote "You may place a picture on the title-page, namely, a head—with a pistol in front of it. This will give you some idea of the music" (Specht 55).

Of course, not all musical symbols are quite so vivid or explicit—and only rarely are they verbalized so directly. Nonetheless, even when composers do not talk or write about their symbolism, it usually informs their creative endeavors. There is, for instance, a phenomenon in the creative process which is experienced by most composers, and probably other artists as well: the intuitive knowledge that the solution or concept is at hand even though the specifics are still missing—in other words, the sense that the piece is composed although the notes are not yet found. Howard Gardner, for instance, relates an anecdote about Walter Piston, one that could be duplicated for many other composers: Piston claimed that a work was almost completed despite the fact that he had not yet selected the notes. Gardner interprets this as meaning that Piston "had planned out the abstract structure of the piece—the number of movements, the principle shifts in orchestral color, the various forms to be employed, and so on—but still had to decide upon the specific vehicles with which to embody his musical conception"

(360). We suspect, however, that Piston may well have meant something quite different. Such technical units—form, number of movements, even general orchestral decisions—often represent the easy part of composition. They have little to do with the meaning of the work. Piston said that the piece was almost completed; notes are generally not filled in without an idea of what one wants to "say" (to invoke a common but ultimately metaphorical usage) in a piece. One may decide midway through the composition of a work to scrap the form and recast it, but rarely will a composer decide to keep the form and fill it in with what he or she perceives as a different "meaning."

Symbolism is not some arcane province of composers: it is intuitively grasped by listeners. If you watch people—be they lay listeners or professional musicians (pedagogues included)—as they listen (or perform), you find that they tap their fingers, bob their heads, and engage in various forms of body movement (subtle and unsubtle) as a response not only to the rhythms or the meter but also to the mood of the moment. Dancers do not dance only to mark the beat. Indeed, pictures of famous performers in symbolic poses—Toscanini in his frenzy, Karajan in his self-absorption, Elvis in his gyrations—are among the major icons of Western music culture. It is not that all composers use the *same* symbolism—indeed, it's precisely the differences in their symbolisms (both the means used and the effects produced) that give us our sense of the differences in their "personalities." But all composers employ *some* symbolism, which they normally hope that the listener—through mutual synthetic operations, through the correct attributive screens applied to the notes at hand—will receive; and all listeners receive *some* symbolic effect, whether or not it is the one that the composer originally intended.

Yet as we have said, the symbolic remains rarely discussed by academic musicians. Richard Wagner described starting out on the study of composition: "[My teacher] had a sorry office in explaining to me that what I took for wondrous shapes and powers were really chords and intervals" (241). In *Dombey and Son*, Dickens describes the literary equivalent, the dreary classroom of Dr. Blimber, for whom "all the fancies of the poets, and lessons of the sages, were a mere collection of words and grammar, and had no other meaning in the world" (134–135). That description comes, appropriately enough, from Chapter 11 of the novel; and it remains, unfortunately, a depressingly accurate commentary on the bankruptcy of much aesthetic scholarship even today.

III

We are not interested in forcing yet another rigid classificatory system on music, much less on art more generally. We recognize that there are other valid descriptive models, that the lines dividing the technical, attributive, and synthetic are ambiguous, and that the three strands interact in complex ways. And since we are offering our model primarily as a conceptual scheme from which to rethink literacy, rather than as a plea for any particular reformation of the canon of world literature, we do not have any specific pedagogical or curricular recommendations to offer to teachers. Nonetheless, we do believe that our model of listening has serious implications for the ways in which literacy, both musical and literary, is addressed.

First, our analysis suggests a need to reconceptualize the relation between literacy and the range of a person's knowledge—or between literacy and the canon. What does a literate person "need" to know? To simplify for a moment, we will say that on the basis of their answers to this question, most critics fall into one of two broad groups, inclusionists and extrapolationists. Inclusionists (Hirsch is a good example) argue for a particular set of works with which one ought to be familiar. But their position is beset by persistent questions about *what* texts belong in this class. There are strong arguments, including those made by Hirsch, that contemporary citizens need a sense of their own (in our case, Western) culture and its history if they are to find their place in the world; given the increasing internationality of culture, there are strong arguments, too, that people need to gain a sense of cultures that are *not* their own. There are arguments for stressing high culture; there are arguments for stressing reasoned study of the popular culture that surrounds most people, but is rarely reflected upon. How can these differences be negotiated?

Extrapolationists try to solve this dilemma by arguing—in line with traditional notions of the liberal arts—that experience with a few choice texts (or works of music) can prepare one to deal with anything else that comes along. But whether or not this solution works depends on how one conceives of those "texts." Certainly, if literacy is envisioned, as we have suggested, as a way of experiencing and thinking about art, then familiarity with what used to be called "the work itself," the technical level alone, is an incomplete base on which to build it. Knowledge of music's technical level is not analogous to knowledge of elementary chemistry. And although proponents of formalistic musical analysis still trumpet universal validity for their principles, the assumption that understanding how to analyze Bachian counterpoint or Mozartian form will enable one to listen adequately to Mahler, or that knowing more generally how to analyze music of the Western high art tradition will necessarily prepare one to listen well to jazz or Japanese music, is false. We are not suggesting, of course, that the technical is unimportant—much less that specialized training for advanced music students should forgo the intense traditional grounding in theory. But to the extent that we are talking about a quality of mind that allows flexible listening, knowledge of the technical *alone* can never be sufficient for adequate extrapolation to new musical experiences.

This principle not only forces a refinement of the extrapolationist position; it also encourages a more dramatic shift in perspective. For once the technical loses its dominant position, knowledge of specific texts—either musical or literary—becomes a secondary concern. Indeed, our model suggests that whatever musical (or literary) texts one experiences, literacy depends on one's knowledge along a different axis entirely. For if one cannot study *any* cultural production without studying the technical *and* the attributive and synthetic strands that it presumes in its audience, then literacy is best conceived in terms of *vertical* reach (the incorporation of all three strands) rather than *horizontal* extent (the range of texts with which a person is familiar).

Thus, for instance, we are not prepared to declare the Shostakovich Fifth either inside or outside any canon. But we believe that if one does choose to deal intelligently with this work at the end of the twentieth century, one has to come to terms with how the listening experience stems not only from the music's technical level (or even the codes of the attributive level)—for instance, the long-term harmonic shift from the opening in D minor to the final measures in D major. The experience grows, too, from the attributive screens that encourage us to hear such minor/major changes as emotional symbols, as well as from the long and conflicted history of Soviet/Western relations—not to mention the listener's own synthetic choice as to whether to hear the music through the mythology that treats it as a hymn to socialism or the counter-mythology that treats it, instead, as a bitter protest against the Soviet State. Likewise, we are not taking a position on whether familiarity with *King Lear* is a prerequisite to cultural literacy in America; but we do believe that a literate reading of *King Lear* is one that is aware not only of the linguistic and thematic structure of the play, but also of the way any reading of Shakespeare is filtered through powerful mythologies about the playwright that influence English-speaking readers from childhood on—as well as of the ways any particular experience of the play works, in part, by the readers' choice of the filters through which to read it.

Second, our model suggests that we need to rethink how we go about making aesthetic judgments. Since the attributive is not a set of unvarying codes, but a set of filters whose availability is partly culturally contingent, partly a matter of individual choice, our model encourages sensitivity to the variety of synthetic responses, and recognition that judgment will necessarily be contextual and provisional. But we would stress that such contextualism need not result in total or anarchic relativism or loss of value; nor need it coalesce the study of art merely to the study of cultural anthropology. Granted, our position, which embeds any work of art in cultural contexts (both of its production and its reception), undermines the notion of an objective, inherent meaning or quality describable in technical terms alone. But in contextualizing the technical, we have not eliminated it; indeed, we would argue that music can no more be reduced to a study of the attributive and synthetic than to a study of the technical. It therefore does not follow that discussion of evaluation is impossible. What does follow is the recognition that if quality *is* to be addressed (and it is hard to see how it can be avoided completely, even if it is only raised as something to be rendered problematic), then it is necessary to develop new evaluative strategies that take *all three* strands of listening into account. The same argument applies to literature as well: recognizing the way that our experience of *King Lear* is embedded in cultural mythology and synthetic choices does not drain the work of its value—it only makes talking about that value vastly more challenging. But literary critics and theorists—at least those who have gotten beyond the notion of universal objective standards—have become increasingly shy about dealing with aesthetic value just at the moment when boldness is necessary; it is therefore no surprise that they have barely begun to embark on such conversations.

Third and most important, our model encourages a reconceptualization of what it means to describe aesthetic artifacts and experiences, for it exposes the attributive nature of a great deal of apparently "descriptive" criticism. When Alan Walker proposes his principles of musical greatness, he asserts global applicability of purely technical observations and insists that the *same* distinction between good and bad music is to be found "cutting across all musical barriers—light, serious, chamber, orchestral, vocal, etc.; cutting across all historical styles; cutting across all shades of opinion, all varieties of taste" (4). In fact, Walker is locked into a very particular, historically limited Germanic style, one that doesn't describe or discover greatness so much as impose it. Such universalizing, an almost inevitable consequence of purely technical discussion, is the very antithesis of literacy in our sense.

The same point needs to be made about literature as well. The New Critics once suggested that their methods were universally applicable, and that mastery of explication as they practiced it—even though it was exemplified through readings of only a handful of selected, canonical, Western male texts—would prepare their readers to meet all future needs. Cleanth Brooks's *The Well Wrought Urn*, for instance, ranges chronologically from Donne to Yeats; "the intervening poems were to be read as one has learned to read Donne and the moderns" (193). Few literary theorists would subscribe to those precise principles today. Yet is knowing how to read through such lenses as narratology or post-structuralism or French feminism or film theory substantially different? Or are they just another series of ways of filtering world literature through fundamentally Western frames of reference?

To put it in other terms: learning to read world literature *as* world literature involves not only reading new texts, but also learning to read in profoundly new ways, unless one wishes to repeat, on a literary level, the error of those listeners who, listening to African music through Western codes and mythologies, hear it as "bitonal." It may be impossible to escape one's own frames entirely—but even if one is trapped, one can learn to recognize the bars on the cage and become self-conscious about the limitations they place upon us.

Notes

1. For discussion, see Eisenberg, 111–112.
2. "Very few specific titles appear on the list, and they usually appear as words, not works, because they represent writings that culturally literate people have read about but haven't read" (xiv); "The information about literature that exists in the minds of literate people may have been derived from conversation, criticism, cinema, television, or student crib sheets like *Cliffs Notes*. The American conception of Sherlock Holmes has been formed more by the acting of Basil Rathbone than by the writing of Conan Doyle. . . . Only a small proportion of literate people can name the Shakespeare plays in which Falstaff appears, yet they know who he is. They know what *Mein Kampf* is, but they haven't read it" (147).

3. For good examples of this shift in perspective, see Newcomb, McClary, Kramer, and Nattiez.

4. For further discussion of this model, see Rabinowitz, "Chord and Discourse" and "Whiting the Wrongs."

5. Obviously, the boundary, like all boundaries, blurs. It is hard to know, for instance, whether Scriabin's more fanciful instructions (e.g., "avec une douceur de plus en plus caressante et empoisonnée," in the Ninth Sonata) constitute part of the technical level or not.

6. The word *refer* in the first sentence is admittedly loose; strictly speaking, it is possible, as will soon be evident, for music to depend on things "outside itself" without referring outside itself. In the total context of Walker's argument, however, it is obvious that he is using the word in a fairly broad way.

7. For further discussion of the formalist underpinnings of analysis, see, for instance, Kerman, Tomlinson, Morgan, and Treitler. Although Subotnik specifically addresses musicology, her arguments apply to analysis as well.

8. Although Piston mentions at the beginning of his book that he is concerned with "the common practice of composers . . . as observed in the eighteenth and nineteenth centuries" (vii), he neglects the Western bias of his sample and often minimizes the historical limitations as well.

9. Of course, some serialists did try to codify harmonic practice; although the code governing registers in Webern's Symphony, for instance, is quite different from anything found in the common practice period, any violation of the code would be as clearly discernible to the composer, performer, or trained listener as it would be in a chorale by Bach. Boulez's technique called "multiplication of intervals," however, seems to work as a code only on the levels of composition and visual analysis. The twelve tones are grouped into chords, which form the set; each chord is then expanded by transposing or "multiplying" its component intervals onto each pitch of the original chord, with all doublings canceled. But if Boulez's rules—in contrast to Webern's—are broken, it is neither likely nor expected that any listener will notice. The code is not really a source of expectations at all, but rather a means of generating previously unused and, by virtue of their intervallic duplications, "non-irrelevant" (a word we have chosen with great care) notes.

10. See also Krehbiel: in multi-thematic works, "A harmony latent in each group, and the sequence of groups is such a sequence as the experience of ages has demonstrated to be most agreeable to the ear" (26).

11. Of course, there are always problems in the physical transmission of musical symbols—handwriting can be hard to decipher, copyists make errors. But the question of whether or not to include the disputed cymbal crash in the Bruckner Seventh is different in kind from the question of what frame of expectations to invoke when listening to a given piece.

12. Quoted from Paul Henry Lang, *Music in Western Civilization* (811). Thanks to Fred Maus for revealing the source of Babbitt's quotation. Bab-

bitt's fiery rhetoric is a reference to the final paragraph of Hume's *Enquiry Concerning Human Understanding.*

13. Of course, the initial provisional distinction between constatives and performatives breaks down by the end of this volume; still, it is useful for our purposes here.

14. For the ways in which this analysis of Babbitt's argument can contribute to a discussion of the ethics of music, see Rabinowitz, "'Three Times.'"

15. Haylock increases the mythological pull of his argument when he explains how to interpret that unity, calling the plainchant theme "Rachmaninov's musical 'spectre.'"

16. One might argue that infants listen directly; we, however, would say that infants, in their initial encounters with sound, are hearing but not listening.

Works Cited

Austin, J. L. *How to Do Things with Words.* 2nd ed. Cambridge, Mass.: Harvard University Press, 1975.

Babbitt, Milton. "The Structure and Function of Musical Theory." In *Perspectives on Contemporary Music Theory,* edited by Benjamin Boretz and Edward T. Cone, pp. 10–21. New York: Norton, 1972.

Banks, Paul. Jacket notes to Mahler *Songs of a Wayfarer and First Symphony* [Virgin Classics VC 7 90703].

Brooks, Cleanth. *The Well Wrought Urn: Studies in the Structure of Poetry.* New York: Harvest, 1947.

Dickens, Charles. *Dombey and Son.* New York: Dutton/Everyman's Library, 1907.

Eisenberg, Evan. *The Recording Angel: Explorations in Phonography.* New York: McGraw-Hill, 1987.

Gardner, Howard. *Art, Mind, and Brain: A Cognitive Approach to Creativity.* New York: Basic Books, 1982.

Hanslick, Eduard. *The Beautiful in Music.* Translated by Gustav Cohen. Edited by Morris Weitz. Indianapolis: Bobbs-Merrill/Liberal Arts, 1957.

Haylock, Julian. Jacket notes to *Sergei Rachmaninov: Etudes-Tableaux* [ASV CD DCA 789].

Henderson, W. J. *What is Good Music? Suggestions to Persons Desiring to Cultivate a Taste in Musical Art.* 3rd ed. New York: Scribner's, 1899.

Hirsch, E. D. Jr. *Cultural Literacy: What Every American Needs to Know, with an Updated Appendix.* New York: Vintage, 1988.

Kerman, Joseph. *Contemplating Music: Challenges to Musicology.* Cambridge, Mass.: Harvard University Press, 1985.

———. "How We Got into Analysis, and How to Get Out." *Critical Inquiry* 7, no. 2 (Winter 1980): 311–331.

Kolodin, Irving. *A Guide to Recorded Music.* Garden City, New York: Doubleday, 1941.

————. *The New Guide to Recorded Music: International Edition.* Garden City, New York: Doubleday, 1950.

Kramer, Lawrence. *Music as Cultural Practice, 1800–1900.* Berkeley and Los Angeles: University of California Press, 1990.

Krehbiel, Henry Edward. *How to Listen to Music: Hints and Suggestions to Untaught Lovers of the Art.* 1896. New York: Scribner's, 1911.

Krenek, Ernst. "Extents and Limits of Serial Techniques." In *Problems of Modern Music,* edited by Paul Henry Lang, pp. 72–94. New York: Norton, 1962.

Lang, Paul Henry. *Music in Western Civilization.* New York: Norton, 1941.

McClary, Susan. *Feminine Endings: Music, Gender, and Sexuality.* Minneapolis: University of Minnesota Press, 1991.

Morgan, Robert P. "Theory, Analysis, and Criticism." *The Journal of Musicology* 1, no. 1 (January 1982): 15–18.

Nattiez, Jean-Jacques. *Music and Discourse: Toward a Semiology of Music.* Translated by Carolyn Abbate. Princeton: Princeton University Press, 1990.

Newcomb, Anthony. "Narrative Archetypes and Mahler's Ninth Symphony." In *Music and Text: Critical Inquiries,* edited by Steven Paul Scher, pp. 118–136. Cambridge, England: Cambridge University Press, 1992.

Parakilas, James. "Classical Music as Popular Music." *The Journal of Musicology* 3 (1984): 1–18.

Peyser, Ethel. *How to Enjoy Music: A First Aid to Music Listeners.* New York: Putnam's, 1933.

Piston, Walter. *Harmony.* 3rd ed. New York: Norton, 1962.

Rabinowitz, Peter J. "Chord and Discourse: Listening through the Written Word." In *Music and Text: Critical Inquiries,* edited by Steven Paul Scher, pp. 38–56. Cambridge, England: Cambridge University Press, 1992.

————. "'Three Times out of Five Something Happens': James Cain and the Ethics of Music." In *Keeping Company: Rhetoric, Pluralism, and Wayne Booth,* edited by Fred Antczak. Ohio State University Press, forthcoming.

————. "Whiting the Wrongs of History: The Resurrection of Scott Joplin." *Black Music Research Journal* 11, no. 2 (Fall 1991): 157–176.

Schuller, Gunther. *Early Jazz: Its Roots and Musical Development.* New York: Oxford University Press, 1968.

Searle, John R. *Speech Acts: An Essay in the Philosophy of Language.* Cambridge, England: Cambridge University Press, 1969.

Specht, Richard. *Johannes Brahms.* Translated by Eric Blom. London: Dent, 1930.

Subotnik, Rose Rosengard. "The Role of Ideology in the Study of Western Music." *The Journal of Musicology* 2, no. 1 (Winter 1983): 1–12.

Suleiman, Susan. "Introduction: Varieties of Audience-Oriented Criticism." In *The Reader in the Text: Essays on Audience and Interpretation,* edited by Susan Suleiman and Inge Crosman, pp. 3–45. Princeton: Princeton University Press, 1980.

Tomlinson, Gary. "The Web of Culture: A Context for Musicology." *Nineteenth Century Music* 7, no. 3 [April 3, 1984]: 350–362.

Treitler, Leo. *Music and the Historical Imagination.* Cambridge, Mass.: Harvard University Press, 1989.

Wagner, Richard. *Wagner on Music and Drama: A Compendium of Richard Wagner's Prose Works.* Translated by H. Ashton Ellis. Edited by Albert Goldman and Evert Sprinchorn. New York: Dutton, 1964.

Walker, Alan. *An Anatomy of Musical Criticism.* London: Barrie and Rockliff, 1966.

11. Informing Adult Readers: Symbolic Experience in Children's Literature

William Moebius

In childhood a book resembled a folding screen. A heap of animals and plants would suddenly pop out at you from behind dreary grey covers and when you shut it, everything vanished again. A book has something of the "magic cap" or the "magic table-cloth." This peculiar property of books was well understood by the old calligraphic scribes, who were sensitive to the need of words to flower into pictures or transform themselves into leafy trees hung with toys. Letters leapt out at you with a roar from the undergrowth of the text, and the book was read slowly, with delicious pauses. The art of the calligraphic scribe cannot be brought back. But we can help the book's age-old longing to be arcane and impenetrable by making its verbal texture so dense that it fairly dances before the reader's eyes, and, catching his breath, he sees little green leaves and the pretty muzzles of red fox cubs running out on to the page from under the black, charred tree stumps of the painter's words.

—Abram Terts (Andrei Sinyavsky), writing without books or family while serving a sentence in the Dubrovlag (15)[1]

And so, in the end, the reader himself stands at the door to his kingdom like a guardian demon, forbidding entrance to anyone who wants to ask impertinent questions; and by using that defense mechanism known as "Oh, that's weird," he is ready to repel any intruder who instigates a rebellion.

When the door shuts behind him, leaving him supposedly secure in that magical, saintly space called children's literature, he won't see the blind alley into which he's stumbled, the blind alley which is his past without history and his future without history. He doesn't see it because someone—the Old Lady; Babar; Huey, Dewey, and Louie; or the reader himself when he becomes an adult and must raise his own children—is painting the four infinite walls, the floor and ceiling, someone is painting on a very hard and very real wall a horizon that does not exist.

—Ariel Dorfman, concluding an essay begun in the Allende years (64)

Whether they see in it little green leaves or a painted horizon, adults no longer take children's literature for granted. It is there. It was there in the beginning, when they first started to read, and it is still there, now that they can read small print. Even the venerable tradition of the ornamented letter, recalled so fondly by Terts, responding as he puts it to "the need of words to flower into pictures," is still there in picturebooks and in such longer works as Michael Ende's *The Neverending Story*. Jacqueline Rose, author of *The Case of Peter Pan or the Impossibility of Children's Literature*, speaks for many adults: "For me children's literature cannot be understood as the passive reflection of changing values and conceptions of the child (images of childhood); instead I see it as one of the central means through which we regulate our relationship to language and images as such" (138).[2]

If children's literature is a "central means," then its close study as literature ought to follow. Until children's literature is studied along with other canonical writings, it remains a part of the precious belief and imagery of childhood without becoming part of the self-knowledge instructors wish to cultivate in their students. Left by itself in the cave, in a "magical, saintly space," it serves to advance the academic careers of such tender and insecure figures as Vinnie Miner: "She is fifty-four years old, small, plain, and unmarried—the sort of person that no one ever notices, though she is an Ivy League college professor who has published several books and has a well-established reputation in the expanding field of children's literature" (Lurie 3).[3] In its "*jugendliterarische Ghetto*,"[4] it circulates quietly and respectably in the children's section of the public library, sells well in the children's corner of the bookstore, and even, as of 1969, boasts its own version of *Books in Print*.[5] While its authors enjoy the adulation of large crowds of adult readers, who often flock to autographing sessions in numbers that might make the author of *Bright Lights, Big City* envious, reviews of the autographed works appear usually after page thirty-six in the *New York Times Book Review*. Contemporary works as well known as *Where the Wild Things Are* or *Make Way for Ducklings* are not eligible for the National Book Award but at best for the Newbery, Caldecott, Hans Christian Andersen, or the Golden Phoenix Awards. Yet this isolation from traditional literary culture cannot obscure one crucial fact: children's literature informs and creates readers. It provides the "symbolic outlining";[6] it leads to "the intensification and enrichment of the individual's esthetic experience" (Rosenblatt 44).[7]

Like a slip of the tongue, the conduct and behavior of children's literature is so central to the way in which adults regulate their relationship to language and image that it is always falling under suspicion, as if it were a foolish dragon watched over by a child warden who should and will know better someday. Like the jury's scribbled "Important," "Not Important," "Important," in *Alice's Adventures in Wonderland*, children's literature evokes ambivalent attitudes toward authors and texts. It is worth studying this ambivalent attitude, for it tells a lot about adult readers' expectations of themselves and of what they hope to gain from reading. The conventional criteria by which they ascertain literary worth don't prepare them for, say, a child's picturebook. They observe, "but there is so little text!" as they might not say when reading a sonnet. If a character is shown urinating or defecating (*My Special Best Words, Mrs. Plug the Plumber, I Have to Go!*), if a crowd is shown tearing a hapless good-natured boy limb from limb (*Once There Was a King Who Promised He Would Never Cut Anyone's Head Off*), if animals are shown maimed, limbs amputated (*Die Bauern im Brunnen*), if the flesh of two hyperactive boys is, in their former outline, shown spread out in lumps on a floor (*Max und Moritz*), adult readers may well be shocked: the very genre has been laid bare and made strange. Is this appropriate for children? Or are these images obscene only to adults like themselves? They are called upon to reconcile very conflicting expectations. Not that these expectations will be the same for every reader. The possible staining of a Longstocking by the uncontrollable "Pippi" of that heroine's first name goes frequently unnoticed, at least among adults, but not among children. Forbidden images fill the central pages of many picturebooks, and forbidden thoughts filter through many longer books for children.

Such ambivalence awakens adults, helps shape them as readers. Whether it troubles their standing as grown-ups, or makes them uneasy in their dignities, is probably not as critical as the doubt it creates about structure and meaning. The adult suspicion of children's literature rests partly, I think, on the question of its agenda within familiar narrative structures. Is it an agenda of freedom or escape from adult control and convention, or one of submission and acceptance? When print and image appear together, their agenda often appear to be entirely opposed, as in *Curious George* or *The Tale of Peter Rabbit*. George smiles as he looks down from the stolen balloons that keep him hovering over the streets below, but the text tells that he is afraid. Peter's naughtiness is documented in picture after picture, not the proper behavior of his three sisters. Yet the kindly narrative voice does not allow his audience to think of him as stupid or greedy, ill-bred or willful, but rather as a child in a good deal of trouble. The familiar structuralist sequence (*Interdiction*: "Thou shalt not" / *Violation*: "I just have to!" / *Consequence*: "You'll pay for this" / *Response*: "Woe is me!" or "I'm learning to like it!") does not in these instances stiff-arm adults into compliance or agreement with those who would establish the interdiction, as might a simpler moral fable (e.g., certain German tales read directly out of Grimm or French tales out of Perrault).

What Anthony Browne's or James Marshall's picturebook versions of "Hansel and Gretel" and "Little Red Hiding Hood," respectively, do to their originals is to tell a different story altogether. In Browne's version, for example, next to the words "The family was always very poor, and when a terrible famine came to the land, they could find nothing to eat," we look at a full page illustration that shows all but one member of the family huddled over the empty dining table. Father and children are in plain, rather drab striped shirts, beneath a bare lightbulb; the picture of an ancestor hangs on a wall to the left; the wallpaper is starting to curl, and the atmosphere is altogether that of a poor genteel family in the "old country." But the stepmother, also at the table, is shown in an attractive pink blouse and not huddled at all. If readers follow her gaze across the table, they see the large screen of a television set; a jumbo jet is in flight. While the text tells of the "terrible famine," the illustration tells a tale of divided parental attention and diverted resources. One might even recognize Margaret Thatcher's composed and commanding presence in the stepmother's sturdy gaze. James Marshall's sturdy Red Riding Hood, like the wolf, speaks in an easy, colloquial manner (e.g., "'Oooh,' she said, 'This is scary'" or "'It is I, your delicious—er—darling granddaughter,' said the wolf in a high voice."); despite the dark overtones, the play in the illustrations is that of light comedy. Readers often fail to notice this tension between word and image, assuming that the illustrations in picturebooks merely amplify the meanings of the words.

But if the agenda is too clear and unambiguous, either compelling a moral interpretation or one that feels compassion for the abyss of the author's soul, readers are likely to have the label "typical children's literature" ready at hand, rather than one that names the offending trait. Hans Christian Andersen's work for children (in its various English translations, at least) often arouses suspicion and even a sense of superiority, not the dynamic ambivalence I suggest is the key to a reading of children's literature at its liveliest and best. Roger Sale's comments on Andersen's writings for children are useful here:

> It is often said of Andersen, and of many later successful storytellers for children, that they never grew up themselves and so could better speak to the young. There is perhaps truth in this, but most of the conclusions one might want to draw from this idea seem false. In Andersen's case it is demonstrable that what retarded his maturing as a person handicapped him as an author, and all his defects, by comparison with the earlier authors of fairy tales, seem the result of an inability to be calm, confident, transparently anonymous, a partaker in a tradition older than he, and wiser.
>
> (73)

Jacqueline Rose's careful commentary on J. M. Barrie's inability to be "transparently anonymous" (68–80) and Robert Leeson's brief treatment of Grahame's *The Wind in the Willows* and A. A. Milne's *When We Were Very Young* as participants in "middle-class history" (10–13) suggest that, whether it be unrequited love or class prejudice that gets in the way, the writers of some children's fiction display their handicaps more offensively than do writers in other genres. And the critical response is, rather benignly, to put such "disfigured" writing in a sort of basement called children's literature, rather than to regard the disfigurement as an indication of authorial ineptitude or confusion.

I will come back to the implications of the social and literary configurations found in many popular children's books. Now I will show a second aspect of the reader's experience of children's literature, what has been called *emotional connectedness*.[8] The college classroom is no longer an unlikely place to find veteran readers of children's literature. College-age readers are likely to have been bred with the works of Sendak, Dahl, Hergé, Lindgren, and others in their blood; to suppose that matriculation is the mother of transfusion, and that all that old blood has been shed or drained away in time is wishful thinking. Some students, like their parents before them, carry a few books with them wherever they live; among these we are likely to find not Homer and perhaps not even the Bible, but books from a more recent childhood. Whether it be E. Nesbit's *The Railway Children* or George Selden's *A Cricket in Times Square*, these books are too precious to leave behind. So precious are they that any attempt to reopen them with adult eyes can lead to tremors approaching those of a born-again school board ready to ban the reading of *A Catcher in the Rye.* It's almost as if those who have invested in children's literature at an early age expect to sustain a childhood through that investment. Touching the interest on that investment somehow means reducing the principal, which is childhood itself. Here, in a strange way, is an untouchable body of texts, removed from public view, a hidden canon, privileged by its exclusion from "assigned" or "required" reading. The phenomenon of radical (back to the roots) dyscanonia, or feeling-for-the-canon-of-that-which-cannot-be-read-in-public, is, as Neil Postman points out in *The Disappearance of Childhood,* one of the ways in which some groups see childhood preserved: "Its [i.e., the Moral Majority's or other Fundamentalist groups'] attempts to organize economic boycotts against sponsors of certain television programs, its attempts to restore a sense of inhibition and reverence to sexuality, its attempts at setting up schools that insist on rigorous standards of *civilité,* are examples of an active program aimed at preserving childhood" (148). Perhaps it is not even childhood that is the principal (principle?) at stake, but a kind of felt stability of meaning, available even, as Hamida Bosmajian has noted, in *A Catcher in the Rye*: "In these and other young adult fictions, the adolescent will find himself or herself momentarily addressed, even to the point of the shock of recognition, but at the same time and by unorthodox means, these narratives lead the rebellious youths to accept the nature of our social order and disorder. Yes, these texts are subversive, but not because of what the censors find in them!" (95). The remembrance of readings undertaken at an earlier age provides a surety against the changes of young adulthood; recollected in tranquillity, the experience mastered by the child reader gives the college-age student a certain confidence. As Rod McGillis has put it, "We must understand that if our students are to acquire literary competence, they must also have confidence. Let us give our students the confidence to express what they already know" (6).[9] A confidence not shared, by the way, by some college faculty as they begin to realize the emotional investment in children's literature that exists among many college students.

Perhaps because of its emotional connection, children's literature often appears a fashionable escape, a kind of summer vacation from the hardships of the academic year.[10] The canon of this idyll is apparent at a glance to those who would examine recent attempts to formulate a list of "touchstones." Whether it is an anthology of "classics" of children's literature or a group of appreciative essays, the exclusionary prejudices that guide the selection of texts presented are no one individual's fault: they are part of a pervasive blindness (the blind alley Ariel Dorfman has, in his way, revealed) peculiar to those for whom children's literature is both a bloodless coup against the literary establishment and an immediate asylum from responsibility for literature as a cultural practice engaging persons of all age and ethnic groups. The sense that children's books, to begin with, are written for another, younger reader, the "fairer still" of an earlier generation adults cannot see in *their* troubled mirror, leads to a process of selection marred by the sins of sentimentality and affection. The romanticism of Terts and of Paul Hazard has its place, which I have tried to identify. Readers cannot ignore that which they have loved best, they cannot grow unless they recognize where they have started from. Many children's books do indeed capture the wonderful freedoms of summer days. It is easy, when one thinks of works such as Arthur Ransome's *Swallows and Amazons*, Philippa Pearce's *Tom's Midnight Garden*, or Claude Roy's *La Maison qui s'envole*, to see how one might link the metaphor of summer flight and fancy with a notion of children's literature as flight-from-the-world, in the pattern of the secular romance described by Northrup Frye in *The Secular Scripture*. Nonetheless, it is not sufficient to linger in the haze if one is to do justice to the breadth and scope, the historical complicities and conscience as well as the imaginative felicities and recompense, of children's literature.

I will now move from the precious legacy of childhood reading, those texts whose dual readership provides a constant puzzle, to the larger question of social and literary configurations. I will focus on two texts which have been widely heralded among children, but have received less favorable attention among adults. Here are, shall I say, two cult objects, to be taken from their shrines and passed around again, reexamined anthropologically and not without an eye to their political overtones. Articles in the press have signaled the continuing significance as cultural artifact of the *Curious George* stories. The repeated airing of the movie version of *Charlie and the Chocolate Factory* and the manufacture and marketing of "Everlasting Gobstoppers" remind readers of the infiltration into the mind- and bloodstreams around them of the powerful thematics of Dahl's book. Both stories are the result of a family collaboration. H. A. Rey and Margaret Rey produced together most of the *Curious George* series and, as Dahl has it, *Charlie and the Chocolate Factory* developed from a story he told his young son Theo, who was convalescing after being hit by a taxi in New York City.[11] That the *Curious*

George stories and *Charlie* have not enjoyed critical acclaim while at the same time proving themselves to be durable properties profitably developed is a fact not to be overlooked.

Curious George is a monkey who has grown up (almost) in Africa. He is captured by a white man in a yellow hat and taken abroad to a zoo. His attempts to get public attention yield the possibility of a future in the movies ("Bedtime for Bonzo?"). The story is complicated by a flaw in the main character: he is too curious for his own good or, for that matter, for anyone else's, except the impatient reader's. Always seeking new highs, always regretting the fall, George looks and looks for an elusive euphoric moment, one that may be represented iconically in the first opening of a pictured "Africa" where he swings on a liane, partially peeled banana in hand. George later identifies with seagulls in their flight and, still later, clutching stolen balloons, he rises above walls and roofs before landing gently on top of a stoplight up against which all the world's traffic is confounded. George's perspective is always that of a little Chaplin in a still silent film; he sees and acts out interesting images but not the laws of society. In the picturebook, he is the wordless observer, for whom the ways of civilization are no more than curious illusions or representations—dolls and toys, at least as George is reported to see them from his place in the sky overhead. Yet the balloon-seller, whose customers are children, also offers for sale miniature marionettes in the likeness of mice and even of a monkey. To his market of children, the monkey is but another expressive form to be possessed and manipulated in miniature; to the society of the man with the yellow hat, George is a piece of exotic commodity to be sold to the zoo. In attempting to master his role as homuncular star, George repeats the gestures of the man with the yellow hat, sleeping in a fancy bed, eating and drinking (red wine) at the table, even dialing the telephone from his owner's desk. But he is never the naturalized citizen, always only a kind of resident alien, often in someone else's custody. George's destiny is to "be for others" the epitome of "otherness," to be a principal sight in the captive carnival at the zoo. Thus, at the end of this first or "expatriation" volume (compare the story of Babar), George is seen to be repeating his past as a still(ed) life of the jungle, a living sacrifice (on a barkless, leafless tree) to the interests of the colonizer,[12] who is not only the man with the yellow hat but also the visitors to the zoo and, of course, the reader. The reader, unlike George or the spectators at the zoo, can learn to decipher all kinds of cultural codes.

Puer aeternus from the heart of darkness, George can be the omi-

nous shadow of unteachable, underdeveloped, backward, "sponta-
neous," and jolly folk, the race of childhood, or of the childlike race,
or he can be an authentic artist striving to bring images alive in an
alien world filled with profiteers, managers of law and order (fire-
men, a jailkeeper), and the drivers of all kinds of earthbound vehicles. In this text, icons of power and pleasure, alienation and suffering abound; the terms of racial oppression and exploitation are
inscribed here, as well as the dynamics of art, both as image-making
and as social commentary.

Whatever grown-ups uncover as they reread *Curious George*,[13]
they are likely to find as much to reflect upon as they are to love.
Whatever it meant before, it cannot mean the same the second time,
even though a child could get it. To read over,[14] reconstruct, reinter-
pret—these are crucial acts for any readers of literature, but not
easily accomplished in the face of so much that is new, as is often
the case in a course in "world literature," where most works are
ones of which students have not even heard. Read in quick succes-
sion, such books may stretch the reader beyond his or her capacity
to be surprised and stimulated, especially if the books also introduce
vast amounts of new information. Jean Piaget's "principle of mod-
erate novelty" may be invoked here for pedagogical reasons (68.1).[15]
And if students are expected to be critical readers, they must learn
to rely on themselves, starting with what may be false confidence in
the fact that they were once children who read a particular children's
book. They may believe that, having become adults, they can handle
children's literature in the way they wish they could handle literature written for adults. And if, as some have written, today's child
never had a Wind-in-the-Willows/Leave-It-To-Beaver childhood,[16]
then the construction of a putative childhood will enable this hypothetical adult to grasp certain elements of imaginative response
that he or she could never afford earlier in life. In other words,
whether the student is rereading a childhood favorite, or reading for
the first time a children's classic, he or she may well be buoyed and
girded by the belief in an innate critical superiority at the start. Such
students are ready to enjoy the children's book because it is non-
threatening: a perfect Adam and Eve scenario.

First published in 1964, revised in 1973, *Charlie and the Chocolate Factory* remains the serpent in the garden of children's literature. Even a brief synopsis may suggest why. For years, the town's
chocolate factory has been closed to the public. Only the ingenious
Willy (Wily?) Wonka, the factory owner, and his dwarfish "Oompa-
Loompahs" work and reside there. Charlie Bucket (an empty vessel

waiting to be filled?—he comes from poverty and has no purchasing power of his own, other than from a bill he finds on the street) has heard delicious stories about Wonka's factory from his Grandpa Joe. Wonka, always the promoter, offers five tickets (to anyone who can find one in a candy bar). Four other children, with the purchasing power of their parents behind them, find tickets. Then frugal Charlie finds his and the grand tour follows. Wonka lays down the rules, but only Charlie (and Grandpa Joe and the Oompa-Loompahs, who offer choral commentaries on such evils as TV and parents who spoil children) obeys them. While the other children are "reprocessed" (earning their "just desserts," as students are prone to observe) and expelled (extruded, in one case) from the factory, Charlie, always meek and restrained, earns the role of Willy's successor. Willy's magical glass elevator lifts Charlie's family out of poverty to live everlastingly wonderfully inside the walls of the factory.

The book has been disparaged by most reviewers and omitted from canonical lists (except those proposed by children) until recently. For example, it is not referred to in Margery Fisher (1986); in Perry Nodelman (1985); in Nancy Larrick (1975); none of the author's work is referred to in Zena Sutherland's editions of *The Best in Children's Books* (1973, 1980). Neither Rey's nor Dahl's work is included in two recent anthologies of children's literature: Griffith and Frey (1987) and Butler (1987). Dahl's work *is* mentioned in Gillespie and Gilbert (1985) and in *Masterworks of Children's Literature* (1986), where it is assigned the following curious qualification: "Unfortunately, this sort of wild hopping about from fancy to absurdity is characteristic of Dahl's fiction for children; it is a tribute to his considerable understanding of things children find exciting that his books are even coherent" (183). Margaret Higonnet (1987), without specifically mentioning Dahl, may have hit on one of the reasons for his exclusion from most lists: "It would seem that, as a specialized children's literature has developed in the modern West, it has been made to carry and inculcate our norms of literary unity and structure. Just as literature written for children reproduces social norms, it also crystallizes formal norms, innate only in appearance, which serve ideological purposes" (52). Dahl's "wild hopping about from fancy to absurdity" would make it "unfortunately" suspect. But not to children, among whom his work has many fans. Aitken and Kearney (1986) report on a survey, taken in twenty local schools, of children's "knowledge of and reactions to a list of adult-approved titles" to which titles by Dahl were then *added. Charlie and the Chocolate Factory* was ranked first; other works by Dahl placed fifth and seventh (48). In 1978, one of his works received the Nene award (to the author of the book receiving the greatest number of votes that year from Hawaiian children in grades 4–6). In 1979, another of his works earned him the Young Reader Medal, decided by the votes of California school children in grades K–12 (the list of nominations was also drawn up by the children).[17] Canonized by children, Charlie's story, refocused on Willy Wonka, has also made its mark with a screen version starring Gene Wilder. *Charlie and the Chocolate Factory* has been called one of the leading "books-that-every-teacher-should-know-because-there-is-probably-no-option" (Bailey and Hollindale 166), an epithet Satan would be proud of and a litany publishers are only too glad to hear. Unless one is a member of an army of teachers and librarians, one may, however, be hard put to say what the book is about, to name and thus exorcise its evil once and for all.

Some readers might say it is about consumption, greed, and self-ishness, if not about impotence, a sort of latter day *Satyricon* or *Golden Ass*. Some might say it is about language; like *Alice's Adventures in Wonderland*, it has the earmarks of a mixed genre such as Menippean satire, with morsels of ludic verse, morality play texture, and a potpourri of people, typefaces, and cultural contexts from the world of Dickens to that of Madison Avenue.[18] Some might even say it is about religion and economics, purgatorial factories, the saintly executive-to-be, the owner as both divine tempter and judge, the underworld "Plutocrat" dispensing a chocolate opiate to the malnourished masses. None of these readings allows us to isolate the text from a literary and social context. Even if turning to a quasi-biographical reading (the author as loving father of a wounded son), one finds unsettling echoes of the author's writing for an exclusively adult audience that reads *Penthouse* and *Playboy*;[19] there are hints of ribaldry and scatology in the description of pink and brown orifices, tunnels and tubes in the earth's bowels, and in the quasi-innocent seduction of a young man by an old boy who boasts of his private yacht: "I made her by hollowing out an enormous boiled sweet! Isn't she beautiful! See how she comes cutting through the river!" Of the female figures portrayed, from Grandmas Josephine and Georgina (whose names are cognate with those of their husbands, Joseph and George, and who are therefore hard to see as distinct individuals) to Violet Beauregarde and Veruca Salt (whose names contain the seeds of their destinies), none proves to be instrumental or effective at what she sets out to do. This may reflect the worldview of a twelve-year-old male, but it is difficult not to see in it the misogynist tendencies of the old pornographer himself.

Charlie's story also situates itself within narrative tradition as a kind of cautionary fairy tale. In this version of the Hansel and Gretel story, all the Gretels are dispensable. There is a male witch, but the temptations are the same, at once sensational and ethereal, heavenly food forever. As in the fairy tale, parents (except for Charlie's), in a famine one might say of selfhood, lust after their own images and tend to manipulate their children according to their own interest in publicity. The sorcerer is cruel and unforgiving, and does not let himself be easily disposed of: he is "much older than you think." Like Hansel, Charlie is developing the ability to substitute symbolic representations for sensory reality; his peers and forerunners, Augustus Gloop, Violet Beauregarde, Veruca Salt, and Mike Teevee, lack this detachment. Charlie has learned about Willie Wonka, the legendary chocolate-maker, from the stories he hears his grandfather tell, and he learns to play the spectator role beautifully,[20] never succumbing to a foolish involvement in events, so that by emulation he may inherit the sorcerer's position. His willingness to be enchanted by this male Circe of capitalism does not lead to piggish behavior but rather to a rapt perception of the unified purpose of all things ("Just you wait and see," he exclaims as he is about to inherit Willie's wealth and power). The other children fall victim to the peculiar vice betokened by their names, and must be reformed and purged of that vice through the same process of liquidation and elimination as governs the making of pure chocolate. This devouring of children is not new in the world of the fairy tale, nor is the promise of a new life without the encumbrances of past mistakes.

It may well be that fairy tale motifs on the subject of hunger and everlasting food supplies make a reading of *Charlie and the Chocolate Factory* the attractive, even seductive experience it is for children. In his *Child and Tale: The Origins of Interest*, André Favat argues that the fairy tale experience is particularly suitable for young children whose life experiences are moving them "from an egocentric to a socialized sphere."

> With its construction of animism, magic, morality of constraint, and its whole egocentric cast, the fairy tale retains in stable form, impervious to change, the very conception of the world the child now finds challenged. In the face of that challenge, with the resultant crisis and regressive impulse, the child under eight must turn to the fairy tale for a reaffirmation of his original con-

ception of the world—a world preserved in the tale, unchanged and unchallenged.

(49)

Yet the fairy tale motifs in *Charlie and the Chocolate Factory* are displaced, repositioned within the framework of a modern technocracy, in which the individual is relegated to the role of consumer of non-essential goods, and in which an Angloid candy manufacturer controls the fate of a whole "third-world" nation, those littler and less educated than the "old-world" chocolate producer himself. Described in the first edition of 1964 as pygmies from Africa, and later (in the 1973 edition) as dwarfs (not an uncompelling representation of those who labor without personal recognition and with only the clothes on their backs), the Oompah-Loompahs serve the research interests of their owner/handler, becoming happily expendable at any time for the greater good of all. They also serve as right-thinking commentators, expostulating in rhymed verse on the evil influences of television or of indulgent, publicity-seeking parents. Charlie's example speaks for itself. Unlike Hansel and Gretel, Charlie takes no initiatives that are not previously approved by an adult. His spectatorship, while honorable in a reader, appears to support a code of unquestioning obedience and submission to authority. Unlike Mike Teevee, who questions Wonka's hypocritical record as purveyor of nourishment (Wonka lives on fish and cabbages, but sells candy for a living), Charlie listens and watches and waits, the perfect child, the lucky consumer, and the next CEO of the chocolate factory. While the "liquidation of lack" signals the happy ending, it does not support a reading of the text as a fairy tale, but as a modern children's book, as disturbing and repellent as it is fascinating and even contagious.

For young readers, *Charlie and the Chocolate Factory*, like a number of rereadable children's books, has the appeal of a box of Froot Loops; for older readers, for whom the fairy tale motifs wear thin, it is a problem text, almost *nefas*, an abomination. For those readers who confront the social and literary aspects of this problem text, it can never be quite as *fas*, or perfect in the sight of heaven, as it might once have been. To reread it is to reexamine one's own pleasures as a reader, indeed to encounter one's identity as problematic, dynamic, multidimensional. Like *Curious George* and a host of other well-known books for children, such a book as *Charlie* tests our adult expectations, forcing us to realize that the kingdom of literature itself is not one but many. Children's literature need not be viewed as a protectorate of the great nation of letters, but as a richly troublesome republic, with worldwide and lifelong influences, always challenging the sanctity of its own borders.

Notes

An earlier version of this paper was delivered at the N. E. H. Summer Institute on "The Theory and Teaching of World Literature" at the University of Massachusetts at Amherst in July, 1987. I am especially grateful to Sarah Lawall for her encouragement and guidance in the revision of that paper.

1. Terts returns several times to a recollection of the childhood experience of reading, notably with this: "*Mystery Island, The Three Musketeers* . . . such titles used to have a wonderful music about them and were, perhaps, more full of meaning than the books themselves. I remember how we spoke of them with bated breath, and I remember the smell of their pages and bindings, and the silvery gleam of the yet unread *Silver Prince*. The pregnancy of words in childhood! Who will restore it to us? . . ." (152f.)

2. For more on the possibility of situating and defining children's literature, see Peter Hunt's excellent chapters "Criticism and Children's Literature"; "The Situation of Children's Literature"; "Defining Children's Literature" (5–64). For more extensive treatments of image in children's picturebooks, see Joseph H. Schwarcz and Chava Schwarcz, *The Picture Book Comes of Age: Looking at Childhood through the Art of Illustration, Children's Literature* (19 and passim), and my "Introduction to Picturebook Codes." Molly Bang, a notable picturebook maker and artist, provides a brilliant introduction to the language of pictures in *Picture This: Perception and Composition*.

3. Other views on pedagogy in the college teaching of children's literature can be found in Glenn Edward Sadler, ed., *Teaching Children's Literature: Issues, Pedagogy, Resources*.

4. Lucia Binder, drawing on terms proposed by Alfred Clemens Baumgärtner, asks "How far in general do critics have the possibility of working against a ghetto-culture—and what does this children's literature ghetto actually consist of?" ["Inwieweit haben die Kritiker überhaupt die Möglichkeit, der Ghettobildung entgegenzuwirken—und worin besteht dieses jugendliterarische Ghetto eigentlich?"] (13).

5. For readers of English, the publication by Bowker in 1969 of *Children's Books in Print* was one milestone. Another was reached in 1980, when, with volume 8, the Yale University Press assumed publication of *Children's Literature*, which claimed to be "the first scholarly journal in the field of children's literature published by a major university press" (1). By 1982, the Modern Language Association had seen fit to grant the study of children's literature "division" status. Following the lead of the Yale University Press, The Johns Hopkins University Press publishes a scholarly journal in the field of children's literature, *The Lion and the Unicorn*.

6. The relation of children's books to literacy is treated with vision and acumen by Margaret Meek in "Symbolic Outlining: The Academic Study of Children's Literature." See also Christa Ellbogen, "Durch Lesen erziehen . . . ? Kinder- und Jugendliteratur im Spannungsfeld von literarischem und pädagogischem Anspruch" and Moebius, "Cultural Entitlement in the New Age."

7. The application of Rosenblatt's statement to children's literature in particular is mine. D. W. Harding's "Ways forward for the teacher . . ." echoes this emphasis.

8. The title of Egoff et al., *Only Connect: Readings in Children's Literature* (after an essay by P. L. Travers), has still not lost its mystique.

9. See also Christa Ellbogen, who emphasizes the making of not only a "*wissender*" (knowledgeable) but also a "*durchschauender*" (perceptive) citizen.

10. This echoes a romantic manifesto summarized by Postman (52–64). For a more detailed discussion, see John Sommerville (120–135, 160–188). Terts, remembering Locke, remarks, "We are too used to thinking of childhood innocence as an absence of something, as a *tabula rasa*. But suppose the reverse is true and this applies rather to those who have lost their innocence?" (162). Gareth Matthews recommends "cultivated innocence" as a way to "puzzle and muse over the simplest ways we have of saying and seeing things," or, in other words, as a prerequisite for philosophical inquiry (94). Lissa Paul comments on a letter to her from Hughes, in which, she reports, he "reaches for the redemptive side of today's New Medievalism. As he sees it, an audience of children and secretly listening adults potentially possesses the best characteristics of both adults and children: access to knowledge of grown-up cultural and linguistic secrets, and the unconditional open-mindedness of children" (55ff.). Cautions against "adultist" views (if they threaten to overwhelm the rights of child readers) are summarized by Hugh Crago (122–140).

11. See Dahl's famous reply to Eleanor Cameron's polemics in "'Charlie and the Chocolate Factory': A Reply" (121ff.).

12. See Dorfman, "Of Elephants and Ducks" (15–64) and J. Rose (50–57), for more on the relation between colonialism and children's literature.

13. For further discussion of this classic, which is not included in any of the anthologies or in Patricia Jean Cianciolo's *Picture Books for Children*, see Moebius "The *Enfant Terrible* Comes of Age."

14. As discussed in Richard Exton's amusing "The Post-Structuralist Always Reads Twice."

15. Discussed (under the heading of "Curiosity," 37–39) by Herbert Ginsburg and Sylvia Opper, who summarize ". . . the novelty principle asserts that what determines curiosity is not the physical nature of the object, but rather the degree to which the object is discrepant from what the individual is familiar with, which, of course, depends entirely on the individual's experience" (39).

16. Postman (5) maintains that the upsurge of studies in the history of

childhood is a sign of its imminent demise. See also C. John Sommerville
(7). Some believe that our post-modern interest in the history of the book
points the same way.

17. See *Children's Books: Awards and Prizes* (57, 115).

18. H. J. Rose calls Menippean satire a "type of popular ethical discourse . . . in prose, but freely interspersed with poetry . . ." (228).

19. For an excellent study of the double-agentry, inherent in children's
book authorship, of those who also write for adults, see Aidan Chambers's
"The Reader in the Book" (esp. 254–257).

20. Revisiting the work of James Britton on the spectator role, Arthur N.
Applebee summarizes: "Our attitude toward such an experience becomes
that of a *spectator*: we look on, testing our hypotheses about structure and
meaning, but we do not rush in to interrupt—to do so would obscure the
relationships and spoil the effect of the whole" (16).

Works Cited

Ahlberg, Allan, and Joe Wright, ill. *Mrs. Plug the Plumber*. New York: Golden Press, 1980.

Aitken, David, and Anthony Kearney. "Children's Books in Teacher Education at St. Martin's College Lancaster." *Signal* 49 (1986): 44–51.

Applebee, Arthur N. *The Child's Concept of Story*. Chicago: University of
Chicago Press, 1978.

Bailey, Jennifer, and Peter Hollindale. "Children's Books in Teacher Education at York University." *Signal* 51 (1986): 156–171.

Bang, Molly. *Picture This: Perception and Composition*. Boston: Bulfinch/
Little Brown, 1991.

Baumgärtner, Alfred Clemens. "'Jugendbuch und Literatur: Überlegungen
zu einem unstrittenen literarischen Phänomen." In *Kinder- und Jugendliteratur*, edited by M. Gorschenk and A. Rucktäschel, pp. 9–19. Munich:
Fink, 1979.

Binder, Lucia. "Kritik, Rezension—oder 'Einstufung'? Einige Fragen zur
Kinderbuchkritik." *1000 und 1 Buch, Zeitschrift für Kinder- und Jugendliteratur* 2 (1987): 12–16.

Bosmajian, Hamida. "Censorship and Acts of Reading." *Children's Literature in Education* 18:2 (1987): 95.

Browne, Anthony, ill. *Hansel and Gretel*. Adapted from a translation from
Grimm by Eleanor McQuarrie. London and New York: Franklin Watts,
1981.

Busch, Wilhelm. *Max und Moritz*. Munich: Südwest, 1979.

Butler, Francelia, Anne Devereaux Jordan, and Richard Rotert. *THE WIDE
WORLD ALL AROUND: An Anthology of Children's Literature*. New
York: Longman, 1987.

Carroll, Lewis. [Charles Lutwidge Dodgson.] "Alice's Adventures in Wonderland." In *Alice in Wonderland*, edited by Donald J. Gray, pp. 1–99.
New York: W. W. Norton, 1971.

Chambers, Aidan. "The Reader in the Book." In *The Signal Approach to Children's Books*, edited by Nancy Chambers, pp. 250–275. Harmondsworth, England: Penguin, 1980.

Children's Book Council. *Children's Books: Awards and Prizes*. New York: Children's Book Council, 1981.

Cianciolo, Patricia Jean. *Picture Books for Children*, 2d ed. Chicago: American Library Association, 1981.

Crago, Hugh. "A Signal Conversation." *Signal* 50 (1986): 122–140.

Dahl, Roald. "'Charlie and the Chocolate Factory': A Reply." In *Crosscurrents of Criticism: Horn Book Essays, 1968–1977*, edited by Paul Heins. Boston: The Horn Book, 1977.

Dorfman, Ariel. *The Empire's Old Clothes: What the Lone Ranger, Babar, and Other Innocent Heroes Do to Our Minds*. Translated by Clark Hansen. New York: Pantheon, 1983.

Egoff, Sheila A., G. T. Stubbs, L. F. Ashley, eds. *Only Connect: Readings in Children's Literature*. Toronto and New York: Oxford University Press, 1969.

Ellbogen, Christa. "Durch Lesen erziehen . . . ? Kinder- und Jugendliteratur im Spannungsfeld von literarischem und pädagogischem Anspruch." *1000 und 1 Buch, Zeitschrift für Kinder- und Jugendliteratur* 2 (1986): 4–9.

Ende, Michael. *The Neverending Story*. Translated by Ralph Manheim. Illustrated by Roswitha Quadflieg. New York: Doubleday, 1983. Originally published as *Die unendliche Geschichte* (Stuttgart, 1979).

Exton, Richard. "The Post-Structuralist Always Reads Twice." *The English Magazine* 10 (1982): 13–20.

Favat, F. André. *Child and Tale: The Origins of Interest*. Research report: National Council of Teachers of English, no. 19, 1977.

Fisher, Margery. *Classics for Children and Young People*. Lockwood, England: Thimble Press, 1986.

Frye, Northrop. *The Secular Scripture: A Study of the Structure of Romance*. Cambridge, Mass.: Harvard University Press, 1976.

Gillespie, John T., and Christine B. Gilbert. *Best Books for Children*, 4th ed. New York and London: Bowker, 1985.

Ginsburg, Herbert, and Sylvia Opper. *Piaget's Theory of Intellectual Development*, 2d ed. Englewood Cliffs, N.J.: Prentice-Hall, 1979.

Grahame, Kenneth. *The Wind in The Willows*. Illustrated by Ernest H. Shepard. London: Chas. Scribner's Sons, 1908.

Griffith, John W., and Charles H. Frey, eds. *Classics of Children's Literature*, 2d ed. New York: Macmillan, 1987.

Harding, D. W. "Ways forward for the teacher (2): making way for the child's own 'feeling comprehension' (Response to literature: Dartmouth seminar report)." In *The Cool Web: The Pattern of Children's Reading*, edited by Margaret Meek, Aidan Warlow, and Griselda Barton, pp. 376–392. New York: Atheneum, 1978.

Higonnet, Margaret. "Narrative Fractures and Fragments." *Children's Literature* 15 (1987): 37–54.

Hunt, Peter. *Criticism, Theory, & Children's Literature*. Oxford: Basil Blackwell, 1991.

Larrick, Nancy. *A Parent's Guide to Children's Reading*, 4th ed. Garden City, New York: Doubleday & Co., 1975.

Leeson, Robert. *Children's Books and Class Society Past and Present*. London: Writers and Readers Publishing Co-operative, 1977.

Lindgren, Astrid. *Pippi Longstocking*. Translated by Florence Lamborn. Illustrated by Louis S. Glanzman. New York: Viking, 1950. Originally published as *Pippi Langstrump* (Stockholm: Rabén and Sjögren, 1945.)

Lurie, Alison. *Foreign Affairs*. New York: Random House, 1984.

Marshall, James. *Red Riding Hood*. New York: Penguin, 1987.

Masterworks of Children's Literature. vol. 8, *The Twentieth Century*. New York: Stonehill/Chelsea House, 1986.

Matthews, Gareth B. *Philosophy and the Young Child*. Cambridge, Mass.: Harvard University Press, 1980.

McCloskey, Robert. *Make Way for Ducklings*. New York: Viking, 1941.

McGillis, Rod. "The Child as Critic: Using Children's Responses in the University Classroom." *Children's Literature Association Quarterly* 10:1 (1985): 4–6.

McInerney, Jay. *Bright Lights, Big City*. New York: Vintage, 1984.

Meek, Margaret. [Margaret Meek Spencer.] "Symbolic Outlining: The Academic Study of Children's Literature." *Signal* 53 (1987): 97–115.

Milne, A. A. *When We Were Very Young*. New York: Dutton, 1924.

Moebius, William. "Cultural Entitlement in the New Age." *The Lion and the Unicorn* 16 (1992): 57–65.

———. "Introduction to Picturebook Codes." *Word and Image* (April-June 1986): 141–158.

———. "The *Enfant Terrible* Comes of Age." *Notebooks in Cultural Analysis* 2 (1985): 32–50.

Munsch, Robert, and Michael Martchenko. *I Have To Go!* Toronto: Annick Press, 1987.

Nesbit, E. *The Railway Children*. Illustrated by C. E. Brock. London: Wells, Gardner, Darton, 1906.

Nodelman, Perry, ed. *Touchstones: Reflections on the Best in Children's Literature*. West Lafayette, Indiana: Children's Literature Association/Purdue University, 1985.

Paul, Lissa. "Inside the Lurking-Glass with Ted Hughes." *Signal* 49 (1986): 52–63.

Pearce, Philippa. *Tom's Midnight Garden*. Illustrated by Susan Einzig. London: Oxford University Press, 1958.

Piaget, Jean. *The Origins of Intelligence in Children*. Translated by M. Cook. New York: International Universities Press, 1952.

Postman, Neil. *The Disappearance of Childhood*. New York: Delacorte Press, 1982.

Potter, Beatrix. *The Tale of Peter Rabbit*. London: Frederick Warne, 1903.

Ransome, Arthur. *Swallows and Amazons*. London: Jonathan Cape, 1930.

Rey, H. A. *Curious George*. Boston: Houghton Mifflin, 1941.

Rose, H. J. *A Handbook of Latin Literature*. New York: E. P. Dutton, 1960.

Rose, Jacqueline. *The Case of Peter Pan or the Impossibility of Children's Literature*. London: Macmillan, 1984.

Rosen, Michael, and Kathy Henderson. *Once There Was a King Who Promised He Would Never Cut Anyone's Head Off*. London: André Deutsch, 1976.

Rosenblatt, Louise. *Literature as Exploration*, 3d ed. New York: Noble and Noble, 1965.

Roy, Claude. *La Maison qui s'envole*. Illustrated by Georges Lemoine. Paris: Gallimard, 1977.

Sadler, Glenn Edward, ed. *Teaching Children's Literature: Issues, Pedagogy, Resources*. New York: Modern Language Association of America, 1992.

Sale, Roger. *Fairy Tales and After: From Snow White to E. B. White*. Cambridge, Mass.: Harvard University Press, 1979.

Salinger, J. D. *A Catcher in the Rye*. Boston: Little, Brown, 1951.

Schwarcz, Joseph H., and Chava Schwarcz. *The Picture Book Comes of Age: Looking at Childhood through the Art of Illustration*. Chicago and London: American Library Association, 1991.

Selden, George. *A Cricket in Times Square*. Illustrated by Garth Williams. New York: Farrar, Straus and Giroux, 1960.

Sendak, Maurice. *Where the Wild Things Are*. New York: Harper & Row, 1963.

Sommerville, C. John. *The Rise and Fall of Childhood*. Beverly Hills, Calif.: Sage Publications, 1982.

Steptoe, John. *My Special Best Words*. New York: Viking, 1974.

Sutherland, Zena, ed. *The Best in Children's Books, 1966–1972*. Chicago: University of Chicago Press, 1973.

———. *The Best in Children's Books, 1973–1978*. Chicago: University of Chicago Press, 1980.

Terts, Abram. [Andrei Sinyavsky.] *A Voice from the Chorus*. Translated by Kyril Fitzlyon and Max Hayward. New York: Farrar, Straus & Giroux, 1976.

Waechter, Friedrich Karl. *Die Bauern im Brunnin*. Zürich: Diogenes, 1978.

12. In the Canon's Mouth: Being Lucid about the Local

Margaret Spencer

No changes in the curriculum of schools, colleges, or universities happen in a vacuum. The revision of the content of courses reflects the ways in which we change our minds as we study what goes on in the world, how we now look at the past, and what we want for the future. The opposing claims of innovation and continuity are hard to reconcile, especially in literature. While we are unlikely to seek a revival of Young's *Night Thoughts*, we are bound to ask ourselves if our neglect of texts in English from the new communities across the world which are at home in our language should not be redressed.

Whatever else it does, literature joins times and places. When she discovered that John Keats was twenty-one before he saw the sea, and that ever thereafter he sought consolation in his recollection of it so that even the movement of wind over a wheatfield could stir him, Amy Clampit, whose childhood was spent by the sea, re-read Keats *through* this contrast and understanding. The result is her network of poems: *Voyages: Homage to John Keats*. As I read these poems, their seascape reads mine, from my childhood by the sea, so that my reading of Keats is renewed by the words of a contemporary American poet. In the terms of this essay I became more lucid about what, for me, is now local: the Keats who lived in London.

I

In May and June I spend my time supervising the first drafts of masters' dissertations being written by my students who are mostly teachers in this city. Their everyday concerns are the literacy and literary competency of children in multicultural classrooms where, in all, 161 languages are spoken. Despite the variation in the titles of their work, the students are asking: What is literacy, now, and how is it schooled? What is literature, now, and how do we choose to read it in this or that classroom? If, in their written examinations, my students are confronted by a question about the literary canon—and goodness knows, in the quirkiness of all examinations they might be—I guess that the mental presence of their pupils might move them to quote from Terry Eagleton's *Literary Theory*, a work which, on the whole, commends itself to them. "The so-called 'literary canon,' the unquestioned 'great tradition' of the 'national literature' has to be recognized as a *construct*, fashioned by particular people for particular reasons at a certain time. There is no such thing as a literary work or tradition which is valuable *in itself*, regardless of what anyone might have said or come to say about it. 'Value' is a transitive term, it means whatever is valued by certain people in specific situations according to particular criteria and in the light of given purposes" (1983).

Is that true about the canon—that it changes as people's opinions change? What counsel should I then give to my student who, after some grubbing in the archives, discovered that every year since the beginning of school examinations in London—the kind of examinations in literature which act as gate-keepings to England's highly competitive university entrance—the poems of John Keats had appeared on every syllabus? (Only Shakespeare rivaled this in appearance, and he is a special case of a *compulsory* text; *hors canon*, you might say). What should I deduce from these repeated appearances? That examiners wanted to keep before the eyes of successive generations of students the literary radicalism of the early Romantic movement? That the verse has some intrinsic virtue for adolescents in their intellectual accidie and sensuous indulgences? What were the reasons for insisting that prospective civil servants of the late nineteenth century, the examinee of those days, should read the *Ode to a Nightingale*? To remember England when they reached outposts of the Empire? Or had it something to do with the sales of Palgrave's *Golden Treasury*, Matthew Arnold's, and some say, Queen Victoria's, favorite poetry book?

In England the canon's proving ground is the examination hall. My accomplice in this idea is Roland Barthes. Literature, he is reported to have said, is "what is taught." I am still asking what has it meant, for a hundred years, *to have read* Keats? How would you, my American readers, view a post-structuralist reading of this field if you were setting examination questions? My advice to my student did nothing to solve the question of Keats's right to a place in the canon. I simply said that if he looked at each of the editions produced in turn over the years and set for school use in the list of recommended books, he might be able to trace the reasons other people had given for keeping Keats there. I added that he was not to balk at the idea that pride, pelf (economics nowadays), or procrastination ("we'll think of something else for next year's") might play a part in this perpetuity.

In English literature in England there are nine hundred years of vernacular texts to choose from, and the choosers have been, traditionally, the *literati*, the lettered, those who had the power to privilege opinion over knowledge. There have been only 120 years of compulsory literacy, always vaguely defined and indefinitely measured or understood. Both literature and literacy have been credited with civilizing influences. Without doubt they have added to judgments of personal worth and contributed to forms of self-regard; but not for everyone. It is right therefore that scholars should ask questions about literacy and literature, such as: Who reads? Whose reading counts?, especially if they have, as I hope they do have, more than the favored few in mind. But has "well-read" any force now as a description of anyone? What does it suggest to you, to us all? What does it convey about the cleverest children in the minority groups in London schools, the Indians?

I have blown my cover at the outset, for my standing as a comparativist scholar is all untried. My temporizing about the canon may prove less than helpful unless I introduce at once my mentor, Frank Kermode, whose book *Forms of Attention* concentrated my mind wonderfully during the preparation of this paper, not the least as the result of his distinction between opinion and knowledge. My modest competences lie in studies of young people reading in ways which are of some concern to me because I believe they are underprivileged in school. My continuing interests stretch through readers to the books they choose to read, and those which they are, in the course of their education, bound to read. My views of literacy include the idea that reading has to be defined as social practice, and both literature and literacy are studied best in the contexts of culture and history. This said, and the canon unmentioned, I am concerned to keep literacy and literature at the heart of the language arts curriculum, not least because they can be shared, productive activities, although they have often been regarded as individual, exclusive ones. English teaching, which has been my life's work, has taught me the necessary relationship between literature and understanding the meaningful aspects of living, that is, most aspects of living.

The problematic in what follows is: How can I teach the tradition of literature as something vital, alive? Therefore I ask, what literary theory takes account of this vitality, and how does teaching, or, as I prefer, helping others to learn, invite students to contribute to its continuance as well as to a criticism of it? My argument is that young people's growth in language and understanding is at the heart of the matter, and that they have powerful allies in those who make books for them, especially the books which offer them the resourceful possibilities of cultural plurality and polysemic texts. The form of attention now to be explicated is how children become readers of literature and what that reading signifies in the contexts of contemporary cultures.

II

I will begin by accepting and extending a proposition enunciated by Professor Lawall during the 1987 Institute on Theory and Teaching of World Literature: that students "should be aware of themselves as holding a historically shaped perspective." I extend this to include their teachers, especially if more than a decade separates teachers and students. Then I ask, what shapes an understanding of the perspective? Is it not, besides the metacognition, language? If all readers bring their reading history to the reading of any text, how does one history compare with another?

I am told I could read before I went to school in the village in Fife on the east coast of Scotland where I was born. That may be my ancestors' insistence; it is also partly my recollection. I could sing the hymns in the Kirk, holding the book open, and the nursery rhymes, and songs my grandparents taught me:

> Ye hielans and ye lowlans
> O whaur hae ye been?
> They hae slain the Earl o' Moray
> And laid him on the green.

On Sundays our walk might take us past the ruins of the castle where Macduff's wife and children were murdered. When we crossed the Forth Bridge by train to Edinburgh, my grandfather, who claimed to have known Robert Louis Stevenson, would tell me the story of *Kidnapped*, which is set in the village beneath the massive steel girders. He would always point out the island in the Firth of Forth where, in Shakespeare's version

> Sweno, the Norways' king craves composition
> Nor would we deign him burial of his men

> Till he disbursed, at Saint Colme's Inch,
> Ten thousand dollars to our general use . . .
>
> *(Macbeth* I, 2, 61–64)

Macbeth was, to me, a local Scottish king before he became the tragic hero of the play Shakespeare wrote for the later Scottish King, James, who succeeded Elizabeth I.

In the town made famous in a ballad, I lived opposite the house of Chaucer's later contemporary, Henryson. In school I read Chaucer, Shakespeare, Milton, the Romantic poets—including Keats—and Matthew Arnold, from whom I learned about poetic touchstones. My own private canon gave honor to Walter Scott and Elinor Brent Dyer, to the writers of Victor Gollancz's Left Book Club proposed by my radical teachers, but whose modernisms I didn't fully understand. Evelyn Waugh, Virginia Woolf, and Aldous Huxley filled the summer when we waited for war to be declared. I left school four years later, a precocious short-sighted pedant, with attestations of fitness in Latin, French, and German, a muddled experience of Dickens and Thackeray (whom I haven't read since), an enormous enthusiasm for Shakespeare, Milton, and Robert Burns, a slight distaste for Keats, admiration of Shelley's anarchic behavior, and a longing to read Baudelaire in the company of someone who understood him.

As an undergraduate in wartime Edinburgh, I was one of the few who were exempt from the obligatory war service that had taken my classmates to learn Japanese, to sail in submarines with my father, or, later, to land on Normandy beaches. In return for the grace and favor of being exempt from these things, I was expected to tackle my reading like a soldier and my French prose like a potential spy. So I applied myself to Anglo-Saxon, Old Norse, and most other things from Beowulf to Virginia Woolf in cold rooms and sometimes in air-raid shelters. Once I was rebuked for reading Byron there instead of the Bible—the latter being thought a more appropriate volume should I be called to meet the author. When I emerged in 1946 I faced the smashed-up postwar world laden with all the weight of the past in European history and philosophy in addition to literary texts, and a wild and wondering excitement, ready to do battle for the role of poetry in the brave new world. That I was thoroughly molded into, trapped in, the Arnoldian hierarchy of the heritage of literature there was no doubt. The one merciful chink in this proof armor was that my tutor hated Arnold's obvious successor, Dr. Leavis, because he had said unkind things about Milton. I have never been a Leavisite. New Criticism I learned in the company of distinguished American teachers in an ancient Salzburg castle where we were fed by the army of occupation. I resisted the New Criticism because, it seemed to me then, it took no account of Coleridge. My canonicals were of the severest kind, baroque and medieval. Keats disappeared early from my reading, except in the exam class, which I taught well, out of guilt.

Three things in those years shaped much of what followed. First, I was female but I had been taught in undergraduate and postgraduate studies as if I were one of the young men in my class who had been returned for reasons of unfitness or wounds. They had been to war. They tempered my idealism with a world-weariness that a reading of *Troilus and Cressida* confirmed. "What is aught but as 'tis valued?" Their historical perspectives were shaped where history was made. Clearly I see now that the men were favored. My reading was what Jane Miller called a "learned androgyny." I was bifocal, bilingual in a special sense, with my engendered perspective on Jane Austen kept well hidden from examination papers.

I realize now that I never expected all that reading, done with pleasure and sometimes with ecstasy, to be about my *life*. The feelings I had were displaced onto the characters I read about; they were my companions, my enemies, my dangerous friends, my tolerable relations. The language of books seduced me because my family never spoke about how they felt, far less about how women feel. It was as if the words gaiety, sorrow, enthusiasm, delight, anger, hate, ferocity, despair, disappointment, wonder had no counterpart in any of them. It simply wasn't done to betray affection and pleasure, any more than it was possible to admit to exasperation and exhaustion. Poetry became a licensed self-indulgence. Like J. S. Mill, I probably owe it my survival.

Two other things in one. The exigencies of war kept elderly scholars at work in the universities, so I read the Scottish ballads and the poems of Donne with Herbert Grierson. Yet Donne has enjoyed a comparatively short period of canonicity, like Botticelli in painting and Monteverdi in music. Donne's poetry emerged from Dryden's dismissal, Dr. Johnson's disregard, and the charge of being "rough" or "quaint" only in 1912 when Grierson published his edition of the poems. It was a remarkable bit of luck to hear this amazing scholar describe that enterprise in 1946. What came from Grierson's edition of Donne was Eliot's approval of Donne's undivided sensibility. So the Eliot canon, which is admired in the States as elsewhere, derives in part at least from the hard editorial slog of a patient Scot who brought to his work the traditions of the Protestant biblical study of his forebears. Here now is Kermode, nearly forty years later: "The preservation and renewal of these masters has become the duty *not* of artists and enthusiasts, carefree adherents of opinion, but of canon-defending theory-laden professors, a fact of some importance." Grierson read Donne with a Scots accent. He thundered the ballads, emphasizing the strong beat of the prosody, and confirmed my local loyalty for ever. Not once have I claimed to be an Englishwoman, for all my London linguistic affectations.

These things are part of the formative history. They show clearly how the Tradition can be a kind of investment for most teachers of literature. I had learned my lessons. They were to prove useful currency, and I lived for some time on the interest. But, as life broke in, I discovered I was old before my time.

The perspectives shaped by this history were hierarchical, privileged by a set of social structures and a dialect of power, Standard English. As I entered teaching, the elitisms of my literary caste were about to be challenged, not least by other teachers. I was to discover that the very studies which had privileged me could render others ineligible, and that what school literature teaching taught them was their ineligibility. Not long into my first teaching job I joined, almost by accident, a group of radical teachers who taught me that English, the *language*, is "the arena where the interaction of language, thought and society is passionately played out" (Rosen).

I had taken for granted that talk, reading, writing, in the way I did these things, was the common lot of humankind. This now amazes me. For all my studies in Middle English I knew nothing of the dialects of modern England beyond the comedy of Shaw's *Pygmalion*, although I was actively bilingual. The steady stream backward toward England, as if history had turned around, of those whose ancestors had been exploited by the readers of Keats in the nineteenth century, was well underway. What were to become "The other languages of England" were already being spoken in London and Midland towns. The faces of my pupils changed. I had to confront what I didn't know. For all my Anglo-Saxon, French, Latin, German, and my research enquiries into how humans understand what they read, I had never actually asked myself: What *is* language, and how do we learn it?

When I realized that the superstructure of my teaching was founded on ignorance so complete as to be dangerous, I entered the intellectual revolution of the late fifties and early sixties and taught both teachers of literature and adults who were considered illiterate. Within months I faced incontrovertible evidence that reading ability and intelligence are not synonymous, that systems of literacy are directly related to distributions of power, that reality is socially constructed, that talk is a powerful mode of learning, and that television would come to play an ever-increasing role in people's lives. My debt to my colleagues James Britton, Nancy Martin, and Harold Rosen in these learning years is fathoms deep. In the schools, in teachers' groups, in learning to rework the living tradition of literature, I learned to reread culture, language, and learning. The monument to these days emerged as *A Language for Life*, what teachers call the Bullock Report.

If scholars turn opinion about texts and authors into knowledge, then teachers face, in their classrooms, the vivid and clamorous reality of language and the energy of children learning to use it. The later linguistic revolution of the sixties and seventies made this plain. The necessity to recognize pluralities was forced on the United States long before it was confronted in England. If British schools avoided mistakes about Headstart programs and the like, it was because teachers in the United States taught us the inadequacy of simple theories of cultural assimilation. Arrogantly, perhaps, I'm disposed to believe that, whatever politicians may claim, it was teachers who saw in what came to be called the *Other Languages of England* a powerful resource rather than an insoluble problem. It was in school classrooms that the need to read other literatures became imperative, not least because the pupils, already culturally displaced, demanded to be valued by finding that their stories, their traditions, had value. Sometimes teachers expressed this need by saying that children from Africa, Asia, the Indian subcontinent, and the Caribbean could not "find themselves" in English books, as if a crude realism were the answer. Even the Greek children whose names were Aristarchos, Ulysses, or Homer seemed to have to reclaim what had been colonized. But Anansi stories could begin to restore a history which linked West Africa to Jamaica in south London. Remarkably, bilingualism and feminism came together in a conviction that "children are not invited to become readers by stories which neglect their lives and their knowledge" (Miller).

Understandings of this kind were rooted in my reading of Vygotsky. *Thought and Language* and *Mind in Society* have had for me, my colleagues, and students, the greatest explanatory power of what confronts us. His work is rich enough to inform most of what we do, including the replacement of the vertical hierarchical model of literature teaching with a horizontal, networking one, a rich pluralism instead of a competitive pecking order. Vygotsky makes plain that neither language nor literature can be abstracted from the social and cultural processes in which they are embedded. Language is not simply the means by which a culture or a history is transmitted. Instead, it generates thought, interacts with it, changes it, holds it. "Words have to be made to mean in developing personal utterance, while they also anchor within developing thought the meanings which are made" (Burgess). When children enter the conversation of humankind they remake it as surely as Dr. Johnson did. When they learn to write, to compose, they are doing the same kind of thing as Tolstoy; when they read they are becoming what we have become—readers.

It now seems to me an impossible thing that teachers of literature, not only in multilingual but in all classes, should have no curiosity about children's developing understanding about the imaginative play and paradoxes that language makes possible. The generative insights of Saussure, and Halliday's linguistic perceptions of language as social semiotic, sit well within the explanatory force of Vygotsky's social theory. Jerome Bruner called him "a titan" of modern developmental understanding. James Britton made his colleagues and students read *Thought and Language* in Bruner's and Cole's edition when it appeared in 1962. This is, in my view, comparative literature of a different but equally significant kind, a kind directly related to the enterprises of literacy and literature.

Teachers embarked on necessary raiding operations in adjoining fields: linguistics, social psychology, ethnography, always to link language and learning. Sooner or later (in my case sooner) the fact that all children become proficient in language before they go to school—in London some children spoke three languages—by being encouraged to make words mean for their own purposes and intentions and not by formal ordered instruction, would have to be turned towards their learning to read. *What* they read would then matter right from the start.

The study of children's language development, with its emphasis on its social nature and the importance of shared meanings, transformed the teaching of English in England. Our multicultural classes pushed us in other ways too, most particularly into the study of *narrative*, not just as an offshoot of structuralism, but in the vein carried by Barbara Hardy's assertion that narrative is "a primary act of mind transferred to art from life." Teachers have rediscovered children's natural genius for storytelling, a genius which *being read to*, in our literate tradition, extends and transforms. Here is Harold Rosen's version:

No one tells us why language development should not include as a central component getting better at telling and responding to stories of many different kinds. We should have been warned. We now know that every Tom, Dick, and Harry [and I know he would now say Ranjit, Cara, Ali] is a master of infinitely delicate language skills from a very early age, rich competences of grammar and modulated language use, and that every Tess, Bess, and Hannah [Amarjit, Yasmin, Dalbir] inherits complex linguistic and semiotic systems of meanings developed in their culture; which includes modes of story telling. We should have been warned that a common possession of human kind was not, ipso facto, of little account but rather an indicator of the functioning of the mind, a part of the deep structure of the mind.

(*Stories and Meanings* 6)

Research makes this good. The apparently simple interactions of a mother and children reading a story together, a teacher reading to children in a nursery class, the efforts of Cochran Smith and Vivian Gussin Paley in the United States and those of Dombey and Fox in England, all these display linguistic competences linked to cultural understandings in ways no teacher of literature can ignore if the reading history of their students is to be given the value it demands. Not only for narratologists, the paid-up readers of novels in universities and colleges, is narrative "a meta code, a human universal on the basis of which transcultural messages about the nature of a shared reality can be transmitted" (White 2). There is nothing exclusive about narrative. Its universality stares one in the face, so all literatures have equal claim to being recognized by opinion and to becoming knowledge. In different cultures there are, as Shirley Brice Heath makes plain, different rules for the telling, rules which are learned early, transformed but never forgotten. Narrative is surely the bedrock of comparative literature, a natural networking of making and meaning, essentially anti-hierarchical, transcanonical, democratic.

Children are tellers and reshapers. Their own language and lore, the carnivalistic parodies and scandals they create when adults are absent, reveal a variety of discourse kinds not found elsewhere (Grugeon). They change the stories adults tell them into versions which suit them better. In London classrooms, they create an *interculture*. Children discover that when someone tells you a story it becomes yours to retell. This is the living tradition. I am equally excited by the power, strength, and diversity of writing done by the young in classrooms. The teachers' problem is to keep this writing alive and not to let it die in the attritions of examination warfare. The importance of literature for the young lies in its *production*, far more than in any system of analysis.

Why am I so emphatic? My education gave me books, taught me to read, and taught me at the same time that writing, real writing, the kind that other people read, was great novels. I saw there was no apparent continuity between these great books and the detective stories I wrote with my brother. I had no Genette to link the discourse of my endless anecdotes with the temporal immortalities of Proust, nor to value the fact that I had been born into a tribe of storytellers, the kind that spoke, when they spoke, in exact particularities of incident and not in the abstractions of essayists. No wonder I welcome back the natural narrative impatience of children to tell the world as they learn how to mean (Paley). Children's narrative skill vindicates my conviction that the problem of literature teaching in schools and colleges stems from the abandonment, by college literature teachers *of* literature, of the continuous teaching of *reading*, and their curious indifference to the ideological nature of literacy (Street).

The history of the teaching of reading in the United States must one day be written to make plain its continuing preoccupation with methodology, its thrall to behaviorist psychology and publishing, its disjunction from literature written for children. The development of children's language, the research into pre-school "literacy events," the need for alignment between the learners' cultural expectations of reading and the school's view of pedagogy have all brought to a head a need to acknowledge that learning to read is not a process of decoding words into sentences. Instead, it is the discovery of discourse kinds, of understandings of the nature of written language composed into texts which are embedded in the social semiotic. For too long in the teaching of reading we have backgrounded the fact that learning to speak includes learning the *local* culture, that narrative is universal, that linguistic competences, both psychological and social, are learned in the contexts of purposeful use and not as lock-stepped fractions of instruction. All of this now appears as central in the way children *learn* to read, however they may be taught. They learn in interaction with others and with texts. Their first texts are not words but *images*. In a powerful study of a child's early narration related to drawing, Myra Barrs speaks of *Maps of Play*. Speaking to themselves, the children spontaneously, to themselves, re-enact the story they have seen on television, an Invaders quest tale, with the help of their puppet dolls. Then, to share their game with an adult, they draw the map of the action in a manner reminiscent of Tolkien (Barrs).

I now want to suggest that children's literacy evolves in interaction with texts, not the texts written for word recognition, but those which depend on a highly organized *metatextuality*. I have to ask the reader to take the evolutionary details of my research as given. One example may prove helpful.

During the process of conducting longitudinal studies of what was involved in teaching inexperienced readers—my colleagues taught the same children for four years—we learned that the first *school* view of what reading is, that is, the messages about reading conveyed by the methodology, is the one that dominates most children's understanding of reading throughout school learning. Thus reading *becomes* the mechanisms of the basal reading scheme. "Getting it right" is then more important than "making it mean" or "discovering how it goes." As we looked for ways to replace this model in the reading contexts we shared with our pupils (now no longer poor, retarded, illiterate, low achieving, etc., but simply, *inexperienced*) we discovered that they had had no means of learning *the lessons that texts teach*; that is, lessons which are the learning-to-read experiences which we all renew as we continue to read, all our lives.

Let me demonstrate this. In a children's picture book called *Rosie's Walk* the artist author tells a story, in thirty-six words and thirty-two pages of pictures, of a hen walking round a farmyard followed by a fox. The text reads simply: "Rosie the hen went for a walk . . ." The fox falls into a trap on every second page, but the word *fox* never appears in the text. The readers have to tell themselves that part of the story from the pictures. In doing so they discover that reading is a narrative game with rules which the author teaches the reader and which the author is also free to change. These are reading lessons which have to be learned but which never appear in basal reading texts designed to teach only word recognition.

It was from Jonathan Culler that I first borrowed the term *literary competences* to explain the vital untaught reading lessons.

We also tend to think of meaning and structure as properties of literary works, and from one point of view this is perfectly correct: when the sequence of words is treated *as a literary work* it has these properties. The work has structure and meaning *be-*

cause it is read in a particular way, because these potential properties, latent in the object itself, are actualized by the theory of discourse applied in the act of reading.

(113)

How then, does a young reader, a beginner, or even an inexperienced twelve-year-old learn "the theory of a discourse"? Not by taught lessons of word recognition, but by acceptance of invitations to take part in certain kinds of meaningful activities involving words and pictures. That's what the inexperienced adolescent readers whom I taught, skilled as they were at word games, recognition sequences, and phonic check lists, had never been allowed to find out. They had never read a joke book; they had no idea that what they had learned in reading a comic related to *The Shrinking of Treehorn.* They had not stayed long enough in any author's company to learn that author's game or how it could be played. Let me show you how children follow Culler's reading instructions and bring to texts an "implicit" understanding of the operations of literary discourse which tells them what to look for.

From the very popular artist-author John Burningham, English children learn what Frank Kermode calls *the secrets of texts* long before they go to school and are taught to read. For example, *Mr. Gumpy's Outing* is a cumulative tale, a form as old as telling and latent in every literary canon. The animals who are Mr. Gumpy's friends ask him whether they may have a ride in his boat. Their requests are formed in different ways but they all mean the same thing. "Please may I . . . Can I come, too. Is there room for me . . ." Mr. Gumpy's response is always "Yes, if you don't . . . ," followed by a condition that suits each animal. The pig is told not to muck about, the rabbit mustn't hop, the chickens are forbidden to "flap," an English term for "become overexcited." The readers learn the stricture very quickly and discover that there are different ways of saying the same thing, and some of these are specially jokey and apt.

They also discover that fiction is a way of exploring the possible safely. Think of how difficult it is to explain embarrassment to children, yet how easily they feel it. In *Would You Rather* Burningham asks searching questions:

Would you rather. . . . an elephant drank your bathwater, an eagle stole your dinner, a pig tried on your clothes, or a hippo slept in your bed?

Some of these questions are the thinkable unthinkable, in pictures! "Would you rather your dad did a dance at school, or your mum had a row in a café?" The images of the imagination which Burningham offers children have to be compared with those that children take for themselves from what they see around them and, now very powerfully, from television. With these they make in their heads a model of the world, essentially fictive, which, as Bruner suggests "guides our perception, thought and talk. In the main, they appear to be diverse, rich, *local*, extraordinarily generative" (my italics). My conviction is that children's picture books teach children not only what reading can be like (and that is no little offering compared with the parsimony, in both text and pictures, of the basal reader) but the *possibilities* latent in both language and mental imagery, the play of words, and the play of the imagination. This is laid down early. I do not claim that it has to be. Far from it. But without early paradigms shot through with pleasure and perceptive understandings, reading becomes a great chore. "The artist creates possible worlds through the metaphoric transformation of the ordinary and conventionally given" (Bruner 49). This is what the artists, who create children's books professionally, know, and what children intuitively learn from them.

Here are more secrets from Burningham. In *Come Away from the Water, Shirley* he demonstrates the picture conventions of realism as the rules of cultural habit, and so-called fantasy as the subversion of cultural habit, or escape. In *Where's Julius?* the rules learned on separate pages of *Shirley* are locked together. Julius cannot come to breakfast, lunch, or supper when the exact menu is announced (*nouvelle cuisine* when his mother prepares it; good old English when his father cooks) because he is making "a little home in the other room with three chairs, the old curtains, and the broom; digging a hole in order to get to the other side of the world; riding a camel to the top of the tomb of Neffatuteum which is a pyramid near the Nile in Egypt; cooling hippopotamuses in the Lombo Bombo River in Central Africa with buckets of muddy water. . . ." Julius's exploits are canonical; the language is strongly bookish. But the artist's concern is where the language stops, in the images of Julius's fantasies. No reading lessons outside the book teach the readers how to read these amazing, glowing pictures. Like his colleagues and contemporaries, John Burningham wants the young reader to have freedom from over-conventionalized expectations of what a book or a story *can* be like. The near-innocence of the beginner who has still to learn what books can be like is the challenge to the artist.

Now, think of how *Paradise Lost* is loaded in every rift with the ore of Milton's learning. Milton assumes that he shares known texts, like the Bible, with his readers. Here, then, is part of the text of a picture book for young children called *Each Peach Pear Plum*, by Janet Ahlberg and Allan Ahlberg. The title is from an eighteenth-century nursery rhyme (Opie).

> Each Peach Pear Plum
> I spy Tom Thumb
> Tom Thumb in the cupboard
> I spy Mother Hubbard
> Mother Hubbard in the cellar
> I spy Cinderella
> Cinderella on the stairs
> I spy the Three Bears.

The very young readers are offered a plurality of texts, the characters from nursery rhymes and fairy tales are hidden in the pictures. There is a new story in the text: Baby Bunting falls into a stream and is later rescued. The whole is a subtle game of "I spy." My point is that the child enters the author's canonical world as surely as Milton's readers did.

Behind all new books for children are centuries of old stories weaving their way in and out of realistic fictions and fictive fantasies. Most of these latent stories come to children the first time as something told rather then written; they span cultures as well as generations. Rosie is the latest of a long line of Pertelotes stretching back to Aesop. The acceptability of this deep and obvious game lies in the fact that the readers, both new and old, have to be inducted into it. (It's hard to imagine university professors taking children's literature seriously unless they felt they could justify their enjoyment of a *divertissement* in terms of theoretical enrichment.) The adults who read with their children learn new reading lessons. The problem is to get the adults to see that's what they are, that the author is the teacher, and to persuade the professors that the canon of world literature is first learned as local, multicultural storytelling.

Janet Ahlberg and Allan Ahlberg have a reputation for linking the traditions of children's literature, a fairy tale, for example, with contemporary subversions of it. *Burglar Bill* is a good example. They also take the model of a store catalogue and transform it into a *Baby's Catalogue* where by reading the lists of words and pictures the youngest readers discover the cultural differences of families who share what is common in our lives. Intertext is at its redoubtable best in an epistolary novel, *The Jolly Postman: Or Other People's Letters*. What is more secret or subversive than this invitation to read? The narrative is in rhyme: the Jolly Postman takes letters to characters from *Mother Goose*. (I hope Arthur Applebee doesn't mind that Cinderella now has an address.) The letters themselves are there, tucked into envelopes. They are written in the full conventional dress of the rhetoric and register of their kind, the things sent and replied to: an invitation, a lawyer's missive, a postcard, an advertising flyer, a publisher's courtesy copy of a book, a birthday card, a letter of apology. The authors know that children, without lessons, can write their own versions of these letters: Humpty Dumpty makes an insurance claim; Jill writes to Jack in hospital, and so on. To write and put a letter in with the others is to play the literacy game, and at the same time to transform the thing that it is.

My experience tells me that the reason students don't read in their school days and have to be inducted by means of the great books course later is that the invitation to read in school is never linked with this kind of enjoyment and the consequent development, of literary understanding, which can come only from reading *many* books of many kinds.

I could now proceed from here to make the case for the untaught reading lessons as primary material in the creation of a poetics of literature created for children. Instead I want to double back, to look at the privileging of the written word in European and, I guess, North American education. One lesson we expect children to learn is that writing acts as a transparent window on established reality. Since Saussure (before, but he gives the knowing credence) we have understood that a sign system of writing does *not* do this. The artists and writers of contemporary books for children are hammering this home. Among the early reading lessons this one is foregrounded. As young readers become participants in the work read, the artist reminds them that they are playing a game, a game of deep play, with rules which are taught and learned in the interaction of the artist with the reader. That understood, all literature becomes in time, accessible.

In the multicultural classroom where the non-hierarchical networking of literacies and cultures goes on, teachers learn to reread our own cultural history alongside those of our pupils. We enter into new readings and devise new cultural makings with the help of the interactions which a variety of texts, both read and written, demand of us. We reveal and criticize the immense presuppositions which the traditions of European literacy have bound us into, presuppositions about power, ideologies, literary theories, educational expectations. Ethnographic studies of literacy have released us from an embarrassing custodial obligation to a narrow view of literature and the ways by which children acquire literary competences. Even if we believe with some college professors that the habit of reading *at all* differentiates a person, we can also agree that the traditionally well-read are not always in the best position to encounter new literary adventures. Children do that best; they are always expecting a story to be a surprise.

As for the canon, it is now dumb, in my hearing. I am reduced to one idea: that to be a reader and a teacher of and in world literature one can best begin by being *lucid about what is local.*

Each of us has a history that makes our theory of literature and pedagogy. We take this theory for granted as knowledge when it is often only opinion. I had to unlearn my privileged view of literature in order to see bilingual children in English classrooms as having the same right of access to powerful words and ideas as I had, the right to their own canon, their chance to turn opinion into knowledge. The multicultural classroom challenges us to teach literature as in a workshop of cultural making, not as custodians of a museum (Reid). Our lives are, more than ever, socially knotted together in the networking of ideas and cultures; that is the multicultural reality into which new readers come. Their allies are powerful, and if we don't prevent them from joining forces, reading and writing will not be lost, for all that the images in new picture books will have to be read with great subtlety, greater acknowledgment. We have an obligation to bring about enabling situations, in literature classes as in all others, to show that there is nothing "natural" or "inevitable" about who reads, and who reads what. Even now, as I read the stories of King Arthur to children, I am struck as never before that as the knight sallies forth to meet something different in the alien world, his duty is to return having reduced the alien to the status of the same. Perhaps that was why the Round Table died away. In-fighting overcame heroism. The true comparative lies in the interplay of what Raymond Williams calls the "emergent" and the "residual."

I have come a long way round to say something that Geertz, the interpretive anthropologist, says better than I ever could and which applies to literature as to every other aspect of culture:

> To see ourselves as others see us can be eye-opening. To see others as sharing a nature with us is the merest decency. But it is from the far more difficult achievement of seeing ourselves amongst others as a local example of the forms human life has locally taken, a case amongst cases, a world among worlds,

that the largeness of mind, without which objectivity is self-congratulation and tolerance a sham, comes.

(16)

III

The autobiographical tone of much of this piece is deliberate. If we believe that literature makes a difference, then we must look at what difference we think it makes, beginning with ourselves.

My concern has been to stress that literature is *constructed* within the cultural and historical domain of those who write and those who read, and that children, from their earliest entry into different types of discourses and signification, are in the same position as their elders. They too learn their culture as they make things mean. They seek out particular kinds of individuality as they enter their social history and learn their language socially. The difference is that children find meaning in the local and the familiar before they discover the nature of a divided society and a divided world. For those who mediate literature to the young (in England they are called *teachers of English* so as to avoid "language arts" being separated from other language functions) the problem is that they teach themselves and their view of the world, while sometimes ignoring the changing world and sticking to the texts as if they *were* the world. We cannot confer permanent modernity on any literature. At best we can rediscover its relevance.

For an English teacher of English, literature now means at least all literature in English, in the world where English is spoken or written and that means Africa and Asia as well as North America and Australia. It also means that the readers' choosing is as important as the teachers'; that bilingual reading becomes the norm rather than the exception. It is, in Michel Foucault's terms, *les mots et les choses*; part of the order of things. So while I cannot read all that has been written, equally I cannot say that the Western tradition is all that counts as literature and feel that my students are well served. Instead they must teach me what there is to be read, and we shall read together. I am salutarily reminded that it was a story by Borges that urged Foucault to shatter the familiar landmarks of his thinking, to disturb and threaten with collapse our age-old distinction between the same and the other, to look for the "possible unconscious of our understandings."

In studying world literature I think that's what readers have to do. I see it being made possible for children in productions like *Where's*

Julius! where the everyday world of meals is challenged in formal linguistic terms by the possibility of thinking *otherly*, without words at all. Television offers the young this chance all the time: to resist, to deflect, to disturb those things that are so obvious that the mind doesn't even formulate their existence.

I have written as if those who read literature have the larger interpretative task. It isn't so, of course. Readers are simply following in the wake of writers. As I was trying to find an example of world literature which set my interior model for me, I discovered with a painful, head-and-heart-racking thrill, a new book by V. S. Naipaul, who, as it happened, arrived in London (on his way to Oxford) from Trinidad in the same year that I came south from Scotland. In *The Enigma of Arrival* I found again my attempts in those days to be assimilated to the London I had read about in books. I recognized, perhaps for the first time, how Henry James, T. S. Eliot, Joseph Conrad, and Vladimir Nabokov must have felt the same kind of splitting. Naipaul writes about living in a cottage in the down country of Wiltshire, in the sunset of the British Empire, but his tale is of change in all things. Here is the Indian from the West Indies writing his way into the consciousness of those whose literature made him want to be a writer. Here is what I shall read at next English harvest time with the teachers who come to our course to confront the multiconsciousness of the plurality of our culture. Here is a world writer.

Naipaul explains that, on the staff of the manor house in the grounds of which his rented cottage stands, there were once sixteen gardeners. Now there is only one. The reader enters the slow dramatic deliberateness of the prose (which I have shortened, undoubtedly to its detriment) where the writer remembers the gardeners of his childhood.

As a child in Trinidad I knew or saw few gardeners. In the country areas, where the Indian people mainly lived, there were nothing like gardens. Sugar cane covered the land. Sugar cane, the old slave crop, was what the people still grew and lived by; it explained the presence, on that island, after abolition of slavery, of an imported Asiatic peasantry. Sugar cane explained the poor Indian-style houses and roughly thatched huts beside the narrow asphalt roads. In the smooth dirt yards of those little houses and huts there were nothing like gardens. There might be hedges, mainly of hibiscus, lining the foul-water ditches. There might be flower areas—periwinkle, ixoria, zinnia, marigold, Lady's Slipper, with an occasional small tree like the one we called the Queen of Flowers. There was seldom more.

There were gardens in Port of Spain, but only in the richer areas, where the building plots were bigger. It was in those gardens that as a child, on my way home from school in the afternoons, I might see a barefoot gardener. And he would be less a gardener, really, less a man with knowledge about soils and plants and fertilizers than a man who was, more simply, a worker in a garden, a weeder and a waterer, a barefoot man, trousers rolled up to mid shin, playing a hose on a flower bed.

This barefoot gardener would be an Indian—Indians were thought to have a special way with plants and the land. And this man might have been born in India and brought out to Trinidad on a five-year indenture, with a promise of a free passage back to India at the end of that time or a grant of land in Trinidad. This kind of Indian contract labour had ended only in 1917—antiquity to me in 1940, say; but to the barefoot waterer in the garden (still knowing only a language of India) a time within easy recall. This kind of gardening was a town occupation, barely above, or merging into, that of "yard boy," which was an occupation for black people, and something so unskilled and debased that the very words were used as a form of abuse.

(224–225)

Here follow details of changes; of the growing of vegetable gardens, like English allotments, "created by accident and not by design; created at the end of the period of empire, out of the decay of the old sugar plantations."

The gardener belonged to the plantation or estate past. That past lay outside of Port of Spain, in the Indian countryside, in the fields, the roads, the huts.

Literature or the cinema (though I cannot think of any particular film) would have given the word different associations. But that knowledge—of swamp and estate and vegetable plot—was the knowledge I took to England. That was the knowledge that lay below my idea of the P. G. Wodehouse gardener and my idea of the gardener in *Richard II* poetically conversing with a weeping queen. There were gardeners in the great parks of London. There was a gardener of my Oxford college, a mild, humorous, pipe-smoking man with (as I thought) the manner of one of the dons. And just as in the allotments beside the railway, I had grown to see the original of the Aranguez plots; so, coming to the manor (with its echoes of the estate big house and servants) and seeing around me the remnants of agricultural life (the reverse, the distorted original of the Trinidad estates), that earlier knowledge revived in me.

(227)

IV

World literature is still about reading and writing, but now we have to do these traditional things in the contexts of more widely shared cultures. In his lucidity about his locality, Naipaul writes the world, just as Keats did in cold London. The Indian children in London may never see India. The Caribbean is no longer "home" to many black Cockney children. Yet, as they read Naipaul, Achebe, Rushdie, Walcott, the Vedic hymns, the retold Greek tales, as they create their own narrative lore and re-create the old English language, the young, now in school, will rewrite and reread world literature. They will follow the example of that very local boy, Will Shakespeare, who listened to fairy tales, read Plutarch and Holinshed, argued with his friends, and emulated the scholars of the Inns of Court, and thought about the New World, where these words now go, with my gratitude.

Works Cited

Ahlberg, Janet, and Allan Ahlberg. *Burglar Bill*. London: Heinemann, 1977.
———. *Each Peach Pear Plum*. Harmondsworth: Kestrel, 1978.
———. *The Baby's Catalogue*. Harmondsworth: Kestrel, 1982.
———. *The Jolly Postman: Or Other People's Letters*. London: Heinemann, 1986.
Applebee, Arthur. *The Child's Concept of Story*. Chicago: University of Chicago Press, 1978.
Barrs, Myra. "Maps of Play." In *Language and Literacy in the Primary School*, edited by Margaret Meek and C. Mills, pp. 105–115. Lewes, Sussex: The Falmer Press, 1988.
Bernstein, Basil. *Class, Codes, and Control*. London: Routledge, 1973.
Britton, James. *Language and Learning*. London: Penguin, 1992 (revised).
Bruner, Jerome. *Actual Minds, Possible Worlds*. Cambridge, Mass.: Harvard University Press, 1986.
Burgess, Tony. "The Question of English." See Meek.
Burningham, John. *Come Away from the Water, Shirley*. London: Jonathan Cape, 1977.

————. *Mr. Gumpy's Outing*. London: Jonathan Cape, 1970.

————. *Where's Julius?* London: Jonathan Cape, 1986.

————. *Would You Rather?* London: Jonathan Cape, 1978.

Clampit, Amy. *What the Light Was Like*. London: Faber, 1985.

Cochran-Smith, M. *The Making of a Reader*. Norwood: J. Ablex, 1983.

Culler, Jonathan. *Structuralist Poetics*. London: Routledge, 1975.

Dombey, Henrietta. "Learning the Language of Books." In *Opening Moves*, edited by Margaret Meek. Bedford Way Papers No. 17. London: Institute of Education, University of London and Heinemann Educational Books, 1983.

Eagleton, Terry. *Literary Theory*. Oxford: Blackwell, 1983.

Foucault, Michel. *Les Mots et les Choses*. Paris: Gallimard, 1966.

Fox, Carol. "Talking like a *Book*: Young Children's Oral Monologues." In *Opening Moves*, edited by Margaret Meek. Bedford Way Papers No. 17. London: Institute of Education, University of London and Heinemann Educational Books, 1983.

Geertz, Clifford. *Local Knowledge*. New York: Basic Books, 1983.

Genette, Gerard. *Narrative Discourse*. Oxford: Blackwell, 1980.

Grierson, Herbert, ed. *The Poems of John Donne*. Oxford: The Clarendon Press, 1912.

Grugeon, Elizabeth. "The Singing Game." Master's thesis. Institute of Education, University of London, 1986.

Hardy, Barbara. *Novel: A Forum on Fiction*. Providence: Brown University Press, 1968.

Heath, Shirley Brice. *Ways with Words*. Cambridge, England: Cambridge University Press, 1989.

Heide, Florence Parry. *The Shrinking of Treehorn*. New York: Holiday House, 1971.

Henryson, Robert (1420?-1506). *The Testament of Cresseid*. Edited by Bruce Dickins. Edinburgh: Porpoise Press, 1925.

Hymes, Dell, ed. *Language in Culture and Society*. New York: Harper & Row, 1964.

Kermode, Frank. *Forms of Attention*. Chicago: University of Chicago Press, 1985.

————. *The Genesis of Secrecy*. Cambridge, Mass.: Harvard University Press, 1971.

Linguistic Minorities Project. *The Other Languages of England*. Edited by M. Stubbs. London, Boston: Routledge and Kegan Paul, 1985.

Meek, Margaret. [Margaret Meek Spencer.] *Learning to Read*. London: The Bodley Head, 1982.

Meek, Margaret and Jane Miller, eds. *Changing English: Essays for Harold Rosen*. London: Heinemann Educational, 1984.

Miller, Jane. *Many Voices*. London: Routledge, 1983.

————. *Women Writing about Men*. London: Virago, 1986.

Naipaul, V. S. *The Enigma of Arrival*. New York: Knopf, 1987.

Paley, V. Gussin. *Wally's Stories*. Cambridge, Mass.: Harvard University Press, 1985.

Reid, Euan. "The Newer Minorities: Spoken Languages and Varieties." In *Language in the British Isles*, edited by P. Trudgill. Cambridge, England: Cambridge University Press, 1984.

Rosen, Harold. *Neither Bleak House nor Liberty Hall*. Inaugural Lecture, Institute of Education, University of London, 1981.

————. *Stories and Meanings*. NATE Papers in Education. Sheffield, 1985.

Saussure, F. de. *Course in General Linguistics*. Translated by Wade Baskin. New York: Philosophical Library, 1959.

Street, Brian. *Literacy in Theory and Practice*. Cambridge, England: Cambridge University Press, 1986.

Vygotsky, L. S. *Mind in Society; The Development of Higher Psychological Processes*. Cambridge, Mass.: Harvard University Press, 1978.

————. *Thought and Language*. Cambridge, Mass.: MIT Press, 1962.

White, Hayden. "The Value of Narrativity in the Representation of Reality." In *On Narrative*, edited by W. J. T. Mitchell, pp. 1–23. University of Chicago Press, 1981.

Williams, Raymond. *Writing in Society*. London: Verso, 1983.

Contributors

Sarah Lawall, professor of comparative literature at the University of Massachusetts at Amherst, is especially interested in literary theories related to structures of world-representation and in literature that experiments with worldviews. She has written on Greek drama, surrealism, contemporary French poetry, literary theory and criticism, and the concept and practice of world literature. Her publications include articles on the previous subjects and *Critics of Consciousness: The Existential Structures of Literature* (1968), the co-edited *Découverte de l'essai* (1974), and a co-authored translation and commentary of Euripides' *Hippolytus* (1986). She is editor of the modern sections of *Norton World Masterpieces* and directed a summer 1987 Institute on the Theory and Teaching of World Literature supported by the National Endowment for the Humanities.

Thomas M. Greene, Frederick Clifford Ford Professor of English and Comparative Literature at Yale University and longtime chair of the Department of Comparative Literature, is a critic and literary historian best known for works on comparative and Renaissance topics such as *The Light in Troy* (1982) and *The Vulnerable Text: Essays on Renaissance Literature* (1986). His recent efforts have included studies of magic and literature; a book on poetry and magic, *Poésie et magie*, was published in 1991.

Charles Segal, professor of Greek and Latin at Harvard University, has been particularly concerned with the interpretation of Greek tragedy, Greek and Roman epic and lyric poetry, and the role of contemporary criticism in the study of classical literature. Among his many books are *Tragedy and Civilization: An Interpretation of Sophocles* (1981), *Interpreting Greek Tragedy* (1986), *Pindar's Mythmaking* (1986), *Language and Desire in Seneca's Phaedra*

(1986), and *Orpheus: The Myth of the Poet* (1989). A study of how poetry and philosophy function together in the Epicurean therapy of the fear of death is the subject of his *Lucretius on Death and Anxiety* (1990). Forthcoming are *Oedipus Tyrannus: Tragic Heroism and the Limits of Knowledge* and *Euripides and the Poetics of Sorrow.*

Nancy Sorkin Rabinowitz, professor of comparative literature at Hamilton College, is the author of *Anxiety Veiled: Euripides and the Traffic in Women* (1993) and the co-editor, with Amy Richlin, of *Feminist Theory and the Classics* (1993). Her articles, on a wide range of subjects in both classics and nineteenth- and twentieth-century women's fiction, have appeared in such collections as *Pornography and Representation in Greece and Rome* and in such journals as *Arethusa, Ramus, Helios, College English*, and *Journal of Narrative Technique.*

Joan Dayan is professor of English and African American studies at the University of Arizona. She writes on both American and Caribbean literature, focusing most recently on Caribbean studies and cultural criticism. During 1990 and 1991 she was a fellow at the Shelby-Cullom Davis Center for Historical Studies, Princeton University, where she continued work on *Haiti, History, and the Gods* (University of California Press, forthcoming). Among her publications are a translation and introduction to the Haitian René Depestre's *A Rainbow for the Christian West* (1977) and *Fables of Mind: An Inquiry into Poe's Fiction* (1987). She is also working on a book-length study of René Depestre to be published by Cambridge University Press.

Maria Tymoczko, professor of comparative literature at the University of Massachusetts at Amherst, is a specialist in early Celtic literature. She has published numerous articles on medieval, Irish, and Welsh literature, and on translation theory. Her study, *The Irish "Ulysses"* (1994) explores James Joyce's use of Irish mythic patterns and narrative forms.

Doris Sommer is professor of Latin American literature at Harvard University. She is author of *Foundational Fictions: The National Romances of Latin America* (1991) and *One Master for Another: Populism as Patriarchal Rhetoric in Dominican Novels* (1984), as well as co-editor of *Nationalisms and Sexualities* (1991). Her current work explores "resistant texts and resisted readers," essays about minority writers and privileged readers.

Janet A. Walker, associate professor of comparative literature at Rutgers University, has published widely on the self in modern Japanese fiction, including *The Japanese Novel of the Meiji Period and the Ideal of Individualism* (1979). Her recent work focuses on the poetics of fiction in Japan and the West and on the question of transcultural genres: "On the Applicability of the Term 'Novel' to Modern Non-Western Long Fiction" (1990).

Eugene Eoyang is professor of comparative literature and of East Asian languages and cultures at Indiana University, where he teaches theory of literature, theory of translation, Oriental fiction and poetry, and comparative aesthetics. As an editor with Doubleday Anchor Books, he launched the Anchor Bible, publishing ten volumes before his departure in 1966. He has contributed over fifty translations to *Sunflower Splendor: Three Thousand Years of Chinese Poetry*, edited by Wu-chi Liu and Irving Lo. He was the editor and chief translator of *Ai Qing: Selected Poems* and is a founding editor of *Chinese Literature: Essays, Articles, Reviews (Clear)*. His most recent publication is *The Transparent Eye: Reflections on Translation, Chinese Literature, and Comparative Poetics* (1993).

Chantal Zabus has been trained in Belgium, Canada, and the United States and is now professor of English literature and the new literatures in English at the University of Louvain-la-Neuve, Belgium. She is a specialist in African literatures and Commonwealth studies and the author of *The African Palimpsest* (1990).

Peter J. Rabinowitz, professor of comparative literature at Hamilton College, divides his time between literary theory and music. He is the author of *Before Reading: Narrative Conventions and the Politics of Convention* (1987) and co-editor, with James Phelan, of the forthcoming *Understanding Narrative*. He has written on a wide variety of topics, including theories of reading, detective fiction, the symphonies of Mahler, and the piano music of Louis Moreau Gottschalk. He is a contributing editor of *Fanfare*. He and Jay Reise are currently completing a book on the act of listening.

Jay Reise is the composer of the opera *Rasputin*, commissioned by the New York City Opera and premiered in 1988. He has also written three symphonies, performed by the Philadelphia Orchestra among others, and numerous chamber works. He is currently professor of music at the University of Pennsylvania.

William Moebius, chair of the Department of Comparative Literature at the University of Massachusetts at Amherst, has written on the verbal and visual languages of children's literature, most recently for *Children's Literature* and *The Lion and the Unicorn*. His translation of Sophocles' *Antigone* is in press. Other translations include Sophocles' *Oedipus at Colonus* (1972) and the poems of Philodemus for *The Greek Anthology* (1973). His *Elegies and Odes* appeared in 1967 with the Swallow Press.

Margaret Meek Spencer learned to read well enough in her Scottish primary school to continue to do it as a student and a teacher. She joined the Department of English in the University of London Institute of Education in 1968 and subsequently became head of English and Media studies and, after her retirement in 1990, emeritus reader. Her teaching life has been influenced by the significant growth in the understanding of children's language and thought; by the production of books for children; by the work of the London and of the National Associations for the Teaching of English; by contact with distinguished colleagues in multicultural London, France, Canada, the United States, Australia, and South Africa; and by research in classrooms and extended studies of children's learning to read and write. Among her many studies of literacy and the teaching of literature at the early levels are *Learning to Read, How Texts Teach What Readers Learn*, and *On Being Literate*. She was awarded the Eleanor Farjeon Prize for services to children's literature.

Index